The Dynamics of 'Race' and Gender

CALCASA RPRC

The Dynamics of 'Race' and Gender:
Some Feminist Interventions

Edited by

Haleh Afshar and Mary Maynard

Taylor & Francis
Publishers since 1798

UK	Taylor & Francis Ltd, 4 John St., London WC1N 2ET
USA	Taylor & Francis Inc., 1900 Frost Road, Suite 101, Bristol, PA 19007

First published 1994

A Catalogue Record for this book is available from the British Library

ISBN 0 7484 0211 X
ISBN 0 7484 0212 8 (pbk)

Library of Congress Cataloging-in-Publication Data are available on request

Typeset in 10/12pt Times
by Graphicraft Typesetters Ltd., Hong Kong

Printed in Great Britain by Burgess Science Press, Basingstoke on paper which has a specified pH value on final paper manufacture of not less than 7.5 and is therefore 'acid free'.

Contents

Contents

Acknowledgments

We would like to thank the Development Studies Association for funding and supporting the Women and Development Study Group. Thanks are similarly due to the University of York's Open Course Series' Committee for facilitating the meetings at which most of these papers were initially presented. We would also like to thank the Centre for Women's Studies and its members for hosting the DSA's Women and Development Study Group's annual meeting and offering kind hospitality to many of the participants.

In addition we would like to thank all our contributors for giving so generously of their time in reading one another's drafts and in coming to several meetings to discuss them. Their incisive criticisms and the good humour with which they were shared were exemplary and have made our collaboration a great pleasure. We would also like to thank those who met the deadlines, promptly delivered and corrected their chapters and then patiently waited for the latecomers.

Last but not least, we would like to thank Maurice Dodson and Bob Coles for holding the fort, and Molly and Ali for giving us the space and occasionally their beds to accommodate colleagues and contributors to this volume.

The Dynamics of 'Race' and Gender

Haleh Afshar and Mary Maynard

During the past decade, feminism and Women's Studies have been forced to acknowledge the diversities of women's experiences, as well as the patriarchal oppression that they share. An emphasis on 'difference' has shattered the illusion of the homogeneity of, and sisterhood between, women, which previously characterized white, middle-class, Westernized feminist politics and analysis. With this has come an awareness that, although women may be oppressed by men within patriarchal relationships, there are also other areas of oppression in their lives, which they experience in a gendered way. Here emphasis has been given to age, class, disability, 'race' and sexuality. Yet, although 'difference' has become something of a catch-all phrase within feminism and is now a term to be found widely in the literature, less attention has been paid to specific analyses of its implications in concrete settings. Further, there is still a paucity of material concentrating on the interrelationship of 'race' and gender, in general, and the consequences of racism, for women of different backgrounds, in particular. It is the aim of this collection to contribute to debate and understanding in this area.

The contributors to this volume are from different religious, cultural and ethnic backgrounds and classify themselves as black, white, Asian, Iranian, African, Irish, European and British. They seek to place an analysis of 'race' and gender issues at the centre of discussion, thereby countering the ways in which such matters are often marginalized in supposedly mainstream debate. The book also aims to challenge the assumption, which is deeply embedded in most Western texts, that 'race' is some kind of minority experience. Not only can it be pointed out that the majority of the world's peoples live in situations where ascriptions as to 'race' are defining features in their lives, it is also the case that to be labelled 'white', in a world context, is also to be allotted a racial category, albeit one which is privileged, unanalyzed, taken for granted and itself a 'minority' status.

Many commentaries on the lives of 'non-white' groups portray their experiences as entirely those of oppression, thus conflating 'race' with racism. We question the assumption that 'race' is necessarily and always experienced in a negative way, for it can also provide a positive context for celebration. Although racism is a highly significant and under-researched issue, in feminism as elsewhere, we contend that there is more to an understanding of black peoples' experiences than can be portrayed by focusing on racism alone. Thus, the chapters of this book, in their various ways, take the lives and experiences of women from a range of ethnic groups as the norm, questioning the values and approaches of host societies which represent such norms as undesirable and homogeneous 'differences'. The authors demonstrate how the lives of women from different cultural backgrounds are multi-faceted, while also suggesting how their experiences have some commonality with those of similar class positions in other societies. At the same time, they indicate the ways in which different cultural perspectives on matters such as marriage, motherhood, employment, loyalty and sense of identity mark the specificities that signal differing priorities for different women and construct distinctions between them.

Although both 'colour' and creed are presented as constants in terminology, the contributors to this book are well aware that the very idea of 'race' is a social construction, the meaning of which varies according to time, place and circumstance. The effects of historical legacy, political context, culture and variables such as class and generation all combine to influence perceptions of what counts as 'white' and 'non-white' and when and where 'non-white' is seen as 'black'. Further, in addition to the definitions and categories which are imposed on 'others' by dominant discourses and those with the power to 'name', there is also the question of individual and collective definitions of self. These, despite the strength of racial stereotyping, may remain flexible and will also vary according to contexts and personal choices, sometimes inevitably leading to a clash between public and private identities. The very term 'black' has itself recently become a contested area of discourse, having been adopted with pride by the politically active, while also sometimes being abandoned, with relief, by those women who find the demands of kin and community too restrictive. Again, different circumstances can dictate different choices for different women.

In focusing on issues to do with 'race' and gender, it is not the intention of this book to suggest that we are referring to two separate systems of racism and patriarchy, which intermesh in some readily comprehensible or simple way. Nor do we argue that there can be a single framework for understanding how racial and gender dynamics interrelate, nor one theoretical formulation for comprehending racialized gendering. Rather, it is the complexities and varieties of the experiences and forms of oppression which are highlighted. This is done in an attempt to contest the one-dimensional, and often benign, portrayal of the impact that 'race' and gender have on each other, which is sometimes to be found elsewhere in the literature.

The book is organized around three main themes and these are reflected in its section headings: 'Issues of Theory and Method'; 'Questions of Identity'; and 'Racism and Sexism at Work'. The first section is concerned with some of the conceptual and methodological issues raised by analyzing the ways in which 'race' and gender interrelate, in differing contexts. This is an important area since, although feminists purport to have taken on board the issue of diversity among women, this is often more at the level of rhetoric and there is still relatively little theoretical work which is gendered and which also takes account of 'race' and racism. Additionally, a concern with the methodological implications of this is virtually uncharted territory, from the point of view of feminist scholarship, where discussions of method and epistemology have been almost silent on the question of 'race'.

In this context, in chapter 1, Maynard questions how useful the notion of 'difference' is for feminism, particularly when dealing with 'race' and ethnicity. While not denying the significance of diversity among women, she is critical of whether a focus on 'difference' alone enables us to explore, not just the ways in which women may be distinguished from each other, but the processes and mechanisms through which distinct and specific forms of subordination are brought about. Maynard argues that simply to emphasize 'difference' runs the risk of masking the conditions that give some forms of 'difference' value and power over others. When concentrating on 'race' and ethnicity, this can lead to the marginalization of issues such as racism, racial domination and white supremacy.

Following on from this, in chapter 2, Bhavnani links concerns about theory with those of methodology in discussing Donna Haraway's arguments about feminist objectivity and situated knowledges. Bhavnani argues that the three elements which Haraway posits as being central to any discussion of feminist objectivity – accountability, positioning and partiality – lead to three questions, which, in turn, frame criteria and principles according to which research may be defined as implementing the goal of feminist objectivity. It is these three criteria, reinscription, micropolitics and difference, which are discussed and defined in the chapter. Bhavnani does this by drawing on her recent research with young working-class people in Britain. In this she reflects on her experiences of interviewing young black people and, as a black female researcher, of interviewing young white men.

The role of the black researcher studying black people also forms part of Wheeler's analysis. Drawing on material from an action research project concerned with service provision for black mental health users, she reflects on the expectations which were had of her and the limits on what she was able to provide. Wheeler frames her chapter with an analysis of statistical and research evidence about black people and mental health. She concludes that this is highly stereotyped and racist in both the assumptions made and the categories employed. Mental health services and psychiatry can thus be seen as mechanisms of social control.

Chapter 4 is also concerned with the ways in which racist assumptions inform the social categories utilized in the collation of official statistics. Focusing on the collection and reporting of information about the spread of HIV/AIDS, Akeroyd shows how this has both made use of and submerged issues of race, ethnicity and gender. This, in turn, highlights issues relating to what we 'know', how we know it, and what is foregrounded, obscured and ignored in research and data collection. Akeroyd argues that some rather arbitrary labelling has helped to shape social perceptions of who is presumed to be vulnerable to, and at risk or safe from, the illness.

With issues of theory and methodology still providing the context, the second section of the book explores the meaning of identity in various contexts where there exists a racialized gender dynamic. The idea that identity should be regarded as both multiple and fragmented, as opposed to previous formulations of it as relatively fixed and uniform, has arisen from both writings on 'difference' and from poststructuralist and postmodernist arguments. The intention in this section is to explore such possibilities in terms both of how identity is represented and how it is experienced. Drawing on empirical research, as well as other forms of knowledge, the contributors demonstrate that current, postmodern, notions of almost endless possibility and plurality in identity formation require tempering by recognition of more material constraints.

In chapter 5, for example, Allen provides a useful overview of the concept of identity and how it has been used in both social science and in popular discourse. She considers what an understanding of identity might mean in relation to the social divisions of race, ethnicity and nationality. Drawing, in particular, on examples from European history and politics, Allen shows how notions of identity can simplify, marginalize and reify crucial aspects of social divisions and inequalities. She argues that a study of the processes by which identity has come to be equated with sameness, and the consequences of this for those who are excluded, is in urgent need of inclusion on the feminist agenda.

Focusing on identity in a rather different context, Skeggs addresses the ways in which it can be challenged and transformed through music. She shows how a group of black American female musicians are using 'rap' to conjure themselves into existence against the powerless positions (both economic and cultural) that are offered to them. She argues that they 'talk back, talk Black' to colonialism, ridiculing masculinity and using sexually explicit language to celebrate female sexuality and autonomy. In drawing upon a long tradition of black female musicians, Skeggs sees these female rappers as turning themselves from sexual objects into sexual subjects. In so doing, she claims, they challenge the basis of the social order which seeks to contain them.

Afshar's work draws on a three-generational study of Muslim women in West Yorkshire, to look at the ways in which different social and economic circumstances offer them different choices in identity terms. Muslim women in West Yorkshire have to negotiate between the restrictive conservative demands of revivalist Islam and the necessity of earning a living and raising a family in a society whose norms and values are different to theirs. Afshar's chapter highlights the choices women make, at different times of their lives, to accommodate contradictory constraints. She argues that it is the process of transmission of ascribed identities which is most difficult, for to teach women who have been born and bred in Britain an Islamic identity and experience is a nearly impossible task.

The third section of the book is concerned with racism and sexism at work. Here, a number of writers demonstrate the relationship between 'race' and women's position in the labour market, examined in a variety of contexts. They are each designed to analyze the ways in which 'race' and gender together construct a subordinated material position for women of different ethnic groups and to highlight some of the differing strategies for resistance that might be available.

For instance, in chapter 8, Brah draws upon interviews with young Muslim women of Pakistani origin to analyze the place of paid work in their lives. Brah argues against developing a general theory of gender that could then simply be applied to specific instances of paid work. Instead, she proposes a framework that focuses on studying the intersections between gender, class, ethnicity, racism and religion, empirically and historically as contingent relationships. The young Muslim women's narratives demonstrate the contradictory interplay of such factors in their lives. Overall, the research shows women's position in the labour market to be inscribed by a multiplicity of factors, including the impact of the global and local economy on local labour markets, cultural ideologies about women and paid work, the role of education in mediating job aspirations, and racism.

Similar considerations inform Phizacklea's discussion in chapter 9, which aims to make debates about the continued gendering of jobs sensitive to the impact of racialization. The first part presents a critical evaluation of the supposed benefits of the single European market for the fifteen million ethnic minority long-term residents of Europe, whose fears about their futures Phizacklea regards as having some justification. The second part of the chapter uses a case study of home-based work to illustrate how it reproduces the occupational segregation of the external labour market, how the ideology of the gendered and racialized worker is constructed and how this is then used by the suppliers of home-based work. Phizacklea also highlights an often overlooked aspect in these processes, which is played by the state.

Lutz also addresses some of these themes in her analysis of the meaning of ethnicity and identity for immigrant women in the Dutch labour market. She focuses on how perceptions of these women's ethnic backgrounds act as a structural constraint on their employment chances. Using data concerning the situation of two groups of immigrant women in the Netherlands, the Turkish and the Creole Surinamese, she explores how they respond to stereotyping and the ways in which they do manage to participate in the labour market process.

In the following chapter, Bunie M. Matlanyane Sexwale focuses on black South African women domestic workers' experiences of violence, at the hands of their employers. Drawing from the words of the domestic workers themselves, she describes the nature of the emotional, sexual and physical violence and how resistance to it is organized through the South African Domestic Workers Union. Matlanyane Sexwale argues that part of the explanation for these violent labour relations lies in South Africa's history of colonization, capitalist penetration and apartheid, all of which contributed to gender relations marked by personal and structural violence and coercion. This has also been affected by the current threat to the white minority of loss of their political power.

Finally, in chapter 12, Moghissi explores the difficulties of exposing sexism and racism within the university system. Based on personal experience, it shows what individuals can expect and prepare for if they decide to break the silence and confront sexism and racism. Moghissi argues that even a small and personal victory can be important. It acts as a reminder that it is still possible to summon the commitment and energy to fight racism and other dehumanizing practices.

Together, the chapters in this book indicate how the processes of 'race' and gender interrelate in highly complex and contradictory ways. They attempt to move beyond simplistic statements that gender just needs to be deconstructed in order for feminists to be able to take account of 'difference'. Instead, this collection demonstrates the benefits to be gained from analyzing the interplay of various axes of differentiation in specific empirical and historical locations. In so doing, it underscores the point that diversity among women cannot be seen as a static phenomenon. Nor can it be understood or explained in absolute terms. Rather, 'race' and gender interact as part of a dynamic process. It is these dynamics which the feminist theoretical, methodological and empirical interventions, described in this book, are designed to address.

Section I
Issues of Theory and Method

Chapter 1

'Race', Gender and the Concept of 'Difference' in Feminist Thought

Mary Maynard

This chapter is concerned with theorizing the interrelationships between 'race' and gender oppression and the extent to which this is furthered by using the concept of 'difference'. It hardly needs stating that second-wave Western feminism has come under sustained criticism for its universalistic, homogenized and 'white' assumptions about women, since so much has been written on the subject (Frye, 1983; Collins, 1990; hooks, 1982, 1984, 1989, 1991; Ramazanoglu, 1989; Spelman, 1988). Much of this critique has concentrated on diversity among women, rather than, as previously, the things that might be said to unite them. Not only do women diverge in terms of how 'race', ethnicity, class, age, sexuality and disability effect their experiences, other factors, such as historical context and geographical location, also need to be part of the framework of feminist analyses.

One of the central ways in which this concern with diversity has developed is through an emphasis on the concept of 'difference'. Although the concept has no one connotation, as will be discussed, its implications of plurality and multiplicity have been regarded by many as providing the necessary antidote to the former unquestioning use of the unified terms 'woman' or 'women'. It is now commonplace to read books and articles, often written by white feminists, exhorting us to remember that there are differences between women and that these need to be taken account of in our work. Less likely to be found, however, are indications of what difference actually means and how it can be made a constructive part of empirical research, theoretical analysis or practical political action in order to bring about change.

My concern in this chapter is to question how useful the notion of 'difference' is for feminism, particularly when dealing with issues to do with 'race' and ethnicity. It should be pointed out from the beginning that I am certainly not denying the significance of diversity among women and the need for feminists to rethink their intellectual and political practice in the light of this. The problem is, rather, the extent to which using ideas about difference enables us to explore, not just the ways in which women may be distinguished from each other, but the mechanisms and processes through which distinct and specific forms of subordination are brought about. I argue that to focus on 'difference' alone runs the risk of masking the conditions that give some forms of 'difference' value and power over others. In the context of 'race' and ethnicity this can lead to the marginalization of issues such as racism, racial domination and white supremacy.

The chapter has five sections. The first section briefly considers some linguistic and terminological difficulties. The second provides a context for those that follow by considering some problems with existing literature and the ways in which Western feminists have grappled with the 'race' and gender dynamic. The third section focuses on the idea of 'difference' and the main ways in which it has been used in the feminist literature of Britain and the United States. In the fourth, attention is turned to some of the problems in discussing 'difference', particularly when focusing on 'race'. The final section suggests some possible ways forward.

Terminological Disputes

It is impossible to embark on any discussion of 'race' without first drawing attention to the problematic nature of the term, along with others associated with it. Disputes on the topic are legion. It has long been recognized that races do not exist in any scientifically meaningful sense. Nonetheless, in many societies people have often acted, and continue to act, as if 'race' is a fixed objective category. These beliefs are reflected, as Solomos has pointed out, in both political discourse and at the level of popular ideas (Solomos, 1989). Common-sense understandings of 'race' have concentrated on such variables as skin colour, country of origin, religion, nationality and language.

Some commentators, such as Miles, have suggested that 'race' should be dispensed with as an analytic category (Miles, 1982). This is partly because the very use of the term reproduces and gives legitimacy to a distinction that has no status or validity. It thus helps to perpetuate the notion that 'race' is a meaningful term. Although this may be the case at one level, to deny the significance of 'race' like this also obscures the ways in which it has 'real' effects, both in material and representational terms (Anthias, 1990). Donald and Rattansi have suggested that instead of starting with the question as to whether 'race' exists, it is more useful to ask how the category operates. 'The issue is not how *natural* differences determine and justify group definitions and interactions, but how racial logics and racial frames of reference are articulated and deployed, and with what consequences' (Donald and Rattansi, 1992, p. 1). Such an approach is useful because it can be used to chart the nature of the concept's shifting boundaries, while also permitting analysis of its ontological effects.

Another major confusion in the literature, as well as in everyday usage, is between the terms 'race' and ethnicity. Anthias distinguishes the two, defining 'race' as relying on 'notions of a biological or cultural immutability of a group that has already been attributed as sharing a common origin' (Anthias, 1990, p. 20). She describes ethnicity as 'the identification of particular cultures as ways of life or identity which are based on a historical notion of origin or fate, whether mythical or "real" ' (*ibid.*). The term ethnicity has been preferred to that of 'race' in some quarters, largely because it is viewed as supposedly having fewer essentialist connotations (Rothenberg, 1990). This overlooks the fact that it is quite possible for the concept to be used in an essentialist way, as Gilroy describes in his discussions of how black people's identification with ethnic absolutism has, indirectly, endorsed the explanations and politics of the new right (Gilroy, 1987, 1992). The idea of ethnicity is also linked to liberal notions of multi-ethnic societies and multi-culturalism, which have a tendency to obscure the force of racism with their celebration of a benign pluralism. Yet, in as much as ethnicity can provide the grounds for inferiorization, oppression, subordination and exploitation, it too may constitute the basis for racism (Anthias, 1990). As Anthias argues, 'the markers and signifiers that racism uses need not be those of biology and physiognomy but can be those of language, territorial rights or culture' (Anthias, 1990, p. 24). For this reason, 'race' and terms such as ethnicity and ethnic group are often used interchangeably. In this chapter the term 'race' is used, with some reluctance, in the same way as by Omi and Winant who see it as 'an unstable and "decentred" complex of social meanings constantly being transformed by political struggle' (Omi and Winant, 1986, p. 68).

A further issue of language which requires clarification relates to the use of the term 'black'. Initially this was employed as a political category to signify a common experience of racism and marginalization and the gulf this creates between white people and those whom they oppress, on both an institutional and a personal basis. Hall has described, for example, how the idea of 'The Black Experience' provided the basis for a new politics of resistance and critique of the way black peoples were positioned as 'other', irrespective of their different histories, traditions and identities (Hall, 1992). Recently, however, usage of the term 'black' has been criticized for the way in which it has tended to refer only to those of sub-Saharan African descent, for its American connotations, for its denial of the existence and needs of other cultural groups, and for assigning the label to those who do not necessarily define themselves in this way (Brah, 1992). Although feminists are beginning to acknowledge these difficulties, there is still a tendency to use the term in a homogenizing way. While the development of black feminism has been significant in challenging the fallibilities and inadequacies of white women's accounts, it is important to remember that such criticisms are not the prerogative of those from particular groups alone, nor do they come solely from those living in Western countries.

Mary Maynard

Understanding 'Race' and Gender: Approaches and Positions

One of the difficulties in trying to establish a perspective from which to consider how 'race' and gender interact is the polarized way in which research and thinking on the two subjects has previously developed. While white feminist work has been much criticized for its silence on matters of 'race', the fact that analyses of 'race' often disregard gender is frequently ignored. The study of racism and of racialized social structures, as Solomos notes, can be traced back to the work of classical social theorists and nineteenth-century political thinkers (Solomos, 1989). As a field of social science enquiry, however, the analysis of 'race' and race relations is usually taken as originating with a number of American social theorists (for example, W.E.B. Du Bois, E. Franklin Frazier, Charles S. Johnson, Robert E. Park, Louis Wirth) who wrote from the 1920s to the 1950s. During this period this group of writers helped to establish what came to be defined as the study of race relations, particularly through their work on segregation, immigration and 'race' consciousness in the USA (Solomos, 1989). It was this body of writing, in particular, which influenced those working on 'race' in post-war Britain and America.

Subsequently the analysis of the social meaning of racial divisions moved through a number of stages. In Britain there was an early concern with the arrival of immigrants, when they were black and from what was called the New Commonwealth, and the problems they supposedly presented in terms of accommodation, integration and assimilation into the host country's customs and mores. This gradually gave way, in the context of the 1970s concern with inequalities, to a focus on institutional and other forms of racism. Much of the emphasis here was on capitalism and/or class analysis and the extent to which an understanding of racial divisions could be subsumed within this. As a result of such debates, attention was eventually turned to the implications, both past and present, of slavery, colonialism and imperialism. More recently work has moved from what had tended to be a preoccupation with economic and material concerns to the role of the state, cultural phenomena and discourses in maintaining and challenging the racialized status quo.

The point about these developments is that, although a vast body of literature on 'race' has been generated, little of it, with a few notable exceptions, has been gendered.[1] When women were included it was often in a highly stereotypical fashion as wives, mothers and daughters. Instead, the focus has been overwhelmingly on the lives of black men, which have also largely been discussed from a white male point of view. It has also tended to concentrate on the public zones of the economy, employment, policing and law and order. The contribution of this work to an understanding of black women's lives, as with that of much of the Western feminist literature, has been minimal.

One field of enquiry which is notable for its concern with non-white, non-Western women's lives has been Development Studies. Although very little of this was recognized before the publication in 1970 of Ester Boserup's *Women's Role in Economic Development*, a considerable body of work on the subject has now been produced. This has been not so much a polemic about the racism of white feminism as a major scholarly intervention which broadens our understanding of the nature of women's lives in various parts of the world. It demonstrates that notions such as the family, citizenship, nation and state mean different things to women in 'third world' situations to those in a white European or North American context. One change in the argument of this literature, which can be perceived over time, is from a perspective which aimed to integrate women into existing development theories and models to one designed to replace these with a more feminist framework (McFarland, 1988). It is interesting, however, that the academic studies of development and of 'race' rarely draw from each other and have tended to progress in parallel. (Work on colonialism and imperialism and, increasingly, on nationality and nationhood would be exceptions here.) In addition, mainstream feminist work, which has concentrated on women in the West, has paid little attention to the ideas and implications of the literature on women and development. Rather, it has tended to treat it as a separate concern, providing the comparative and contrasting examples to Western phenomena which are regarded as more central and mainstream. Thus the polarized nature of many approaches to issues of 'race' and of gender has obscured questions of the possible relationships which might exist between them.

It is the critiques of white feminism made by black feminists which have forced consideration of the implications of 'race' and racism for the study of women. Black feminists have pointed to the inherent racism of analyses and practices which assume white experiences to be the norm, use these as the basis from which to generate concepts and theories, and fail to acknowledge the internal differentiation of black women (Amos and Parmar, 1984; Anthias and Yuval-Davis, 1983; Collins, 1990; hooks, 1984). Yet early attempts to theorize the interconnection of 'race' and gender have themselves been criticized. These merely add 'race' into the already existing feminist theoretical frameworks. They imply that 'race' simply increases the degree of inequality and oppression which black women experience as women and that oppression can be quantified and compared (Collins, 1990). This ignores the fact that 'race' does not simply make the experience of women's subordination greater. It qualitatively changes the nature of that subordination. It is within this context that writers have turned to the idea of 'difference' as a concept with the potential to encompass the diversities which ensue.

The Concept of 'Difference'

The concept, 'difference', has a long history in relation to Western feminism. Although the word was not used, as such, by first-wave feminists, the degree to which women were the same as or different from men, as well as divided by factors such as class, formed the basis of discussions about their roles, their rights and their potentialities in nineteenth-century society (Gordon, 1991). Subsequently, second-wave feminists have, implicitly or explicitly, employed the term to point to the inequalities and disadvantages that women experience when compared to men, as well as to revalue some aspects of femininity that had previously been denigrated. Thus there have been analyses of women's language and conversational styles, discussions as to whether they have different ways of writing, as well as research into, for example, their servicing of the household, discrimination in paid employment and risks from male violence. Recently, however, 'difference' has been used with another connotation by Western feminists, referring to the differences between women themselves, rather than just between two genders. There have been two formulations of this: one which focuses on the diversity of experience, the other concerned with difference as informed by postmodernist thinking.

One way of conceptualizing difference, then, is in experiential terms. The idea that women's experiences should be fundamental to its work has been one of feminism's central tenets. A focus on experience has been seen as a way of challenging women's previous silence about their own condition and in doing so confronting the 'experts' and dominant males with the limitations of their knowledge and comprehension. Feminism must begin with experience, it has been argued, since it is only from such a vantage point that it is possible to see the extent to which women's worlds are organized in ways which differ from those of men (Smith, 1988). Focusing on black women's experiences highlights the ways in which 'race' plays an important part in their social and economic positioning.

It has been shown, for example, how 'race' significantly affects black women's experiences of and treatment in areas such as education, the health service and the labour market (Brah, 1991). The influence of 'race' on how black women are represented in popular culture and the mass media has also been demonstrated (Modleski, 1986). 'Race' also has profound consequences in terms of the kinds of environments and circumstances in which women live around the world, as witnessed by the appalling famines in Africa and ethnic cleansing in the former Yugoslavia. All these things are, of course, mediated by other factors, such as class, nationality and able-bodiedness.

Focusing on how different experiences can result from the influence of 'race', however ascribed and perceived, has also made difference visible in two other senses. The first is an acknowledgment that the impact of 'race' may mean that the chief sites of oppression are not the same for black and white women. Black feminists have shown, for example, that for some women the family can be an arena for resistance and solidarity against racism and does not necessarily hold such a central place in accounting for women's subordination as it may do for white women (Carby, 1982; hooks, 1984). The second way in which a previously hidden form of difference has become visible is in the fact that 'race' is not a coherent category and that the lives of those usually classified together under the label 'black' can themselves be very different. Thus, culture, class, religion, nationality etc., in addition to gender, can all have an impact on women's lives. In Britain, for instance, there are many differences *within* the cultures of people of South Asian, African and African-Caribbean descent, as well as between them (Brah, 1992). The idea of difference, therefore, emphasizes differentation and diversity. It challenges the homogeneity of experience previously ascribed to women by virtue of being 'black'.

Some commentators, particularly those sympathetic to postmodernist thought, have argued against a notion of difference based on experiential diversity. Barrett, for instance, criticizes this formulation, in a general sense, for being rooted in an unproblematized and taken-for-granted notion of common sense and for its implicitly relativistic view of knowledge (Barrett, 1987). Black writers, however, have emphasized the importance of recognizing that experience does not necessarily equal 'truth'. Rather, it provides the basis from which to address both the similarities and the contradictions in women's lives and to develop theories as to how these might be understood collectively (Brah, 1992; Collins, 1990). As Brah says, the notion of experience is important 'as a practice of making sense, both symbolically and narratively; as struggle over material conditions and over meaning' (Brah, 1992, p. 141). She makes the useful distinction between 'the *everyday of lived experience* and *experience as a social relation*'. Experience in the former sense relates to an individual's biography. In the latter sense it refers to collective histories and the ways in which groups are positioned in social structural terms (Brah, 1991, 1992). Brah argues that although the two levels are mutually interdependent, they cannot be reduced to each other. 'Collective experience does not represent the sum total of individual experiences any more than individual experiences can be taken to be a direct expression of the collective' (Brah, 1991, p. 172). She thus alerts us to some of the tensions and complexities of discussing difference in terms of experience.

The second way in which the concept of difference is employed is in the work of postmodernists. It goes without saying that there is little agreement over what the term means and much dispute as to whose work should or should not be included within its rubric.[2] While not dismissing the legitimacy of these debates, it is possible, for the purposes of this chapter, to describe some common themes.

The postmodernist position is, broadly speaking, characterized by the view that there is no objective social world which exists outside of our pre-existing knowledge of or discourse about it. There is, thus, much scepticism about the possibility of distinguishing between 'real' aspects of the social world, on the one hand, and the concepts, modes of understanding and meanings through which they are apprehended, on the other. Postmodernism is locked into confrontation with modernist modes of thought, which are premissed upon the search for grand theories and objectivity and the assumption of a rational and unified subject. In contrast, postmodernism emphasizes fragmentation, deconstruction and the idea of multiple selves. It decentres the subject, reducing it to a mere nodal point at the intersection of a plethora of discourses (Felski, 1989). Such an approach offers both a critique of conventional epistemology, of how we gain knowledge about the social world (this includes, at its extreme, a complete disavowal that this is possible), and a view of subjectivity as both ephemeral and transitory (Baudrillard, 1990; Boyne and Rattansi, 1990; Foucault, 1989; Lyotard, 1984; Nicholson, 1990).

Postmodernism is, then, about difference in a number of senses. It can include 'differance' in the Derridean sense of the disjuncture between objects of perception and the meanings these have as symbols or representations (Derrida, 1978). Hence, phenomena such as objects or identities depend upon language, 'which simultaneously stands for and stands *in the place of* the things words represent' (Poovey, 1988, p. 51). It can refer to the multiplicity of voices, meanings and configurations which need to be considered when trying to understand the social world and which, supposedly, negate the possibility of any particular authoritative account (Lyotard, 1984). Postmodernism can also relate to the multitude of different subject positions which constitute the individual. It challenges the perceived essentialism of modernist thinking by positing difference as being at the centre of the postmodern world and by championing deconstruction as the method through which this is to be analyzed. In all of this *discourse*, rather than the supposedly modernist concern with structure, is the central conceptual preoccupation (Walby, 1992). Although postmodernist writing tends to be very abstract, ungendered and indifferent to issues such as those of 'race', some black and white feminist writers have contemplated its significance for their work (Barrett, 1992; Flax, 1987; Hall, 1992; hooks, 1991; Nicholson, 1990; Poovey, 1988; Spivak, 1988, 1990).

The two connotations of difference which have been discussed, that based on experience and that on a postmodernist fragmentation, are clearly separate and rooted in what might be regarded as oppositional philosophies. Yet, their consequences for the study of 'race' and gender, and what makes them so appealing, are surprisingly similar. To begin with they both share an emphasis on heterogeneity, together with, quite rightly, a distrust of analyses which make sweeping generalizations and develop grandiose theoretical frameworks about the nature of 'race' and gender oppression. Both challenge the unquestioning, fixed polarizations of black versus white and the heterosexist male versus female. In the diversity-of-experience approach this enables consideration of oppressive relationships between women and between men, dispelling the idea that oppression only occurs between white and black people and between men and women. It also allows for the possibility, as black women have argued, that not all men are 'enemies' and that men and women can unite in struggle (hooks, 1991).[3]

Both formulations of difference, in varying ways, subvert the unity and meaning of terms such as 'race', 'black', 'patriarchy' and 'woman'. (It is interesting that 'white' and 'man' seem to have been relatively untouched by such deconstructionist treatment.) The implication is that these kinds of categories are too internally differentiated to be useful. This, in turn, has led to a concern with subjectivity and identity. hooks, for example, whose recent work incorporates strands of both the difference of experience and the postmodernist approaches, argues for the necessity of reformulating outmoded notions of identity (hooks, 1991). These impose an essentialist, narrow and constricting idea of 'blackness', often related to colonial and imperialist paradigms. Similar arguments have been made about the deterministic and stereotyped definitions of womanhood and of femininity. Instead, an emphasis on difference allows for multiple identities and can open up new possibilities for the construction of emancipatory selves. The likely liberatory effects of this have been outlined both for black peoples (for example, Hall, 1992; hooks, 1991) and, through the deconstruction of femininity and celebration of its multiple forms, for women (Flax, 1987; Skeggs, 1991a). One constructive consequence of this is that 'blackness' and 'womanhood' come to be associated with some positive connotations and are not just seen in terms of oppression (Brah, 1991). Difference, then, not only challenges the passive labels of 'black woman' or 'white woman', it transcends such classifications, suggesting alternative subject formulations.

The Dangers of Difference

The previous discussion has indicated some of the reasons why Western feminists have seen the idea of difference as attractive, particularly when considering how to analyze the implications of 'race' and gender for each other. Yet there are dangers in accepting the concept uncritically in either of the two formulations described. What Poovey has referred to as 'this brave new world of the reconceptualized subject' may be implied by the term, but it does not necessarily follow from how it is used in current practice (Poovey, 1988, p. 60). Numerous writers, for instance, have pointed to, and been critical of, the political conservatism that characterizes much postmodernist thinking, arguing that it is incapable of making any statements of an evaluative or ethical nature and has masculinist underpinnings (Callinicos, 1989; Habermas, 1987; Hartsock, 1987; Norris, 1992; Skeggs, 1991b). Others have criticized the difference-as-experience approach because of its 'us' and 'them' connotation. It can imply the existence of a supposed norm that applies to some women but not to others, so that it is the women who are not white who are the different ones (Spelman, 1988). Whiteness here is not itself seen as a racialized identity and one that, additionally, may need to be deconstructed. White people are not racialized in the way that black people are and 'race' is seen to be a problem for the latter and not for the former. Such a stance leads to the proliferation of discrete studies of a wide variety of experiences, but makes no effective challenge to the categories or frameworks within which they are discussed. Acknowledging that 'race' gives rise to forms of difference, for example, is not the same as paying attention to *racism* as it exists in the social world or feminist work. As Spelman argues it 'suggests a setting of tolerance, which requires looking but not necessarily seeing, adding voices but not changing what has already been said' (Spelman, 1988, p. 162). This runs counter to the expressed aim of making diversities visible, in that the power to name and define still resides with white women at the 'centre' (hooks, 1984).

Another difficulty inherent in using the idea of difference, in both the experience and postmodernist forms, is the endless possibilities for diversity which are created. There are several dangers associated with this. One relates to a potential slide towards the much critiqued position of liberal pluralism which sees the social world simply in terms of an amalgam of differing groups or individuals (Allen, 1972). In such pluralism difference tends to be treated as existing all on one plane or on the same level. All forms of diversity are lumped together as examples of difference, implying that they are similar phenomena with similar explanations. This kind of parallelism was heavily critiqued by Hazel Carby over a decade ago (Carby, 1982). So many forms of difference are created that it becomes impossible to analyze them in terms of inequality or power, except in the Foucauldian sense of discourse. Under pluralism, differences in access to resources or life chances etc. become largely explicable in terms of personal culpability or luck. The possibility of offering more structured socio-political explanations disappears, except in a localized sense, because these, necessarily, must be rooted in generalizations which cannot be made. There is, therefore, the danger of being unable to offer any interpretations that reach beyond the circumstances of the particular.

There are other problems also related to the pluralistic assumptions of difference. For instance, it tends to emphasize what divides women, at the expense of those experiences that they might possibly share or have in common. Yet since cultural differences are not absolute, the similarities as well as the diversities need to be acknowledged. Pluralism also encourages a cultural relativism of the 'anything goes' variety in its approach to diversity. In discussing this, Berktay has argued that some feminists, in their struggle to overcome ethnocentric bias, both tolerate and rationalize practices towards women in other societies which they would not find acceptable in their own (Berktay, 1993).

One of the reasons for these difficulties is that difference, as an organizing concept, tends to detract from our ability to consider the relationships between things and the possible consequences in terms of domination and control which ensue. Writing about American society, Gordon claims that it is, therefore, 'a step backward to think about the experiences of minority and white women as merely different. They have intersected in conflict, and in occasional cooperation but always in mutual influence' (Gordon, 1991, p. 106). Thus feminist concerns about 'race' and about gender should, necessarily, be based not so much in understanding difference, as it is currently articulated, as in getting to grips with hierarchy and power (MacKinnon, 1987). The force of racism, as Rothenberg points out, is in the assigning of *value* to difference, which is then used to justify denigration and aggression, and not in difference per se (Rothenberg, 1990). Yet there is a tendency in some of the current writing to discuss and deconstruct both 'race' and gender as if they have no links to racism and patriarchal oppression. It is the argument of this chapter that a focus on difference alone is not sufficient to take account of these latter dimensions of power.

Finally, some further points need to be made about politics and the debate about difference. One difficulty that has been discussed in the literature concerning difference in terms of experience is that of political agency and the basis from which women might 'act' politically. Much has been written about the pitfalls of identity politics, in which women have retreated into ghettoized lifestyle politics defined in terms of personal experience and shared subjectivities alone (Adams, 1989; Brah, 1991, 1992; Harriss, 1989; hooks, 1991; Parmar, 1989). This has been criticized for using the language of 'authentic subject experience', an emphasis on the accumulation of oppressed identities leading to a hierarchy of oppression, and being divisive, thus making it difficult to work collectively across experiences (Parmar, 1989). Instead, Brah has recently advocated a politics of *identification*. This regards coalitions as politically possible through the recognition of the struggles of other groups and not just those of one's own, including, on a global scale, those of communities who may never actually meet face to face (Brah, 1991).

For the postmodernist accounts of difference, however, the position is even more vexed. The deconstruction of the self into multiple modes and forms of identities, existing only at the intersection of discourses, raises questions about self-conscious activity. Paradoxically, although everything is about the subject, no one in postmodern analyses actually appears to *do* anything. Subjectivities are seemingly overdetermined by the discourses in which they are constituted, and thus lacking in both intentionality and will. How far are individuals aware of the possibilities which, it is said, some of the recent discourses of the new ethnicities and femininities open up to them (Brah, 1992; Hall, 1992; Skeggs, 1991a, 1991b)? Are these discourses available to all women and black peoples in the same way? Or is it, perhaps, only some, the more privileged, who are in a better position to take advantage of and use the new forms of representation which ensue?

These are not intended to be idle questions, for behind them lies an important point. The deconstruction of categories such as race and gender may make visible the contradictions, mystifications, silences and hidden possibilities of which they are made up. But this is not the same as destroying or transcending the categories themselves, which clearly still play significant roles in how the social world is organized on a global scale. Thinking through and imagining beyond labels such as 'race' and gender, for those in a position to do so, is one important part of challenging both their legitimacy and their efficacy. A reworking of language alone, however, does not make them go away.

Mary Maynard

Rethinking Difference

The concept of difference is not sufficient or weighty enough to encompass all the dimensions that analyses of 'race' and gender need to include. This is not to suggest that it has not been of enormous *political* significance to black peoples especially, both in terms of naming their oppressions and in forming identities which can provide the bases for collective struggle (Brah, 1992; Parmar, 1989). Rather, it is as an *analytical* tool that its value is limited. Although usefully drawing attention to diversity, it cannot, on its own, account for power; how this comes to be constructed as inferiority and the basis for inequality and subordination. There is, therefore, a need to shift the focus of analysis from difference alone to the social relations which convert this difference into oppression (Bacchi, 1990).

Amid the contemporary theoretical hype about postmodernism, such a position stands likely to be accused of an unfortunate hankering after a, supposedly, discredited form of modernist thought. Barrett has recently written, for example, about an 'extensive "turn to culture" in feminism' with a corresponding shift away from a social structural model, focusing on 'capitalism, or patriarchy, or a gender-segmented labour market or whatever' (Barrett, 1992, p. 204). Instead the emphasis is, she claims, on culture, sexuality, symbolization and representation. Yet, it is one thing to argue that such a change has taken place (and it is certainly debatable as to whether it has occurred to quite the degree suggested) and something completely different to imply that this renders a concern with materiality redundant. It is, after all, possible to acknowledge the significance of culture and discourse and some of the problems to which they may give rise in speaking about the social world, without denying that events, relations and structures do have conditions of existence and real effects outside the sphere of the discursive (Hall, 1992). To recognize that how things are represented is constitutive and not merely reflexive of how they appear to be is, surely, to do no more than accept another version of a concern for the methodological difficulties of studying social phenomena with which the social sciences have always been plagued.

Feminist analyses which are concerned with 'race' and gender, not just as subjects for study, but for the power relations to which they give rise and which need actively to be challenged, thus need to take account of several things. The first is the material, as well as the cultural, dimensions of social life and the social relations which emerge from and interact with these. This does not mean a return to the old mechanistic assumptions, embedded in non-Marxist as well as Marxist thought, in which culture, beliefs and subjectivity are determined by social structure or the economic. It *does* mean that access to and quality of resources (such as food, shelter, money, education), as well as the restrictions resulting from the lack of them and from violence, harassment and abuse, need to be taken into account. The interaction between these things, how they are represented and their relationship to more specifically cultural phenomena may be complex and contradictory. They are, nonetheless, mediating factors in any social circumstances and cannot be ignored in analyzing the situations of black and white women.

A second important issue in considering race and gender is to problematize the label 'white' (Ware, 1992). It was pointed out earlier that whiteness is not seen as a racial identity. When questions of 'race' are raised this usually means focusing on black peoples, its victims, who are thereby constructed as 'the problem'. Yet the processes of racism and racial oppression might be better understood by concentrating, as well, on the exercise and mechanisms of white privilege and power. This does not necessarily mean focusing only on situations where black and white peoples interact. It is as important to look at the taken-for-granted everydayness of white privilege, as well as circumstances in which it is more directly expressed. Also significant in this context is the process of unravelling what the term 'white' actually means, for it is by no means a homogeneous category. It should not be forgotten, for instance, that it is not necessary to be black to experience racism, as the experiences of the Jews and the Irish and current events in Europe testify. Further, the meanings of the categories black and white are not constant. Those labelled one way under certain socio-cultural conditions may find the label changes under others.

A third matter of significance in the analysis of 'race' and gender is the need to end the continual splitting of racial and gender identities and positions, as if they can be dichotomized. It is necessary, instead, to focus on the ways in which each is implied in and experienced through the other, and not separately. Much of the work of hooks, for instance, has focused on how both 'race' and class influence the degree to which male domination and privilege can be asserted and how racism and sexism are interlocking systems of domination which uphold and sustain one another. It thus does not make sense to analyze 'race' and gender issues as if they constitute discrete systems of power. For this reason Gordon has suggested concentrating analytically, instead, on such questions as the racialized aspects of gender, gender as a concept with class characteristics, the racialized aspects of class, and so on (Gordon, 1991).

Such an approach is likely to involve concentrating on culturally and historically specific circumstances, reversing the flow of theory away from the grand abstract theorizing of the metanarrative type dismissed (yet still used) by postmodernists. This does not mean, however, that generalizations about the relationship between 'race' and gender can never be made, as some have claimed (Knowles and Mercer, 1992). While it is clear that *universalizations*, with their implications for the whole world, are untenable, it is possible to talk in qualified terms about general properties, and through comparison to highlight differences and similarities, where these clearly arise from substantive material.

Finally, this chapter has argued that the current tendency to treat difference as *the* major organizing category in understanding 'race' and gender is misplaced. Although diversity is clearly one important element, to focus on this alone is to marginalize other issues, not least of which are those of racism, power and other forces of oppression. It is not the case that women are constructed differently in any absolute way and clearly evident that they share experiences across cultures. Nor is it necessary to abandon categories, such as woman or 'race', in order to recognize that they are internally differentiated. These categories may not be unitary, but this does not mean that they are now meaningless. As Stanley has argued, such terms stand for 'the social construction of a particular set of people facing – albeit with large internal differences – a common material reality because [it is] one based in a common oppression/exploitation' (Stanley, 1990, p. 152). This material reality is taken to include representations and categorizations themselves, as well as physical material circumstances. Thus there is no need to conclude, as many now seem to, that such a position leads to essentialism (Riley, 1988). For if the argument depends, as it does, on the idea of social construction, then it is obvious, as Brah reminds us, that it is 'commonality derived from historically variable experience and as such remaining subject to historical change' which is involved (Brah, 1992, p. 174). Discussions of difference have, rightly, drawn attention to serious problems which existed in the narrowly defined nature and overgeneralizations of previous work about women by Western feminists, one from which a concern for 'race' was almost entirely lacking. Their overemphasis on fragmentation, however, offers neither political nor intellectual support in confronting the oppressions with which feminism has historically been concerned. It runs the risk, in fact, of overlooking the very existence of such oppressions.

Notes

The author is grateful to Haleh Afshar, Anne Akeroyd, Sheila Allen, Bunie Matlanyane Sexwale, Bev Skeggs and Erica Wheeler for comments on an earlier draft of this chapter.

1   Some of the notable exceptions would include Davis, 1981; Gutman, 1976; Morrissey, 1989; Phizacklea, 1983, 1990; Westwood and Bhachu, 1988.
2   It is possible, for instance, to distinguish the poststructuralist work of someone like Foucault, which emphasizes how meanings and subjectivity are constituted through discourse, from the postmodernism of Baudrillard and Lyotard which sees the social world in terms of wholesale disinformation and manipulation and the construction of language games. Felski points out that the latter are more likely to situate what they regard as a crisis of truth and representation as occurring within a particular period. Thus it may be linked to a supposedly new stage

of capitalist development, variously described as late capitalism, post-capitalism or disorganized capitalism (Felski, 1989).

3   This argument was foreshadowed by other writers, for example Rowbotham (1972).

References

ADAMS, M.L. (1989) 'There's No Place Like Home: On the Place of Identity in Feminist Politics', *Feminist Review*, no. 31.

ALLEN, S. (1972) 'Plural Society and Conflict', *New Community*, vol. 1, no. 5.

AMOS, V. and PARMAR, P. (1984) 'Challenging Imperial Feminism', *Feminist Review*, no. 17.

ANTHIAS, F. (1990) 'Race and Class Revisited – Conceptualising Race and Racisms', *Sociological Review*.

ANTHIAS, F. and YUVAL-DAVIS, N. (1983) 'Contextualising Feminism: Gender, Ethnic and Class Divisions', *Feminist Review*, no. 15.

BACCHI, C.L. (1990) *Same Difference: Feminism and Sexual Difference*, Sydney, Allen and Unwin.

BARRETT, M. (1987) 'The Concept of Difference', *Feminist Review*, no. 26.

BARRETT, M. (1992) 'Words and Things: Materialism and Method in Contemporary Feminist Analysis', in BARRETT, M. and PHILLIPS, A. (Eds) *Destabilizing Theory: Contemporary Feminist Debates*, Cambridge, Polity.

BAUDRILLARD, J. (1989) *Selected Writings*, ed. M. Poster, Cambridge, Polity.

BAUDRILLARD, J. (1990) *Revenge of the Crystal: A Baudrillard Reader*, London, Pluto.

BERKTAY, F. (1993) 'Looking from the "Other" Side: Is Cultural Relativism a Way Out?', in DE GROOT, J. and MAYNARD, M. (Eds) *Women's Studies in the 1990s: Doing Things Differently?*, London, Macmillan.

BOSERUP, E. (1970) *Women's Role in Economic Development*, London, Allen and Unwin.

BOYNE, R. and RATTANSI, A. (Eds) (1990) *Postmodernism and Society*, London, Macmillan.

BRAH, A. (1991) 'Questions of Difference and International Feminism', in AARON, J. and WALBY, S. (Eds) *Out of the Margins*, London, Falmer Press.

BRAH, A. (1992) 'Difference, Diversity and Differentiation', in DONALD, J. and RATTANSI, A. (Eds) *'Race', Culture and Difference*, London, Sage.

CALLINICOS, A. (1989) *Against Postmodernism: A Marxist Critique*, Cambridge, Polity.

CARBY, H. (1982) 'White Woman Listen! Black Feminism and the Boundaries of Sisterhood', in CENTRE FOR CONTEMPORARY CULTURAL STUDIES *The Empire Strikes Back*, London, Hutchinson.

COLLINS, P.H. (1990) *Black Feminist Thought*, London, Unwin Hyman.

DAVIS, A. (1981) *Women, Race and Class*, London, The Women's Press.

DERRIDA, J. (1978) *Writing and Difference*, London, Routledge and Kegan Paul.

DONALD, J. and RATTANSI, A. (Eds) (1992) *'Race', Culture and Difference*, London, Sage.

Mary Maynard

FELSKI, R. (1989) 'Feminist Theory and Social Change', *Theory, Culture and Society*, vol. 6.

FLAX, J. (1987) 'Postmodernism and Gender Relations in Feminist Theory', *Signs*, vol. 12, no. 4.

FOUCAULT, M. (1989) *The Archaeology of Knowledge*, London, Routledge.

FRYE, M. (1983) *The Politics of Reality: Essays in Feminist Theory*, New York, The Crossing Press.

GILROY, P. (1987) *There Ain't No Black in the Union Jack*, London, Hutchinson.

GILROY, P. (1992) 'The End of Antiracism', in DONALD, J. and RATTANSI, A. (Eds) *'Race', Culture and Difference*, London, Sage.

GORDON, L. (1991) 'On "Difference"', *Genders*, no. 10.

GUTMAN, H. (1976) *The Black Family in Slavery and Freedom, 1750–1925*, New York, Vintage.

HABERMAS, J. (1987) *The Philosophical Discourse of Modernity*, Cambridge, Polity.

HALL, S. (1992) 'New Ethnicities', in DONALD, J. and RATTANSI, A. (Eds) *'Race', Culture and Difference*, London, Sage.

HARRISS, K. (1989) 'New Alliances: Socialist Feminism in the Eighties', *Feminist Review*, no. 31.

HARTSOCK, N. (1987) 'Rethinking Modernism', *Cultural Critique*, Fall.

HOOKS, B. (1982) *Ain't I A Woman*, London, Pluto.

HOOKS, B. (1984) *Feminist Theory: From Margin to Centre*, Boston, South End Press.

HOOKS, B. (1989) *Talking Back*, London, Sheba.

HOOKS, B. (1991) *Yearning*, London, Turnaround.

KNOWLES, C. and MERCER, S. (1992) 'Feminism and Antiracism: An Exploration of the Political Possibilities', in DONALD, J. and RATTANSI, A. (Eds) *'Race', Culture and Difference*, London, Sage.

LYOTARD, J-F, (1984) *The Postmodern Condition*, Manchester, Manchester University Press.

McFARLAND, J. (1988) 'The Construction of Women and Development Theory', *Canadian Review of Sociology and Anthropology*, vol. 25, no. 2.

MACKINNON, C. (1987) *Feminism Unmodified*, Harvard, Harvard University Press.

MILES, R. (1982) *Racism and Migrant Labour*, London, Routledge and Kegan Paul.

MILES, R. (1989) *Racism*, London, Routledge.

MODLESKI, T. (Ed.) (1986) *Studies in Entertainment: Critical Approaches to Mass Culture*, Bloomington and Indianapolis, Indiana University Press.

MORRISSEY, M. (1989) *Slave Women in the New World*, Lawrence, Kansas, University Press of Kansas.

NICHOLSON, L. (Ed.) (1990) *Feminism/Postmodernism*, London, Routledge.

NORRIS, C. (1992) *Uncritical Theory*, London: Lawrence and Wishart.

OMI, M. and WINANT, H. (1986) *Racial Formation in the United States*, London and New York, Routledge and Kegan Paul.

PARMAR, P. (1989) 'Other Kinds of Dreams', *Feminist Review*, no. 31.

PHIZACKLEA, A. (Ed.) (1983) *One Way Ticket: Migration and Female Labour*, London, Routledge.

PHIZACKLEA, A. (1990) *Unpacking the Fashion Industry*, London, Routledge.

POOVEY, M. (1988) 'Feminism and Deconstruction', *Feminist Studies*, vol. 14, no. 1.
RAMAZANOGLU, C. (1989) *Feminism and the Contradictions of Oppression*, London, Routledge.
RILEY, D. (1988) *'Am I That Name?' Feminism and the Category of 'Women' in History*, Basingstoke, Macmillan.
ROTHENBERG, P. (1990) 'The Construction, Deconstruction, and Reconstruction of Difference', *Hypatia*, vol. 5, no. 1.
ROWBOTHAM, S. (1972) *Women, Resistance and Revolution*, London, Allen Lane.
SKEGGS, B. (1991a) 'A Spanking Good Time', *Magazine of Cultural Studies*, no. 3.
SKEGGS, B. (1991b) 'Postmodernism: What is all the Fuss About?', *British Journal of the Sociology of Education*, vol. 12, no. 2.
SMITH, D. (1988) *The Everyday World as Problematic*, Milton Keynes, Open University Press.
SOLOMOS, J. (1989) *Race and Racism in Contemporary Britain*, London, Macmillan.
SPELMAN, E. (1988) *Inessential Woman*, London, The Women's Press.
SPIVAK, G.C. (1988) *In Other Worlds*, London, Routledge.
SPIVAK, G.C. (1990) *The Post-Colonial Critic*, London, Routledge.
STANLEY, L. (1990) 'Recovering Women in History from Feminist Deconstructionism', *Women's Studies International Forum*, vol. 13, nos 1/2.
WALBY, S. (1992) 'Post-Post-Modernism? Theorizing Social Complexity', in BARRETT, M. and PHILLIPS, A. (Eds) *Destabilizing Theory*, Cambridge, Polity.
WARE, V. (1992) *Beyond the Pale: White Women, Racism and History*, London, Verso.
WESTWOOD, S. and BHACHU, P. (Eds) (1988) *Enterprising Women: Ethnicity, Economy and Gender Relations*, London, Routledge.

Chapter 2

Tracing the Contours:
Feminist Research and Feminist
Objectivity[1]

Kum-Kum Bhavnani

The projects of feminist research are frequently thought of as having episte-mological concerns at their centre (Michele le Doeuff, 1987), these concerns having posed challenges to the practices and theories of the human sciences within the academy. Many writers have been working on these issues in the past two decades (Stanley and Wise, 1979; Mies, 1983; Eichler, 1988; Grosz, 1987; Harding, 1991; Hartsock, 1983; Haraway, 1989; Collins, 1990; Rose, 1983; Smith, 1988; Stacey, 1988) and it is generally agreed upon that issues of objectivity and their relationship to 'science' are issues which are at the fore-front of the projects of feminist research. Simultaneously, arguments which look critically at positivist approaches to knowledge have impinged upon the disciplines of sociology (Abbott and Wallace, 1990), history (Alonso, 1988; Passerini, 1987) and social psychology (Squire, 1989) to name but a few examples. These universes of discourse have been informed by feminist approaches, which means that questions are raised, for example, within psy-chology about the apparent objectivity of the experimental method (Sherif, 1987). This, in turn, has brought into focus the arguments about the limited value of quantitative analyses in providing insights into issues of human rela-tionships (e.g. Griffin, 1985) and about power inequalities within the research process (Bhavnani, 1988). Such discussions have frequently focused on the *methods* deployed in the generation of insights in the human sciences. What has often flowed from these discussions are broader challenges which inter-rogate empiricism and positivism.

Such challenges mean that scientific activity as neutral and value-free has gained academic credence (see, e.g., Rose and Rose, 1976) although not a widespread academic acceptance. If, however, it is accepted that scientific insights are social in origin, then these origins may be analyzed by tracing the historical development of such insights. Thus, a historical approach can facil-itate answers to questions such as *why* a particular issue is investigated at a particular point in time. For example, *why* was it that the end of the nineteenth century and the turn of the twentieth saw considerable interest in relying on arguments about the brain size of black people and white women to explain apparent differences in cognitive abilities between these groups and white men (Griffiths and Saraga, 1979)? A historical approach may also facilitate the posing of questions as to *how* such knowledge is produced – that is, who produces it and how it becomes privileged. The logic of this argument is that a historical approach encourages questions to be raised about the political economy of knowledge production. In this way, a historical approach can eliminate the idea of total knowledges; thus, objectivity and truth come to be seen as concepts which are historically situated and situationally specific.

Knowledge production is, therefore, a historical process. My argument is that feminist epistemologies, in the process of continuing challenges against positivism, have always placed questions and issues about the historical relationships between science and society at the centre of our work. Feminist theorizing has always argued that there is a necessity for scientific work to examine its practices, procedures and theories through the use of historical insights, for it is these insights that bring into focus the ways in which knowledge production is a set of social, political, economic and ideological processes (e.g. Acker *et al.*, 1983).

The arguments about the historicization of knowledge, embraced by many writers (e.g. Bhaskar, 1989; Fraser, 1989) lead me to ask of feminist studies – is feminist work being developed with an adequate historical sense of differences amongst women?

The work in the US of, for example, black writers such as Angela Y. Davis (1971, 1981) and Patricia Hill Collins (1990) and in Britain writings such as those by Bryan *et al.* (1985), Grewal *et al.* (1988) and Ware (1992) has shown that the histories of the feminist movement in both of those countries are fraught with racisms and exclusionary practices. These arguments continue by suggesting that an important consequence of these histories is that racialized, gendered and class-based inequalities are embedded into the creation of knowledge. What often occurs in the process of presenting feminist arguments for the historicization of knowledge is that the points about racisms, exclusion and invisibility of women of colour become silenced (see Haraway, 1989, for an exception). Thus the questions that charges of exclusion and invisibility pose of feminist studies begin to disappear, the projects to create feminist knowledges become weak and fragmented and history gets re-enacted. It is sometimes implied that inclusion of racism in feminist work can lead to fragmentation of feminist projects. My argument is that far from an analysis of racism leading to fragmentation, it is the process of not engaging with the consequences of racialized inequalities which weakens the projects of feminisms.

Thus, I argue that challenges from feminist writers and analysts to positivist approaches to knowledge raise an issue central to knowledge production, namely, that such production is a historical process. I suggest, however, that many of those working on feminist epistemologies have often developed inadequate arguments about such historicity by erasing, denying, ignoring or tokenizing the contradictory and conflicting interests which women may have – often seen most clearly in the writings of women from all over the world (Bhavnani, 1993). Such conflicting interests can mean that different stand-points develop which are in sharp opposition to each other. For example, the history of white women's suffrage in the United States demonstrates these conflicting interests in that such suffrage was often argued for at the expense of black suffrage (Davis, 1981). This way of writing history, that is that conflicting interests amongst women are made visible, can lead to questions arising about objective knowledges. In other words, this approach can demonstrate that objective knowledges are situated and partial, not impartial or disembodied, and neither are they transcendent.

While the above arguments are not new, nor specific to feminist critiques of the social sciences, it is Donna Haraway (1988) who has recently recast and reframed them in her representation of feminist objectivity. Her sense of objectivity is in opposition to positivist discussions of this concept, and is also distant from the absolute relativism embodied in the view that all truths are equally valid. She says 'Feminist objectivity means quite simply *situated knowledges*' (p. 581). In describing feminist attempts to grapple with dis-cussions of truth, she convincingly points to ' "our" problem [which] is how to have *simultaneously* an account of radical historical contingency for all knowledge claims' (p. 579), while still retaining a sense of the material or 'real' world. She suggests that feminists could view objectivity as a 'particular and specific embodiment', rather than as a 'false vision promising transcend-ence of all limits and responsibility' (Haraway, 1988, p. 582), and that 'Femin-ist objectivity is about limited location and situated knowledge, not about transcendence and splitting of subject and object. It allows us to become answerable for what we learn to see' (Haraway, 1988, p. 583). She continues later by stating that 'We seek those ruled by partial sight and limited voice – not partiality for its own sake, but, rather, for the sake of the connections and unexpected openings [which] situated knowledges make possible. Situ-ated knowledges are about communities, not about isolated individuals' (Haraway, 1988, p. 590).

What may be derived from this is that partiality of vision need not be synonymous with partiality of theorizing, and, indeed, may be desirable, for the partiality she discusses could lead to greater insight for feminist analyses. Thus, she argues that not only are positioning and partiality two key elements of feminist objectivity, but 'becom[ing] answerable for what we learn to see' requires that a third element, that of accountability, should be present as well. The strength of this argument is that she engages with difference, and, indeed, uses difference as the springboard from which to transform feminist arguments about objectivity.

Her emphasis on accountability, positioning and partiality is helpful, for this accentuation can permit a clearer approach to analyzing and developing feminist insights into objectivity. Further, her argument that these elements, when emanating from feminist frameworks, can provide some dynamic and creative connections in the production of knowledges is both exciting and timely. If these elements do permit the development of creative and dynamic connections, then it is appropriate to pose the question: 'by what means do these elements permit the making of such connections?' What are the implications to be drawn from the three elements – accountability, positioning and partiality – for the ways in which knowledge production can be faithful to the notion of 'feminist objectivity' outlined by Haraway? What are the principles that flow from these elements and which, in turn, indicate criteria according to which research can be evaluated as 'feminist'?

A question which consistently haunts feminist researchers – especially those of us working within the social sciences – is whether it is possible to identify principles which could frame the development of criteria for the conduct, evaluation and dissemination of feminist work in the social sciences. Is there, indeed, anything which is particular to feminist enquiry in the social sciences, after having specified that the main agent of the enquiry be a woman, or women? This question has been raised many times (recently by Jayaratne and Stewart, 1991) and yet it has still not been thoroughly interrogated. Most readers of this article would agree that research is not necessarily feminist if it is conducted by a woman, nor that the subjects of the enquiry need be only women, but surely it is valid to state that the main agent of any research which claims to be feminist must be 'woman'. However, while that is a necessary condition for feminist work it is not a sufficient one. It is necessary because 'feminist' is derived from 'feminism', which is a political movement comprised of women, but it is not sufficient because there is a clear distinction between 'woman' and 'feminist'. Neither category is unitary nor singular (see Sandoval, 1991), but neither are they collapsible into each other – for 'feminist' is an achieved status, or, more precisely, a continuous accomplishment.

If it is not sufficient that women are the key agents in any work which is defined as feminist, then how can one identify work as feminist in the sense of furthering the aims of feminist objectivity – that is, creating situated knowledges – as laid out by Haraway? I suggest that questions be developed, and principles delineated in order to set up markers against which any social scientific enquiry could be evaluated for its claim to be feminist.

The first principle which flows from Haraway's insistence on accountability as an element within feminist objectivity is that any study whose main agent is a woman/women and which claims a feminist framework should not reproduce the researched in ways in which they are represented within dominant society – that is, the analyses cannot be complicit with dominant representations which reinscribe inequality. In other words, the accountability of the research is not only to specific individuals, but also to the overall projects of feminisms. For example, feminist work often struggles to make the agency of women visible, while not presenting this agency as deviant (e.g. Essed, 1990). So, when people are in positions of structural subordination, research which is defined as feminist must, at the very least, reflect upon whether the analysis presented in the work reinscribes the researched into the dominant representations of powerlessness, into being viewed as without agency, into being defined as abnormal. The question which flows from Haraway's first element is: 'does this work/analysis define the researched as either passive victims or as deviant – does it reinscribe the researched into prevailing representations?' If that is the case, as in, for example, some studies which have been published about South Asian women living in England (see Brah, 1987, for a commentary about this; and see Brah and Shaw, 1992, for an example of a study which avoids such a trap), then it seems to me that regardless of whether the research focuses on women, or is conducted by women, or both, it may not be defined as being informed by *feminism*. If research is unable to achieve such a definition, then, it cannot implement the project of furthering feminist objectivity. I am not, for one second, suggesting that women researchers provide romanticized analyses of people who are frequently in positions of structural subordination. Rather, I am arguing that for feminist objectivity to be enhanced, and for knowledge production to be explicitly understood as a historical process, it is incumbent on women researchers to pose the above question of our/themselves, and to deal with it in the analysis. When this is done, then the work may be claimed as fashioning feminist objectivity.

The second question emerging from Haraway's arguments about positioning is whether the research report, however and wherever it is presented, discusses, or, at its most minimal, makes reference to the micropolitical processes which are in play during the conduct of research. In short, the question is, how and to what extent does the research conduct, write-up and dissemination deal with the micropolitics of the research encounter – what are the relationships of domination and subordination which the researcher has negotiated and what are the means through which they are discussed in the research report?

The third question, analogous to her element of partiality, is centred upon 'difference'. In what ways are questions of difference dealt with in the research study – in its design, conduct, write-up, and dissemination?

It is these three questions – are the researched reinscribed into prevailing notions of powerlessness? are the micropolitics of the research relationships discussed? and how are questions of difference engaged with? – which I suggest flow from Haraway's discussion of feminist objectivity, and which provide reference points through which principles may be delineated and, thus, research projects evaluated. The three questions generate principles and criteria which permit the creation of sufficient conditions, beyond the necessary one that the main agent is a woman. It is the combination of these necessary and sufficient conditions which can then provide the framework for evaluating research as feminist.

I shall use these three questions as reference points – reinscription, micropolitics and difference – to frame the second section of my paper. This is an examination of a research study I conducted in Britain in 1984 and 1985, of which the write-up was completed in early 1988 (Bhavnani, 1991). I shall use the lens of feminist objectivity combined with the questions raised above to comment on that work and to discuss in what ways it stands under the umbrella of feminist objectivity.

The research study explored the ways in which young, working-class people in Britain discussed issues in the domain of the political. Much of the psychological work on young people in Britain has discussed youth as a homogeneous group, focusing on insights derived from biology and conventional psychology (e.g. Conger, 1973). Such work has therefore disguised the ways in which the transition between childhood and adulthood is a social transition (Bates *et al.*, 1984). The transition is presented as a 'natural' one. From this vantage point, when the political views of young people have been discussed, most often using survey methods, young people have been presented as either politically apathetic or politically rebellious (see, e.g., Furnham, 1985, for a review). The definitions which have been used to tap political views have tended to focus exclusively on the parliamentary process in Britain and on potential voting behaviour. Whilst not *all* work with young people has done this – see, for example, the work which came from the Centre for Contemporary Cultural Studies at the University of Birmingham in England (e.g. Hall and Jefferson, 1975) – there is an overwhelming set of discourses about white young men in particular (much of this work had been done with men) suggesting that working-class young men in Britain are not interested in politics. That is, the argument implies, young working-class men are not political. In this way, the direction of such research ends up reproducing discourses which, in general, cast young working-class men as social victims. The work from the Birmingham Centre, and their approach to young people, mostly men, relied on ethnographic and quasi-ethnographic methods. The use of ethnographic approaches, combined with feminist work with young women, as in for example, the work of Angela McRobbie (1982) and Christine Griffin (1985) demonstrated to me that it was possible to take the perspective of young people seriously within an academic research project. But I did not assume that I should automatically take the young people's perspective at face value.

The study took as a starting point that politics is the means by which human beings regulate, attempt to regulate and challenge, with a view to changing, unequal power relationships. It did not define 'politics' only as the arena in which voting, political parties and knowledge of the official political processes in Britain are discussed. Such an open definition of politics required that I think hard about the topics to be discussed within the study, as well as the ways in which these topics would be discussed with young people. As a result, I conducted pilot work in Sheffield, a town in Northern England, in which I used a formal questionnaire, with closed questions, as well as 'hanging out'[2] in the largest shopping mall in the centre of Middleton,[3] where youth often gather on weekday afternoons and on Saturdays. I also spent considerable time in youth centres in Middleton – where young people come to play pool and table tennis, to listen to music and to talk. From the four months I spent immersed in this style of work, that is, a constant seven days a week engagement with young people, I quickly saw that young women, black and white, were not very present in either the malls or the youth centres, except, in the latter case, when there were 'girls' nights' or special sessions set up for young women of South Asian origin. As I had wanted to discuss issues within the domain of the political with both young men and young women, I decided to move the main study to schools in Central and South Middleton. I firstly conducted single-sex group discussions with ninety 16-year-olds in their final year of school in early 1985. The discussions covered a range of issues having 'to do with society' as I explained it, and I used a frequency count of the topics which were raised by the school students to include in the individual interviews. I also wanted to discuss issues which are more frequently thought of as political, such as the parliamentary parties, and so I included this as well into the individual interviews.

The decision to move away from adopting quantitative analyses to the study was informed by my personal history of work in developmental and social psychology as well as by my pilot work. The agenda for the open-ended individual interview schedule which I used was a negotiation between myself and the young people who were the potential interviewees of the study, and the use of open-ended interviews, based on prior group discussions, was a means whereby that negotiation could occur. There was no indication that the young people did not want to discuss the issues within the domain of the political which they and I had negotiated together, and so suggestions of political apathy remain marginal for any analysis of this work. They also talked at length – as the thousands of pages of transcripts show.

I interviewed seventy-two young people in this way, half of whom were men. Approximately one-third of the interviewees were of Afro-Caribbean origin, one-third were of South Asian origin, and the remaining third were white. The topics covered in the individual interviews were derived from the group discussions and included employment, unemployment, training for young people, racism, democracy and voting, marriage and violence against women and children and the miners' strike in Britain of 1984/5. Sixty of the seventy-two interviewees were interviewed by me six months later, the issues being life since leaving school, employment, unemployment and training schemes, recent rebellions by youth in Britain, their futures and party politics. In this way, these interviews about issues in the domain of the political were situated in the context of the movement of these young people from school to unemployment or the labour market. These 132 interviews, each of forty to forty-five minutes in length, were tape-recorded and then transcribed.

I have been reflecting on the points I made earlier about furthering the project of feminist objectivity because there have been times, when I have discussed my research in public forums, when I have been asked 'But what has this project got to do with your interests in "race" [for which read difference] and gender [for which read feminist studies]?' A question which requires specification of how feminism and difference are implicated within this enquiry is certainly a helpful question, for any response to it has to lay bare some of the assumptions, and hence the criteria according to which academic work may be claimed as feminist. The criteria are clearly not obvious in this study, for apart from my self-definition as a black feminist in Britain in the past two decades, there is apparently very little in any initial outline to indicate that the work is based on and aims to develop feminist work. The research explored issues in the domain of the political – not specifically a feminist preoccupation, nor, indeed, part of the common sense of 'women's issues'. I also interviewed both men and women. In what ways, therefore, can it be defined as a feminist enquiry, and hence as something which could help in the elaboration of feminist objectivity?

My previous discussion suggested three questions – focusing on reinscription, micropolitics and difference – which generate principles and criteria from which research conducted and written by women can be evaluated for claims to feminism. Below, I shall discuss my research according to the these questions, and I shall also draw on insights from Haraway's suggestion that feminist objectivity provides unexpected openings and connections.

The first principle I discussed was that of reinscription. Let me point to the ways in which this research project may have been partly successful in avoiding reinscribing the researched as without agency, and as 'politically apathetic' – that is, in avoiding a representation of young working-class people as cultural dopes. I would not want to claim that it was totally successful, but I should like to present the reasons for my thinking that it was partly successful.

Many of the young people, when discussing party politics, organized their arguments through the theme of intelligence ('don't think I'm a brain box' was the way in which one young woman said it). The suggestion was implied by many of the interviewees that their views about, for example, the Labour Party were not legitimate because the speaker did not see her/himself as intelligent. Thus, intelligence came to be seen as a necessary requirement for being able to comment on parliamentary parties. This link between democracy and 'intelligence' provided by the interviewees led to an unexpected opening. That is, the young people in this study were not necessarily politically apathetic, but they understood the playing out of democracy in relation to levels of intelligence, and thus defined themselves as *unable* to present *legitimate* opinions about party politics. It was not that there was no interest there – but there was an implicit and explicit wondering whether their views were legitimate. This unexpected opening can then permit a connection to intelligence.[4] The point for the present argument is that the young people in this particular research project were not politically apathetic or politically disinterested, but rather, that there were distinct and comprehensible reasons why they appeared to not discuss many issues in the domain of the political. In taking the stated views of young people seriously, but not necessarily at face value, it did not reinscribe the researched into dominant representations – namely, that young working-class people are social victims. In avoiding such a reinscription, the study may lay claim to furthering feminist objectivity and, therefore, suggest a more productive way of understanding the construction of politics by this group of young people.

The second question which I have suggested could be used to indicate whether the project of feminist objectivity is beginning to be implemented is related to the micropolitics of the research process. Again, let me take my research as a case study through which I can show what I understand by this.

The power of the researcher in relation to the researched – a set of power relationships which is bounded by the imperatives of resource availability – can define the parameters of the theoretical framework, can control the design of the study, and can inform how the study is conducted, analyzed and written up. That is, the researcher is positioned in a particular relationship of power in relation to the researched. Frequently, research which has been influenced by the arguments of feminist writers such as Helen Roberts (1981) or Liz Stanley (1990) will note this positioning of the researcher. My argument, however, is that the micropolitics of the research situation need to be analyzed and not only noted. For example, relationships within this research flowed from the socially ascribed characteristics, such as 'race', gender and class, as well as age, of the interviewer and interviewee. These socially ascribed characteristics carry hierarchical loadings of their own. Many times, the sensitive social scientist has tried to regulate this unevenness in the social characteristics by ensuring that women interview women and that black researchers interview black people. In fact, it may even have been expected that I would have designed a research study in which I set up such 'matching' – that is, that I only interviewed South Asian women, or black women, or black women and white women. I knew, however, from the start of this study that I wanted to interview white men – because I wanted to see 'what would happen'. Rosenthal's (1966) work on the experimenter effect is often cited to justify the matching of researcher and researched, and work such as that by Zenie-Ziegler (1988) is an example of a study which merely noted the position of the researcher in relation to the researched. I suggest that both matching and noting can take the gaze of the analyst and reader away from the micropolitics of the research encounter. This is because matching and noting cannot explicitly take account of the power relationships between the researcher and the researched, and yet both processes imply that unevenness between the two sides in a research study has been dealt with. In the research study discussed in this paper, such matching was never present – because I was always a woman who was fifteen to twenty years older than the interviewees. This age non-matching was interwoven with matches or non-matches of culture, 'race' and gender. For example, when interviewing young white men, the frequently encountered imbalance of power between white men and black women was potentially both inverted and reproduced in the interviews. My role as student researcher, my age, and my assumed class affiliation may have been taken as sources of potential domination. However, my racialized and gendered ascriptions suggested the opposite. That is, in this instance, the interviewees and myself were inscribed within multi-faceted power relations which had both structural domination and structural subordination in play on both sides. This interplay of subordination and domination on the part of both interviewer and interviewee was a consistent feature of my study.

Let me compare this to a study for which I have considerable respect, but which, as I reflect upon it, I seem to want to add to. Paul Willis (1978) conducted an ethnographic study which deployed participant observation, discussion and individual conversation with a group of young working-class men in Britain in the mid 1970s. He wanted to analyze the ways in which, as they moved from school to the labour market, working-class men obtained and stayed within 'working-class jobs'. One part of his study showed that when the boys talked about their girlfriends, they discussed them in objectified and frequently very dismissive ways. This notion of how this group of young men discuss issues of heterosexual relationships forms part of some forms of academic conventional wisdom – white working-class men are overwhelmingly and offensively sexist. None of the young men I interviewed talked about women in that way. Clearly, there is an important question to be dealt with here – which is why the young men in my study did not talk to me in the way in which they talked with Willis.

The first answer which is often presented is 'well, you're a woman and they thought they should not be rude to you, the *woman* researcher'. Such a comment implies that my interviews with these young men are not authentic – and thus that work such as that of Willis is authentic about young men. This notion, that *some* kinds of work are 'authentic', and therefore, by implication, others are inauthentic, has been sufficiently discredited to make that kind of explanation unsatisfactory. What such a notion does, however, is to reinscribe a Willis-type study as 'natural', as *the truth*. What I am saying is that Willis, a white man, becomes a marker for a universalistic insight whilst I, a black woman, become particularized. (See Barbara Christian's (1987) discussion of a similar issue when 'race' and theory are under scrutiny.) In other words, I argue that the questions which may be addressed to me about my work also need to be put to Willis. When one begins to think of it in this way, then it is possible to analyze the micropolitics of the research process. That is, when the socially ascribed, hierarchically organized characteristics of the researcher and researched have structural domination and structural subordination in play on both sides in a manner which inverts the usually encountered imbalances, *this* set-up can provide an opening for an analysis of the micropolitics. I am not suggesting that men interviewing women is a consequence of my argument, for that is merely a replication of the most frequently encountered power imbalances in research studies. What I am suggesting is that an inversion of this 'normal' power imbalance in research studies – from the conception right through to the analysis – can permit a sharper analysis of the micropolitics of research, so that *feminist* objectivity can be implemented. So, any text which emerges in a research encounter cannot be taken for granted.

The third question which can be posed is to ask in what ways issues of difference are seen and dealt with explicitly. Ironically, this has been the one that has been the most difficult one for me to address explicitly in the context of this paper. I have again taken my lead from Donna Haraway's account of partiality, which does not imply partiality of theorizing. Many readers will be familiar with the argument, often, but not exclusively, presented by women of colour, that studies that have women as researchers and women as the researched group have ignored or glossed over differences amongst women (e.g. Bridenthal *et al.*, 1984; Hewitt, 1985; Lazreg, 1990). This research study did point to many continuities of experience for the young people, who had shared experiences of their schools, their housing, and the relationship of their household to the local state. However, it is clear that there were also non-shared experiences and accounts such as those of racism, culture and gender. If difference is understood as difference of interests within this study – that is, that there are material reasons for the discontinuities of experience and identities put forward by the young people – then the ways in which the young people talked about racism provides an entry point for such a discussion. On the whole, the young white people in this study did not express explicit racism, although some of their comments were situated within discourses which can lead to a reproduction of racism. An example of this would be 'I don't care what colour they are – they're just my friends'. In general, however, most of the white interviewees claimed to be against racism by utilizing the theme of 'we're all humans, aren't we?' This appeal to a common biology and naturalness led the white interviewees to suggest that racism was also 'natural'. For example, many white interviewees said 'it's human nature' and, therefore, implied that little could be done to eliminate it by society.

In contrast, many young black people identified a number of the ways through which some of the contradictions of racism could be considered, thus indicating one type of strategy for challenging racism. Examples of the identification of contradictions were points such as 'why do they want a tan when they criticize us because of our colour?' Or reference was made to the arranged marriage between Prince Charles and Diana as being publicly lauded, while official statements in Britain about arranged marriage within South Asian cultures condemned the practice. Some of the young women of South Asian origin suggested that, as marriage was a 'natural' consequence in their lives, then one could defend the *concept* of arranged marriage, because the logic was that 'if you're going to get married anyway', an arranged marriage was preferable to a love marriage. When asked why, one young woman said:

PN11: Cos you don't have to go out looking for someone – I couldn't.
KKB: You couldn't?
PN11: No, must be like a hunter with a spear and net, hunting for a husband.

This strategy of pointing to contradictions within racist arguments was one which was developed by the black interviewees. This is one way of beginning to examine difference – in the sense of pointing to the contradictions within racist arguments. However, the young black people also discussed racism through suggesting explicit strategies to tackle it. Such strategies included 'I told my teacher', 'I wanted to grab and choke them', and 'I ignored them', this last implying that ignoring was one strategy out of a repertoire of strategies available to her. The interweaving of a concept of strategy into their discussions suggested that these speakers thought that racism could be altered by being challenged, either by pointing to the contradictions or by suggesting explicit means to tackle racism. In suggesting that patterns of racist behaviour can be altered and eliminated, there is a consequent implication that, therefore, racism is not natural. That is, it is implied that racism is a result of social definitions rather than a biological inevitability of 'human nature'.[5] It is this discontinuity of both identity and experience which can be generated if a sense of difference is built into the research process.

In conclusion, it is clear that feminist projects which trace the contours of feminist objectivity are a central means by which it may be possible to escape from the impasse over questions of 'objectivity' and 'truth' which at present hounds many discussions of research practices. Further, I suggest that *feminist* objectivity, with its principles of accountability, partiality and positioning, leads to a set of questions which, in turn, frame principles and criteria for the evaluation of research studies – criteria of whether or not subjects are reinscribed into powerlessness, of how the micropolitics of the research are discussed and of how 'difference' is made integral to a research study.

The point can be made most concisely using the following extract from an interview conducted for the study:

KKB: What's your ideal job?
PN60: I'd like the job of the Queen.
KKB: Why? What does she do?
PN60: Well, put it like this, she gets paid for breaking bottles against ships and we get arrested for breaking bottles on the street!

Notes

1 This paper was originally published in *Women's Studies International Forum*, vol. 16, no. 2, 1993, pp. 95–104.
2 This is a common technique used in participant observation and ethnographic research where the researcher spends time with the researched on their territory, sharing their work, leisure or home environments.
3 This is the fictional name for the large town in the North of England where I conducted the study.
4 The concept of intelligence has been widely criticized for at least the past two decades as being a means by which economic, social and racialized inequalities

are both reproduced and therefore sustained (see Richardson *et al.*, 1972) – that is, notions of intelligence can undermine the goals of a democracy. Clearly, a question which can then be raised, from the interviews with the young people, is what it is in official discourses about public-domain politics which legitimates this view.

5   One can ask why it was that the young black interviewees discussed racism with me in these ways, and why the white interviewees did so in a different way, and I have dealt with that type of argument earlier.

References

ABBOTT, PAMELA and WALLACE, CLAIRE (1990) *An Introduction to Sociology: Feminist Perspectives*, London, Routledge.

ACKER, JOAN, BARRY, KATE and ESSEVELD, JOKE (1983) 'Objectivity and Truth: Problems in Doing Feminist Research', *Women's Studies International Forum*, vol. 6, no. 4, pp. 423–35.

ALONSO, ANA MARIA (1988) 'The Effects of Truth: Representations of the Past and the Imagining of Community', *Journal of Historical Sociology*, vol. 1, no. 1, pp. 33–58.

BATES, INGE, CLARKE, JOHN, COHEN, PHIL, FINN, DAN, MOORE, ROBERT and WILLIS, PAUL (Eds) (1984) *Schooling for the Dole? The New Vocationalism*, London, Macmillan.

BHASKAR, ROY (1989) *Reclaiming Reality*, London, Verso.

BHAVNANI, KUM-KUM (1988) 'Empowerment and Social Research', *TEXT*, vol. 8, no. 1, pp. 41–51.

BHAVNANI, KUM-KUM (1991) *Talking Politics: A Psychological Framing for Views from Youth in Britain*, Cambridge, Cambridge University Press.

BHAVNANI, KUM-KUM (1993) 'Talking Racism and the Editing of Women's Studies', in RICHARDSON, DIANE and ROBINSON, VICKI (Eds) *Introducing Women's Studies*, London, Macmillan.

BRAH, AVTAR (1987) 'Women of South Asian Origin in Britain: Issues and Concerns' *South Asia Research*, vol. 7, no. 1, pp. 39–54 (reprinted in BRAHAM, P., RATTANSI, A. and SKELLINGTON, R. (Eds) (1992) *Racism and Antiracism*, London, Sage).

BRAH, AVTAR and SHAW, SOBIA (1992) *Working Choices: South Asian Young Muslim Women and the Labour Market*, London, Department of Employment (Research Paper No. 91).

BRIDENTHAL, RENATE, GROSSMAN, ATINA and KAPLAN, MARION (Eds) (1984) *When Biology Became Destiny: Women in Weimar and Nazi Germany*, New York, Monthly Review Press.

BRYAN, BEVERLEY, DADZIE, STELLA and SCAFE, SUZANNE (1985) *The Heart of the Race*, London, Virago.

CHRISTIAN, B. (1987) 'The Race for Theory', *Cultural Critique*, Spring, pp. 51–63.

COLLINS, PATRICIA HILL (1990) *Black Feminist Thought: Knowledge, Consciousness and the Politics of Empowerment*, Boston and London, Unwin Hyman.

CONGER, JOHN (1973) *Adolescence and Youth: Psychological Development in a Changing World*, New York, Harper International Edition.

DAVIS, ANGELA (1971) 'Reflections on the Role of the Black Woman in the Community of Slaves', *Black Scholar*, December, pp. 3–15.

DAVIS, ANGELA (1981) *Women, Race and Class*, London, The Women's Press.

EICHLER, MARGRITTE (1988) *Non-Sexist Research Methods*, London, Allen and Unwin.

ESSED, PHILOMENA (1990) *Everyday Racism*, Claremont, CA, Hunter House.

FRASER, NANCY (1989) *Unruly Practices: Power, Discourse and Gender in Contemporary Social Theory*, Minneapolis, University of Minnesota Press.

FURNHAM, ADRIAN (1985) 'Youth Unemployment: A Review of the Literature', *Journal of Adolescence*, vol. 8, pp. 109–24.

GREWAL, SHABNAM, KAY, JACKIE, LANDOR, LILIANE, LEWIS, GAIL, and PARMAR, PRATIBHA (Eds) (1988) *Charting the Journey: Writings by Black and Third World Women*, London, Sheba Feminist Publishers.

GRIFFIN, CHRIS (1985) *Typical Girls? Young Women from School to the Job Market*, London, Routledge and Kegan Paul.

GRIFFITHS, DOROTHY and SARAGA, ESTHER (1979) 'Sex Differences and Cognitive Abilities: A Sterile Field of Enquiry?', in HARTNETT, O., BODEN, G. and FULLER, M. (Eds) *Sex Role Stereotyping*, London, Tavistock, pp. 17–45.

GROSZ, ELIZABETH (1987) 'Feminist Theory and the Challenge to Knowledges', *Women's Studies International Forum*, vol. 10, no. 5, pp. 475–80.

HALL, STUART and JEFFERSON, TONY (Eds) (1975) *Resistance through Rituals: Youth Subcultures in Post-War Britain*, London, Hutchinson.

HARAWAY, DONNA (1988) 'Situated Knowledges: The Science Question in Feminism and the Privilege of Partial Perspective', *Feminist Studies*, vol. 14, no. 3 (Fall), pp. 575–600.

HARAWAY, DONNA (1989) *Primate Visions*, London, Routledge.

HARDING, SANDRA (1991) *Whose Science? Whose Knowledge?*, Ithaca, Cornell University Press.

HARTSOCK, NANCY (1983) 'The Feminist Standpoint: Developing the Ground for a Specifically Feminist Historical Materialism', in HARDING, S. and HINTIKKA, M. (Eds) *Discovering Reality: Feminist Perspectives on Epistemology, Metaphysics, Methodology, and Philosophy of Science*, Dordrecht, Reidel.

HEWITT, NANCY (1985) 'Beyond the Search for Sisterhood: American Women's History in the 1980s', *Social History*, vol. 10, October.

JAYARATNE, TOBY EPSTEIN and STEWART, ABIGAIL (1991) 'Quantitative and Qualitative Methods in the Social Sciences: Current Feminist Issues and Practical Strategies', in FONOW, MARY MARGARET and COOK, JUDITH A. (Eds) *Beyond Methodology: Feminist Scholarship as Lived Research*, Bloomington, Indiana University Press, pp. 85–106.

LAZREG, MARNIA (1990) 'Feminism and Difference: The Perils of Writing as a Woman on Women in Algeria', in HIRSCH, MARILYN and KELLER, EVELYN FOX (Eds) *Conflicts in Feminism*, New York, Routledge, pp. 326–48.

LE DOEUFF, MICHELE (1987) 'Women and Philosophy', in MOI, TORIL (Ed.) *French Feminist Thought: A Reader*, Oxford, Basil Blackwell, pp. 181–209.

Kum-Kum Bhavnani

McRobbie, Angela (1982) 'The Politics of Feminist Research: Between Talk, Text and Action', *Feminist Review*, no. 12, pp. 46–62.

Mies, Maria (1983) 'Towards a Methodology for Feminist Research', in Bowles, Gloria and Duelli Klein, Renate (Eds) *Theories of Women's Studies*, pp. 117–39.

Passerini, Luisa (1987) *Fascism in Popular Memory*, Cambridge, Cambridge University Press.

Richardson, Ken, Spears, David and Richards, Martin (Eds) (1972) *Race, Culture and Intelligence*, Harmondsworth, Penguin.

Roberts, Helen (Ed.) (1981) *Doing Feminist Research*, London, Routledge and Kegan Paul.

Rose, Hilary (1983) 'Hand, Brain and Heart: A Feminist Epistemology for the Natural Sciences', *Signs*, vol. 9, no. 1.

Rose, Hilary and Rose, Stephen (Eds) (1976) *The Radicalisation of Science: Ideology of/In the Natural Sciences*, New York, Macmillan.

Rosenthal, Robert (1966) *Experimental Effects in Behavioural Research*, New York, Appleton.

Sandoval, Chela (1991) 'US Third World Feminism', *Genders*, no. 10, Spring, pp. 1–24.

Sherif, Carolyn Wood (1987) 'Bias in Psychology', in Harding, S. (Ed.) *Feminism and Methodology*, Milton Keynes, Open University Press, pp. 37–56.

Smith, Dorothy (1988) *The Everyday World as Problematic: A Feminist Sociology*, Milton Keynes, Open University Press.

Squire, Corinne (1989) *Significant Differences: Feminism and Psychology*, London, Routledge.

Stacey, Judith (1988) 'Can there be a Feminist Ethnography?', *Women's Studies International Forum*, vol. 11, no. 1, pp. 21–7.

Stanley, Liz (Ed.) (1990) *Feminist Praxis*, London, Routledge.

Stanley, Liz and Wise, Sue (1979) 'Feminist Research, Feminist Consciousness and Experience of Sexism', *Women's Studies International Forum*, vol. 1, no. 3.

Ware, Vron (1992) *Beyond the Pale: White Women, Racism and History*, London, Verso.

Willis, Paul (1978) *Learning to Labour*, London, Saxon House.

Zenie-Ziegler, Wiedad (1988) *In Search of Shadows: Conversations with Egyptian Women*, London, Zed Books.

Chapter 3

Doing Black Mental Health Research: Observations and Experiences[1]

Erica Wheeler

Introduction

Published empirical research on services available to 'black and ethnic minority groups'[2] after discharge from psychiatric hospitals[3] is painfully thin. Given the government's plans for care in the community, it is vital to know what services are being provided in order that local authorities, health authorities, and family health service authorities can be monitored to ascertain whether they have discharged their statutory responsibilities to 'promote the development of domiciliary, day and respite services to enable people to live in their own homes wherever feasible and sensible' (Secretaries of State for Health, Social Security, Wales and Scotland, 1989, p. 5). Beyond this general responsibility, it is necessary to discern whether the obligations to recognize the distinctive characteristics of and make specific provision for ethnic minorities are being met. The White Paper quoted above recognizes that

> minority communities may have different concepts of community care and it is important that service providers are sensitive to these variations. Good community care will take account of the circumstances of minority communities and will be planned in consultation with them. (Secretaries of State for Health, Social Security, Wales and Scotland, 1989, p. 10)

I wish to argue in this chapter that the rhetoric of the White Paper ignores the 'political' realities in which the shift of mental health resources away from the majority, white indigenous population to cater to the mental health needs of black and ethnic minority users requires a change in the power relationship between black users and (largely) white providers. In order for this shift to take place without a struggle it would have to be seen as legitimate by the persons responsible for implementing it. My observations and experiences have led me to believe that this shift may only come about in a limited way (especially in the face of financial constraints placed on health and social services departments) unless black groups become more actively involved in setting their own health agendas. I do not see this struggle as either brief, or easy, but the pledge of the government to give consumers more choice and access to information about resources available must be used in as effective a way as possible.

I wish to proceed by: (a) laying down the conceptual framework for the discussion of my experiences and observations; (b) using the mental health/ illness literature on both women and black people to illustrate the context in which service provision has been and is taking place; (c) using women's actual experience of the services, coupled with and followed by my own observations and experiences. I wish to make women the focus of my comments initially, but to also include my own observations which refer to the research process itself, from which I hope other black researchers can learn.

Conceptual Framework

The view being taken in this chapter is that the black mental health service users seen during this research, like other working-class users of mental health services, exercise little power over the 'resources' which are defined by professionals as necessary for their recovery. By definition, therefore, black users are unequal, in many cases oppressed, within this relationship. This inequality in the power structure is generated and maintained by a socio-political view of black people and ethnic minority people in which they are still seen as 'immigrants'. This term both ignores the existence of black and ethnic minority people who are British, and continues to carry the connotation of inferiority in the way in which it is used both in the popular press and in some types of academic literature.

It is little wonder that in the psychiatric discourse too, black and ethnic minority persons are viewed in a negative way as 'different' and 'special' (i.e. problematic), a view which leads to the pathologization of our experiences and ignores our 'richness' and diversity. Thus 'culture' and colour become the focus of the 'ills' of many mental health users, and the 'resources' on which they depend comprise the vehicle through which power continues to be exercised.

Many black and ethnic minority women feel the negative impact of this power most keenly, subject as they are to the combined effects of 'race' and gender. Nicki Thorogood, in an article on Afro-Caribbean women's experience of the Health Service (1989), picks up on the theme of 'resources' as being wider than that which refers only to coping strategies (through for example, social networks). She draws on the work of Giddens (1979) in which he sees resources as the 'media through which power is exercised routinely' in social interaction and through which structures of domination are reproduced; these structures of domination are experienced as relations of class, race and gender (Giddens, 1979, pp. 91–2).[4]

Some of the racial stereotypes which black women have to face subjugate them by defining their roles in narrow and uncomplimentary terms. A popular stereotype imbues the Asian female with traits of submissiveness and compliance, in which she is viewed as living in an extended family and therefore as more 'naturally' family-oriented. The Afro-Caribbean female, on the other hand, is seen as aggressive, and family ties are viewed as volatile because of their 'weak culture'. The impression given is that this results in a breakdown of authority with no clear definition of roles. This view is, however, juxtaposed with the image of matriarchal domination. Husband (1986) in a chapter on 'Racism, Prejudice and Social Policy' succinctly traces the historical development of stereotypes of black people in Britain.

With regard to women in general, the perception of mental illness taken from the literature must be included, since it too explains the oppression that women are subjected to in the receipt of or exclusion from mental health services, and therefore cannot be ignored. There are two main theoretical approaches taken by feminist sociologists to viewing the reasons for the gender bias which exists in mental illness statistics: the causation and labelling approaches. Those feminists who put forward the causation approach have argued that the depressive disorders women suffer from are real (Penfold and Walker, 1984). This is because women have more reasons to be depressed. This is primarily attributed to their disadvantaged position in society in relation to men, and the disadvantages faced by women in education, employment and so on in comparison to men have been well documented. Therefore, from a causation approach some feminist writers link certain features of the social structure (i.e. the dominant-subordinate relationship between men and women) to causes of neurotic disorders in women.

The labelling approach takes the view that more women are diagnosed as neurotic because of the attitude of their 'labellers', for example male GPs and psychiatrists. In other words the medicalization of female problems by the male-dominated medical profession allows for the enforcement of the status quo, where women are seen primarily in terms of their domestic roles. This then allows disorders to be defined in terms of their deviation from this role. It should be noted that the two approaches are not mutually exclusive and I would suggest that elements of both can be found in an examination of black women's experiences. The next section takes a look at the evidence on the sex-role stereotyping that is part of the female experience of mental health provision.

Erica Wheeler

Women and Mental Illness

Although it is not the purpose of this chapter to deal in depth with the literature on women and mental illness, it is important that the place of women in the literature is mentioned. The reasons for this are twofold. Firstly, it illustrates how gender stereotypes permeate perceptions of mental illness and ultimately affect diagnostic decisions. Secondly, it reveals the neglect of studies on the aftercare experiences of black women leaving psychiatric hospitals. Their needs therefore remain largely invisible. They remain a minority within 'minorities'.

Mental health and mental illness are not concepts that can be defined with precision, yet the literature on these subjects has been presented as though mental disorder is more 'normally' a characteristic of women. Evidence of the existence of sex-role stereotypes is abundant in American literature. One of the most widely quoted of these studies (Rosenkrantz *et al.*, 1968) studied perceptions of male and female characteristics and identified a number of stereotypical characteristics assigned to men and women. Stereotypically masculine traits were more often perceived as more 'socially desirable' than were attributes which were stereotypically feminine. Another widely quoted study (Broverman *et al.*, 1970) in which mental health professionals were asked to denote characteristics of the healthy male, female and adult, showed that they too held different standards for the mental health of men compared to women. Healthy women differed from healthy men by being: more submissive, less independent, less adventurous, more excitable in minor crises, more emotional, more easily hurt, less competitive, less aggressive, more concerned about their appearance and less objective.

Mental illness statistics show that more women than men are identified as being mentally ill or experiencing emotional problems, and that gender differences are particularly significant in the rates of neurotic disorders. For instance DHSS (1986) figures show that women are admitted to psychiatric hospital at the rate of 468 per 100,000 compared to men at 364 per 100,000. In line with gender stereotyping, women are more likely to be diagnosed as suffering from psychological problems (e.g. depression) by their GPs (Goldberg and Huxley, 1980). These gender stereotypes, which influence diagnosis, are reflected in the subsequent treatment. In a Canadian study of valium users, Cooperstock and Lennard (1979) found that the basis for prolonged prescription of valium for women was to maintain them 'in a role which they found difficult or intolerable without the drug'. This role was the domestic role. Similarly Barrett and Roberts (1978) discovered that British doctors aimed at readjusting their 'depressed' middle-aged female patients to their domestic role. Hence, it is not surprising that two-thirds of persons taking anti-depressive drugs are women (Curran and Golombok, 1985).

However, there is limited accurate and accessible statistical information about the differential diagnosis between and among black and ethnic minority women who either migrated to or were born here, and white women born here. There is even less about their comparative and/or specific needs after leaving psychiatric hospital. The impact on the lives of black women of racism, gender oppression and possible misdiagnosis goes largely unnoticed.

Mental Health Service Provision for Black Women

The health district in which the research to which I am referring was conducted had a glaring absence of mental health service provision for black and ethnic minority women. If the percentage of all black and ethnic minority persons discharged over the year of the study (48 per cent)[5] is anything to go by, then it shows the extent of the neglect. Maybe this lack of services is not so surprising, given that there were no community-based statutory or voluntary sector services which catered in particular for the mental health needs of black and ethnic minority persons anyway. The only women's counselling and therapy service which existed in the district had to close its doors during the study because of the cessation of charitable funding on which it relied.

The services referred to here are counselling and therapy services (post-discharge) in both the statutory and voluntary sectors. There are five community based (statutory) mental health resource centres in the health district, but at the time of the study none of them made any provision for counselling and therapy in any other language but English, thus denying persons whose first language was not English access to such resources. There was the additional problem of lack of choice for Asian females who did speak some English, but who would prefer to see a female counsellor or therapist who had some cultural understanding of their background, which is sometimes invaluable in the therapeutic process. There was also the case that due to lack of resources, training and knowledge about mental illness, there were no black organizations in the voluntary sector in that health district (where there were workers with the relevant language skills), who were equipped to provide counselling and/or therapy for black and ethnic minority persons who were emotionally distressed or had mental health problems.

Despite this absence of provision, I soon realized that, whereas men discharged from hospital were looked after by their wives (the majority of persons discharged were married), women did not appear to enjoy reciprocal care, despite their label as 'mentally ill'. No one interviewed was in full-time employment and only two persons (both women) were in part-time employment. None could therefore afford to hire help in the home. Women were clearly being sent back home to continue to have responsibility for full-time care of the home and children. Contrary to the stereotype of the extended family which gave support to women, only some 5 per cent of persons seen overall did in fact live with in-laws or parents.

I wish to refer to three in-depth interviews, conducted either by the female Asian interviewer or by myself, which indicate some of the problems of isolation and neglect faced by women, based on what I believe to be health care professionals' acceptance of their 'natural' roles as wives and mothers. This in turn has led to the needs of such women for practical help, as well as some form of therapy, becoming invisible.

The pressure to discharge women back home (and in many cases without follow-up) can come from two sources. Firstly, in keeping with what the studies previously quoted show, male psychiatrists may well see home as the most 'natural' place for women – back to their roles as mothers and carers. Secondly, there are still some households where the expectations of family members are also in keeping with those of the mental health professionals. The following case can be used as an example of both.

In this particular case, a mother-in-law whose daughter-in-law had been into hospital because she was suffering from post-natal depression had this to say when questioned about how she saw her daughter-in-law's role in the household:

She should stay at home. She is out all day. That's what she wants to do, go out all day. She should wear eastern clothes and feed the children herself instead of just putting their dinners in front of them. She should live life as a daughter-in-law. If we say the least bit to her she says, I am leaving, I have many friends. She spends my son's salary on Western clothes.

The daughter-in-law mentioned suffered severe post-natal depression after the birth of both her children, but it became worse after the birth of her second child. She had felt under considerable pressure to conform, and had felt isolated and disillusioned as a result of her marriage, and her change in roles. In a very short period of time she went from being a prospective college student to having the responsibilities of marriage and motherhood. However, based on the information she gave, what for her amounted to traumatic changes did not appear to be given serious consideration by her family or during her treatment. Her role of wife and mother was seen as paramount and she was rehabilitated in order to be returned home to her duties.

The experience of separation from her family at the age of 17 and the sense of isolation she felt, however, were real. She said:

I don't think anybody should have to go through this [i.e. getting married so young]. It's so hard, you know, growing up in one place, getting married and moving to another place ... after seven years I've adjusted, but my sister never has.

Of her own shattered expectations she lamented, 'I was still very young at heart, young in the mind, full of ideas of my own about what I wanted to do, wanted to be'. After her marriage she found:

things were really weird, different. He wasn't the person I thought he was, he was more strict . . . I just felt it was totally not what I expected, not what they expected me to be . . . it was like going from one time warp into another [from domination by her father to domination by her husband].

She did attempt to get out of the marriage (thereby shattering the stereotype of the docile Asian female) both after the birth of the first child (taking him with her) and after the second (leaving them both behind), but was forced to return because of the pressures placed on her by her parents and brothers, coupled with her inability to support herself financially.

At the time of her 'breakdown' (after she returned home for the second time) she did not feel that she had benefited from her time in hospital. All she wanted was to 'get out of there'. However, her on-going 'treatment' after her discharge (carried out by a male psychiatrist) appeared to have led (by the time I saw her) to her acceptance of her role as wife and mother. She appeared also to have come to accept her husband's authority over her. She has not, however, always been happy about it. Although, for instance, she stated that she did not mind not having control over her own finances, or even an account of her own (she had a part-time job but gave all her money to her husband), she also had this to say:

but that's one thing I hate, I have to ask for it. If I want some money I have to ask him. He's like my mum, what do you want it for? I hate that. I say, you have a whole wad in your pocket and I never ask *you* what's that money for.

Her 'treatment' has been considered a success.

The next case is that of an Afro-Caribbean woman, who in this case wanted to be reunited with her son who had been taken away from her as a baby because of her (mental) illness. Her son was subsequently fostered by a white family. She felt bitter that she was not allowed access to him and has spent much of her time since he was taken away trying, first, to get him back, and when that failed, trying to gain access to see him. She voiced her fears that 'he will be brought up as a white child, I am afraid of the consequences when he is an adult. How will he regard himself? What problems will it cause?' These questions have gone completely unanswered and unaddressed.

The decision to place her son with white foster-parents was more painful because it came at the time when both she and her older son were experiencing racial abuse and harassment in the council property in which they were living. Her windows were smashed and her older son was regularly called 'black wog' and other abusive terms. This, together with the break-up of her marriage, led to her moving house to a smaller one-bedroom flat which is where I interviewed her. By this time she had been into hospital on ten occasions and had attributed many of her worries to (1) her inability to get her son back and (2) lack of another woman to talk to about her problems, even if she could not help her solve them now. She felt let down by her psychiatrist and the hospital system as a whole, and seven years later she still felt

> not satisfied with life at all. If I die tomorrow I wouldn't mind! They've not left me with much to live for, they've taken my son away. My solicitor is trying to get access to him.

What she wanted more than anything was to

> have my son at home. No one should have the right to take your child off you unless it's being abused. It's no fault of your own [if you are ill]. It brought me to the brink of killing myself. They don't realize it's embarrassing and painful to have your child taken off you.

She felt that over the years her (white, male) psychiatrist had consistently ignored her requests for help in pleading her case for allowing access to her younger son, or giving weight to her request for a two-bedroom flat in order that, if it ever became possible, her son could eventually spend weekends with her. She pointed out that 'Every time I try to talk to him [the psychiatrist] about what is troubling me, he tells me to try and think of something else and asks about my medication!' What it felt like to her was that the views of the male psychiatrist took precedence over her own. At the time of my last visit she added yet another toy to her display of toys she had bought for her son over the last seven years in the hope that one day she would see him.

The final case concerns a female, Afro-Caribbean single parent. Far from fitting the stereotype of the domineering, matriarchal, West Indian female who can 'cope' because of some wider family network, she and her family had been suffering financially and emotionally for many years since her husband died. Despite her illness and some twenty-odd admissions to psychiatric hospital, she had managed to raise her two sons to adulthood. Although she has for many years been the sole breadwinner, she felt under pressure as the mother of two male teenagers to 'be a good mother to them'. It would be difficult to say how much of her desire to be a good mother (which to her meant 'doing everything') was compensation for the amount of time she spent away from home and in hospital, and how much she herself accepted it as her maternal role.

She had no family other than her two sons, and struggled on her meagre income from a succession of part-time, low-paid jobs, and said she had never received or expected assistance in seeking employment from her social worker. Of the difficulties in finding and keeping employment she had this to say:

> Some [employers] are better than others, but most of them as soon as they know that you're not too good in the head, they don't want to have anything to do with you.

Her sons too have been left to cope as well as they could, and no one has ever spoken to them or advised them about their mother's longstanding illness. The hospital personnel did not even ensure that she received any form of 'home help' after discharge from hospital.

I would like to end this section on the experiences of black women by referring to the comments made to me by an Asian female worker in one of the smaller Asian groups in the voluntary sector. She shared her concerns with me about the fact that elderly people and women were particularly disadvantaged since they tended to be more isolated and less fluent in English. She therefore needed to spend time accompanying them to medical appointments. She found herself being an advocate for those women unable to speak for themselves. She thought that many women felt somewhat humiliated having to be dependent on workers, and their sense of humiliation was reinforced when medical (male) personnel chose to ignore them, and address her (the worker) rather than their female client during consultations.

It is noteworthy among the general findings of the research that only a small percentage of black people were referred to residential or nursing home facilities after discharge from hospital. There was also a significant under-representation of Asian women (as a proportion of all Asian women discharged during the study). One Asian social worker interviewed was of the view (which was echoed by some of her colleagues within the same organization) that there was a need for a confidential service for women, provided by women who were not part of the local community. In addition to a formal therapeutic environment, such as that provided by a specialized counselling service, for some Asian women, Asian community centres (Bangladeshi, Pakistani and Indian) were seen as suitable for less intensive and/or sensitive group work. This was suggested mainly because they are venues where women tend to meet for diverse reasons, whether it be language classes, vocational courses or social events, and which are regarded as safe and familiar.

Although there were glimpses of problems (some serious) with other women encountered during the research, it was not possible to say how widespread they were since not everyone was subject to an in-depth interview. It was during such discussions that more serious problems tended to surface. It is my belief, however, that the observations made and the issues highlighted were only a fraction of the problems which remained largely hidden during the study.

Mental Illness in the Black Population: The Literature

From the 1960s onwards the literature on mental illness in black communities in Britain has been based on epidemiological studies. The main finding that runs through all of these studies is the increased risk of mental hospital admission for 'immigrant' groups. The data also shows that those persons born in the Caribbean, and their offspring born in England, have dispropor-tionately higher rates for schizophrenia than the 'native' white population. These epidemiological studies were largely based on hospital admissions, and confined to hospitals within particular geographical regions.

One of the earliest studies was undertaken by Hemsi (1967) who analyzed first admissions to seven psychiatric hospitals serving the local boroughs of Camberwell and Lambeth. Diagnoses were based on the author's criteria and these were applied to information obtained from case notes. Although it was recognized that (a) because of the pattern of migration to this country from the Caribbean, calculation of the size of the Afro-Caribbean population was imprecise, (b) there was inadequate socio-economic and demographic data on the control group, and (c) a number of patients had 'atypical psychoses' which were 'reassigned' to one or other of the standard diagnostic categories, results claimed to show a fivefold excess of schizophrenia in Afro-Caribbean men compared to the native population.

The results of other small studies (Pinto, 1970; Cochrane and Stopes-Roe, 1981) were published in the 1970s on Asians. Based on interviews with thirty-three patients, Pinto estimated that the prevalence of schizophrenia was just over four times greater for Asians compared to natives of Camberwell. The study by Cochrane and Stopes-Roe, which was carried out in the 1970s but published in 1981, examined non-psychotic conditions among Indian and Pakistani residents of Birmingham, using a method of scoring (the Langner scale), and found these types of conditions were lower in both Asian groups compared to their British controls.

In the 1970s there were two large-scale studies on admissions to psychiatric hospitals which included data on ethnicity. One of these studies, carried out in 1971 (Cochrane, 1977), looked at 'Mental Illness in Immigrants to England and Wales: An Analysis of Mental Hospital Admissions 1971'. This study found that admission rates for Scottish, Polish and Irish born persons were higher than for persons born in England. For persons born in India, Pakistan and the Caribbean admission rates were almost the same as for persons born in England. The rate for Afro-Caribbean women, however, was four times that of 'native' women. The second study, done in the South-East of England in 1976 (Dean *et al.*, 1981) came up with different findings for first-time admissions to hospital. It showed higher admission rates for Afro-Caribbeans of both genders. The incidence rate for schizophrenia for Afro-Caribbean men was found to be five times the British rate. Afro-Caribbean women also showed a fivefold increase in rate compared to British women. Both studies concentrated on place of birth as an indicator of ethnicity, therefore omitting black persons born in the UK.

Other smaller studies published in the 1980s (for instance, Carpenter and Brockington, 1980; Hitch and Clegg, 1980; Bebbington *et al.*, 1981; McGovern and Cope, 1987) also looked mainly at first admissions to psychiatric hospitals. They all showed higher incidence rates for schizophrenia among

Afro-Caribbeans. The study by Bebbington *et al.* (1981), which looked at mania in 'immigrant' patients, found it to be three times higher in Afro-Caribbean men and five times in Afro-Caribbean women compared to the native rate. McGovern and Cope and Harrison *et al.* (1988) included a high proportion of what the literature refers to as 'second-generation immigrants' in their samples.

In a very enlightening paper prepared for the Royal College of Psychiatrists in 1989, Dr Sashidharan, a prominent black psychiatrist, who works extensively in the black community in Birmingham, took a critical look at the published research mentioned above on the psychiatric epidemiology of ethnic minority groups. His paper showed the racism inherent in the way in which the methodological inconsistencies in the research in this field (which if it were to be believed shows an epidemic of schizophrenia in the black population) have gone unquestioned. He pointed to the biases in the choice of numerators and denominators used in such studies which render them unreliable and open to severe criticism. He argued that if the statistics produced from the study by Hemsi in 1967 and those of the study by Harrison *et al.* in 1988 were to be believed, then what we see is a threefold increase in the incidence rates for schizophrenia for the 15–54 age group in Camberwell and Lambeth over some twenty-five years while the rates for whites have remained almost the same.

Sashidharan in an article, entitled 'Schizophrenic or Just Black?' (1989b), also argues the point that it is Western concepts of psychiatry which need to be questioned. Figures show that a diagnosis of schizophrenia is given four to ten times more frequently in black people than in their white counterparts when they first contact, or are admitted to, psychiatric facilities. Yet, as he goes on to say, if admissions for schizophrenia and related disorders are set aside, then 'it is clear that black people are under-represented as users of psychiatric in-patient facilities'.

Research has appeared to show that a diagnosis of schizophrenia means different things in black and white patients (diagnosis for black patients is often arrived at without 'core symptoms' being present). It should be noted, however, that these core symptoms such as withdrawal, language aberrations, hallucinations or delusions are not absolute or concrete, but are open to interpretation by the psychiatrist. Furthermore, the initial diagnosis for black patients is more likely to be changed subsequently than it is for white patients, and Dr Sashidharan argues that we should look towards the 'interpretative framework' of psychiatry to explain the apparent high incidence of schizophrenia. He argues that it is 'ethnocentrism that informs the theories and practices of most institutional agencies [which] is also reflected at a critical juncture within clinical practice – that of diagnosis' (Sashidharan, 1989b, pp. 14–15).

It is no wonder, therefore, that black Britons are critical of the treatment received at the hands of mental health services, and see psychiatry as a form of punishment or social control. The theory of social control appears to be borne out by the life experiences of many black people. A member of the Black Health Workers and Patients Group complained that black communities are subject to inferior treatment, misdiagnosis, and lack of statutory provision (Mercer, 1984). A former chair, and later Director of the Afro-Caribbean Mental Health Association (ACMHA), regards psychiatry as one of a range of social mechanisms which include schools, the courts, police and social welfare among these control mechanisms (Francis, 1989).

Planning for Whom? – Inadequate Data Sources

Given the inconsistencies in the epidemiological data on mental illness in black communities and the increased likelihood of misdiagnosis on admission to mental institutions, and all the other factors mentioned above, black researchers and black groups seeking to change the health agenda to one which takes the needs of black and ethnic minority persons into account need accurate and appropriate information.

One of the first difficulties I faced in obtaining accurate demographic data was the lack of information relating to ethnicity from either the purchasers or providers of mental health services.[6] In drawing up community care plans the recent White Paper (1989) calls for joint planning between social services departments (SSDs), district health authorities (DHAs), and family health services authorities (FHSAs), and, as noted above, special attention to the needs of minority communities. The question which needs to be asked, therefore, is how planning can take place in the absence of information which covers all sections of the population served by these three authorities? The lack of information on ethnicity persisted up to the time of this research, despite the existence of a specialized hospital team (which called itself the 'Transcultural Unit') established since the early 1970s, specifically set up to address the mental health needs of black and ethnic minority groups in the district.

Although there was, during the time of this research, an information system under development for this specialized unit which recorded ethnicity, a similar system of recording clients of other consultants not a part of this 'Unit' did not exist. The recording systems for clients of approved social workers from the social services department were no more helpful in locating persons, since there was no clear understanding of the definition of 'black and ethnic minority persons'. Furthermore there were no systematic records for those clients who were seen by social workers, but for whom there were no statutory obligations to make reports, as there was for those persons 'sectioned' (i.e. detained) under the 1983 Mental Health Act.

Towards the end of the study the FHSA (in conjunction with the SSD and the DHA) was arranging discussions with an Asian GP about the mental health needs of his Asian clients. Hitherto there was no work commissioned for the purpose of discovering the mental health needs of black and ethnic minority persons in the district.

Some black authors have highlighted the fact that, even when the collection of 'race data' is carried out (of which Ethnic Record Keeping and Monitoring (ERKM)[7] is a part), it is not necessarily used in a beneficial way to improve services to black and ethnic minority communities. A negative view is that it may become part of a 'numbers game' used either against black communities or as a tool to control and abuse them (Ohri, 1988). A different argument, in the area of health research, is that the collection of statistics can function as a substitute for, and therefore as a hindrance to, the development of an anti-racist practice (Sheldon and Parker, 1992). What I would argue for is the collection of data which has a direct impact on health care delivery, without which glaring inequalities continue to go unnoticed, since they cannot be picked up and used by black user groups, professionals or researchers.

Consultation

Section 46 of the Community Care Act (1990) requires local authorities in preparing community care plans to consult with, *inter alia*, DHAs, FHSAs, housing authorities, and voluntary organizations representing users and carers. Like 'resources', lack of true consultation can be used as a tool to exclude black communities from decision making, or used as a token to display a pseudo-commitment to changing services.

What I discovered was that those persons who were aware that there was such thing as a consultation process knew this because of previous experience of being 'involved' in discussions with, for instance, the health authority (although not in discussions around mental health). However, such 'consultation' was viewed with great scepticism by black groups since many persons recalled being invited to meetings, being given tea and samosas, asked their views, only to discover after the meetings that there was no feedback, and there appeared to be no subsequent changes in service provision.

Indeed, what I found was that very few of the representatives of the community groups and black organizations in the voluntary sector who were interviewed had even a basic understanding of what mental illness was, or of what services were available to help persons suffering from emotional distress or a mental disorder.

With regard to what happened within the provider units (e.g. hospital) among mental health personnel it was mainly the relevant managers and administrators who were *au fait* with most of the requirements of the care programme approach[8] which forms the cornerstone of community care for persons with a mental illness. However, the same could not be said with confidence at that time of 'front-line' professionals such as psychiatrists and community psychiatric nurses, who were responsible for implementing the

care programme approach. This uncertainty applied equally to persons working in the specialized unit based at the hospital who were drawn from a
variety of disciplines (psychiatric nursing, social work, psychology, psychiatry, and attendant medical staff).

These health and social care professionals were, less than a year before
the final implementation date of 1 April 1993, and almost exactly two years
after the requirements were issued in relevant government circulars in
September 1990, unclear about how the requirements of community care
plans could or would affect their practice. They were also unsure about their
relationship with fundholding GPs, especially in the light of the extension of
the GP fundholding scheme.[9]

What proved even more worrying was the 'siege mentality' under which
black and ethnic minority staff in the statutory sectors operated (although
this was more true of health than social services). The impact of community
care changes on the specialized unit in particular was very worrying for the
staff employed there, because they felt they were facing an uncertain future
which could ultimately end in 'disbandment'. Although the black nurses and
social workers interviewed for the research were happy to talk to me as
another black person about their views on the quality and accessibility of the
service for black clients, which they viewed as inadequate, they did not feel
that knowledge of government changes would necessarily be beneficial to
black clients. There was instead a feeling that much 'lip service' was being
paid to the mental health needs of black clients despite the existence of a
special unit.

My observation was that not only was the unit underfunded, in relation
to the volume of its work with black and ethnic minority clients, it was under-
staffed as well. Of a total of eight professional staff, three permanent staff
were black (there was one Asian community psychiatric nurse, 80 per cent of
the time of a 'Section 11'[10] funded Asian social worker, and one Asian clinical
assistant). These three members of staff were meant to deal with all referrals
of clients who, according to the 1991 Census classification, were not white,
and who came from an extensive catchment area which included Afro-
Caribbeans and Chinese, not to mention a range of Asian groups from the
Indian subcontinent and Africa.

One of the main criteria for accepting such clients was that they were
insufficiently fluent in English to be referred to the 'regular' wards or consultants at the hospital. However, it should not be forgotten that the remit of the
specialized unit was meant to be much wider and, according to Anna Greenwood, in presenting the argument for a specialist unit:

> A sane person may be diagnosed as mentally ill . . . because their re-
> sponse to stress differs from indigenous expectations. A mental health
> worker's unspoken dislike or contempt towards a person's ethnic
> group can undermine the person's self-respect or evoke a negative
> response which is then seen as 'unprovoked aggression'. . . .

She went on to say:

> The term 'ethnic minority' refers to people of varying backgrounds, including Asian families, black British teenagers, immigrants from Romania. . . . When their mental health is being questioned, any and all of these (and indeed, anyone black and/or of a non-mainstream culture and/or with no English or English as a second language) may be 'up against it'. . . . A black person is likely to be seen as an 'outsider', even if British-born and wholly British in culture. . . . Contacts with 'standard' mental health services can be *disabling* for ethnic minorities, hence the need for special attention. (Greenwood, 1993, pp. i–ii)

Faced by what over the years had become a marginalized service to black and ethnic minority persons, although still committed to the idea of a specialized unit, black nursing and social service staff had become disillusioned about the political will to address the questions of adequate and accessible care for black and ethnic minority users of mental health services. Given the negative feelings of many of these persons it was surprising that black health and social service professionals and persons in the voluntary sector consented to be interviewed, but maybe the key to this is, as a few persons in the voluntary sector indicated, that it was because the interviewers were black. However, being a black researcher did give rise to problems of its own.

When Being a Black Researcher Is Not Enough

It is not uncommon that research whose stated aim is to improve service provision may lead to a rise in expectations on the part of service users. However, one of the dilemmas which I faced was the conflict between my identity as a black person doing research among a disadvantaged group of people, with whom I felt an affinity because of our shared experiences of being 'foreigners', and therefore a moral obligation to help (and being expected to!), and that of a researcher with a limited capacity to do so.

It was very easy to identify with Joyce Ladner (1971), who analyzed the growing into womanhood of low-income adolescent black girls from a large metropolitan centre in the USA. She referred to her 'inability to be *objective* about analyzing poverty, racism and disease'. My dilemma was not due to any conflict between whether I should become involved in the lives of respondents or not, for in a sense the commitment to do 'action research' is in itself a political decision which the research team made at the outset. Rather it was the dilemma faced between being a black social scientist wanting to help to make a difference in their lives through my research, and one recognizing that the problems they experienced reflected larger socio-economic issues.

The types of problems individuals and families were experiencing were of a wide-ranging nature, and many of them may have been contributory factors to their poor mental health, for example, mortgage arrears, poor housing conditions, inadequate income, and unemployment, all symptoms of their underlying poverty, and an almost complete reliance on state benefits as their only means of subsistence. Since few of the service users interviewed (27 per cent) had a social worker after discharge, there were requests to find out about appropriate employment, to make phone calls to the DHSS office to enquire about social security benefits, to fill out poll tax forms, or to find out about alternative housing and accommodation.

What made it more painful was that it was not uncommon for the re-searchers to be regarded as a sister, daughter or son, and indeed it was not difficult to imagine oneself in a similar light. Not only did it make me feel powerless but somehow I felt I was taking away something from them by 'intruding' into their lives, without being able to give anything immediate or tangible in return, or to give any guarantees about service improvement.

In some cases I was acutely aware that my ability to provide advice and practical assistance was the yardstick by which I was judged, rather than what appeared to be an intellectual exercise in information gathering, regardless of how 'action-oriented' the project was meant to be. The inability to provide such help was greeted on return for follow-up interviews some months later (fortunately for the project only in a minority of cases) by 'there is no point in talking to you, you have done nothing to help me'. This, in some instances, was a painful and bitter truth. What some individuals and families needed was immediate help, and anything less seemed pointless.

Conclusion

What was necessary and, fortunately, an integral aspect of this particular piece of research, was to be able to speak on behalf of service users and carers in a critical but constructive way at statutory sector forums, while the research was in progress. In this way one could lobby for changes before the completion of the research project, and keep voluntary sector organizations and black and ethnic minority professionals informed of findings, which they in turn could use to exert pressure for changes in service provision. This applies in particular to black women, the extent of whose needs is largely hidden.

Given the time-limited nature of such research it is inevitable that some of the momentum is lost on completion of the project. However keeping channels of communication open in the manner described above lends greater credibility to the research and makes it more accessible to black pressure groups.

One of the greatest benefits which could come out of doing black research is the provision of data which can be used by black pressure groups, in conjunction with black health and social service professionals, to lobby for changes and to help set the agenda for services which they see as important. The White Paper states that services should be tailored to fit users and carers, and black groups should take advantage of the rhetoric and try to turn it into a reality. To do this they have to take more responsibility for determining their own needs rather than wait for them to be dictated by statutory services.

I may be optimistic in thinking that if black groups played a more active role in monitoring service provision and demanding changes, they in turn could decide what type of research into their needs is necessary, and insist that research contains an element of financial commitment to meeting those needs. It may therefore be more realistic to have small-scale studies which target a particular area with the intention of providing a service during the research rather than wait for promises of improvement which may or may not come later. Any such need for service provision uncovered by the research can then be incorporated into mainstream provision following the end of the research project. This can have several benefits. It allows the persons doing the research to be able to provide some degree of practical assistance, and the incorporation of needs uncovered during the project which can subsequently be addressed following the research would help to restore some degree of credibility to statutory organizations, who after all have statutory obligations to the community which they serve. It would also allow black professionals given a special brief to work with ethnic minorities to help to make service provision a reality. Black and ethnic minority people have a right to mental health services which address their needs but it is only by being more organized and systematic, and with the help of relevant information, that they can challenge and expose the inequalities in the system and begin to shift the balance of power.

Notes

1   The research on which these observations and experiences are based was funded by the Joseph Rowntree Foundation and was conducted between August 1990 and November 1992. The completed Report for the district for which I was primarily responsible is due for publication in the last quarter of 1993. The research team was based at the Department of Social Policy and Sociology at the University of Leeds. Although this chapter is based on the aforementioned research the views expressed here are entirely my own.

2   This is the definition used to refer to all persons from the Caribbean, the Indian subcontinent, the Far East and Africa, as well as those persons born in Britain

who share this ancestry. Such groups are taken to suffer discrimination and sub-ordination in society. It is therefore not necessary for a group to be a numerical minority to qualify as a minority group. For the sake of comparison with future research the 1991 Census categories were used.

This is not to say that the Census categories were not without complications. As authors such as Ahmad (1992) and Sheldon and Parker (1992) point out, 'conflated concepts and confused categories' are used in the 1991 Census. They argue that cultural, geographical and nationalist notions of race dressed up as ethnicity and colour were used in the 1991 Census.

3 This chapter dips into and expands some of my observations and experiences from the research on housing, support and aftercare from psychiatric hospitals in two adjacent health districts. The comments refer to the health district for which I was primarily responsible during the study, and with which I have maintained connections as result of my work there.

The research was concentrated solely on persons who were former in-patients of psychiatric hospitals and it was

(a) conducted by black researchers who obtained users' consent in a face-to-face meeting prior to the interview (only 3 per cent of persons approached in this way refused, compared to 17 per cent who could not be met personally). The views of persons whom the user identified as a carer were also obtained. In both cases questionnaires were used, and for a small sample of mental health service users in-depth interviews were also conducted;

(b) in keeping with 'good' academic research, where interviewers and respondents were matched as far as possible by language, ethnicity, and gender. As an Afro-Caribbean, I interviewed corresponding users and carers. Interviews with Asians were either conducted by a colleague, or by an interpreter in my presence;

(c) conducted in the privacy of users' homes, where there was no attempt made to enforce textbook notions of 'confidentiality' by excluding other family members (some of whom appeared to visit especially for the interview) from the room.

(d) deliberately angled at incorporating the views of black and ethnic minority workers or representatives of a cross-section of: black voluntary sector organizations, mosques, black workers in white voluntary organizations, persons in the (statutory) youth and com-munity service based at community centres. The intention was (i) to obtain the views of workers or community representatives, who, in the course of their work, would come into contact with black users of mental health services; (ii) to find out if there was any mental health service provision specifically offered by the black voluntary sector.

4 Giddens' view of resources as being integrally related to power seems particularly apt in the mental health field. At the 'macro' level the power to give or not to

give services in general is held by health and social services institutions, at the 'micro' level it is the health and social service professionals who exercise this power over individuals.

5   This percentage is taken from the 81 names of black and ethnic minority persons discharged over a period of one year. The figure was given by professionals, upon whom the interviewers relied, and has hence been used for the purposes of the study. However, it was later discovered, by a subsequent check of medical records, that the actual number of black and ethnic minority persons discharged over the study period was 98.

6   The term purchasers is used to refer to health authorities, and providers to NHS Trusts, which in the case of this research were responsible for provision of all mental health services. It should be noted that the social services department was also in the process of splitting up the purchasing and the providing elements of its services. Their responsibility to mental health users is for provision of social care needs.

7   ERKM – a system of record keeping by local authorities which includes the ethnic origins of clients, the purpose of which is to monitor and review procedures and practices to ensure equal opportunities in service provision.

8   The care programme approach is meant to be led by the needs of users of mental health services. According to government guidelines it must contain systematic arrangements for: assessing and reviewing health and social care needs, and effective systems for ensuring agreed services are provided to persons who can be treated in the community.

9   This would require consultant psychiatrists to have a closer working relationship with GPs who are the primary referrers. From 1 April 1993 GPs have been given the power to purchase mental health services. This puts GPs in a more powerful position vis-à-vis consultants (i.e. it sets up a new purchaser-provider relationship).

10 Section 11 funding gives local authorities the power to recruit specialist workers under provisions of Section 11 of the 1986 Local Government Act. This permits the Home Office to fund 75 per cent of a post of which at least 50 per cent should be devoted to work with residents who are defined as originating from the 'New Commonwealth'. These posts carry the danger that work with minority communities can become marginalized. Many authorities, rather than examine the scope and relevance of mainstream provision, define work with such communities as a specialism and leave it to junior workers. For a further exploration of some of the problems and attitudes around Section 11 funding see Ballard (1979).

References

AHMAD, W.I.U. (Ed.) (1992) *The Politics of Race and Health*, Race Relations Research Unit, University of Bradford.

BALLARD, R. (1979) 'Ethnic Minorities and the Social Services', in SAIFULLAH KHAN, V. (Ed.) *Minority Families in Britain*, London, Macmillan.

BARRETT, M. and ROBERTS, H. (1978) 'Doctors and their patients: the social control of women in General Practice' in SMART, C. and SMART, B. (Eds) *Women, Sexuality and Social Control*, London, Routledge and Kegan Paul.

BEBBINGTON, P., HURRY, J. and TENNANT, C. (1981) 'Psychiatric Disorders in Selected Immigrant Groups in Camberwell', *Social Psychiatry*, 16, pp. 43–51.

BROVERMAN, D., CLARKSON, F., ROSENKRANTZ, P., VOGEL, S. and BROVERMAN, I. (1970) 'Sex-Role Stereotype and Clinical Judgements of Mental Health', *Journal of Consulting and Clinical Psychology*, 34, pp. 1–7.

BUTT, J., GORBACH, P. and AHMAD, B. (1991) 'Equally Fair?', London, Race Equality Unit.

CARPENTER, L. and BROCKINGTON, I.F. (1980) 'A Study of Mental Illness in Asians, West Indians and Africans Living in Manchester', *British Journal of Psychiatry*, 137, pp. 201–5.

COCHRANE R. (1977) 'Mental Illness in Immigrants to England and Wales: an analysis of Mental Hospital Admissions 1971' *Social Psychiatry*, 12, pp. 2–35.

COCHRANE R. and STOPES-ROE, M. (1981) 'Psychological Symptom Levels in Indian Immigrants to England – A Comparison with the Native English', *Psychological Medicine*, 11, pp. 319–27.

COOPERSTOCK, R. and LENNARD, H. (1979) 'Some Social Meanings of Tranquillizer Use', *Sociology of Health and Illness*, 1, 3, p. 33.

CURRAN, V. and GOLOMBOK, S. (1985) *Bottling it up*, London, Faber and Faber.

DAVIS, A. (1981) *Women, Race and Class*, London, The Women's Press.

DEAN, G., WALSH, D., DOWNING, H. and SHELLEY, E. (1981) 'First admissions of native-born and immigrants to psychiatric hospitals in south-east England in 1976' *British Journal of Psychiatry*, 139, pp. 506–512.

FRANCIS, E. (1989) 'Black People, "Dangerousness" and Psychiatric Compulsion', in BRACKX, A. and GRIMSHAW, C. (Eds) *Mental Health Care in Crisis*, London, Pluto.

GIDDENS, A. (1979) *Central Problems in Social Theory*, London, Macmillan.

GOLDBERG, D. and HUXLEY, P. (1980) *Mental Illness in the Community: The Pathway to Psychiatric Care*, London, Tavistock.

GREENWOOD, A. (1993) 'Ethnic Minorities' Mental Health: The Case for a Specialist Unit', *Ethnic Minorities Current Awareness Bulletin*, vol. 4, part 2 (March 1993), pp. i–ii.

HARRISON, G., OWENS, D., HOLTON, A., NEILSON, D. and BOOT, D. (1988) 'A Prospective Study of Severe Mental Disorder in Afro-Caribbean Patients', *Psychological Medicine*, 18, pp. 643–57.

HEMSI, L.K. (1967) 'Psychiatric Morbidity of West Indian Immigrants', *Social Psychiatry*, 2, pp. 95–100.

HITCH, P.J. and CLEGG, P. (1980) 'Modes of Referral of Overseas Immigrant and Native-born First Admissions to Psychiatric Hospital', *Social Scientific Medicine*, vol. 14A, pp. 369–74.

HOOKS, B. (1981) *Ain't I a woman?*, London, Pluto.

HUSBAND, C. (1986) 'Racism, Prejudice and Social Policy', in COOMBE, V. and LITTLE, A. (Eds) *Race and Social Work: A Guide to Training*, London, Tavistock.

LADNER, J.A. (1971) *Tomorrow's Tomorrow*, Garden City, N.Y., Doubleday.

LITTLEWOOD, R. and LIPSEDGE, M. (1982) *Aliens and Alienists*, Harmondsworth, Penguin.

McGOVERN, D. and COPE, R.V. (1987) 'First Psychiatric Admission Rates of First and Second Generation Afro-Caribbeans', *Social Psychiatry*, 22, pp. 139–49.

MERCER, K. (1984) 'Black communities experience of psychiatric services', *International Journal of Social Psychiatry*, 3, 1 and 2.

OHRI, S. (1988) 'The Politics of Racism, Statistics and Equal Opportunity: Towards a Black Perspective', in BHAT, A., CARR-HILL, R. and OHRI, S. (Eds) *Britain's Black Population*, Aldershot, Gower.

PENFOLD, S. and WALKER, G. (1984) *Women and the Psychiatric Paradox*, Milton Keynes, Open University Press.

PINTO, R.T. (1970) *A Study of Psychiatric Illness among Asians in the Camberwell Area*, unpublished MPhil thesis, University of London.

ROSENKRANTZ, P., VOGEL, S., BEE, H., BROVERMAN, I. and BROVERMAN, D. (1968) 'Sex-Role Stereotypes and Self-Concepts in College Students', *Journal of Consulting and Clinical Psychology*, 32, pp. 287–95.

SASHIDHARAN, S. (1989a) 'Epidemiology, Ethnicity and Schizophrenia', paper given to Special Committee on Psychiatric Practice and Training in British Multi-Ethnic Society, Royal College of Psychiatrists.

SASHIDHARAN, S. (1989b) 'Schizophrenic or Just Black?', *Community Care*, 5 October.

SECRETARIES OF STATE FOR HEALTH, SOCIAL SECURITY, WALES AND SCOTLAND (1989) *Community Care in the Next Decade and Beyond: Policy Guidance*, London, HMSO.

SHELDON, T. and PARKER, H. (1992) 'The Use of "Ethnicity" and "Race" in Health Research: A Cautionary Note', in AHMAD, W.I.U. (Ed.) *The Politics of Race and Health*, Bradford, Race Relations Research Unit, University of Bradford.

THOROGOOD, N. (1989) 'Afro-Caribbean Women's Experience of the Health Service', *New Community*, 15(3), April, pp. 319–34.

Further Reading

BARNES, M. and MAPLE, N. (1992) *Women and Mental Health: Challenging the Stereotypes*, Birmingham, Venture Press.

BHAT, A., CARR-HILL, R. and OHRI, S. (1988) *Britain's Black Population: A New Perspective*, Aldershot, Gower.

COPE, R. (1989) 'The Compulsory Detention of Afro-Caribbeans under the Mental Health Act', *New Community*, 15(3), April, pp. 343–56.

CONNELLY, N. (1988) *Care in the Multiracial Community*, London, Policy Studies Institute.

Erica Wheeler

GUTTENTAG, M., SALASIN, S. and BELLE, D. (Eds) (1980) *The Mental Health of Women*, New York, Academic Press Inc.

HOWELL, E. and BAYES, M. (1981) *Women and Mental Health*, New York, Basic Books Inc.

MILES, A. (1981) *The Mentally Ill in Contemporary Society*, Oxford, Blackwell.

MILES, A. (1988) *Women and Mental Illness*, Brighton, Wheatsheaf.

SKELLINGTON, R. and MORRIS, P. (1992) *'Race' in Britain Today*, London, Sage, in association with the Open University.

Chapter 4

Gender, Race and Ethnicity in Official Statistics:
Social Categories and the HIV/AIDS 'Numbers Game'

Anne Akeroyd

During its first decade the HIV infection/AIDS pandemic has caused an estimated 500 000 cases of AIDS in women and children, most of which have been unrecognised.... The social, economic, and demographic impacts on women and children have until now been largely neglected.... *The major reason for such neglect was that during the early 1980s most AIDS cases were in young and middle-aged men.* (Chin, 1990, p. 224, emphasis added)

Statistics on AIDS represent the subject of AIDS: they themselves constitute sets of discursive practices. (Bloor, Goldberg and Emslie, 1991, p. 136)

This chapter is concerned with aspects of HIV/AIDS research and data collection which shape understandings about women and the human immunodeficiency virus (HIV) and the acquired immune deficiency syndrome (AIDS). It discusses the classifications employed in official statistics which may highlight or mask certain social and sexual categories and misrepresent the situation in respect of women. Brief references to official figures and responses in the mass media provide easy access to the 'facts' and help to induce public awareness.

For the 'public' of Britain, HIV and AIDS have only recently become issues for women, due to the publicity about the increased numbers of women diagnosed with AIDS, plus the initial results of the anonymous testing of pregnant women in antenatal clinics. (Scharf and Toole, 1992, p. 64)

In America, too, warnings about the 'neglected tragedy' of women with AIDS have only recently appeared in daily news and scientific coverage (Ickovics and Rodin, 1992, p. 1). However, coverage in the mass media, especially of *causes célèbres*, and confusion over the meaning and accuracy of the numbers may also compound public confusion. The misunderstandings are all the greater in respect of issues affecting women or having a bearing on racial and ethnic minorities.

Questions of sameness and difference come to the fore in feminist debates: as Maynard (this volume) points out, the sameness of women had been taken for granted in the feminist literature until black feminists challenged this assumption. This chapter focuses on a subject which has commonly been construed from the outset, and not least in the mass media, in terms of difference, of 'otherness' in racial, gender, sexual or behavioural terms. The major distinction commonly made between 'us' and 'them' is between those who are (commonly presumed) not to be at risk of being infected with HIV, who don't/won't/can't get or be got by HIV/AIDS (depending on the view taken of the *modus operandi* of the virus) and the others, those who are, who do/will/can become infected. This dichotomy recurs in many contexts, whether the other has been defined *inter alia* in terms of sexual orientation and behaviours, lifestyle, morality, race, nationality, and/or geographical distance. Yet, almost from the outset there was evidence that HIV did not select the sex of its host, and that gender, race, ethnicity and heterosexuality offered no protection against infection. As HIV infection spreads, however, and as more deaths are classified as 'AIDS deaths', so the need to subsume everyone under the 'other' has become the message of the health educators. Yet the numbers currently infected (especially in Britain), the hyperbole in the reporting and interpretations of the statistics, have made that message hard to get across, hard to believe, and even harder to evaluate in terms of social and personal relevance.

Reports and the (In)visibility of Women

The Centers for Disease Control (CDC) reported on 7 January 1983 on two cases of immunodeficiency in female sexual partners of males with AIDS in New York, referred to forty-three other women who had developed opportunistic infections typical of AIDS, and suggested that heterosexual transmission of the putative 'AIDS agent' was a possibility (CDC, 1983). The first report of heterosexual patients including a woman had actually occurred in August 1981, however, only two months after the report about *Pneumocystis carinii* pneumonia (PCP) in homosexual men in California which started the investigations which led to the identification of HIV and the naming of AIDS. By 15 September 1982 heterosexual females accounted for 5.7 per cent of the

593 cases of AIDS reported to the CDC, 62.5 per cent of whom were intra-venous drug users as were 60 per cent of the heterosexual males (CDC, 1982). The age, sex and race distributions remained fairly constant in the USA, with women comprising some 6 to 7 per cent of the adult AIDS cases until the revision of the AIDS case definition in September 1987 incorpor-ated a broader spectrum of diseases, one effect of which was to increase the number of AIDS cases in women.

Throughout the 1980s and 1990s in the USA women comprised a growing proportion of total reported AIDS cases, reaching 12.8 per cent by 1992, and the proportion of female cases attributed to heterosexual contact each year rose from 30 per cent in 1988 to 37 per cent in 1991 (Stone and Peterson 1992, p. 520). AIDS was expected by 1991 to be in the five leading causes of death in women aged 15–44 years, who account for 85 per cent of all cases in women (CDC, 1990). The case figures for January–March 1993 show that the large increase in female cases in the USA has continued, with women comprising 14 per cent of new cases and cases in women rising 132 per cent faster than in men (Murrain, 1993) – and that is before the latest change in the AIDS case definition has begun to have any impact.

Almost from the beginning, then, there was evidence of HIV infection and AIDS amongst women in the USA (a matter to which Treichler (1988) and Campbell (1990) among others have also drawn attention). (In sub-Saharan Africa the effects on women were even more marked: there the sex ratio has been approximately equal from the outset and heterosexual contact the main mode of transmission.) However, scientific and lay awareness of the ways in which HIV/AIDS affects women and the difference and similarities between men and women, between homosexuals, bisexuals and heterosexuals is still inadequate. Women have been frequently compared to all men, includ-ing homosexual and bisexual men; this may create a bias and tend to make women's position seem to be worse than that of men (Ellerbrock *et al.*, 1991). Women may be less likely to know their HIV status or to be aware that they may be at risk, as personal narratives have attested. Recent estimates suggest that three-quarters of the women (but only 29 per cent of HIV-seropositive homosexual and bisexual men) in London found through anonymous screen-ing to be HIV-infected will not know their HIV status (Hall, 1993). Some learn of it when a perinatally infected child is ill (CDC, 1990). A number of studies have shown that '[c]urrently women appear to be diagnosed late or misdiagnosed or even not diagnosed at all' (Scharf and Toole, 1992, p. 65). This is amply borne out by a study of an emergency room in the Bronx which found major differences in the recognition of HIV infection as between men and women.

Despite the presence of HIV infection across a broad age range for both sexes (from 13 to 87 years), HIV was completely unrecognised among all adolescent, young adult, and older women (25 years of age or less and 45 or over). (Schoenbaum and Webber, 1993, p. 366)

This, the researchers suggest, might be the result of preconceptions about the ages of women at risk for HIV derived from the known ages of women with AIDS in New York, 87 per cent of whom fell into the 25–49 age group, whereas cases were recognized in men across the age range.

In 1992 Scharf and Toole (like most writers discussing women) still needed to draw attention to the paucity of data on women and HIV/AIDS, to the ways in which the stereotypic social roles of women are reflected in images of women in relation to HIV, to the inequalities in the position of women manifested in relation to HIV/AIDS, and to the low priority given to women's needs and issues in research. In particular, they noted the invisibility or 'statistical insignificance' of women in HIV/AIDS statistics and the consequent biases in the provision of treatment, services, planning, statistics, and medical research. Drawing some lessons from the USA, they pointed out that nearly half the women who die of HIV infection do so before they are diagnosed, they appear to have a shorter life span after diagnosis of AIDS, poor and black women are disproportionately affected, and the illnesses and conditions that appear to affect women more than men are not included in the AIDS and HIV definitions.

There have been improvements, however, as evidenced in the growth of biomedical and social science research, and in literature reviews on HIV/AIDS in women (e.g. Ellerbrock *et al.*, 1991; Minkoff and DeHovitz, 1991; Sherr, 1991), though much of this did not start until the beginning of the 1990s. The Seventh International Conference on AIDS in Florence in 1991 was the first time that

> there was an obvious presence of research highlighting the impact of HIV on women and children. The number of papers on children far outweighed those on women, yet the women issues were acknowledged and not simply subsumed under the heading of family or pregnancy. (Sherr, 1991, p. 423)

However, women may still be treated as a means to an end. Nicoll, for example, considers that

> [w]omen and children can provide unique surveillance of data on the heterosexual epidemic. Unlinked anonymous testing for anti-HIV among pregnant women or young babies soon after birth can . . . provide a proxy measure of HIV seroprevalence among sexually active women. (Nicoll, 1991, p. 214)

One outcome of the new interest in women and gender issues has been the reversal of some of the 'accepted wisdom' and an increased awareness of the problems making it hard for women to protect themselves from infection. A very large number of papers on women were presented at the Eighth International Conference on AIDS in Amsterdam in 1992; *inter alia* they indicate that the progression of HIV infection to AIDS and the survival of HIV-infected persons do not seem to differ significantly between women and men. As previously observed in cohorts of HIV-infected men, age influences HIV disease progression in women. (Castro *et al.*, 1992, p. 1466)

Numbers, Names and 'Knowledge'

Numbers have been of the essence from the outset: uniquely among diseases, AIDS statistics are cumulative – national and global totals of cases include people who have already died.[1] 'Body counts' have been foregrounded by the dominance of epidemiological concerns and preoccupation with vital statistics for AIDS and HIV infection, with national and international forecasts and with projecting trends into the next millennium. HIV/AIDS surveillance[2] and forecasting exemplify the assertion that 'Numbers provide the rhetoric of our age' (Keyfitz, 1987, p. 235), reflecting the need to have a picture of the future whilst recognizing the impossibility of knowing the future (Keyfitz, 1987, p. 237).

Counts and measures of HIV/AIDS (notably in relation to heterosexual transmission) have been hotly contested as recent debates in the UK over the revision of AIDS and HIV estimates show (*The Lancet*, 1993). Quantitative social scientists have challenged the CDC's use of non-random samples, arguing that this affects representation of sub-populations in the surveillance system (Oppenheimer, 1992, pp. 68–75). Using the 1988 General Social Survey, Laumann *et al.* (cited in Oppenheimer, 1992) found that the national surveillance system displayed class, race and geographical biases, and significantly underestimated the prevalence in the white middle class and in the Midwest and overestimated it in blacks, Latinos and in the East (Oppenheimer, 1992, p. 69). The numbers also display a gender bias, as do other statistics (see Anderson, 1992); and there are reasons to doubt some aspects of the racial/ethnic figures as well (see below). However, as Treichler (1992, p. 387) points out, though there may be questioning and denunciation of specific numbers, their overall use is not questioned.

The problems of under-reporting of AIDS cases and HIV infection are considerable (see Evans *et al.*, 1991; Gertig *et al.*, 1991; Buehler, 1992; Winn and Skelton, 1992). Most studies examine male cases and fail to examine problems of actual or potential gender biases in the surveillance and treatment systems (but see Schoenbaum and Webber, 1993). A recent investigation of reports of deaths in women in the US underlying-cause-of-death vital records and AIDS surveillance systems concluded that they identified 55–80 per cent and 67–97 per cent respectively of HIV-related deaths in women aged 15–44 years in 1988 (Buehler *et al.*, 1992a). Other studies on female deaths and AIDS surveillance criteria in the USA, some 'prompted in part by media reports that have misinterpreted vital statistics data', are cited by Buehler *et al.* (1992b, p. 262).

There are problems with the official statistics which may cause confusion and misunderstandings, only a few of which can be mentioned here. First, the case definition of AIDS in the USA (which was mainly based on symptoms in gay men) has changed several times, each change adding to the numbers of cases and altering the proportions of the sub-populations recorded in the exposure categories which indicate the probable transmission route/source of infection. Part of the increase in AIDS cases in women and heterosexual men between 1983 and 1987 was the result of the 1987 revision (Ellerbrock *et al.*, 1991, p. 2972). That also increased the numbers of patients who were black or Hispanic, or were injecting drug users, and the proportion of reported cases which were female also increased (CDC, 1989). The inclusion of a CD4+ lymphocyte count[3] criterion in the USA in 1992 will increase the numbers of people living with AIDS by 30–100 per cent (according to different studies), and the diagnosis of AIDS is made some eighteen months earlier, thus lengthening survival times. The gender and racial implications of this have yet to be fully comprehended; but it may increase the numbers of identified cases in women and injecting drug users (Stanton *et al.*, 1992) and there may be some racial differences in the decline of CD4 cell counts (Easterbrook *et al.*, 1992). The latest revision, from January 1993, further redresses the gender bias, by adding invasive cervical cancer to the HIV classification system and AIDS surveillance case definition (CDC, 1992).

The second factor is the labelling and ranking of the exposure categories, the allocation of almost all reported cases to a single category, and the changes in the categories over time. The new format in the UK, introduced in 1991, shows the annual increase in new cases for twelve-month periods and emphasizes the probable way in which people acquired HIV by rearranging and relabelling the exposure categories.

Information on past behaviour, hierarchically ordered, is used to decide how infected persons probably acquired HIV-1. If infected adults have two or more exposure categories they are assigned for these tables to a single exposure category in the following order: blood factor treatment, blood and tissue transfer, injecting drug use (IDU), IDU and sexual intercourse between men, sexual intercourse between men, sexual intercourse between men and women.[4]

The exposure categories may also contain ranked sub-categories, as is the case with the category for 'sexual intercourse between men and women' which is further subdivided by the ranked 'risk' statuses of the partner(s). However, 'there is an unfortunate tautological element here: multiple risk cases are categorized to the riskiest transmission category and become in turn components in epidemiological analyses which identify the riskiest transmission categories' (Bloor *et al.*, 1991, p. 135). There are inconsistencies in the hierarchical rankings of exposure categories and different countries and research studies may rank the categories differently. Other information such as race/ethnicity may be included, as in the US statistics which identify race/ethnic categories. Such differences complicate cross-national comparisons and the assessment of findings in different studies and over time.

Third, the dissemination of national or international totals of AIDS cases, and the simplified, short summary list of cases by probable exposure category/source of infection which is used by the mass media (and even in publications such as the *AIDS Newsletter*) may account for at least some of the confusion and misunderstandings about the statistics, especially about risks posed to and by heterosexuals. Official recording techniques may be misleading, and cross tabular representations would bring out more information (see Bloor *et al.*, 1991). The reporting of global statistics is also unhelpful: WHO global statistics refer to total numbers only, and are not broken down by e.g. gender or age in its *Weekly Epidemiological Record* updates.[5]

The transmission/exposure categories reflect the dominance of epidemiological concerns and the lack of attention paid to the social and political consequences of such classifying and grouping of individuals, particularly the marginalizing of certain groups such as Haitians (Oppenheimer, 1988, pp. 282–3). In the early years, for example, one way of handling HIV-infected children, whether or not there was evidence to support the contention, 'was to link them to established classifications through their mothers, who were characterized as either drug-addicted or, like gay men, promiscuous' (*ibid.*; p. 284). Women with AIDS were literally 'otherized' by inclusion in the 'Other' category (Treichler, 1988, p. 194).

The exposure categories appear to identify 'risk groups' even though it is both misleading and counterproductive to refer to risk groups rather than to risky practices/behaviour. Small sub-populations such as recipients of blood and tissue products are singled out for statistical visibility, but the major division is between homosexuals/bisexuals and heterosexuals. Although these terms are used as shorthand for modes of transmission ('homosexual' frequently seeming to stand as a euphemism for anal intercourse) in practice, following the earlier usage by the CDC of 'risk groups', the terms have come to stand for sexual identities and thus in common parlance for 'groups'. The addition to the British statistics of categories referring to the sexual orientation of adults of 15 years or over may also perhaps reinforce the notion of 'risk groups' by rendering invisible risks for lesbians/bisexual women/women-who-have-sex-with-women (see note 4). In these tables, only three categories are differentiated: women and heterosexual men are grouped together and homosexual men and bisexual men are separated out. Bisexual men are regarded as 'bridgeheads' into the 'general population': by having sex with men they risk becoming infected with HIV and then transmitting the virus to their (imputedly) heterosexual female partners. Same-gender sex with women and female bisexuality are not documented in the published statistics: women are lodged firmly in the heterosexual camp.

The question of risks for lesbians and women-who-have-sex-with-women is, however, increasingly the focus of debate as concern about HIV/AIDS in women grows. Accounts in the medical/behavioural literature of the possibility of transmission of HIV between lesbians have been few and references to bisexual women even fewer (but see McCombs *et al.*, 1992). The early feminist discussions of the potential risks of some lesbian sexual practices appear not to be widely known.

Petersen *et al.* (1992) have assessed the evidence for female-to-female HIV transmission for 106 of the 144 HIV-seropositive women identified among nearly one million female blood donors in twenty blood centres in the USA in 1990 (same-gender sex contact does not exclude women from donating blood whereas it does men). None had had sex only with women since 1978, and only three had reported sex with both women and men (bisexual men and/or male injecting drug users) since then. They concluded that the risk of female-to-female transmission is a potential one but probably very uncommon: the major risk to lesbian women lies in heterosexual contacts and injecting drug use. Similar findings were made by Chu *et al.* (1992) who investigated the 18,199 cases of AIDS in adult women reported to the CDC from 1 June 1980 to 30 June 1991. They identified 164 women (0.9 per cent of the total) whose reported sexual contacts were only with women. Almost all (93 per cent) were injecting drug users; the other 7 per cent had received blood transfusions before March 1985. They too concluded that female-to-female transmission could not be excluded but seemed to be extremely rare.[6] HIV transmission might occur via vaginal secretions and menstrual blood, and women who have sex with women need to be aware of the risk behaviours of sexual partners, but prevention efforts should focus on drug use.

The size of the female injecting drug user population in the USA practising female-to-female sex is unknown; but some interesting issues are raised by the study by Magura *et al.* (1992) of a random sample of thirty-nine female heroin users in New York City's central jail in 1989–90. Fifteen (38 per cent) disclosed a current sexual relationship with a woman though none identified as 'lesbian' and only four as 'gay'/'in the gay life'/'bisexual'. As most of the women had previously had heterosexual relationships and 80 per cent had children, the researchers characterized them as 'bisexual'. Of the 'bisexuals' 73 per cent were black, 7 per cent Hispanic and 20 per cent white, and of the heterosexuals 50 per cent were black, 29 per cent Hispanic and 21 per cent white. They found that 'bisexual' women were much more likely to share injection equipment; and they also identify some risky sexual practices.

These papers raise crucial questions about identity. Magura *et al.* emphasized that 'asking about *sexual orientation* is not the same as inquiring about *sexual partnerships and attachments*' (1992, p. 188, their emphasis). Likewise, Chu *et al.* (1992), who refer to lesbians and bisexual women, the two categories which do not appear in the official statistics, sounded another cautionary note:

Finally, our data are based on reported sexual behaviors, not self-identified sexual orientation. Women who identify as lesbians may have sex with men. Programs to prevent HIV transmission among women who identify as lesbian should be aware that, as with bisexual and heterosexual women, lesbian women can also acquire HIV from heterosexual transmission. (Chu *et al.*, 1992, p. 319)

Confusion between reported sexual behaviour, self-identity and sexual orientation has bedevilled the question of HIV/AIDS from the outset, partly because of the initial focus on 'risk groups'. The use of 'homosexual' (rather than 'gay') and subsequently 'men-who-have-sex-with-men' was adopted to overcome this problem. As with racial/ethnic categorizations, the question of self- or observer-attributions is an important one, and so is the question of self-identity for health prevention measures. The complexities and timing in the process of identification as a lesbian or bisexual woman discussed by Rust (1993) place in stark relief the simple categories used in much survey-based research and quantitative studies, a matter also pertinent to questions of heterosexual identity and to racial and ethnic classifications.

Whilst it is hard to find information about HIV/AIDS in women-who-have-sex-with-women, the stress on race/ethnic categories in the US statistics and in research protocols has made African-Americans and Latinos in the USA, male and female, highly visible. The disparity between the prevalence of HIV infection and AIDS in these two sub-populations compared with other racial/minority groups has long been evident, though the ratio of black (and ethnic) cases to white ones has varied over time; and among women of childbearing age (15–44 years) these categories accounted for a disproportionate share compared with their racial proportions in the US population as a whole (Gayle *et al.*, 1990). Ellerbrock *et al.* (1991, p. 2972) found that between 1981 and 1990 the cumulative incidence rates of AIDS for black and Hispanic women were respectively thirteen and eight times greater than for white women; that over half of the women with AIDS were black, about a quarter white and a fifth Hispanic; and that even though the numbers of women with AIDS had increased, the proportion who were black had stayed much the same, but the white and Hispanic proportions had respectively decreased and increased. They also found similar racial distributions among heterosexual men and cumulative incidence rates twelve and nine times respectively greater for black and Hispanic men than for white men. The CDC has consistently drawn attention to the over-representation of racial and ethnic minorities, especially women, recently pointing out that 72 per cent of all US women diagnosed with AIDS have been black and Hispanic though these are only 19 per cent of all US women, and the death rate from

HIV infection in 1988 was nine times higher for black women than for white ones (CDC, 1990). Many of the women were of lower socio-economic status, a fact to which the CDC drew attention because of the reliance in these sub-populations on public provision for prevention efforts, health care and social services (CDC, 1990). (Data about poor women and AIDS are summarized in Shayne and Kaplan, 1991.) HIV/AIDS is indeed linked to poverty and deprivation; but this may be masked or overlooked by the focus on race or ethnicity, or be taken for granted and therefore underplayed.

There are, however, reasons to be cautious about such racialized/ethnicized data and analyses. The use of race (and ethnicity) as a variable is deeply ingrained in American medical research, and may often have deleterious consequences. In their review of this topic, Osborne and Feit (1992) found 'a predilection for making comparisons between black and white patients, particularly with diseases associated with promiscuity, underachievement, and antisocial behaviour' (p. 275); and comment that 'Predictably, comparative ethnic research with AIDS . . . started shortly after its recognition. In fact, HIV infection has become one of the most popular subjects for racial comparison' (p. 277). Among the adverse consequences of race-related research and the constant focus on African Americans and Hispanics, they suggest, are the tendency to fail to address 'other, more virulent societal problems that predispose to disease' (*ibid.*, p. 278), the possibility that findings may serve to reinforce prejudices and to affect medical diagnoses and care, that they imply misleadingly that race is more important than other factors as a determinant of disease, and that the conclusions are very likely to be incorrect. They recommend that authors make clear the 'distinction between race as a risk factor and race as a risk marker' (*ibid.*, p. 276).

There are other shortcomings in the deployment of race and ethnicity in HIV/AIDS research. Particularly limiting is the restricted set of categories used in official records and many research studies which may hamper investigations of cultural similarity and diversity within and between the macro categories.[7] This is a problem that pervades all US federal population and health statistics on the evidence presented by Hahn (1992). The current standards for statistical classification of racial and ethnic groups were set in 1978 by the Office of Management and Budget in Directive 15, 'Race and Ethnic Standards for Federal Statistics and Administrative Reporting', which gave brief rules for the classification of people into four racial categories of American Indian/Alaskan Native, Asian/Pacific Islander, black, and white, and for two ethnic categories (applied to blacks and whites) of Hispanic or non-Hispanic.[8]

There is much scope for error, bias and variation in American racial/ethnic health statistics. States may use race-ethnicity coding categories differently; morbidity rates are based on data from relatively few states, which might not be representative for some racial/ethnic groups; the quality and completeness of reporting may also vary by racial or ethnic group; and the reporting of race/ethnicity is incomplete (whereas 99 per cent of reports specify gender) and varies widely between states (Buehler *et al.*, 1989). Variations in attributions may occur partly depending upon whether they are based on the perception of the respondent or of the interviewer/observer (Hahn, 1992, pp. 269; see also Yu and Liu, 1992; Stanfield, 1993).[9] A potential source of spurious or erroneous comparisons is the change in 1989 to classifying a newborn infant by the racial/ethnic category of its mother alone in the CDC's National Center for Health Statistics (NCHS). This will affect future comparisons by increasing the numbers of white infants in published statistics (previously only infants with two white parents were considered white) though since 1984 in statistics on Hispanic origin newborns have been assigned to their mother's origin (Hahn, 1992, p. 269). The basis for contrasting blacks and whites, for inferring the over-representation of blacks in HIV/AIDS statistics – particularly common in papers on women – is frequently a comparison with national census figures for population groups, numbers which also present considerable problems (see Petersen, 1987; Yu and Liu, 1992; Lee, 1993).

The imprecision of the race/ethnic categories, the aggregation of very diverse groups into one category, and the attributions and 'misattributions' of people with HIV infections and AIDS (before and after death) have been discussed in various papers concerned with the accuracy of AIDS surveillance systems and vital statistics. Such misattributions may mean that the over-representation of minorities among AIDS cases may be even greater than current data suggest. Yu and Liu (1992, p. 1647) (summarizing a recent study) point out that inconsistencies in coding the race of deceased infants have been found to be lowest for whites (1.2 per cent) and blacks (4.3 per cent) and very high for other races (43.2 per cent) (and exceptionally so for Filipinos with a 78.7 per cent error rate). The status of newborns depends on parental status; assignation on death depends on information about identity provided by the next of kin or on independent assessments by funeral directors (Hahn, 1992). During life an individual may switch identities or select one according to the situation. And who knows what method and criteria for attributions were used by researchers? We are rarely given details.

That 'individuals may be assigned a different race at birth, during the course of life, and at death' (Hahn, 1992, p. 269; see also Yu and Liu, 1992, p. 1648) must further undermine confidence in the statistics. Whether there might be any gender implications is not clear, and this might repay investigation. Whilst discrepancies and shifts in personal identities should not surprise a social scientist, there may be little widespread appreciation that these are issues, let alone the extent to which changes in identity may occur both for personal/political reasons and/or as artefactual consequences of different classification systems. It is difficult indeed to realize the fuzzy nature of the categories when faced with apparently 'hard' statistical data about HIV and AIDS presented in racial and ethnic boxes.

Reframing the Agenda

Despite the evident need for gender-sensitive and women-centred research, and despite feminist critiques such as those of Patton (1986) and Treichler (1988) it is only recently, ten years into the pandemic, that detailed attention has been paid to the problems of HIV and AIDS of and for women.

Clearly, in some respects there has been a change for the better. Women are increasingly on the agenda – even if too often the stress is still on women as mothers and on women of childbearing age. i.e., 15–49 years old.[10] By (belatedly) incorporating women-specific indicators into the case definition of AIDS, the Centers for Disease Control have finally succumbed to the pressure to be more gender-sensitive and to take cognizance of the growing body of evidence that women manifested different opportunistic infections, that the natural history of HIV infection might differ in women and that they were often diagnosed late (if at all).[11] An increasing volume of research on HIV/AIDS in women is now being undertaken, and no longer mainly by social scientists. There is also a growing awareness in the USA, at least, of the ways in which gender bias pervades not only HIV/AIDS research but all medical science and drugs trials,[12] which should lead to improvements and, given the dominance of US concerns and research into HIV/AIDS, may well influence researchers in other countries as well.

Gender is a key factor, as the current projections of the impact of HIV/AIDS upon women demonstrate. The continuing perception among the public (and some doctors) and specifically among women at risk that AIDS is a disease of gay men, and the stress on condom usage as the prime preventive measure, a measure fraught with gendered implications, further support this. Identifying gender differences in respect of HIV/AIDS, though, is no easy matter, as Treichler (1988) has demonstrated. Medical, scientific and epidemiological research has tended to pay little detailed attention to the specific differences which gender might make; and it is often impossible to discern from the literature whether and how gender might be implicated or, indeed, even to discover the sex of the researchees.[13] Even when differences relating to women have been noticed, these are not always investigated nor may they always result in differences in treatment and care.

Another factor is the issue of race and ethnicity and the disproportionate HIV/AIDS burden borne by minority women in the USA to which reference is frequently made. A focus on race and ethnicity, which at first sight the data might seem to justify, seems more problematical on closer examination. Here I have focused not so much on the data collection practices in respect of HIV/AIDS, but rather on the wider issues of racial classification in the USA to which they are linked. The question of racism and HIV/AIDS has been addressed by feminist researchers such as Patton (1986, p. 17) and Treichler (1992). Schneider suggested that increased racism in the USA in the 1980s set the environment for discussing HIV/AIDS in the context of race and ethnicity, and pointed out that 'Race framed the epidemiological targeting of an entire nationality, the Haitians, as a 'high-risk' group, ... it is likely that the focus on the Haitians diverted attention from U.S. racial/ethnic groups' (1992, p. 32). This is a problem that goes beyond medicine, though it is acute in that field. Stanfield points out that 'the presumptuous embrace and utilization of such categories by social scientists generates a number of dilemmas' (1993, p. 17);[14] and that in race-centred societies such as the USA 'Race-saturated everyday language (verbal and nonverbal) reflects and determines how Americans describe themselves and others' (*ibid.*).

The differential impacts of HIV/AIDS related to class or socio-economic status is a third factor, though one which I have mentioned but briefly. Little detailed attention has been paid to class issues: and, too often, even when the class or socio-economic status of researchees has been identified, the detailed analysis of findings ignores that aspect altogether, the focus instead being on categories of sexuality. An additional difficulty for accounts referring to the USA, according to Krieger (1993), is that medical researchers may use the terms 'social class', 'socio-economic status' and 'insurance status' interchangeably and may also subsume racial/ethnic differences under class, rather than examining separately the effects of racial discrimination within socio-economic strata.

Gender, race and class factors are becoming more important though we still have too few accounts in which they are all paid due attention (but see Osmond *et al.* (1993) who designed their study of low-income culturally diverse women in South Florida to examine the interaction between these factors). Schneider (1992) has reviewed the situation for the USA, looking at both men and women; and Treichler has suggested that analyzing *inter elia* 'the intersections of gender, race, and class in relation to an illness profiled in terms of nonintersecting categories' is one area in which feminist analyses of AIDS would be a useful contribution (Treichler, 1988, p. 232–3).

There is still a very long way to go, though, particularly in relating HIV/AIDS policies, programmes, research and theoretical work to women's daily lives. Reid (1992) argues that there has been a failure to take full account of the existing knowledge about women's real-life situations and the forces and relationships shaping and constraining them,[15] and draws attention to the fact that in all the disciplines involved in the HIV research and programme agendas men have predominated.[16] This gender bias in personnel is the more serious, because, as she points out, 'A serious constraint to progress is that women are more aware than men that experience and knowledge are gender-based, that social, political, moral, research, policy, program, and other agendas are drawn up on the basis of men's experiences' (Reid, 1992, p. 664). In a racialized and ethnicized world, too, the agendas often also reflect not the concerns of racial and ethnic minorities but those of the dominant majority and of the politicians who are also involved in politically 'ring-fencing' their domains to control the poor, the dispossessed, the non-white migrants and refugees, and those with HIV infection and AIDS.

Notes

1 That this is so is not often obvious. The UK statistics published in the Communicable Disease Report now show numbers of deaths as well. AIDS is also unique in being the only example of a syndrome which is recorded like a disease. The list of opportunistic infections in the definition of AIDS has undergone various redefinitions and also varies between geographical areas.

2 Surveillance is 'the systematic collection of data pertaining to the occurrence of specific diseases, the analysis and interpretation of these data, and the dissemination of consolidated and processed information. . . . Such information is essential for monitoring the spread of the [AIDS] epidemic, allocating health resources and assessing the effectiveness of preventive measures' (Gertig *et al.*, 1991, p. 1157). Various sources of information are utilized – death certificates, cohort studies, vital records, medical records, HIV tests (such as the recent anonymous testing of blood taken from women in antenatal clinics in England), some of which may raise questions of human rights, privacy, confidentiality and voluntariness. For examples and methods used in calculating the numbers of HIV/AIDS cases, incidences, prevalences and projections based on the situation to mid 1992 see Mann *et al.* (1992).

3 Cells carrying CD4 molecules, especially the T-lymphocyte CD4+ 'helper' cells, are the main targets of the virus. Monitoring the CD4+ cell count is a way of measuring the immunosuppressive effect of HIV infection; a count of fewer than 200 cells per microlitre is taken as an indicator of AIDS (Buehler, 1992). CD4+ cell counts are not being adopted in Britain and Western Europe, so discrepancies between national and regional totals of cases may become more marked.

4 'Change of AIDS/HIV reporting', *The AIDS Letter*, No. 23, Feb/Mar 1991, p. 6 (citing *Communicable Disease Report* 1, 1991).

5 Bernard (1991) has attempted to identify age/gender profiles on a global basis for AIDS and HIV infection using official government reports and secondary tabulations from Regional WHO Offices.

6 Most papers on lesbians do not rule out female-to-female sexual transmission of HIV but regard it as a remote possibility. This may be the consequence of scientific procedures and the use of probabilistic statements; as the null hypothesis cannot be proved a scientist will not rule out theoretical but unlikely possibilities of transmission, but '[l]ay people may misinterpret this phrasing, however, to mean that such transmission is possible or somewhat likely' (Herek and Glunt, 1988, p. 889).

7 I use the American accounts for illustrative purposes. Ethnic and racial statistics for HIV/AIDS figures in the UK are hard to come by; HIV/AIDS and health education among minority groups has only recently been officially addressed. If the prevailing official categories are used then we too will have 'official' knowledge on health matters (as in other domains) about only a few very broad ethnic/racial categories.

8 The National Center for Health Statistics (NCHS) has used nine race code

categories since the 1970s – White, Black, (American) Indian, Chinese, Japanese, Hawaiian, Filipino, other Asian/Pacific Islander, and other races. The 'other Asian/ Pacific Islander' category includes at least twenty-one other ethnic identities, which Yu and Liu (1992, p. 1646) consider renders that category 'nebulous, meaningless, and scientifically useless' for programme-planning and research purposes.

9   Yu and Liu (1992) address problems of 'race' coding practices, under-enumeration, ways of improving the quality of information, and matters of research methodology, sampling problems etc.

10   Data are often restricted to adults in the 15-to-49-year-old category (e.g. Mann *et al.*, 1992, Appendix 2.2H). Data about children are rarely gendered (but see R-P. Bernard's analyses in his *AIDS Feedback* series).

11   See, e.g., Campbell, 1990; Ellerbrock *et al.*, 1991; Minkoff and DeHovitz, 1991; Sherr, 1991.

12   The Governing Council of the American Public Health Association adopted 'Policy Statement 9115: Support for Women's Health Research' in its 1991 meeting (American Public Health Association, 1992, pp. 485–6), and applauded the establishment of an Office for Research on Women's Health at the National Institutes of Health.

13   Webb (1993) summarizes papers presented to the 1993 meeting of the American Association for the Advancement of Science, which confirm my impressionistic judgement of marked gender bias in the HIV/AIDS literature. Vita Rabinowitz *et al.* showed that in 180 studies of HIV reported in *AIDS* and *The Journal of AIDS* in 1991, about 25 per cent did not give the gender of the subjects, over 50 per cent applied results inappropriately or questionably to both sexes, and some 75 per cent which looked for gender differences found them; only two out of five studies on HIV in *Science* in 1991 gave gender and all five made inappropriate generalizations from their findings. Jeri Sechzer analyzed papers in *Science* from 1984 to 1991; in experimental studies and drug tests male animals were often used, frequently the sex of the animals was not given, and inappropriate or questionable generalizations to both sexes occurred in the majority of papers.

      Minority groups are also frequently excluded from or under-represented in drug trials. African-Americans often live in poverty-stricken urban areas, and their social needs hamper participation in trials even if attempts have been made to recruit them; and the problems are compounded for women with young children (El-Sadr and Capps, 1992). Funding for the first drug trials involving ethnic minorities and women was only allocated in 1991 (*AIDS Newsletter* 1991, 6 (2), p. 16, no. 146).

14   Among the problems he mentions are the uncritical use by quantitative researchers of official racial categories; the question of objective and subjective racial identifications; and the neglect of the identities of Euro-Americans.

15   She calls this a failure of epistemic responsibility (following Lorraine Code), a failure to be open to the acquisition of knowledge, to question assumptions, to seek alternative sources, to acknowledge different perspectives and to recognize

Anne Akeroyd

the contingent nature of some kinds of knowledge and their relation to (gendered and socially) mediated experiences (Reid, 1992, p. 658).

16 Epidemiology seems hardly to have been affected by feminist concerns and debates about methodology. Scientists are also far less likely to read the social scientific literature than vice versa, and it is in social scientific literature that many of the papers on women and feminist issues have appeared. This is compounded by the poor coverage of social scientific and feminist studies in AIDS indexing journals and bibliographic databases.

References

ALONSO, W. and STARR, P. (Eds) (1987) *The Politics of Numbers*, New York, Russell Sage Foundation.

AMERICAN PUBLIC HEALTH ASSOCIATION (1992) 'Policy Statements Adopted by the Governing Council of the American Public Health Association November 13, 1991', *American Journal of Public Health*, vol. 82, no. 3, pp. 476–94.

ANDERSON, M. (1992) 'The History of Women and the History of Statistics', *Journal of Women's History*, vol. 4, no. 1, pp. 14–36.

BERNARD, R-P. (1991) 'AIDS/HIV by Age/Gender: Global Review in 22 Panels', *AIDS-Forschung*, vol. 6, no. 11, pp. 577–93.

BLOOR, M., GOLDBERG, D. and EMSLIE, J. (1991) 'Ethnostatics and the AIDS Epidemic', *British Journal of Sociology*, vol. 42, no. 1, pp. 131–8.

BUEHLER, J.W. (1992) 'The Surveillance Definition for AIDS', *American Journal of Public Health*, vol. 82, no. 11, pp. 1462–4.

BUEHLER, J.W., STROUP, D.F., KLAUCKE, D.N. and BERKELMAN, R.L. (1989) 'The Reporting of Race and Ethnicity in the National Notifiable Diseases Surveillance System', *Public Health Reports*, vol. 104, no. 5, pp. 457–65.

BUEHLER, J.W., HANSON, D.L. and CHU, S.Y. (1992a) 'The Reporting of HIV/AIDS Deaths in Women', *American Journal of Public Health*, vol. 82, no. 11, pp. 1500–5.

BUEHLER, J.W., BERKELMAN, R.L. and STEHR-GREEN, J.K, (1992b) 'The Completeness of AIDS Surveillance', *Journal of Acquired Immune Deficiency Syndromes*, vol. 5, no. 3, pp. 257–64.

CAMPBELL, C.A. (1990) 'Women and AIDS', *Social Science and Medicine*, vol. 30, no. 4, pp. 407–15.

CASTRO, K.G., VALDISERRI, R.O. and CURRAN, J.W. (1992) 'Perspectives on HIV/AIDS Epidemiology and Prevention from the Eighth International Conference on AIDS', *American Journal of Public Health*, vol. 82, no. 11, pp. 1465–70.

CENTERS FOR DISEASE CONTROL (1982) 'Update on Acquired Immune Deficiency Syndrome (AIDS) – United States', *MMWR – Morbidity and Mortality Weekly Report*, vol. 31, no. 37, pp. 507–8, 513–14.

CENTERS FOR DISEASE CONTROL (1983) 'Immunodeficiency among Female Sexual Partners of Males with Acquired Immune Deficiency Syndrome (AIDS) – New York', *MMWR*, vol. 31, no. 52, pp. 697–8.

CENTERS FOR DISEASE CONTROL (1989) 'Update: Acquired Immune Deficiency Syndrome – United States, 1981–1988', *MMWR*, vol. 38, no. 14, pp. 229–36.

CENTERS FOR DISEASE CONTROL (1990) 'AIDS in Women – United States', *MMWR*, vol. 39, pp. 845–6.

CENTERS FOR DISEASE CONTROL (1992) '1993 Revised Classification System for HIV Infection and Expanded Surveillance Case Definition for AIDS among Adolescents and Adults', *MMWR – Recommendations and Reports*, vol. 41, no. RR-17.

CHIN, J. (1990) 'Current and Future Dimensions of the HIV/AIDS Pandemic in Women and Children', *The Lancet*, vol. 336, no. 8709, pp. 221–4.

CHU, S.Y., HAMMETT, T.A. and BUEHLER, J.W. (1992) 'Update: Epidemiology of Reported Cases of AIDS in Women Who Report Sex Only With Other Women, United States, 1980–1991', *AIDS*, vol. 6, no. 5, pp. 518–19.

EASTERBROOK, P.J., MARGOLICK, J., SAAH, A.J. *et al.* (1992) 'Racial Differences in Rate of CD4 Decline in HIV-1 Infected Homosexual Men', Abstract MoC 0064 in *Index File: V1: Final Programme and Oral Abstracts*, Eighth International Conference on AIDS, Amsterdam, 19–24 July, Amsterdam, CONGREX Holland B.V.

EL-SADR, W. and CAPPS, L. (1992) 'The Challenge of Minority Recruitment in Clinical Trials for AIDS', *Journal of the American Medical Association (JAMA)*, vol. 267, no. 7, pp. 954–7.

ELLERBROCK, T.V., BUSH, T.J., CHAMBERLAND, M.E. and OXTOBY, M.J. (1991) 'Epidemiology of Women with AIDS in the United States, 1981 through 1990', *Journal of the American Medical Association (JAMA)*, vol. 265, no. 22, pp. 2971–5.

EVANS, B.G., GILL, O.N. and EMSLIE, J.A.N. (1991) 'Completeness of Reporting of AIDS Cases', *British Medical Journal*, vol. 302, no. 6789, pp. 1351–2.

FEE, E. and FOX, D.M. (Eds) (1988) *AIDS: The Burdens of History*, Berkeley, CA, University of California Press.

FEE, E. and FOX, D.M. (Eds) (1992) *AIDS: The Making of a Chronic Disease*, Berkeley, CA, University of California Press.

GAYLE, J.A., SELIK, R.M. and CHU, S.Y. (1990) 'Surveillance for AIDS and HIV Infection among Black and Hispanic Children and Women of Childbearing Age, 1981–1989', *MMWR – Morbidity and Mortality Weekly Report*, vol. 39, no. SS-3, pp. 23–30.

GERTIG, D.M., MARION, S.A. and SCHECTER, M.T. (1991) 'Estimating the Extent of Underreporting in AIDS Surveillance', *AIDS*, vol. 5, pp. 1157–64.

HAHN, R.A. (1992) 'The State of Federal Health Statistics on Racial and Ethnic Groups', *Journal of the American Medical Association (JAMA)*, vol. 267, no. 2, pp. 268–71.

HALL, C. (1993) 'Many People with HIV "Do Not Know They Are Infected"', *The Independent* (London), 1 February, p. 3.

HEREK, G.M. and GLUNT, E.K. (1988) 'An Epidemic of Stigma: Public Reactions to AIDS', *American Psychologist*, vol. 43, no. 11, pp. 886–91.

ICKOVICS, J.R. and RODIN, J. (1992) 'Women and AIDS in the United States:

Anne Akeroyd

Epidemiology, Natural History, and Mediating Mechanisms', *Health Psychology*, vol. 11, no. 1, pp. 1–16.

KEYFITZ, N. (1987) 'The Social and Political Context of Population Forecasting', in ALONSO, W. and STARR, P. (Eds), *The Politics of Numbers*, New York, Russell Sage Foundation.

KRIEGER, N. (1993) 'Analyzing Socioeconomic and Racial/Ethnic Patterns in Health and Health Care', *American Journal of Public Health*, vol. 83, no. 8, pp. 1086–7.

LANCET, THE (1993) 'Heterosexual AIDS: Pessimism, Pandemics, and Plain Hard Facts', Editorial, 3 April, vol. 341, pp. 863–4.

LEE, S.M. (1993) 'Racial Classifications in the US Census: 1890–1990', *Ethnic and Racial Studies*, vol. 16, no. 1, pp. 75–94.

McCOMBS, S.B., McCRAY, E., WENDELL, D.A., SWEENEY, P.A. and ORONATO, I.M. (1992) 'Epidemiology of HIV-1 Infection in Bisexual Women [Letter]', *Journal of Acquired Immune Deficiency Syndromes*, vol. 5, no. 8, pp. 850–2.

MAGURA, S., O'DAY, J. and ROSENBLUM, A. (1992) 'Women Usually Take Care of Their Girlfriends: Bisexuality and HIV Risk among Female Intravenous Drug Users', *The Journal of Drug Issues*, vol. 22, no. 1, pp. 179–90.

MANN, J., TARANTOLA, D.J.M. and NETTER, T.W. (Eds) (1992) *AIDS in the World: A Global Report*, Cambridge, MA and London, Harvard University Press.

MINKOFF, H.L. and DeHOVITZ, J.A. (1991) 'Care of Women Infected with the Human Immunodeficiency Virus', *Journal of the American Medical Association (JAMA)*, vol. 266, no. 16, pp. 2253–8.

MURRAIN, M. (1993) 'New stats on women and AIDS with new definition', *Discussion on Women's Studies List*, WMST-L@UMDD.BITNET, 14 June.

NICOLL, A. (1991) 'Global HIV/AIDS: Women and Children First', *Current AIDS Literature*, vol. 7, no. 6, pp. 213–14.

OPPENHEIMER, G.M. (1988) 'In the eye of the storm: The Epidemiological Construction of AIDS', in FEE, E. and FOX, D.M. (Eds) *AIDS: The Burdens of History*, Berkeley, CA, University of California Press.

OPPENHEIMER, G.M. (1992) 'Causes, Cases, and Cohorts: The Role of Epidemiology in the Historical Construction of AIDS', in FEE, E. and FOX, D.M. (Eds) *AIDS: The Making of a Chronic Disease*, Berkeley, CA, University of California Press.

OSBORNE, N.G. and FEIT, M.D. (1992) 'The Use of Race in Medical Research', *Journal of the American Medical Association (JAMA)*, vol. 267, no. 2, pp. 275–9.

OSMOND, M.W., WAMBACH, K.G., HARRISON, D.F., BYERS, J., LEVINE, P., IMERSHEIN, A. and QUADAGNO, D.M. (1993) 'The Multiple Jeopardy of Race, Class, and Gender for AIDS Risk among Women', *Gender & Society*, vol. 7, no. 1, pp. 99–120.

PATTON, C. (1986) *Sex and Germs: The Politics of AIDS*, Montreal and Buffalo, Black Rose Books.

PETERSEN, L.R., DOLL, L., WHITE, C., CHU, S. and the HIV BLOOD DONOR STUDY GROUP (1992) 'No Evidence for Female-to-Female HIV Transmission among 960,000 Female Blood Donors', *Journal of Acquired Immune Deficiency Syndromes*, vol. 5, no. 9, pp. 853–5.

PETERSEN, W. (1987) 'Politics and the Measurement of Ethnicity', in ALONSO, W. and STARR, P. (Eds), *The Politics of Numbers*, New York, Russell Sage Foundation.

REID, E. (1992) 'Gender, Knowledge and Responsibility', in MANN, J., TARANTOLA, D.J.M. and NETTER, T.W. (Eds) *AIDS in the World*, Cambridge, MA and London, Harvard University Press, pp. 657–67.

RUST, P.C. (1993) ' "Coming Out" in the Age of Social Constructionism: Sexual Identity Formation among Lesbian and Bisexual Women', *Gender & Society*, vol. 7, no. 1, pp. 50–77.

SCHARF, E. and TOOLE, S. (1992) 'HIV and the Invisibility of Women: Is there a Need to Redefine AIDS?', *Feminist Review*, no. 41, pp. 64–7.

SCHNEIDER, B.E. (1992) 'AIDS and Class, Gender, and Race Relations', in HUBER, J. and SCHNEIDER, B.E. (Eds), *The Social Context of AIDS*, Newbury Park, CA, SAGE Publications.

SCHOENBAUM, E.E. and WEBBER, M.P. (1993) 'The Underrecognition of HIV Infection in Women in an Inner-City Emergency Room', *American Journal of Public Health*, vol. 83, no. 3, pp. 363–8.

SHAYNE, V.T. and KAPLAN, B.J. (1991) 'Double Victims: Poor Women and AIDS', *Women & Health*, vol. 17, no. 1, pp. 21–37.

SHERR, L. (1991) 'Women and Children', *Aids Care*, vol. 3, no. 4, pp. 423–32.

STANFIELD, J.H. II (1993) 'Epistemological Considerations', in STANFIELD, J.H. II and DENNIS, R.M. (Eds) *Race and Ethnicity in Research Methods*, Newbury Park, CA, SAGE Publications.

STANTON, D., CHAISSON, R.E., RUCKER, S. *et al.* (1992) 'Impact of the 1992 AIDS Case Definition on the Prevalence of AIDS in a Clinical Setting', Abstract PoC 4460 in *Index File: V2: Poster Abstracts*, Eighth International Conference on AIDS, Amsterdam, 19–24 July, Amsterdam, CONGREX Holland B.V.

STONE, K.M. and PETERSON, H.B. (1992) 'HIV, Heterosexual Transmission, and Women', *Journal of the American Medical Association (JAMA)*, vol. 268, no. 4, pp. 520–3.

TREICHLER, P.A. (1988) 'AIDS, Gender, and Biomedical Discourse: Current Contests for Meaning', in FEE, E. and FOX, D.M. (Eds) *AIDS: The Burdens of History*, Berkeley, CA, University of California Press.

TREICHLER, P.A. (1992) 'AIDS and HIV Infection in the Third World: A First World Chronicle', in FEE, E. and FOX, D.M. (Eds) *AIDS: The Making of a Chronic Disease*, Berkeley, CA, University of California Press.

WEBB, J. (1993) ' "Gender Offenders" Skew Results in Many Studies', *New Scientist*, 20 February, vol. 137, no. 1861, p. 8.

WINN, S. and SKELTON, R. (1992) 'HIV in the U.K.: Problems of Prevalence, Sociological Response and Health Education', *Social Science and Medicine*, vol. 34, no. 6, pp. 697–707.

YU, E.S.H and LIU, W.T. (1992) 'US National Health Data on Asian Americans and Pacific Islanders: A Research Agenda for the 1990s', *American Journal of Public Health*, vol. 82, no. 12, pp. 1645–52.

Section II
Questions of Identity

Chapter 5

Race, Ethnicity and Nationality: Some Questions of Identity

Sheila Allen

The aim of this chapter is to suggest some possible ways in which feminist perspectives on identity can be developed to take account of the complexities of racial, ethnic and national divisions. It considers the kinds of approaches that have been adopted by social scientists and looks at the current use of the term in popular discourse.[1] It makes no claim to be exhaustive in terms of the literature. This is not out of some sense of false modesty, nor is it simply that the literature which could be drawn on is voluminous. It reflects rather the current situation in which identity has become a recurring referent in popular media discourse. We are confronted daily with events which are interpreted, at least in part, as matters of identity. Is identity used when there is no under- standing or no readily available explanation of events or of the actions of others? Is this more likely to be the case in times of rapid social change accompanied by widespread disruption?

Identity also appears with increasing regularity in academic discussions. For example, at a conference on women's role in building the 'new' Europe, with participants from across Europe and the former Soviet Union, held in Athens in the autumn of 1991 it was constantly stated that everyone needs a national identity (Allen, 1991). This unqualified statement was extremely puzzling to me. A woman from Cyprus, one born in Tashkent, living and working in Moscow, and I were the only ones to ask what this meant and to raise doubts about its relevance, especially for women. Either our queries were met with blank incomprehension, or its meaning and relevance were taken to be so self-evident as to need no explanation. The emergence or re-emergence in Europe of nationalisms, and of exclusive ethnicities reinforcing racialized structures and practices, pose a considerable challenge to many understandings and explanations developed by social scientists, including feminist scholars. Given the widespread use of the term identity, the ways in which it has been conceptualized and its use as a tool of analysis deserve close attention. The questions raised by its current usage are much more than intellectual puzzles. They are intimately related to issues of human action, moral purpose and the range of choices available. The social conditions and the individual circumstances in which choices are embedded are relevant to the interpretations made about identity/identities.[2] I first consider theories of what I will call the identity problematic and the ways in which it has been conceptualized and investigated. I then discuss perspectives from feminist approaches which modify, and in some cases significantly reshape, the ways in which this problematic is discussed. Finally I take up some issues in the current popular discourse which are of particular relevance to women.

Identity in the Social Sciences

The use of the term identity has not been widespread in social science until comparatively recently. However, the identity problematic, all those ideas of how human beings see themselves and relate to others, in groups, quasi-groups, communities and societies has been at the core of much European social thought over at least the past four centuries.

There are two major ways of conceptualizing the problematic. One is where each human being is seen as an individual entity separate from others, not living in isolation, but in association with them. The problem to be investigated then starts with the individual who exists prior to and outside the social, and the explanation is couched in terms of the links between the individual and society. The second way depicts individuals as part of the social relations in which they engage, both in the sense of direct personal interaction and indirectly as part of wider structures, of which they are not necessarily aware. The task then becomes one of explaining how the mechanisms of social interaction and social structure operate to create human beings as social persons and how in turn these social persons influence the structures of which they are a part. In addition to these broader conceptualizations, but integral to them, is a range of questions about the individual's/social person's understanding or perception of her/himself. It is around these that the narrower concept of identity has been focused. There is a further assumption to be noted, which is not always made explicit, but is incorporated into theoretical models and into common-sense thought, that of mind and body dualism. It is not my intention to pursue the ramifications of this assumption in any systematic way in this chapter though I recognize their importance to a feminist unravelling of mainstream depictions of women.

In order to set the context for the later discussion of feminist approaches I examine some of the work and the insights we can draw from across relevant mainstream disciplines.

In the sociological literature reference to identity is relatively scarce. This is due in part to the discipline tending to eschew over long periods anything which might be interpreted as psychological or individualistic reductionism. If we look to the identity problematic, however, we find that this is theorized, albeit at different analytical levels and within very different paradigms, in the work of many nineteenth- and twentieth-century social theorists (for an overview see Burkitt, 1991, and for the philosophical underpinnings see Benton, 1977). Marx, for instance, develops ideas about the relations of individuals to themselves, to others and to the natural world as part of his work on theorizing capital and labour power (Marx, 1973). His concept of alienation was not simply, or primarily, a psychological state or feeling, but integral to the structuring of the forces and relations of production in the development of capitalism. How far he carried it forward into his later work has been a matter of considerable debate, which need not concern us here. According to Gouldner (1971, p. 189) there was a limited convergence between the young Marx and the early writings of Parsons 'in their view of man as a striving, goal seeking creature'.[3] Their differences arose from the balance they saw between such striving and the social conditionality, which led Marx to emphasize the state of alienation and Parsons to stress voluntarism. 'To Parsons men are free to strive, but are not free to *achieve* what they strive for. Men make a difference but not the difference they intend. This indeed is the picture of Marx's alienated man. But what for Marx is an historic pathology is for Parsons the unavoidable and eternal condition of man' (*ibid.*, p. 193).

Durkheim deals with the possibilities of linkages among individuals in complex societies, marked by high levels of the divisions of labour, where direct relations to significant others are narrowed and the larger structures of economics, politics and religion appear as external, controlling and oppressive. A state of normlessness, or *anomie*, Durkheim argues, characterizes societies in transition, where there appear to individuals to be no moral structures to regulate their actions. Though he comes close to an individualist explanation he does not adopt the utilitarian view that the pursuit of self-interest brings the greatest good for the greatest number. On the contrary, he finds the basis of moral action in this type of society in the interdependences associated with complex divisions of labour which members come to recognize as *social facts*, external to and constraining any one individual. Industrial societies cohere through this form of solidarity which he termed organic, as opposed to those with simpler divisions of labour which were mechanically solidaristic.[4]

Weber distinguished between traditional social orders, where individuals inherited their social status, lived in local situations within taken-for-granted authority structures, and modern societies where the processes of rationality took precedence. Production relations, markets and bureaucratized authority structures encapsulated individuals and mediated human relations, so that a loss of meaning ensued. Weber borrowed Schiller's phrase, the 'disenchantment of the world', to describe these processes of secular rationalization and their effects on social relations. Individuals, while being freed from the constraints of 'traditional' obligations and the security these provided, are caught in much wider systems over which they have no control. Simultaneously they are expected to produce and reproduce organizations fitted to material and cultural tasks, and themselves as capable social actors.

Despite the differences in these approaches and differences of emphasis within them, all were concerned with explaining the construction of self as part of societal order and change. Their ideas have been developed by others and the problems addressed remain central concerns (see, for instance Bauman, 1978; Elias, 1982). Burkitt (1991), after reviewing a wide range of social theorists, argues against any division between society and the individual and concludes that 'there are many levels of dynamic agency within the personality . . . . These different levels are always interwoven with and determined by social relations and activities of production, communication and power. . . . Only if we begin from the study of social relations and activities can we truly understand how individuals are social selves' (p. 215).

Over the past few years the problem has been addressed, particularly with regard to gender and race, within the context of debates on modernism and postmodernism. It is claimed that the dominance in Western social science of theoretical approaches which saw in industrialization a pattern of social change which subordinated all social statuses to the market and production relations created a mode of theorizing inappropriate to the late twentieth century. Without going into any further detail at this point we have to note that most theorizing of change and development, whether of a Marxist or liberal variety, presumed that ethnicity, race and other statuses were subordinate to those produced by economic rationalization and ever more centralized systems of power.[5] In most accounts of the development of Western industrial economies neither capitalists nor labourers were depicted as having any gender, ethnicity, race, religion or nationality. It was not that these social attributes did not exist, but according to the models of development adopted they belonged to 'traditional' societies and through the processes of industrialization were marginalized and so became less and less relevant to understanding societal relations.

Much about this model of development has a clear purchase on the creation of modern societies and I would not wish to suggest that we cast it aside. Rather the task is to hypothesize and investigate how and when the processes and structures of modernization/industrialization construct and incorporate statuses such as those related to gender, ethnicity, race, religion and nationality. Although sociologists were antipathetic to seeing ethnicity as anything more than a relic of 'traditional' societies and did not incorporate it into core theorizing, it was not by any means totally neglected. When ethnic groups or categories were recognized as relevant they were explained by exogenous factors and as instrumentally functional. Moreover, they were also conceived as situationally specific, applicable to and used in relations outside the market. Thus while structuring personal, religious, cultural or kinship boundaries and actions, they were absent in market relations. In some situations they could be externally imposed by dominant others, defining some or all relations between dominant and subordinated categories, a set of ethnic labels emerging or disappearing according to other political or socio-economic forces. Identity structuring was absent from much sociological work on race and ethnic relations: for example, Rex (1986), Goulbourne (1991) and Schermerhorn (1970) do not discuss it and the emphasis is on group processes and boundary maintenance in what were variously labelled plural or heterogeneous societies.

There was, in addition, a scepticism of ethnic identities claiming long histories or authenticities derived from primordial ties (see Smith, 1986; Allen and Macey, 1994); a scepticism by no means altogether misplaced. Whether considering traditions (cultural beliefs, rituals, ceremonies, ways of doing things) or collective memories of shared pasts, as nations, tribes, peoples or clans, a degree of scepticism is appropriate. Many such claims turn out to be recent, modern inventions or reinventions; the products of conflicts of material interests or struggles over 'authentic' identities linked to claims to civil, political and social rights (Hobsbawm, 1984). McCrone (1992) in his discussion of late-twentieth-century Scotland and the phenomenon of nationalism refers to the selective remembering involved in nationhood. 'Events can be linked across centuries so that the "Scottish people" can stretch across centuries. "Remember Bannockburn" may seem a daft stricture in the late twentieth century when no-one can imagine what it was like to be there' (p. 198). But the stress is on continuity and McCrone argues that 'social scientists and historians have little power to prevent this selective remembering, and con-fronting myths with "facts" has little impact because myths survive almost in spite of facts' (p. 199). For the sociologist the task is to explain under what conditions the mythical past is brought into play and how it is constructed and reconstructed in terms of the present.

One of the most pressing current examples to which such analyses are to be applied is that of the former federal state of Yugoslavia. The ethnic map, here as elsewhere, deals with majorities/minorities but can be used as an exclusionary tool in the hands of majoritarian politicians. The reality in many of the Yugoslav republics is somewhat different. Bosnia, for instance, at the time of its recognition as an independent nation in 1992, had a population of Yugoslavs with a mixture of ethnicities and religions. Bosnians were those born or living in Bosnia; they were Slavs and Croat and if they had a religious affiliation, the Croats were Catholics and the Slavs were either Orthodox Christians or Muslims.[6] The reality was, as many now know, by no means this simple. Patterns of intermarriage were common, so that many had not only partners from 'other categories', but also parents from 'different' religions or ethnicities. All of these were neighbours and kin, especially but not only, in urban contexts, sharing their daily lives over several generations. The description and explanation of who is killing whom and why is interpreted in terms of ethnicity/religion and nationalism. Selective remembering is part of this process not only by the powerful parties directly involved, but by most reporters and commentators. Ethnicity linked to nationalism and religion is claimed to have overridden all other identities in the conflict. Other descriptions, explanations and interpretations, in which these are used as symbols to mobilize support in struggles for political and economic dominance, are by and large ignored.

In an unusually reflexive article on the reporting of the fighting in the former Yugoslavia the situation was described not only as highly dangerous for journalists, but as facing them with a moral quagmire 'in a brutal multisided conflict' (Keating, 1993). One journalist admitted the difficulties of reporting the complexities in which at times 'you had to approach people carefully [*sic*] and say "Excuse me are you Croats? Oh sorry you're Muslims . . . you're shooting at . . . um . . . Serbs? Oh, the Croats!"' Despite this, she went on to argue that viewers at home 'like to identify with one side. Where are the good guys? Who are the bad guys? . . . and if it is not clear, then people lose either sympathy or interest' (Adie, 1993). Constructing clarity where none exists, albeit in order to hold an audience, may be seen as necessary by some reporters, and as such it tells us something about how exclusive categorizations are imposed and transmitted. But it tells us nothing about the identities of those involved and borders on disinformation of a highly dangerous kind. What is clear is that identity is not simply an individual matter, but a social product located in time and space. It is not a fixed static entity, but has to be seen as a dynamic process.

It is in order to make sense of the present that a historical perspective, including the role of mythical pasts and a comparative approach building on the most rigorous theories and methods developed by social scientists, is essential. Before taking these points further, I shall explore work which deals with identity in terms of individual perception or understanding of self.

The discussion of identity *formation* is predominantly to be found in the field of psychology, especially in developmental psychology, psychoanalysis and social psychology (Kelly, 1955; Laing, 1965; Harré, 1979, 1983). A range of studies have used a narrow concept of self and attempted to construct measures which will tell us from what 'self-concept' is derived, how it is constituted and in some cases whether it accords with or deviates from 'reality'. The doll experiments carried out in North America to establish racial identity and preferences considered black children who were seen to be identifying with or preferring white dolls to be misidentifying and to have a preference not only to be white but to be with whites. The criticism of this methodology and the interpretations put on the findings have tended to remain an intra-professional debate and consequently are still being used in a some-what modified form to establish racial identities (see for example, Wilson, 1987). While some social psychologists now add on gender, class, region, and religion as well as race (skin colour), they still rely heavily on the same mechanistic (non-reflexive) theories of socialization which do not disturb the overall model (see Hutnik, 1992, for a review of the psychological literature on ethnic identities).

Moreover, the view that identity is formed during childhood or in adolescence and only marginally modified later, if at all, is still accepted relatively uncritically. For example, a recent study of 16-to-19-year-olds maintains that self-concept/personality 'is largely formed before the age of 16. What happens after then may damage or strengthen it, but only to a fairly small extent' (Banks *et al.*, 1992, p. 126). This very large claim may well have reflected the findings of the research, but the lack of a critical discussion about whether it was a product of the approach and methods adopted or of the specificities of the 16 to 19 age band is surprising. The authors claim that their approach integrates structural and developmental analyses, but there is no reference to work on contemporary society and self-identity such as that by Giddens (1991) or Burkitt (1991). Here we can note that evidence that their claim is less than universally valid is not hard to find. Bauman, for instance, discussing the stages at which Jewishness played a role in his life, says: 'there are three stages in which Jewishness played some role in my life. On the whole, for most of my life and the greater part of it, Jewishness played a very small role, if at all' (1992, pp. 226–7).[7] My awareness of my Irishness developed largely in my thirties and forties and its significance has changed many of the ways I see the world and feel about my identity. Henry (1983) details the processes by which she, long settled in North America, chooses as an adult to look into her national/ethnic roots. Many members of the former Yugoslavia have recently found their ethnic, national or religious affiliations eclipsing all the others. After 1991 these have been made to carry very different meanings and consequences for those involved and for those reporting on them in the media. While it is impossible to know whether the imposed exclusive categorization becomes a matter of self-identity, those trapped in such situations are faced with few options but to conform to them.

Occasionally voices are heard which relate different stories. Two, both from Radio Four, can be taken as examples. The woman in Sarajevo, described by the reporter as a Muslim, crying 'what do I care about the mosque? It is my neighbours who are with me living in cellars, we are all together Serbs and Muslims, that I care about' (1992). Or the young student from Sarajevo university (described by the interviewer as a Muslim) now living in Edinburgh who explained that her friends were drawn from all religious/ethnic groups and it was the same for her parents living in Tuzla. Religion had not been an important defining characteristic, but sharing in the many religious holidays did mean you could enjoy cake provided by your or your friends' grandmothers (1993).

The methods employed to establish empirically how individuals define themselves, especially in conflict situations, raise a number of questions. Arguably the most ambitious attempt by a psychologist in Britain to operationalize the concepts of racial and ethnic identity for empirical research is the body of work produced over the past two decades by Weinreich (1986, 1989).[8] His approach to identity centres on the individual and the identifications, re-identifications and new identifications that individuals form with others. He puts forward statements about the socio-psychological processes which occur in situations of conflicted identifications or the formation of new ones. These relate to specific situations and can be confirmed or disconfirmed by his approach, which he calls the Identity Structure Analysis (ISA), only if there has been no radical change in the socio-historical circumstances. From a sociological point of view, this qualification is a considerable limitation, as taking social change and its implications for explanation and prediction into account is one of the main tasks in theorizing and investigating identity formation. A further problem with the ISA approach arises from the ambiguity which surrounds the basic conceptualization of self/society. Weinreich assumes a distinction between personal and social identity and sees them as related, but does not theorize this relationship.

There is one further question about the methods used widely by psychologists to investigate identity, which relates to a more general methodological problem. The use of questionnaires or even one-off interviews is, I would argue, inappropriate in many contexts. These methods have been the subject of extensive discussion and debate over many decades (Phillips, 1971; Roberts, 1981). Briefly they present two problems, one concerning the subject matter of the investigation and the other the interpretation of the results. (I am not discussing here the different levels of professional expertise which are to be found in the designing of questionnaires/interviews. This is important only when it is assumed the method is appropriate.) One illustration of the problems is to be found in studies carried out in Northern Ireland using questionnaires. These produced findings which suggest that few define themselves in religious terms (Hutnik, 1992).[9] Hutnik, who was critical of the questionnaire method, developed a Twenty Statements Test (TST) in which individuals are asked to complete ten 'I am . . .' and ten 'I am not . . .' statements, which she used to establish ethnic identification among young people in England. Although less directive, this method presents similar problems of interpretation to those found in Northern Ireland. The effectiveness of any method has to be assessed by how its findings advance our knowledge. In the case of Northern Ireland, Heaney's poem entitled 'Whatever you say, say nothing' indicates the complexities of interpretation in situations of long-running conflict. Maybe the fact that religious definitions were used by few is an indication, not of the irrelevance of religion, but of its centrality to the lives of the respondents. Understanding what is not said, reading the silences, is a crucial aspect of any investigation of identity, but one not available through questionnaires or tests. The complexities of social life are part of the processes of data collection and these cannot be encapsulated in twenty statements either by the respondent or the researcher. It is because of such limitations that these methods appear to be inappropriate and distorting, especially where conflict exists and mixed and multiple identities carry personal and social costs. Milner's comment that 'Identity is a concept which has been much used and abused in psychological theory. The term "identity" has been a repository for a variety of imprecise ideas about what people are and how they see themselves. It has been all things to all theorists' (1975, p. 45) remains at least partially applicable.

The perspectives of interactionism and symbolic interactionism have in a variety of ways been concerned with combining 'the subjective aspects of group life with an appreciation of its objective features' (Lal, 1986). Drawing as it does on the intellectual histories of sociology, as well as social psychology, it cannot be said to represent one coherent or consistent set of perspectives (see Fisher and Strauss, 1978, for a fuller discussion). Nevertheless, the theories of Mead (1934) and the work of Blumer (1969) on method are useful. In essence, Mead argued that the self was to be conceptualized as having two components, the I and the me, and it was through the dialogue between them that a sense of self develops. Again we are dealing with a process, not a static entity, and the potentiality for multiple selves over time or location is not to be seen as in contradiction to an integrated self. This potentiality is not limitless (or random). It is precisely the structuring of the limits which sociologists investigate. Additionally, there is no necessity for the self I think and feel I am to be either that which others assume me to be, or the same as the groups with which I behaviourally identify. The discrepancies between my concepts of myself and those that others hold of me may be of great significance to me, but how far I can act on them in any situation is not only up to me, but a matter of structural and cultural location.

Blumer stressed the need for methods to bridge the structural approaches to social research and the accounts given by individuals of their sense of self and their world. In particular, following not only Mead but also Park, he worked on the level of group interaction and advocated forms of participant observation which facilitated the researcher in 'developing a familiarity with what is actually going on in the sphere of life under study' (1969, p. 39). In his approach questionnaires or tests, requiring a finite number of statements about identity, given in one place at one time, were seen as totally inadequate methods of investigation.

A criticism frequently made about symbolic interactionism, that it derives from a particular view of the role of individual agency in North America, is strongly rejected by Lal. She argues that the ideas and methods of the Chicago School, which she equates rather simply with symbolic interactionism, exemplify this approach and neglect neither the history nor the structure in which the individual is located. She cites the studies of Polish immigrants as an example in which documentary evidence, including personal letters, as well as field observational techniques are combined to produce analyses of situated selves (Thomas and Znaniecki, 1918–20). The variety of methods used in investigating a wide range of problems, including race relations, urban communities, industrial relations and collective behaviour, carried out by innumerable sociologists demonstrated the strengths of the traditions and offers a great deal more insight into the social bases of identity than the narrow ones pursued in much psychology. It does not, however, go far enough conceptually.

Interactionism also shares some of the features of the ethnographical approaches used by, among others, anthropologists. Some of their studies have been justly criticized for lack of attention to the asymmetrical power structures in which their subjects are located (see Jarvie, 1964; Mason, 1986). But not all studies have neglected these aspects. Those, for instance, of Mirpuris in Bradford and Pakistanis in South London demonstrate the strength of an urban anthropology which pays close attention to the concerns with and meanings derived from 'homelands', the translation of these in minority situations and the imposition of majority perceptions (Saifullah Khan, 1974, 1976, 1977, 1979). The work of some anthropologists is of particular relevance in exploring conceptualization of identity and these will be considered in the final part of this section.

Epstein (1978) made the concept of identity central to his discussion of ethnicity and ethnic groups in North America and Africa. He argues that when this is done 'new perspectives on old dilemmas' are possible. He points out what should be obvious to social scientists, that ethnic identity is only meaningful where those of different ethnic origins are brought together in a common social context and is only one among many possible identities. While ethnicity is conceptualized as a social mechanism classifying groups or categories, frequently involving relations of dominance, hierarchy and social stratification, he sees the generating of ethnic identity as a psychosocial process. Epstein stresses early childhood experiences and influences in ethnic identification and the security, trust and affirmation of oneself that association with fellow ethnics confers in polyethnic situations and assumes that ethnic identity carries a heavy affective charge. These assumptions may be justified as starting points; however, as ethnic identity is only one of many possible identities he argues that whether it is taken up is partly a matter of choice, but a choice always within social and unconscious elements of constraint.

Epstein's three brief but carefully crafted essays are interesting and insightful and deserve much closer attention than they have received in debates on race and ethnicity in Britain. Barth (1969) has been accorded more prominence than Epstein, but he is concerned with relations between ethnic groups, particularly boundary maintenance and permeability, and according to Fox (1990, p. 6) uses an ethnocentric market model which 'strips cultural identities of their constituting effect on individuals'. Cohen (1969, 1974) was also critical of Barth's approach and in his work on Nigeria developed a two-dimensional model in which the symbolic and the political are autonomous, but dialectically interrelated in such a way that ethnic solidarity and awareness mesh together in social action. He carries these ideas forward in his study of Creole identity as an elite in Sierre Leone (1981).

Carrithers (1992), who is concerned to explain cultural and social diversity, draws attention to research in psychology which describes intersubjectivity, and he uses the concept of human intentionality to conclude that from birth 'the central matter of human life . . . is the way in which we are not so much self-aware as self and other aware' (p. 60). One of the major strengths of anthropology and sociology in investigating the structuring and perception of action has been the stress on fieldwork and ethnograhic studies.

Identity and Feminism

The 'politics of identity', both within feminist social science and in women's movements during the 1980s, have to be rethought. In the first, the concept of difference has been stressed (see Barrett, 1987; Maynard, this volume) and in the second, differences, most notably of class, race, ethnicity and sexuality, used as grounds for exclusion. In the late 1980s and even more in the 1990s differences of religion and nationality have been given a higher profile.

I am not arguing that differences between women do not exist. The recognition of them is an important corrective to earlier Eurocentric, particularly white north American, approaches (Allen *et al.*, 1991). The need to be sensitive to, and appreciative of, the different experiences of women across and within states is now, if not taken for granted, well argued in much of the literature. This clearly indicates that neat boundaries and arbitrary lines cannot encapsulate the specificities of subordination. Concentrating on difference served to highlight how in mainstream social science gender has remained unincorporated in analyses of social formations. Interpreting gender as though the relations of inequality between men and women are one-dimensional has not been helpful. Some women do have greater power and resources than some men, but not as far as men in their own social groups, however defined, are concerned. In attempting to discuss feminist perspectives on gender and to incorporate race, ethnicity and nationality we need to bear in mind the degree to which, both in social science and in practice, women have been defined as the 'other' (de Beauvoir, 1974). This perception has been so taken for granted that women are defined in relation to men, particularly as mothers, wives, sisters and daughters, while men are taken to be representative of a non-gendered subjectivity, of non-gendered human beings.

A reflexive awareness about oneself and others is anchored to day-to-day activities in which we produce and reproduce 'appropriate' behaviours. It is unnecessary for us to think actively about much of this in order to carry on 'as normal'. If asked, we could describe in some way who we are, what we are doing and why. Such descriptions are not just in our minds, but combine our thoughts and feelings, our presuppositions of the enquirer's expectations and our relative statuses. In developing an understanding of the processes involved in the creation and reproduction of ourselves, from a feminist perspective, questions about the presumptions underlying and the common-sense knowledge associated with 'normal' human activities have constantly to be raised. Otherwise the distortions embedded in dominant modes of social thought and everyday language that male equals human are reinforced.

In the creation and reproduction of the self, gender is a fundamental dimension in all societies. Psychology, psychoanalysis, philosophy and sociology have not ignored this altogether, but have fairly systematically neglected or distorted it (Sherif, 1987). As Harding (1987) warns, 'if grounds for accepting knowledge claims are in perfect fit with the claim advanced, we should worry about what kinds of knowledge are being suppressed, subjugated, sent underground' (p. 187). This cautions us to question the taken-for-granted presuppositions of man-made science and the man-made world. For example, for some white, middle-class, educated women in North America and Northern Europe, Friedan's (1963) attempt to explicate 'the problem that has no name' changed their ways of seeing/knowing/understanding themselves. It did not change their 'objective' situation. It facilitated the connections between the personal and public spheres encapsulated later in the statement 'the personal is the political' and led to a range of further questions. These were not only about white middle-class women's identity formation, but about women in different classes and cultures and about women of colour.[10]

Friedan and others argued that only when alternatives are available can women first see that there is an unnamed problem and, second, move towards the issues of what she terms self-actualization. Underlying this train of thought is a culturally and historically specific conception of available alternatives, of choice and self-actualization, that of voluntaristic individualism. If these specificities are not recognized and addressed, serious distortions enter feminist theorizing. Three points, in particular, need to be borne in mind, all of which relate to the self/society debates discussed above. First, available alternatives exist in all societies, as comparative and historical work has shown: it is not only in modern societies that women have alternatives. The questions to be investigated are those which have been central in mainstream social science, reshaped to include women, such as 'under what conditions are alternative ways of acting perceived?' Second, when perceived, what are the cultural and material barriers to be overcome, what resources are available, what are the costs and gains involved in any particular course of action and how do these vary for different groups of women?

The third point relates to Friedan's conception of self-actualization. Self-actualization is not simply or necessarily an individual project as she indicates. Her view is that of white, liberal North America, to a much greater extent than that adopted by the researchers of the various strands of the Chicago School. The conceptualizations of the self as socially constructed are to be understood and realized through collective/group/community activities. The contribution of feminist thought lies in the recognition that all these activities are gendered and so are social selves. In feminist practice, therefore, any moves towards self-actualization include others. The debates on difference within feminism have been around two issues, one about which women to include/exclude and the other about whether women have more in common with men and children in their own group than with women defined as different.

A range of political and intellectual positions has been taken on both these issues. For instance, it has been argued that other divisions, most notably those of class, colour, ethnicity, religion and nationality, cut across those of gender so that only women sharing one or more of these have a common basis with which to identify and act. In modernist theories, as noted above, class relations take precedence so that men and women of the same class are assumed to have common interests as against those of another class. Within this general approach, some of those concerned with race and ethnicity argued that *within* classes fractions developed along racial and ethnic lines, but neglected to theorize their articulation with gender. In postmodernist discussions, multiple differences are posited as central to the understanding of the realities of social divisions, inequalities and disempowering exclusions (Seidman, 1992). However, where patriarchy and the capitalist market not only remain, but are in the ascendancy, the adoption by feminists of post-modernist and deconstructionist perspectives and vocabularies is arguably premature. Virginia Woolf's statement 'As a woman I have no country' provides a starting point for thinking about what feminist analyses have to offer in the present context.

Identity and the Suppression of Difference

In the heterogeneous societies of the contemporary world the postmodernist critiques of universalism carry an attractive plausibility into which the concept of identity neatly fits. However, identity denies and suppresses differences *within* socially created categories and emphasizes differences *between* them. Identity x only has meaning in relation to a not-x identity and logically assumes a categorical equivalence of all xs and a categorical difference from all not-xs. Such logic does not describe any social reality. If we accept that individuals derive their identity from their history, from parents, grandparents and significant others, and from their biography in which the particular combination of relationships and experiences is unique to each individual, then the simple dichotomy of sameness and difference quickly evaporates. We are left to deal with variabilities within categories and similarities across them. In postmodernist discourse some identities are listed but not explained, described but not ordered. To overcome these shortcomings requires an exposition of multiple identities, latent or otherwise, and a theorizing of the social relationships in which they are embedded and through which they may be activated.

One of the critiques of dominant social thought consistently put forward by feminists is that it defines women as other. This is exactly what discussions of identity produce, unless the complexities of social divisions and their ordering are addressed directly, without employing the common dichotomous approach of self/other, mind/body, subject/object and nature/culture. Recognizing and theorizing the interconnections across boundaries is both an intellectual and practical task of considerable difficulty, especially as in European societies, as well as in social thought, dichotomous categorizing abounds impeding the development of fruitful dialogue and a plurality of non-threatening identities.

If we examine the current conflicts and war discourses among politicians and in the media we can see the stark outcomes when '[identity] turns the merely different into the absolutely other' (Young, 1990). In feminist thought the subordination, oppression and exploitation of women are not respecters of national boundaries. On the contrary, women are used in defining boundaries, and asserting the dominance of some men over other men through the protection of 'their' women (Guy, 1992). Societies always portray their women as more virtuous than women of other groups and therefore in need of protection, according to Obbo (1989). The notions of protector and protected are central constructs of war (Stiehm, 1982). To protect 'their' women they engage in violent conflict and rape the women of 'their' enemies. The frequent use of rape in the discourse of men warring over national boundaries is not a recent phenomenon. Nor is the use of gendered language to describe a nation unusual. Nations are raped by others or, as in colonial situations, said to be waiting to be raped by others. For feminist scholars the recognition of male discourses and praxis in this regard is essential. The current attempt to gain international recognition of rape as a war crime grew out of the reporting of rapes in the former Yugoslavia and elsewhere. While agreeing with this attempt to internationalize the criminality of rape and a whole battery of other crimes against women and young girls, it is important to recognize the functions of the male discourse on rape, including war rape. Rape in war serves two functions: one as a rite of passage where soldiers prove their loyalty to the nation by raping the women of the enemy, and the other as a means of attacking the enemy through his women.[11] All women share a common interest in not being raped by the male 'enemy' just as they do in not being raped by their 'protectors'. If we recognize that in national, ethnic or race conflicts rape functions to divide and disunite women, then we, along with Virginia Woolf, begin to question the meaning of such statements as 'Everyone needs a national identity'.[12]

Issues of Exclusion and Marginality

An understanding of the many differences which mark heterogeneous societies leads to an acknowledgment that any simple dichotomous categorizing carries with it mechanisms of exclusion and marginality. In my concluding section I shall take two examples of these from Britain that have not so far been dealt with by feminists, but to which, in my view, their analyses are of particular relevance.

There is general agreement that historically the ideologies of nationalism and racism have been intertwined in British imperialism and that in the post-war period we have witnessed a growth in British or, more particularly, English nationalism as an exclusionary force to deny racialized minorities a

British/English identity with full rights of citizenship (Gilroy, 1987; Miles, 1987a, 1987b; Solomos, 1989). The British nation is a myth, relying heavily on Anglo-Saxon origins and ignoring the different racial, linguistic, cultural and national composition of those living in the British Isles over many centuries. The British state is a reality. In its imperial mode this state defined all those living in the UK or one of its colonies as British *subjects* with varying rights according to gender and race/ethnicity. The post-imperial phase, first through immigration control legislation and then through legal categories of nationality, has produced a progressive reduction of rights for those not holding full British citizenship, with gender and patriality playing crucial and continuous roles in the construction of Britishness by the British state. The *de facto* exclusion of the black British from such constructions raises important political and sociological questions (see Allen, 1989a, 1989b; Allen and Macey, 1994; Goulbourne, 1991). This is a specific example of much wider phenomena, including the plight of refugees, asylum seekers and migrant workers in Western and Central Europe and the situation of many groups of ex-citizens of the former Soviet Union. To construct the problem as one of national identity, rather than one of legitimate claims to citizenship rights within state structures, is to accept ideological constructions of nationhood which function to deny such rights (Morokvasic, 1991, 1992).

Identity when construed as unidimensional, rather than as composed of shared attributes and part of social relations, leads to a marginalization of those who do not fit the categories of 'x' and 'not-x'. The example in Britain which most readily comes to mind is the division of people into black and white. This is highlighted in the politics and policies surrounding transracial adoption and fostering.[13] The arguments for 'same-race' adoption are couched in a variety of terms, but identity has always been prominent among them. Differences of, for instance, class, of parents or siblings of 'mixed' origins, or of birth mothers of the 'wrong' category all become subsumed under a genetically-based dichotomous orthodoxy. This acknowledges little of the multiple characteristics of selves in a society divided horizontally and vertically, where power differentials are central, and so the issue remains clouded. Practitioners leave it unexplored, policy-makers adopt politically expedient solutions and academic researchers, including feminists, do not confront it. At present it is only in the writings of people like Jackie Kay (1991) that the harshnesses and the strengths of the circumstances surrounding, and the feelings involved in 'transracial' adoption in Britain are given a reality and a veracity. In a racially ordered society there are very serious questions to be addressed, but these require not simple dichotomies or claims and counterclaims of racism, but the painstaking hard work of rethinking in non-exclusive ways the experienced vulnerabilities, particularly of women and children, in a patriarchal and class-divided society.

The concept of identity not only marginalizes those categories taken as not fitting a norm which confers sameness, but excludes all those individuals and families of 'mixed' descent or affiliation. Research into those for whom this 'mixed' condition is a normal way of being and living is scarce. What research exists tends to pathologize them, seeing them as abnormal individuals with identity problems, as threatening to ordered social relations in crossing dominantly construed boundaries, and thus strongly reinforces populist stereotypes (see Alibhai-Brown and Montague, 1992; Spickard, 1989; Stahl, 1992). In Europe many people have mixed affiliations and origins. Social scientists need to explore the conditions under which these are productive and creative and those which promote them as destructive and alien.

Unless we ground our discussion and research in as rigorous analyses as we possibly can and risk offending those with particularistic interests or beliefs, which we are almost inevitably bound to do, we shall be unable to contribute to the understanding of present problems and the specific ways in which they affect women across Europe. Insights and theoretical propositions derived from the many attempts by feminist scholars to develop an epistemology and research methodologies which treat women as central actors, not as 'other', are especially relevant to devising research which will take 'mixed' conditions as normal. I see no difficulty in accepting that some people, including myself, think of themselves simultaneously as an outsider and insider, a stranger and an in-group member in ethnic, national and class terms. How we are perceived is a different matter. The study of processes by which identity has come to be the equivalent of sameness and to command such a dominant position in social thought and practice with all the consequences of exclusion and marginality constitutes an urgent research agenda to which feminist analyses have much to offer.

Notes

I would like to thank the many colleagues, students and friends who have discussed earlier drafts of this chapter with me, especially Marie Macey and Mary Maynard for their detailed comments.

1 The current widespread use of the term identity in relation to race, ethnicity and nationality indicates that its analytical status needs close attention.
2 The term choice is problematic. There is no consensus on its meaning. In some voluntaristic models it is conceptualized *as though* individuals make choices in a social vacuum, abstracted from the constraints of the socio-economic, gendered and racialized structures in which they live. This is clearly not adequate.
3 It would be tedious to comment each time on quotations which use the term man to mean the universal subject. The lack of comment does not mean agreement with this use.
4 For a critical discussion of Durkheim's approach see Benton (1977). He does concede, however, that 'the epistomological point that Durkheim makes [that

social life is not spontaneously intelligible to those who live it, and that it can only be known through scientific investigation . . . is important and defensible' (p. 94).

5   Race and ethnicity have been conceptualized in a variety of ways (for a discussion of these see Anthias, 1992). In this chapter they are used as social constructs embedded in social relations, not as unchanging attributes of individuals, voluntaristically chosen. Both can be major social markers between categories, imposed by dominant others, and may provide bases of solidaristic relations. The processes by which these potentials are turned into social realities can only be explained within broader theories of social relations. The increasing use of the term identity in relation to both is highly problematic and, as I argue in this chapter, has to be seen as a particular variant of the general question of the mutually interactive relations of self and society.

6   The Bosnian Muslims are like the Serbs 'ethnically' Slavs. The boundaries drawn in the public discourse use a mixture of religious, ethnic and national markers and so compound the confusion. There are also people of other religions who are rarely mentioned.

7   These were the eruption of anti-semitism in Poland in 1968, the publication of Janina Bauman's book on her experiences in the Warsaw ghetto (1986) and later when he 'discovered that peculiar condition in which Jews were cast during the period of rapid modernization and assimilation in the second half of the nineteenth century'. See also Bauman, 1991.

8   Weinreich maintains that the Identity Structure Analysis (ISA) synthesizes concepts on the socio-psychological processes of identity development derived from psychodynamic, personal construct and symbolic interactionist perspectives. Moreover, he claims that his method incorporates the distinction between an internally recognized categorization of self as being a member of an ethnic group (with an emphasis on ethnic identity) and externally ascribed definitions by others of self as being a member of a general category (with an emphasis on an imposed racial identity). He argues that he makes a distinction between personal and social identity, but recognizes that these are not to be divorced in an artificial way (1986, p. 299).

9   Ethnographic accounts give a rather different picture, that of a public avoidance of issues such as religious affiliations which may provoke anger or embarrassment in others. Such avoidance is confirmed by my own experience in Northern Ireland and the rest of Ireland where my religious affiliation is assumed (always wrongly) and ignored. I am never questioned about it. Outside Ireland among the Irish diaspora (both protestant and catholic) it is raised usually, but not always, with hostility.

10   The range of diverse conditions in which women are located is vast, but these differences are neither random nor absolute. See Spivak (1992) for a particularly vivid portrayal of the experiences of a daughter of a bonded labourer in decolonized India. She analyzes through these the global meanings of '[t]he persistent agendas of nationalisms and sexuality, encrypted [on the gendered body] in the indifference of super-exploitation' (p. 113).

11   One comment on an earlier version of this chapter, in relation to the media, was

that frequently the first question asked by journalists as they arrived in war zones was 'Is there anyone here who has been raped and speaks English?'

12 It has been customary in Western Europe to use the term nation-state, which implies that the state is coterminous with the nation. This is by no means so in innumerable cases (see Allen and Macey, 1994, for further discussion). The state can be multi-national and a nation can exist without being a state (see McCrone, 1992).

13 These emerged only some twenty years after religion ceased to be the excluding criterion used by almost all agencies.

References

ADIE, K. (1993) contribution to KEATING, R. 'When Reporters Go Over the Top', *The Guardian*, 18 January.

ALIBHAI-BROWN, Y. and MONTAGUE, A. (1992) *The Colour of Love*, London, Virago.

ALLEN, S. (1989a) 'Social Aspects of Citizenship', Public Lecture, Queen's University, Belfast, May.

ALLEN, S. (1989b) 'Women and Citizenship: The British Experience', paper presented to the International Seminar on The Participation of Women in Politics and Decision Making Processes, Istanbul, December.

ALLEN, S. (1991) 'Diversity and Commonality: Building a Dialogue', paper presented at the International Conference 'Building a Europe without Frontiers: The Role of Women', Athens, November.

ALLEN, S. and MACEY, M. (1994) 'Some Issues of Race, Ethnicity and Nationalism in the "New" Europe: Re-Thinking Sociological Paradigms', in BROWN, P. and CROMPTON, R. (Eds) *A New Europe: Economic Restructuring and Social Exclusion*, London, UCL Press.

ALLEN, S., ANTHIAS, F. and YUVAL-DAVIS, N. (1991) 'Diversity and Commonality: Theory and Politics', *Review Internationalede Sociologie*, 2.

ANTHIAS, F. (1992) *Ethnicity, Class, Gender and Migration*, Aldershot, Avebury.

BANKS, M., BATES, I., BREAKWELL, G., BYNNES, J., EMLER, N., JAMIESON, L. and ROBERTS, K. (1992) *Careers and Identities*, Milton Keynes, Open University Press.

BARRETT, M. (1987) 'The Concept of Difference', *Feminist Review*, no. 26.

BARTH, F. (1969) *Ethnic Groups and Boundaries*, London, George Allen and Unwin.

BAUMAN, J. (1986) *Winter in the Morning*, London, Virago.

BAUMAN, Z. (1978) *Hermeneutics and Social Science*, London, Hutchinson.

BAUMAN, Z. (1991) *Modernity and the Holocaust*, Cambridge, Polity.

BAUMAN, Z. (1992) *Intimations of Postmodernity*, London, Routledge.

BENTON, T. (1977) *Philosophical Foundations of the Three Sociologies*, London, Routledge and Kegan Paul.

BEAUVOIR, S. DE (1974) *The Second Sex*, Harmondsworth, Penguin.

BLUMER, H. (1969) *Symbolic Interactionism: Perspective and Method*, Englewood Cliffs, N.J., Prentice-Hall.

BURKITT, I. (1991) *Social Selves: Theories of the Social Formation of Personality*, London, Sage.

CARRITHERS, M. (1992) *Why Humans Have Cultures*, Oxford, Oxford University Press.

COHEN, A. (1969) *Custom and Politics in Urban Africa*, Berkeley, University of California Press.

COHEN, A. (1974) *Two Dimensional Man*, Berkeley, University of California Press.

COHEN, A. (1981) *The Politics of Elite Culture*, Berkeley, University of California Press.

ELIAS, N. (1982) *State Formation and Civilisation: The Civilising Process*, vol. 2, Oxford, Blackwell.

EPSTEIN, A.L. (1978) *Ethos and Identity*, London, Tavistock.

FISHER, B.M. and STRAUSS, A.L. (1978) 'Interactionism', in BOTTOMORE, T. and NISBET, R. (Eds) *A History of Sociological Analysis*, London, Heinemann.

FOX, R.G. (Ed.) (1990) *Nationalist Ideologies and the Production of National Culture*, Washington, American Anthropological Association.

FRIEDAN, B. (1963) *The Feminine Mystique*, London, Gollancz.

GIDDENS, A. (1991) *Modernity and Self Identity*, Cambridge, Polity.

GILROY, P. (1987) *'There Ain't No Black in the Union Jack'*, London, Hutchinson.

GOULBOURNE, H. (1991) *Ethnicity and Nationalism in Post-Imperial Britain*, Cambridge, Cambridge University Press.

GOULDNER, A.W. (1971) *The Coming Crisis of Western Sociology*, London, Heinemann.

GUY, D.J. (1992) ' "White Slavery", Citizenship and Nationality in Argentina', in PARKER, A., ROSSO, M., SOMMER, D. and YAEGER, P. (Eds) *Nationalisms and Sexualities*, New York, Routledge.

HARDING, S. (Ed.) (1987) *Feminism and Methodology*, Milton Keynes, Open University Press.

HARRÉ, R. (1979) *Social Being: A Theory for Social Psychology*, Oxford, Blackwell.

HARRÉ, R. (1983) *Personal Being: A Theory for Individual Psychology*, Oxford, Blackwell.

HENRY, F. (1983) *Victims and Neighbours: A Small Town in Nazi Germany Remembered*, Vergin and Garvey.

HOBSBAWM, E. (1984) 'Mass-Producing Traditions: Europe, 1870–1914', in HOBSBAWM, E. and RANGER, T. (Eds) *The Invention of Tradition*, Cambridge, Cambridge University Press.

HUTNIK, N. (1992) *Ethnic Minority Identity: A Social Psychological Perspective*, Oxford, Clarendon Press.

JARVIE, I.C. (1964) *The Revolution in Anthropology*, London, Routledge and Kegan Paul.

KAY, J. (1991) *The Adoption Papers*, Newcastle, Bloodaxe.

KEATING, R. (1993) 'When Reporters Go Over the Top', *The Guardian*, 18 January.

KELLY, G.A. (1955) *The Psychology of Personal Constructs*, New York, Norton.

LAING, R.D. (1965) *The Divided Self*, Harmondsworth, Penguin.

LAL, B.B. (1986) 'The "Chicago School" of American Sociology, Symbolic Interactionism, and Race Relations Theory', in REX, J. and MASON, D. (Eds) *Theories of Race and Ethnic Relations*, Cambridge, Cambridge University Press.

McCRONE, D. (1992) *Understanding Scotland: The Sociology of a Stateless Nation*, London, Routledge.

MARX, K. (1973) *Grundrisse*, Harmondsworth, Penguin.

MASON, D. (1986) 'Introduction Controversies and Continuities in Race and Ethnic Relations Theory', in REX, J. and MASON, D. (Eds)*Theories of Race and Ethnic Relations*, Cambridge, Cambridge University Press.

MEAD, G.H. (1934) *Mind, Self and Society, from the Standpoint of a Social Behaviourist*, Chicago, Chicago University Press.

MILES, R. (1987a) 'Recent Marxist Theories of Nationalism and the Issue of Racism', *British Journal of Sociology*, vol. XXXVIII, no. 1.

MILES, R. (1987b) 'Racism and Nationalism in Britain', in HUSBAND, C.H. (Ed.) *'Race' in Britain: Continuity and Change*, London, Hutchinson.

MILNER, D. (1975) *Children and Race*, Harmondsworth, Penguin.

MOROKVASIC, M. (1991) 'Fortress Europe and Migrant Women', *Feminist Review*, no. 39.

MOROKVASIC, M. (1992) 'Chez nous, la Guerre', in MOROKVASIC, M. (Ed.) *Yugoslavie: Logiques De L'Exclusion, Peuples Méditerranéens*, Paris, Revue Trimestrielle, no. 61.

OBBO, C. (1989) 'Sexuality and Economic Domination in Uganda', in ANTHIAS, F. and YUVAL-DAVIS, N. (Eds) *Women, Nation, State*, London, Macmillan.

PHILLIPS, D.L. (1971) *Knowledge from What? Theories and Methods in Social Research*, Chicago, Rand McNally and Co.

REX, J. (1986) *Race and Ethnicity*, Milton Keynes, Open University Press.

ROBERTS, H. (Ed.) (1981) *Doing Feminist Research*, London, Routledge and Kegan Paul.

SAIFULLAH KHAN, V.J. (1974) *Pakistani Villagers in a British City: The World of the Mirpuri Villager in Bradford in his Village of Origin*, unpublished PhD thesis, University of Bradford.

SAIFULLAH KHAN, V.J. (1976) 'Perceptions of a Population: Pakistanis in Britain', *New Community*, 5.

SAIFULLAH KHAN, V.J. (1977) 'The Pakistanis: Mirpuri Villagers at Home and in Bradford', in WATSON, J.L. (Ed.) *Between Two Cultures*, Oxford, Blackwell.

SAIFULLAH KHAN, V.J. (1979) 'Work and Network: South Asian Women in South London', in WALLMAN, S. (Ed.) *Ethnicity at Work*, London, Macmillan.

SCHERMERHORN, R.A. (1970) *Comparative Ethnic Relations*, New York, Random House.

SEIDMAN, S. (1992) 'Postmodern Social Theory as Narrative with a Moral Intent', in SEIDMAN, S. and WAGNER, D.G. (Eds) *Postmodernism and Social Theory*, Oxford, Blackwell.

SHERIF, C.W. (1987) 'Bias in Psychology', in HARDING, S. (Ed.) *Feminism and Methodology*, Milton Keynes, Open University Press.

SMITH, A.D. (1986) *The Ethnic Origins of Nations*, Oxford, Blackwell.

SOLOMOS, J. (1989) *Race and Racism in Contemporary Britain*, London, Macmillan.

SPICKARD, P.R. (1989) *Mixed Blood: Intermarriage and Ethnic Identity in Twentieth Century America*, Madison, University of Wisconsin Press.

SPIVAK, G.C. (1992) 'Woman in Difference: Mahasweta Devi's "Douloti the Bountiful"', in PARKER, A., ROSSO, M., SOMMER, D. and YAEGER, P. (Eds) *Nationalisms and Sexualities*, New York, Routledge.

STAHL, A. (1992) 'The Offspring of Interethnic Marriage: Relations of Children with Paternal and Maternal Grandparents', *Ethnic and Racial Studies*, vol. 15, no. 2.

STIEHM, J.H. (1982) 'The Protected, the Protector, the Defender', *Women's Studies International Forum*, vol. 5, nos 3/4.

THOMAS, W.I. and ZNANIECKI, F. (1918–20) *The Peasant in Europe and America*, 5 vols., Chicago, Chicago University Press.

WEINREICH, P. (1986) 'The Operationalisation of Identity Theory in Racial and Ethnic Relations', in REX, J. and MASON, D. (Eds) *Theories of Race and Ethnic Relations*, Cambridge, Cambridge University Press.

WEINREICH, P. (1989) 'Variations in Ethnic Identity: Identity Structure Analysis', in LIEBKIND, K. (Ed.) *New Identities in Europe*, Aldershot, Gower.

WILSON, A. (1987) *Mixed Race Children*, London: Unwin Hyman.

YOUNG, I.M. (1990) *Justice and the Politics of Difference*, Princeton, Princeton University Press.

Chapter 6

Refusing to be Civilized:
'Race', Sexuality and Power

Beverley Skeggs

Is this all you got?
one minute and you go pop
yous a big disgrace
I don't mush you all in yer face
telling me lies like you a real good lover
yous a two-minute brother
I hate guys who talk a lot of shit
how they last long and got good dicks
talking shit and telling me lies . . . the best lover?
they all two-minute brothers

Black girl kick it, Black girl just kick that shit (rep x6)
BWP in effect once again for all you females across America.
(Bytches with Problems, 'Two Minute Brother', 1991)

So much for supporting the male ego, doing the work of emotional management, being unable to express sexuality and being unable to directly challenge the male performance. The above lyrics demonstrate not the reproduction of femininity but a refusal to be contained by it. These lyrics explore the fraudulent myths of male sexual performance. They come from Black women who have no economic and/or emotional investment in men. They don't pander to politeness; this is an all-out battle within sexual politics. They speak that which should not be spoken by women. They speak sexuality *with* power. They challenge both the silencing of Black women's cultural responses and the silencing of women's sexuality. Whilst other women are contained by discourses of shame and honour, these rappers refuse to even pander to such terms. Whilst other women try to overcome powerlessness by finding some self-worth and dignity in the ascribed identities of femininity and motherhood, these rappers just take the difficult discourse of sexuality (which frequently objectifies and disempowers women) and assume their power within it. Ultimately, they refuse to be civilized.[1]

Bytches with Problems (Bytches = Beautiful Young Thing College Honeys en' Shit, otherwise known as BWP), a New York rap group, also deal with feminist slogans such as 'No means No'.[2] They are famous for the revenge fantasies that they put to an ironic reworking of 'gangsta' rap music.[3] Their name is a reappropriation of the denigratory terminology used to oppress them. Just as both female and male Black slaves were able to reappropriate the term 'nigga', BWP challenge the language that is used to define and confine them by investing it with new meanings. Hoes (American terminology for prostitutes) is used to similar effect by Hoes wit Attitude (HWA).[4]

BWP draw from a long tradition in Black women's resistance, popularized in music. 'Two Minute Brother' has its legacy in blues music, which drew in part from slave songs and is, Russell (1982) argues, a coded language of resistance. In the 1920s Ida Cox made a test recording of 'One Hour Mama' (it was never released) which uses humour in a similar way to BWP to mount an irreverent attack on male sexual prowess, whilst also claiming the right to a powerful, expressive, autonomous female heterosexuality:

I'm a one hour mama, so no one minute papa
Ain't the kind of man for me
Set your alarm clock papa, one hour that's proper,
Then love me like I like to be

I don't want no lame excuses,
Bout my loving been so good
That you couldn't wait no longer
Now I hope I'm understood

I can't stand no greenhorn lover
Like a rookie goin to war
With a load of big artillery
But don't know what it's for

I don't want no imitation
My requirements ain't no joke
Cause I got pure indignation
For a guy what's lost his stroke

I may want love for one hour
Then decide to make it two,
Takes an hour fore I get started
Maybe three fore I'm through

Ida Cox's lyrics are less confrontational and do not reference directly the collective experience of Black women as do BWP, yet they refer to a similar sexual politics. Hazel Carby (1986) argues that the challenges of the blues singer were resurrected in a different moment of Black power in the sixties. Here, I argue that rap now provides the expression of a similar debate within another formation of Black power; one which uses the currently available cultural resources. Rap is now the major popular site for the expression of Black experience (West, 1992). As Ice Cube (infamous LA rapper, ex-member of Niggas with Attitude and star of the film *Boyz in the Hood*) argues, 'To White kids rap ain't nothing but a form of entertainment. For Blacks its a strategy on how to manoeuvre through life'.[5]

The female rappers are filling a social void identified by numerous Black writers who identify the silencing of Black cultural responses, in particular those of Black women (Christian, 1990; hooks, 1989; Spillers, 1984). Michelle Wallace (1992) notes the structural silencing of women of colour within the sphere of production of knowledge worldwide and Angela Davis (1990) maintains that the marginal representation of Black women in the documentation of African-American cultural developments does not reflect women's participation adequately. Female rappers are filling this void with music.

Angela Davis (1990) and bell hooks (1989) argue that Black women's musical legacy is a way to understand history and contemporary Black women's consciousness. Queen Latifah's[6] 'All Hail the Queen', rapped with Monie Love[7] (her European sister), retells Black women's contribution to history: 'I wanted to show the strength of Black women in history. Strong Black women ... I wanted to show what we've done. We've done a lot; it's just that people don't know it'.[8] The accompanying video to this track uses images of Angela Davis, Winnie Mandela and Sojourner Truth, with footage of African women running with sticks raised above their heads towards armed oppressors. She also includes other female rappers in the video.[9]

The central argument of this chapter is that female rappers, drawing from a long feminist tradition, identified by Adrienne Rich, display their disloyalty to civilization (Rich, 1984). They 'defiantly speak' and 'talk back, talk Black' (hooks, 1989) to the White[10]-Western civilizing system (constructed through slavery and colonialism) which attempts to contain the expression of women's sexuality through the moralizing discourses of conduct: politeness, respectability, caring, duty and responsibility. In so doing, they speak against the power of masculinity to fit femininity to its fantasies (Walkerdine, 1989). This dialogue occurs within heterosexuality and to some extent reproduces it. It does, however, address more general issues of institutionalized heterosexuality. For instance, the Black female rappers speak against the objectification of women's bodies. They speak against the silencing of women's sexuality. They speak against the misogyny that is a ubiquitous part of everyday life for most women. In this way they can be seen to be speaking for all women. Talking back actually produces a social reality, rather than reproducing the given power relationships; it is part of the dialogic process of naming, claiming and recontextualizing that provides us with different meanings for the subject positions that we occupy.[11]

The sections that follow begin by examining how, firstly, the White, western, civilizing structure and, secondly, the 'alternative' civilizing structure position Black women. I explore the challenges made by the Black female rappers to these structures. In the final section I examine to whom the refusal to be civilized speaks, arguing that Black female rap constitutes an important feminist intervention in popular culture.

Civilizing Difference

The term civilization has always been loaded with both racist and sexist connotations. Lillian Smith (1962) notes how:

'Freud said once that woman is not well acculturated; she is, he stressed, retarded as a civilised person. I think what he mistook for her lack of civilisation is women's lack of *loyalty* to civilisation. Southern women have never been as loyal to the ideology of race and segregation as have southern men. . . . Many of them have been betraying White Supremacy for two hundred years but most who have done so could not reason with you as to why. (quoted in Rich, 1984, pp. 277–8)

The term civilization has specific European origins. When first used as a verb 'to civilize' in the early nineteenth century in France and Germany it was related to a hierarchy of social order, defined with refinement (for the aristocracy) against barbarity and savagery (the poor) (Febvre, 1973).[12] Elias (1982) notes how in France and England during the nineteenth century White aristocratic women were able to *display* civilized conduct, yet were not considered to be civilized because of their perceived links with nature and irrationality. Nineteenth- and early-twentieth-century anthropology served to make the distinctions more precise by classifying savagery through colour coding. During this period barbarity continued to have dual meaning applying to both the indigenous poor and the 'others' of colonialization.[13] The meaning of the term civilization is completely dependent on definitions of the 'other'. In a major English treatise on civilization in 1928, Bell admits that the only way he can write about the term is by defining what it is not. Not surprisingly, in his account, sexual practice and sexual morality feature heavily as do the 'facts' of 'admirable anthropologists'. So we can see that historically the discourses of civilization render specific legacies for the positioning of gender, 'race' and class.

The contemporary White, Western, civilizing system is a system of classification, a process of regulation and normalizing, which, drawing upon historical legacies, has always defined Black women as 'other', 'different' and sexual. This civilizing system establishes divisions between women through its classification of explicit sexual behaviour as uncivilized (Elias, 1982). For instance, as Ware (1992) notes, during the nineteenth century middle-class White women were able to locate themselves within a pure and proper femininity, precisely because Black and White working-class women were defined and designated as impure, dangerous and sexual. How they are, we are not and this tells us how we are. White working-class women are able to distance themselves from the sexual only through recourse to respectability; respectability being defined through the legacy of bourgeois standardization (Bourdieu, 1986). The links between Black and White working-class women are blurred in respect to sexuality: Black female sexuality became equated with White working-class prostitution in the nineteenth century (Gilman, 1992). In contemporary terms Black women have consistently been marketed by the music industry (and other areas of film and popular culture) to represent *the* sexual (Young, 1990). From this location within the sexual Black women have historically been constructed as objects of male fantasy. The female body is thus the representational map onto which distinctions of order and dis-order are drawn. White, Western systems of social order are marked by distinctions (of power, economic and cultural resources), coded through *distance to and from* 'civilization'. The White-Western civilizing system can hold no worth for Black women, for as Lola Young (1990) notes, Blackness itself connotes 'difference'; when the subject is also a Black woman the difference is reinforced. But there is an alternative.

Alternative Civilizing?

For the female rappers associated with the Nation of Islam,[14] they, too, have a civilizing system to fit into which, whilst being anti-racist and pro-Black, prescribes a traditional position for women: as reproducers and upholders of the Black Nation, heterosexual and supportive of men and which still constructs distinctions between women depending on their proximity to and distance from the explicitly sexual. West (1992) argues that rap is a cultural form of moral guidance. The Poor Righteous Teacher's (a non-'gangsta', softer, educationalist male rap group) track 'Shakiyla' illustrates the not-so-different Black civilizing system. It praises the strength and moral rectitude of the Black woman and allocates her to a position of sanctity: all of this within a debate between which man (good or bad) has access to her:

> You're no hooker, no slut, you're no bitch and she listens
> You're the *mother of civilisation*
> I hate them snakes who disrespect you
> They often disrespect you when they cannot sex you

Shakiyla's *civilised* and she's despised to drudge herself
Shakiyla's the Black woman and she loves me like to death . . .
She's mine, mine, mine,
Wake up the Black Queen's mine
(1991, 12″ mix, Profile Records)

In a similar way to the White, western civilizing system, this track creates
distance from the sexual by condemning those women who are directly associated with it, asserting the civilizing duty of women and claiming the power
of ownership. It is a message of discipline and righteousness for Black women
not dissimilar to that of male-dominated Western capitalist-Christian societies. This may be because early Black nationalism in the States from the mid
to the late nineteenth century was 'absolutist, civilisationist, elitist and based
on Christian humanism'.[15] Black nationalist men supported the development
of women's educational opportunities because they believed it would be a
means of bettering civilization. Black women played an important and leading role, historically, in the Black nationalist struggle, but this was always
dependent on their acceptance of the 'alternative' civilizing moral order (Scott,
1992).[16] Part of the Black Nationalist critique of White knowledge was to
claim that the earliest civilization (in ancient Egypt) was actually Black (Diop,
1974). Interestingly, Queen Latifah locates herself within this alternative civilizing system, taking care to distance herself from the vulgarity of BWP:

> I like some of what BWP does. That one song *Coming Back Strapped*
> where some guy is beating up this woman and she comes back with
> a gun and blows him away . . . I like that . . . I tend towards more
> subtle, let's talk it out, way of doing things, but sometimes direct
> action – abrupt and nasty – that's the best way. BWP are just saying
> 'stand up for yourself and don't be bullied by any man'. I just have
> some problems on the vulgar way they say certain things.[17]

Note how her use of 'vulgar' and 'subtle' confirm Bourdieu's measurements
of civilization.[18] Abrahams (1976) suggests that in order to maintain respectability one must monitor and compare others' presentational techniques. So,
the choice for female rappers, it seems, is to place oneself either within the
alternative civilizing system, or to completely reject any of the moralizing
discourses used to contain women and the expression of their sexuality.

In order to be seen to be civilized, distance has to be drawn not only
from the sexual but also from the popular and the artificial. Ironically, Queen
Latifah (located in the popular music industry, and even using samples from
Madonna on her last album), disassociates herself from the frivolity of pop
music. She wants her music to be seen as serious. Many rappers draw distinctions between their authenticity and the more obviously pop-rap music
of MC Hammer.[19] Often this distinction is embodied through women. The
mapping onto the division of serious/trivial by those with political claims has

111

a long history; Wallace (1979) documents how the militants of Harlem had no patience with the singing and dancing of the Black Nationalists who they considered were trivializing serious political issues. Now musicians positioned with the Nation of Islam want to impose similar distinctions within popular music itself.[20] To claim serious intent and authenticity the artifice, vulgar, feminine and frivolous must be distanced. The music industry uses the dichotomy of serious/trivial to target groups and market effectively. Music critics use similar distinctions to construct their credibility. This dichotomy is overlayered by others such as authentic/commodified, natural/artificial, and, as Hebdige (1988) has shown, masculine/feminine. The hard-core 'gangsta' rappers always disassociate themselves from the feminine: for example, Ice T's 'Some Of You Niggas Is Bitches Too' suggests that even men can 'stoop' to the levels of women. The educationalist rappers are able to do the same; they are just more subtle. 'Shakiyla' by the Poor Righteous Teachers provides an example:

> Shakiyla's not attracted to material things
> She's the perfect presentation of a wise Black queen
> With no stupid chains on her neck
> She's what a woman should be
> Silly suckers still sweat but
> She's devoted to me
> (1990, off the album *Holy Intellect*, Profile Records)

However, to claim authenticity is to misunderstand the operations of the popular because authenticity is itself commodified, it is just packaged differently. The marketing of Queen Latifah as a serious African woman in popular music just means that a different, older audience is being targeted.[21] To promote distinctions between authenticity and the popular limits the potential audience that could be addressed; it restricts the forms that could be used to articulate Black experience and it assumes a pure, singular, homogeneous Black expression (Bailey and Hall, 1992). To reproduce the association of Blackness with nature and authenticity is also racist, Gilroy (1987) argues, because it confines a homogeneous Black experience to natural expression. So, to claim authenticity is to define oneself through opposition to that which is seen to have less social value. In so doing, differences, inequalities and distinctions are reproduced in the name of 'taste cultures'.

Bourdieu (1986) argues that civilization is an ideological category that operates to maintain and legitimate social distinctions and the allocation of power in the name of 'taste'. In this process issues of access to knowledge and cultural capital are obfuscated:

> The denial of lower, coarse, vulgar, venal, servile – in a word, natural enjoyment, which constitutes the sacred sphere of culture, implies an affirmation of the superiority of those who can be satisfied with the

sublimated, refined, disinterested, gratuitous, distinguished pleasures for ever closed to the profane. (p. 7)

So, when female rappers explicitly address sexual practice as direct pleasure and fun they locate themselves against good taste, polite conduct and civilization. In this sense they are dangerous. They embody a threat to the moral and social order. Mercer and Julien (1988) note how definitions of sexuality are deeply linked to racism because

> Sex is regarded as that thing which *par excellence* is a threat to the moral order of Western civilisation. Hence one is civilised at the expense of sexuality, and sexual at the expense of civilisation. Moral order, they argue, has always been set against the 'chaos' of sexual abandon, which constitutes a threat to the social order. (pp. 107–8)

Challenging Civilization

Racism, Angela Davis (1981) argues, has always drawn strength from its ability to encourage sexual coercion. In order to construct a threat to the moral order of civilization, the Black female rappers have to use and subvert the only language available for the equation of sex with power: the language of masculinity, objectification and conquest. For instance:

> Is this all I get?
> Is this supposed to be good dick?
> Damn
> You said you was a good lover
> But yous a two minute brother
> Nigga I ain't even bust a sweat
> Not to mention I ain't came yet
> I was about to be cool for what with it rocking
> But his shit shrivelled up like a Vienna sausage
> Now I'm hot and got an attitude
> It's time for dinner and I'm serving seafood
> On you knees motherfucka, let your tongue stroke
> Put it on that bit till it hits my throat
> (BWP, 'Two Minute Brother', 1991)

By removing themselves from the feminine subject position of passive receivers of male prowess and performance, they take up places within a masculine subject position and invest the male sexual discourse with new meanings. By using what Audre Lorde (1984) defines as the 'master's tools', masculine language, the female rappers deny the power of the original language to position them as its objects. They use all the discursive resources available to them to create a discursive shift by disempowering the male meaning. This shows that these young women are able to use their knowledge of masculinity to challenge the regulative mechanisms inherent within it, effectively creating a female power/knowledge position. For instance, they draw on the Black musical traditions of slackness, rudeness, toasting and boasting (Spillers, 1984) by using the strategies of the trickster

> who inverts the universe of the master because the master fails to understand the words on the tongues of the oppressed can become tools that initiate a reversal of roles and subversion of the system which he (the master) has so carefully crafted. (Scott, 1992, p. 305)

The female rappers also assert control over their own sexuality by shifting from a receptive position to a demanding position. Rather than defining female sexuality as 'lack', 'invisible', 'subjective annihilation' or 'objectification' or by 'eroticizing their own degradation' (as some feminist theorists would have it), they are defining themselves by defiantly speaking their own sexuality. BWP use explicit sexual language to demand the fulfilment of their sexual desire in a straightforward statement of want.

To not speak sexuality, when one is positioned within it (by gender, 'race' and class) would mean that Black and White working-class women were fitting themselves into modes of behaviour and *conduct* designed for those with greater access to power and economics. Trying to fit into categories of respectability has operated as a most effective form of social and psychic regulation of working-class women for decades. Speaking of sexuality directly exposes the distinctions that exist between women. Only those who are culturally and economically safe can ignore it. The women who are continually defined as the embodiment of sexuality (for example, Black and White working-class women) have to find a way to deal with this continual categorization. That women have been exploited through their sexuality does not necessarily mean that they cannot experience it as something positive and controllable.

Black female rappers are well aware that, in a racist and sexist society divided by class, sexual relationships are underpinned by power, control and objectification. They want to have power and control over their own sexual relationships, as did the blues singers who used it to construct *themselves* as sexual subjects:

> The 'Classic Blues' of the 20's and 30's is a discourse that articulates a cultural and political struggle over sexual relations: a struggle that is directed against the objectification of female sexuality. . . . which also tries to reclaim women's bodies as the sexual and sensuous objects of women's song. (Carby, 1986, p. 12)

Angela Davis (1981) identifies the difficulty for Black women in this recuperation process from object to subject because enslavement relegated Black women's sexuality to the marketplace of the flesh. The blues singers attempted recuperation by teaching Black women much that is positive about their sexuality (Spillers, 1984). Russell (1982) notes of Bessie Smith (the protégé of Ma Rainey):

> With her Black women in American culture could no longer just be regarded as sexual objects. She made us sexual subjects, the first step in taking control. She transformed our collective shame at being rape victims, treated like dogs, or worse, the meat dogs eat by emphasising the value of our allure. In so doing she humanised sexuality for Black women. The importance of this is often lost. (p. 131)

BWP are continuing this recuperative process. They challenge the long tradition of exoticizing and taming the Black woman singer, of coding her as animalistic. In 1984 Tina Turner's tour poster had her rushing towards the camera, in a skirt made from animal fur, with tails hanging from her waist; the caption read 'Captured live'. Grace Jones was similarly portrayed on all fours, caged and snarling at the viewer (Steward and Garratt, 1984). BWP also challenge wider representations of Black women as dutiful servants and comforting or restraining mothers (Bobo and Seiter, 1991).

The assertion of sexuality is also constructed with irreverence and humour. These female rappers are young women enjoying themselves, taking pleasure from their inability to be controlled, and from the disturbance they cause. Even Russell Simmons (chair of Def Jam records, manager of Public Enemy and chair of Rush Associated Labels that finally released the BWP album *The Bytches*) refused to release the album unless a line was deleted from 'Two Minute Brother'.[22] Some theorists argue that, when women speak sexuality using sexually explicit language, they are just colluding in the male pornographic position. In fact, for Black and White working-class women, sexuality is one of the few cultural resources that they can use for the construction of embodied self-worth. Speaking of sexuality is not a privilege, as some theorists have suggested, but a means of collapsing the dichotomy between public and private spheres and exposing the power relationships that control women. Hurtado argues that the public/private dichotomy is relevant only for the White middle class because, historically, the (American) state has intervened constantly in the private lives and domestic arrangements of the working class. The political consciousness of women of colour, she argues, stems from an awareness that the public is *personally* political (Hurtado, 1989).

Female rappers make a distinction between overtly expressing sexuality and being available for sexual usage. This equation between usage and expression has been particularly effective in silencing the expression of women's sexuality (Lees, 1986) and informs much legislation against women. All the female rappers make it abundantly clear that they are not available for use;

their expression of sexuality is solely a matter for themselves. In 'Shake Your Thang', for example, Salt 'n' Pepa force a wedge between overt female sexual expression and the presumption that such expressions are intended to attract men.

It would be very difficult to think that any men could have control over any of the female rappers; they are more of a male nightmare than a male fantasy. Their demand discourses do not sit neatly alongside the feminine and maternal discourses of caring, duty, obligation and responsibility. The only responsibility that BWP will take is for themselves against HIV and pregnancy (Jimmy must wear a raincoat). This is quite different from the majority of the young, White working-class women with whom I did research who, in a similar way, had a great deal of knowledge about masculinity and were able to undermine and challenge male power (Skeggs, 1991).[23] Yet, because of their investments in the duty and responsibility discourses of caring they were unable to express their own sexuality and place themselves into a demand discourse. Not surprisingly, they were condemnatory of those who could.

The ability of BWP to speak sexuality needs to be set against what Fine (1988) defines as the 'missing discourse of desire'. She charts the way in which women learn to suppress any articulations of sexual desire; how the language we have for articulations of desire is inadequate, leading to the promotion of female sexual victimization rather than autonomous expression; and how we learn to frame sexual expression through institutionalized hetero-sexuality (for example, romance and marriage). Thompson (1990b) suggests that it is rare for young women to embark on sexual encounters feeling in possession of their sexuality. Rather they feel that sex is something that is done to them. The female rappers directly challenge this suppression. They provide a new irreverent but demanding articulation for those who have not invested in discourses of respectability.

BWP also refuse to take emotional responsibility for the management of the male ego and relationships. In so doing, Carby (1986) argues, they are challenging the racist process that displaces female desire onto female duty:

> Black female sexuality was frequently displaced onto the terrain of the political responsibility of the Black woman. The displacement of female desire onto female duty enabled the negotiation of racist constructions of Black female sexuality but denied sensuality and in this denial lies the class character of its cultural politics. (Carby, 1986, p. 12)

BWP would never gain the independence and autonomy they want by trying to fit into those notions of duty and caring which sublimate the expression of sexual desire. They refuse to see their sexuality as a duty.

By addressing sexual practice explicitly many female rappers are making a complete disavowal of shame. Shame, as Elias (1982) points out, is one of the central regulative mechanisms of civilization. He demonstrates how shame produces the ultimate coercion because it produces defencelessness against the external construction of superiority. It is the means by which institutional constraints (such as the organization of the hetero/sexual moral economy) become embodied through self-constraint and self-responsibility. The discourse of shame is one of the most insidious means by which women come to regulate and control themselves through their bodies. It involves intensive self-regulation of sexual relations and sexual conduct, which Elias identifies as psychosocial surveillance, a key characteristic of civilization. The female rappers are refusing to take part in this psychic regulation, which will always condemn them to be measured as inferior by the legacies and values of the White-Western civilizing system.

Feminist Rap?

Paradoxically, the music industry, famous for its sexism and racism, has had to provide a space for the feminist challenges of the Black female rappers. In order to market what is happening 'on the street' back to a wider audience, it must take account of what is happening there. The anger, rage and frustration coded through violence, glamour and sexuality is marketable to a White audience who can take voyeuristic delight, whilst remaining safe. Rap is also marketable for other reasons:

> Black expressive culture has decisively shaped youth culture, pop culture and the culture of city life in Britain's metropolitan centres. The White working-class has danced for forty years to the eroticism and gender conflict enjoyed within Black folk culture. Their Rabelaisian power to carnivalise and disperse the dominant order through an intimate yet public discourse on sexuality and the body has drawn many outsiders into a sense and complex network of Black cultural symbols. (Gilroy, 1990, p. 273)

Gilroy argues that it is emotional realism and the candid, expressive voicing of sexual desire that accounts for the immense popularity of Black music amongst Whites in Western societies.

Rap is one area of the music industry where women hold power: Sylvia Robinson of Sugarhill was instrumental in getting the original 'Rapper's Delight' into circulation in 1979; Monica Lynch is president of Tommy Boy Records, the core of Time Warner's rap industry; Carmen Ashurst Watson is president of Def Jam; Ann Carlyle is senior vice-president of Jive; Pat Chardonnay runs Priority Records. Virgin Records benefit from Black women such as Cledrah White who have made it into the industry through Black radio stations. Debi Fee edits the American rap magazine *Yo!* which has international distribution and Lady B, a Philadelphia DJ who was the first recorded rapper in 1978, is founder and Editor-in-Chief of *Word Up!*, a tabloid devoted to Hip-Hop. Queen Latifah and Sha Kim together have established their own record label and Queen Latifah has her own record company. Female rap sales are small in comparison to male rap, but not insignificant: MC Lyte's 1988 'Paper Thin' sold over 125,000 copies in the first six months and Salt 'n' Pepa's first single 'Expressions' went gold in the first week and stayed in the number one position on *Billboard*'s Rap Chart for over two months.

The female rappers speak in a way that is unlikely to be associated with feminism. Firstly, this is because the use of pop music (rap is just one variety) is associated with entertainment and with the frivolous. Secondly, only a few Black women are feminists in the sense understood by White middle-class women (Ngcobo, 1988). Numerous Black writers have documented the way in which feminism is seen by Black women as a White ideology and practice that is anti-men in a way that is incompatible with the Black struggle against racism (Amos and Parmar, 1984; Bryan *et al.*, 1985; hooks, 1989; Joseph and Lewis, 1981). In the interviews with Tricia Rose, Queen Latifah, MC Lyte and Salt were all reluctant to define themselves as feminist, although they admitted to supporting feminist political struggles and ideals (Rose, 1990). Barbara Christian (1987) argues that people of colour have always theorized, often in narrative forms, riddles and proverbs, and through play with language which unmasks the power relations of the world; rap is just one example of that theorizing.

BWP may not speak to any established White feminisms but they both represent and speak to the experience of the group of young Black women interviewed by Sharon Thompson (1990a), who pride themselves on their ability to use and abuse men in their search for autonomy, fun and pleasure. Thompson analyzed narratives of sex, romance and pregnancy gathered from interviews with over 400 African-American young women. She documents a small group whose everyday activities sound remarkably similar to the lyrical expressions of Black female rappers. This group define themselves as part of the long herstory of Black tricksters. They 'multiply contradictions, play all sides of paradox, pursue probabilities and though with marginality, they downplay it as they do with all vulnerability . . . they brag that they are difficult to pin down; moody; nasty; slick . . . they transform weakness into strength' (1990a, p. 271). Thompson argues that explicit sexual intentionality distinguishes this group of narrators. They excel in being 'nasty' and cold, being beyond romance, able to take or leave it. They describe their sexual appetites as insatiable. Proposing that this insatiability drives them to all types of sex, they see themselves as dangerous, proclaiming their sexual appetites and practices as potentially deadly weapons.[24] They are 'uncivilized' and ungovernable. Overall, they portray themselves as invulnerable. They are strong young women who take their pleasure and defend their bodies and their rights. Their lives are what Thompson (1990a) describes as 'drastic entertainments'. Hence, they are not representative of all young Black women. Rather, they are located within specific socio-economic circumstances, informed by Black history and cultural capital, which they use to their advantage to deal with their disadvantages.[25]

Conclusion

The Black female rappers demonstrate that responses to racism are gendered and classed. They draw on the long history of Black female musical resistance and on their current cultural resources to talk back to racism creatively. In so doing they theorize, in their own terms, their positioning as Black women in heterosexual, colonialist-capitalist relations. They also break the silencing imposed on the expression of female sexuality by its location in civilizing moral discourses. They demonstrate that sexuality is a cultural and economic resource as well as an institutional discourse and practice. Thus, access to the discursive subject positions of the civilizing systems (such as respectability and femininity) are related to locations in the social formation. Cultural capital is always gendered, 'raced' and classed.

The female rappers defiantly talk back to a dominant civilizing system of distinctions which always positions them as 'other', as different and as inferior. For representations of otherness are not just textual; they have been firmly anchored in the solid grounds of slavery, colonialism and capitalist practices (Venn, 1992). The female rappers are not able to challenge their structural positioning, but can subvert relations of domination and subordination by using the same language that has been employed to condemn and objectify them and by investing it with new meanings.

Bhabha (1983) emphasizes the basic ambivalence at the heart of colonial discourse which both fixes and assigns its place to the 'other', yet strives to capture an otherness which it conceptualizes as wild, chimerical, excessive and unknowable. The female rappers make it difficult for those who carry the legacy of the White male colonizer to capture, locate and legitimate the positioning of them as the powerless other. They make it clear they are ungovernable and difficult and cannot be fashioned in the image of male fantasy and fear of White civilization. They cannot be normalized or disciplined. It is this attack on 'reason' that Walkerdine identifies as most disruptive, as it will not allow the conversion of conflict into discourse (Walkerdine, 1987). In this sense, female rap constitutes a representational threat to the moral and social order of civilization that endeavours to keep women firmly in their place. The female rappers are putting themselves into existence against powerlessness.

The racism of the music industry provides a space for Black women to be sexual.[26] Rather than reproducing the animalistic, exotic images of Black women that the music industry usually circulates, the female rappers trade on their ordinariness. By challenging the location of women in the moral discourses of caring, obligation, duty and responsibility, which posit support for the male ego, they expose the fraudulent myth of male sexual prowess. They speak directly of two-minute brothers and shrivelled dicks. They strike fear into the heart of most male insecurities. The demand discourse they use defines them as independent (if heterosexual) and autonomous.

By fully embracing the popular they speak to the widest audience possible, refusing to be contained by racist equations of Black equals authentic. It is unlikely that they will speak (in a dialogic way) to those who have made investments in respectability. They do, however, speak directly to those who have the least to lose through challenges to regulative systems.

The female rappers, along with the White middle-class 'Riot Grrrls'[27] and young women's magazines such as *Just Seventeen* and *Mizz*,[28] create a discursive shift which allows young women to be positively associated with the term 'stroppy'. This now describes a whole lifestyle from clothes to music to attitude, enabling the construction of new subjectivities. In this sense female rap is feminism without formal academicized theory. It is proto-feminist pop. Probyn (1992) would describe it as the popular use of transformative spaces: doing the feminist struggle on the popular front. Just as official institutions have had to engage with feminism, so too have young women; contemporary research suggests an increase in feminist sensibilities (Mac an Ghaill, 1988; McRobbie, 1991; Frazer, 1988; Skeggs, 1991). Harding (1986) suggests that feminism is seeping through into everyday practice but she doesn't know where it is coming from. I would argue that popular music is one site. And whilst BWP represent an extreme position with only limited distribution, their lyrics and attitude are incorporated into more mainstream acts such as those of Madonna and Neneh Cherry. As Vron Ware (1992) has shown, Black women have a long history of enabling the White feminist struggle.

BWP have created a popular space for women to speak a sexuality which is about *their* desires in a way which is ungovernable and impossible to contain, yet which is located with fun, autonomy and independence. They speak against all the institutional, structural and discursive attempts to control the expression of women's sexuality. Female rap music illustrates vividly the discursive nature of the boundaries through which Black women define themselves in struggle. And the struggle continues.

Notes

1   The (white) Yeastie Girls (off the Consolidated album) have released 'You Suck', an equally sexually explicit song about oral sex. It provides detailed information on how to do oral sex, comments about safe sex, yeast infections and getting

pubic hairs stuck in your teeth. It combats male resistance, but unlike BWP it registers a dependence upon men for pleasure and is far less irreverent and undermining. It may, however, be the product of BWP's influence.

2   They also challenge the racism of white female employers in a very non-feminist way in a song called 'Kotex', demonstrating how the concept of sisterhood is underpinned by 'race' and class relations. This track, however, operates as a revenge fantasy over racism and powerlessness at work.

3   'Gangsta' rap is hard, aggressive, abrasive 'in yer face' music combined with lyrics of violence and macho bragging. It mainly consists of conquests achieved through big guns and big dicks. Ice T and Ice Cube are probably the most popular. There is an obvious intertextuality between the 'gangsta' rap music and the Blaxploitation films of the seventies such as *Shaft* and *Superfly*. Contemporary films such as *New Jack City*, *Trespass* and *Boyz in the Hood* use rappers for major roles. The music of BWP is used to great effect to provide support for their lyrics, so when a sex scenario is being voiced in 'Two-Minute Brother', the music corresponds, reaching a climax and then slowing to make space for the astounded voice 'is that it?'

4   The popularizing of this form of abbreviation has now hit the mainstream with the singers SWV (Sisters with Voices) and rappers TLC, an ironic move on 'Tender Loving Care'. Their riposte to Color Me Badd's 'I Wanna Sex You Up' is not in the least bit tender, loving or caring.

5   *Hip-Hop Connection*, no. 36, January 1992, p. 15.

6   Queen Latifah is one of the most famous of American female rappers. She is part of the Native Tongues grouping produced by the Flavor Unit, who espouse an African-centric philosophy. Whilst she sings very powerful songs about African history and female autonomy, her management company also manages two exceedingly misogynist rap outfits: Naughty by Nature and Apache.

7   Monie Love is a British rapper who had to move to the States to have her music widely distributed. It is exceptionally difficult for female rappers to make it in Britain where even the male rap scene is small.

8   From an interview with Tricia Rose (1990), p. 123.

9   It is practically impossible to find this video in Britain where, other than Salt 'n' Pepa, a market has yet to be developed to make the distribution worthwhile. This points to the centrality of the industry in providing access for the defiant speech of the female rappers.

10   Capitals have been used for the terms Black and White to de-normalize their usage as biologically reducible categories in order to make their ideological functions explicit. See (charles) (1992) for the full argument.

11   Hall (1992) argues that events, relations and structures have conditions of existence and real effects, outside of the sphere of the discursive, but that only within the discursive, and subject to its specific conditions, limits and modalities, do they have or can they be constructed with meaning. How things are represented and the 'machinery' and regimes of representations in a culture do play a *constitutive*, and not merely a reflexive, after-the-event role. The scenarios of representation thus have a formative place in the constitution of social and political life.

12   See Burke (1973) on Febvre. Chapter 10 discusses the evolution of the word

civilization. He could not find the term civilization in any French text published prior to the year 1766, although the verb to civilize appears first in 1631. Quoting Mazzini, he argues that the term was evoked by France, by the French spirit, at the end of the eighteenth century.

13 These were not always Black groups, as the Irish experience of colonization has shown.

14 The Nation of Islam is based on the readings of Elijah Muhammad in the 1970s, of which Malcolm X was once a part before he formed the Organisation of Afro-American Unity. They are Black Muslims, who promote Black unity and Black education in preparation for the development of a Black nation. Many Black rappers are associated with the Nation, forming different factions such as the 'five percenters'. Rappers such as KRS1 maintain that their rap is part of a programme of learning and education.

15 Wilson Jeremiah Moses quoted by Scott (1992).

16 This is represented in popular culture through the film *Malcolm X* where Malcolm X's partner Betty Shabazz is portrayed firstly as one of the female workers of the Nation of Islam then becomes the house-bound, morally pure mother.

17 *Hip-Hop Connection*, Feb. 1992, p. 29.

18 There is one small contradiction, however. Queen Latifah manages a rapper called Apache who has recently released a track called 'Gangsta Bitch' which refers to women and rappers like BWP in such a way as to incorporate them into fantasies of male control: he recognizes that they are strong, but also believes that they are there for him and are dispensable and replaceable.

19 MC Hammer initially took the hardcore-macho sounds of rap and mixed them with images of cartoons and dancing. He wore flamboyant flowing trousers of vibrant colours as opposed to the street styles or combat gear of the 'serious' rappers. He is often referred to as the aerobic dance music of rap; hence combining insults to the feminine and to the frivolity of dance in one definition.

20 This is not dissimilar to academics who dismiss the value of popular music for as Tricia Rose (1990) notes, 'If I were to suggest that rap music produced some of the most important contemporary Black feminist cultural criticism you would surely bemoan the death of sexual equality' (p. 110).

21 This possibly accounts for the limited distribution of BWP's album.

22 See inside sleeve of album cover. This also suggests that the whole censorship issue may have been a publicity scam.

23 This was an ethnographic study with eighty-three young White women over a period of ten years. The majority, through lack of alternatives, had made social and emotional investments in a caring identity. They had also developed a considerable knowledge about masculine heterosexuality from their readings of young women's magazines and viewing of TV and film. The lack of any equivalent knowledge about female sexuality appeared to be due to the paucity of material available; what there was reproduced the women as passive and acquiescent.

24 The interviews with Sharon Thompson were part of a six-year study (1980–6) and were gathered and written up before the moral panic surrounding HIV and AIDS.

25 Different use is made of restricted access to economic and cultural resources by

the young Black women interviewed by Ladner (1972); Mac an Ghaill (1988); Fuller (1980); Riley (1981); and Mirza (1992).

26 White women are rarely given the same space. Madonna's power and control over her sexuality has increased in relation to her distance from the everyday. The less real she appears the more space she has to play with sexuality.

27 'Riot Grrrls' are groups of White (predominantly) middle-class American 'indie' musicians, some of whose mothers were radical feminists, who draw on collective support and produce fanzines for similar-minded women in the music industry. Some use shocking tactics to confront the sexism of their audiences. They declare their feminism openly. See *New Musical Express*, 6 and 13 March 1993, for more details.

28 McRobbie (1991) and Winship (1985) suggest that young women's magazines such as *Mizz* and *Just Seventeen* have played an important role in the increased feminism of young women.

References

ABRAHAMS, R.D. (1976) *Talking Black*, Bowley, Mass., Newbury House Publishers.

AMOS, V. and PARMAR, P. (1984) 'Challenging Imperialist Feminism', *Feminist Review*, no. 17, pp. 3–19.

BAILEY, D.A. and HALL, S. (1992) 'The Vertigo of Displacement', *Ten 8*, vol. 2, no. 3, pp. 15–23.

BELL, C. (1928) *Civilisation*, Harmondsworth, Penguin.

BHABHA, H. (1983) 'The Other Question . . .', *Screen*, vol. 24, no. 6, pp. 18–36.

BOBO, J. and SEITER, E. (1991) 'Black Feminism and Media Criticism: The Women of Brewster Place', *Screen*, vol. 32, no. 3, pp. 286–302.

BOURDIEU, P. (1986) *Distinctions: A Social Critique of the Judgement of Taste*, London, Routledge and Kegan Paul.

BRYAN, B., DADZIE, S. and SCAFE, S. (1985) *The Heart of the Race: Black Women's Lives in Britain*, London, Virago Press.

CARBY, H. (1982) 'White Woman Listen! Black Feminism and the Boundaries of Sisterhood', in CENTRE FOR CONTEMPORARY CULTURAL STUDIES *The Empire Strikes Back*, London, Hutchinson, pp. 212–36.

CARBY, H. (1986) 'Sometimes It Jus Bes Dat Way', *Radical America*, vol. 20, pt. 4, pp. 9–22.

(CHARLES), H. (1992) 'Whiteness – The Relevance of Politically Colouring the "Non"', in HINDS, H., PHOENIX, A. and STACEY, J. (Eds) *Working Out: New Directions in Women's Studies*, London, Falmer Press.

CHRISTIAN, B. (1987) 'The Race for Theory', *Cultural Critique*, Spring, pp. 51–63.

CHRISTIAN, B. (1990) 'What Celie Knows That You Should Know', in GOLDBERG, D.T. (Ed.) *Anatomy of Racism*, Minneapolis, University of Minnesota Press, pp. 135–45.

Davis, A. (1981) *Women, Race and Class*, London, The Women's Press.
Davis, A. (1990) 'Black Women and Music: A Historical Legacy of Struggle', in Braxton, J.M. and McLaughin, A.N. (Eds) *Wild Women in the Whirlwind: Afro-American Culture and the Contemporary Literary Renaissance*, New Jersey, Rutgers University Press, pp. 3–12.
Diop, C.A. (1974) *The African Origin of Civilisation: Myth or Reality*, USA, Lawrence Hill & Co.
Elias, N. (1982) *Power and Civility (The Civilising Process, vol. 2)*, New York, Pantheon Books.
Febvre, L. (1973) *A New Kind of History and Other Essays* (ed. by P. Burke, trans. by K. Folia), London, Routledge and Kegan Paul.
Fine, M. (1988) 'Sexuality, Schooling and Adolescent Females: The Missing Discourse of Desire', *Harvard Educational Review*, vol. 58, no. 1 (Feb.), pp. 29–53.
Frazer, E. (1988) 'Teenage Girls Talking about Class', *Sociology*, vol. 22, no. 3, pp. 343–58.
Fuller, M. (1980) 'Black Girls in a London Comprehensive School', in Deem, R. (Ed.) *Schooling for Women's Work*, London, Routledge and Kegan Paul, pp. 52–66.
Gilman, S.L. (1992) 'Black Bodies, White Bodies: Towards an Iconography of Female Sexuality in Late Nineteenth Century Art, Medicine and Literature', in Donald, J. and Rattansi, A. (Eds) *'Race', Culture and Difference*, London, Sage, pp. 171–98.
Gilroy, P. (1987) *'There Ain't no Black in the Union Jack'*, London, Hutchinson.
Gilroy, P. (1990) 'One Nation Under a Groove: The Cultural Politics of "Race" and Racism in Britain', in Goldberg, D.T. (Ed.) *Anatomy of Racism*, Minneapolis, University of Minnesota Press, pp. 263–83.
Hall, S. (1992) 'New Ethnicities', in Donald, J. and Rattansi, A. (Eds) *'Race', Culture and Difference*, London, Sage, pp. 252–60.
Harding, S. (1986) *The Science Question in Feminism*, Milton Keynes, Open University Press.
Hebdige, D. (1988) *Hiding in the Light*, London, Comedia.
Hebdige, D. (undated) 'Reggae, Rastas & Rudies: Style and the Subversion of Form', Stencilled Occasional Paper, no. 24, Race Series, Birmingham, Centre for Contemporary Cultural Studies.
hooks, b. (1989) *Talking Back: Thinking Feminist, Thinking Black*, London, Sheba Feminist Publishers.
hooks, b. (1992) discussion of C. West 'The Postmodern Crisis of Black intellectuals', in Grossberg, L., Nelson, C. and Treichler, P. (Eds) Cultural Studies, London, Routledge, p. 700.
Hurtado, A. (1989) 'Relating to Privilege: Seduction and Rejection in the Subordination of White Women and Women of Color', *Signs*, vol. 14, no. 4, pp. 833–55.
Joseph, G. and Lewis, J. (1981) *Common Differences: Conflicts in Black and White Feminist Perspectives*, New York, Anchor Press/Doubleday.
Ladner, J. (1972) *Tomorrow's Tomorrow*, New York, Anchor Books.
Lees, S. (1986) *Losing Out*, Harmondsworth, Penguin.
Lorde, A. (1984) *Sister Outsider*, New York, The Crossing Press.

Mac an Ghaill, M. (1988) *Young, Gifted and Black: Student-Teacher Relations in the Schooling of Black Youth*, Milton Keynes, Open University Press.

McRobbie, A. (1991) *Feminism and Youth Culture: From 'Jackie' to 'Just Seventeen'*, London, Macmillan.

Mercer, K. and Julien, I. (1988) 'Race, Sexual Politics and Black Masculinity: A Dossier', in Chapman, R. and Rutherford, J. (Eds) *Male Order: Unwrapping Masculinity*, London, Lawrence and Wishart, pp. 97–165.

Mirza, H.S. (1992) *Young, Female and Black*, London, Routledge.

Ngcobo, L. (Ed.) (1988) *Let It Be Told: Essays by Black Women in Britain*, London, Virago.

Probyn, E. (1992) 'Technologising the Self: A Future Anterior for Cultural Studies', in Grossberg, L., Nelson, C. and Treichler, P. (Eds) *Cultural Studies*, London, Routledge, pp. 501–12.

Rich, A. (1984) *On Lies, Secrets and Silence: Selected Prose 1966–1978*, London, Virago.

Riley, K. (1981) 'Black Girls Speak for Themselves', *Multiracial Education*, vol. 10, no. 3, pp. 3–12.

Rose, T. (1990) 'Never Trust a Big Butt and a Smile', *Camera Obscura*, vol. 123, May, pp. 110–31.

Russell, M. (1982) 'Slave Codes and Liner Notes', in Hull, G.T., Scott, P.B. and Smith, B. (Eds) *All the Women Are White, All the Blacks Are Men, But Some Of Us Are Brave*, New York, Feminist Press, pp. 129–41.

Scott, J.H. (1992) 'From Foreground to Margin: Female Configuration and Masculine Self-Representation in Black Nationalist Fiction', in Parker, A., Russo, M., Sommer, D. and Yaeger, A. (Eds) *Nationalisms and Sexualities*, New York and London, Routledge, pp. 296–312.

Skeggs, B. (1991) 'Challenging Masculinity and Using Sexuality', *British Journal of Sociology of Education*, vol. 22, no. 3, pp. 343–58.

Smith, L. (1962) 'Autobiography as a Dialogue between King and Corpse', quoted in Rich, A. (1984) *On Lies, Secrets and Silence: Selected Prose 1966–1978*, London, Virago.

Spillers, H.J. (1984) 'Interstices: A Small Drama of Words', in Vance, C. (Ed.) *Pleasure and Danger: Exploring Female Sexuality*, London, Pandora, pp. 73–101.

Steward, S. and Garratt, S. (1984) *Signed, Sealed and Delivered: Of Women in Pop*, London, Pluto.

Thompson, S. (1990a) ' "Drastic Entertainments": Teenage Mothers' Signifying Narratives', in Ginsburg, F. and Lowenhaupt-Tsing, A. (Eds) *Uncertain Terms: Negotiating Gender in American Culture*, Boston, Beacon Press, pp. 269–81.

Thompson, S. (1990b) 'Putting a Big Thing Into a Little Hole: Teenage Girls' Accounts of Sexual Initiation', *Journal of Sex Research*, vol. 27, no. 3.

Venn, C. (1992) 'Subjectivity, Ideology and Difference: Recovering Otherness', *New Formations*, no. 16, pp. 40–62.

Walkerdine, V. (1987) *Surveillance, Subjectivity and Struggle: Lessons from Pedagogic and Domestic Practices*, University of Minnesota, Center for Humanistic Studies.

WALKERDINE, V. (1989) 'Femininity as Performance', *Oxford Review of Education*, vol. 15, no. 3, pp. 267–79.

WALLACE, M. (1979) *Black Macho and the Myth of the Superwoman*, London, John Calder.

WALLACE, M. (1992) 'Negative Images: Towards a Black Feminist Cultural Criticism', in GROSSBERG, L., NELSON, C. and TREICHLER, P. (Eds) *Cultural Studies*, London, Routledge, pp. 654–72.

WARE, V. (1992) *Beyond the Pale: White Women, Racism and History*, London, Verso.

WEST, C. (1992) 'The Postmodern Crisis of Black Intellectuals', in GROSSBERG, L., NELSON, C. and TREICHLER, P. (Eds) *Cultural Studies*, London, Routledge, pp. 689–706.

WINSHIP, J. (1985) ' "A Girl Needs to get Streetwise": Magazines for the 1980s', *Feminist Review*, no. 21, Winter, pp. 25–47.

YOUNG, L. (1990) 'A Nasty Piece of Work: A Psychoanalytic Study of Sexual and Racial Difference in "Mona Lisa" ', in RUTHERFORD, J. (Ed.) *Identity: Community, Culture, Difference*, London, Routledge, pp. 188–207.

Chapter 7

Muslim Women in West Yorkshire: Growing up with Real and Imaginary Values amidst Conflicting Views of Self and Society[1]

Haleh Afshar

Identity, the knowledge of who one is and where one belongs is a powerful denominator of selfhood. We all need to know who our friends and foes are and which are the safe spaces where we can rest; who are the supports on whom we can rely and whom we should distrust. Yet, these definitions, which are central in providing a sense of security and self-knowledge, are not always clear, permanent or entirely reliable. Some, such as sex, or colour of skin, may well remain with us for the rest of our lives. But other identifiers like marital status, political and even kin allegiance and religious adherence are more changeable. Even if the actual definition of belief does not change, what we understand by being a Muslim at 9 would be different from what we understand by it at 19, 39 or 99. Age, history, social contexts and what we generally call life combine to alter virtually all senses of self and identity over time and place.

In this flexible changing context, women's identities are the most transient.[2] We do not even have a name of our own. We are known by our father's name when we are born, by our husband's when we marry and for many by our son's name when we give birth. In the context of universally transient selves and self-definitions, men by their very existence still form the core in the lives of women; and women, who have given birth to and created that core, remain peripheral.

The self-knowledge gained and developed as a 'daughter', dutiful or otherwise, is, for many of us, merely a preparation for becoming a future wife, for acquiring a name not yet known, a home not yet found, a man not yet met and perhaps a mother-in-law as well. The values prescribed at home are merely a path towards this unknown future; a path that may well change radically once the 'right' man has been found. I have met grandmothers who had been sent to boarding schools in India, before the partition, to acquire knowledge and manners to make them a suitable wife for their future husband – a high-ranking civil servant in one case and a business man with British trade connections in another. I have also met young women born and raised in Britain who have had to 'return' to the homes their parents had left, as part of arranged marriages. In each case old identities were difficult to discard and the new identities had proved hard to acquire.

Yet for centuries women everywhere had to a large extent accepted the ascribed values of marriage and motherhood as important signifiers of their identity and their sense of fulfilment. This cultural norm is enhanced ideologically amongst Muslims through endorsement by the Prophet of Islam and the Holy Quran; these include statements that place heaven at the feet of mothers, that demand of children to respect their mothers and of husbands to pay mothers to suckle their babies. The celebration of sexuality within marriage by Islam and its abhorrence of celibacy have all contributed to the positive values that Muslim societies have traditionally placed on marriage and motherhood.

But for Muslim women born and raised as minorities in a non-Islamic Western world, it is harder to internalize these values without question. Nevertheless, in the wake of an international revivalism of Islam, many are choosing to adopt the Islamic identity, donning the scarf and sharing the strength bestowed by a powerful, universalist Islamic identity.

This chapter addresses the contradictory impacts that the politicized adopted Islamic identity have made on a group of immigrant women in West Yorkshire. The work is based on nearly a decade of research by the author with women living in three-generational households in the region. Identified by the snowball method,[3] these households, consisting of grandmother, bride and granddaughter, were selected because it was assumed that they would form the most conservative group of immigrants, where the presence of the older generation was expected to exercise a firm cultural and emotional control. It had been the hypothesis of the research that the youngest generation in these households would show the greatest resistance to old norms and values and would be most likely to 'rebel' against traditional notions of Islam and the kinds of identities that it would have imposed on the family.

Much of the material for this chapter is based on interviews conducted by Mrs Usha Verma, a researcher who speaks Urdu and does not live in the locality where the respondents reside. The author is aware of the multi-faceted problems that such research, conducted by more than one person and in more than one language, poses. Many of the problems have been discussed in great depth in the first chapters of this volume. While acknowledging the obstacles, the author has done her best to come to the conclusions offered here. The intention is to allow the voices of the women themselves to be heard. Since all but one of the interviews were taped, those who spoke in English have been reported verbatim; those who did not have had their words interpreted as closely as possible to the original. This project seeks to express the views of these women, even though these views contradicted much of the assumptions of the researchers.

The work brought in many surprises, not least that the hypothesis had been wrong. History had intervened, as had deteriorating economic conditions and political exigencies, to alter many of the parameters. Most surprising of all, the researcher, who had set out to look at education and the labour market, had to come to terms with the reality that marriage and motherhood were frequently perceived as more important by the women concerned. As a result this chapter will be primarily concerned with these issues.

It must also be noted that although the chapter is about Muslim women, and this was both a self-definition and one that was used by the researcher, the women concerned belonged to different schools of Islamic thought. All were from the mainstream Sunni schools and not the minority Shias. But none specified which particular school they came from. This may well be because the Islamic schools are largely transparent, the differences being not in terms of religious rituals and practices, which are universal for all Muslims, but more in terms of particularities of legal definitions of Sharia (religious laws) which on the whole did not impinge on the lives of immigrant women living in a non-Muslim country. It may also be because of the current revivalist position which claims that all Muslims are part and parcel of the same community (*umma*), regardless of their regional or legalistic differences. Islam is embraced as an empowering badge of unity and adopted and adapted to the perceived needs and aspirations of its adherents.[4]

By contrast the class background of the women and their regional areas of origin, particularly whether they had come directly from the subcontinent or were second-time migrants from Uganda, did make a marked difference in their perceptions of self, society and the economy. These will be noted in the text.

Women, Honour and Identity

Amongst Muslims, women have traditionally been the appointed site of familial honour and shame and the representatives of the public face of the society's apparent commitment to its faith. Thus Muslim women are both guardians and guarded. They are the custodians of the religious beliefs, even though for centuries it has been men who have been the interpreters of norms, values and practices according to that belief. Women, whether they have wished it or not, have been required to reflect the religious commitment of the group in their attire and behaviour as well as in most aspects of their lives. This has not been a painless or a static process. At different times and places Muslim women have come to different arrangements and have struck different bargains with the patriarchal structures within which they find themselves (Kandiyoti, 1991).

At times of hardship, particularly when the Muslim community has perceived itself as a beleaguered minority, women have had to submit to much
greater degrees of restrictions than at times of success and prosperity, or when
the community had expected such a prospect, as in the case of much of the
Middle East in its modernization phase. Furthermore, given the undisputed
core of eternal belief embodied in the text of the Quran, Muslims have been
able to claim an adherence to immovable and absolute laws enacted at the
inception of the faith and followed ever since. At times of crisis, the return
to this position is often articulated in terms of stricter controls and merciless
rejection of those who fail to conform. This study seeks to find a path towards
creating greater understanding between those women who have not lived up
to the expectations of their brethren and the men and women who have felt
threatened by such transgressions and have insisted on casting them out.

Of course not all Muslim women are equally affected. The accord about
Islamic values is more illusory than real and there are marked divisions
amongst Muslims here and elsewhere. These divisions are, as ever, most
marked along class lines, as well as cultural, national and traditional ones.
Old aristocratic and wealthy families, though Muslim, have frequently found
money a useful vehicle for *rapprochement* with the host society. Those who
chose the route of integration had, in the earlier prosperous decade of the
1960s, adopted egalitarian values towards their sons and daughters.

Many had sent their daughters, as well as their sons, to British boarding
schools where the values taught and lived were quite different from those
enunciated within the natal families. Talking to these young women, in the
past ten years, I find them much like their British counterparts. They talk,
dress and behave in much the same way (Lutz, 1991), but many are burdened
with guilt and shame for failing to fulfil their filial duties. In particular their
selected routes towards romance, cohabitation and marriage meet with severe
reprimands and often lead to painful ostracization. By contrast the young
men in these families are not discouraged from pursuing the young women
of their choice, and engaging in numerous flirtatious relationships. It is assumed that in due course the woman they choose to marry will be suitable,
submissive and obedient. Besides, mothers-in-law still maintain the belief
that they can ensure the good behaviour of any wayward daughter-in-law
who might come into the family.

I found this to be a valid claim. Amongst the many Muslim brides that
I interviewed in West Yorkshire only one was white and British. Like the
other daughters-in-law that I talked to she lived with her mother-in-law.
However, her daughter was the only granddaughter I met who could actually
say the *namaz*, the daily prayer, correctly. The same grandmother was
considerably less diligent where her other granddaughters were concerned.
She assumed that where both parents were of Pakistani descent, the children
would be raised as Muslims.

This idea of teaching by osmosis is of course part and parcel of the
general assumptions made about mothering. Women are the perceived

transmitters of cultural values and identities and are the standard-bearers of the group's public and private dignity. Yet women themselves are burdened with a diversity of values and identities which may not always converge to produce a rich entirety. Furthermore, so far as religious teaching is concerned, traditionally Muslim women have not been particularly well versed. They have been barred from *ijtihad*, religious discourse and interpretation, and some are even today not permitted to pray in mosques or take part in public religious debates.

Marriage and Identity

Marriage as an institution marks an important change of identity, a landmark in a woman's progression away from the paternal home to a joint partnership. But the values ascribed to marriage and its impact on women's identity differ to some degree from group to group and nation to nation. This chapter will discuss some of the ways in which conflicting views about the process of adulthood are negotiated by Muslim women living in a non-Muslim community, their approaches to marriage and motherhood and the ways that these impact on their views on identity and employment in West Yorkshire.

For most of our respondents marriage has been seen as a move towards independence, and not, as many feminists would see it, a move towards a different dependence or at best an interdependence. Of course marriage denotes a changed identity for the women concerned and they did not question the reality that for men the change was not quite as overt nor as complete. It is normal and commonplace that men do not change their name or their legal identity. The women we talked to did not consider it problematic that men frequently either exchange the services received from their mothers for those received from their wives, or add their spouse's labour to that of the household.

Once married, women are required to assimilate. In the West, for centuries they legally lost their name, their property and their identity; they became the chattel of their husbands. The Muslim women have been proud of the Quranic rights given to women, which protect their property, give them inalienable rights of inheritance and frequently allow them to keep their name, that is, the name of their fathers.

Furthermore, it is often argued[5] that this core of identity and property is secured and enhanced by parental vigilance; that arranged marriages ensure the suitability of future husbands, and enable women to move into households of similar standing and hence similar values. This provision is frequently endorsed as an 'Islamic' requirement:

> Equality between the two spouses in certain matters is a condition for the validity of marriage. . . .

> Equality, which can be defined as parity of status, is considered by the Hanafis in six matters: lineage, Islam, freedom, property, trade or craft, and piety.
>
> The Malikis require equality in religious piety, freedom from defects, and lineage in that the husband should have a known father and should not be a foundling whose parents are unknown.
>
> The Shafiis' requirements regarding equality are freedom from defects, lineage, chastity, craft, and solvency.
>
> The Hanbalis require equality in religious piety, lineage, solvency, and craft. . . .
>
> The Shia Ithna-Asharis also consider equality in marriage from the husband's side who must be at least equal to the woman in lineage. . . .
>
> The Syrian Law entitles the guardian to apply for the annulment of the marriage if the woman marries a person who is not her equal, without the guardian's consent. (Nasir, 1990, pp. 18–19)

Unquestionably the Islamic marriage recognizes men and women as partners in life and its contractual nature defines their respective roles, obligations and even the charges they can make, pay or deduct for performing their duties. But just as certainly the agreement is one that is made between the 'guardian' of the woman and the future husband or his 'guardian'. It is more about kinship alignment than about marital happiness. Women are 'guarded' by their male kin and are handed over from one male to another in the expectation that the protection will continue. Ayatollah Khomeini even advocated that the changeover should occur before girls reach puberty, to ensure that the men continue to exert a firm influence.[6]

Nevertheless, it can be argued that the Islamic marriage is a contractual agreement, one negotiated by the kin with the best interests of the next generation in mind; one that secures cohesion and traditional norms. For women it is a contract which provides security for the job of wifehood and motherhood; one that recognizes and rewards women's labour of love; it is a move towards complementarity. Men are required to pay the *mahre*, before the consummation of marriage. 'Apart from a valid marriage contract, which makes, *per se*, the dower an established right of the wife, consummation, with the semblance of the right to have intercourse . . . shall also render the wife entitled to a dower' (Nasir, 1990, p. 48). This payment ratified by the marriage contract is 'a sort of exchange', whereby 'in return for the right of sexual union, a woman is entitled to receive a certain amount of money or valuables' (Hilli, 1968, p. 517).

But the payment of *mahre* is subject to different customs and practices; it is not necessarily paid on marriage, more often it becomes a debt repayable on divorce, even though, according to Nasir,

> It is unanimously agreed by the Sunnis that the whole dower shall become due to the wife on the occurrence of either of two events:

(i)   the actual consummation of marriage; or
(ii)   the death of either spouse before consummation. (Nasir, 1990, p. 49)

Although theoretically women are entitled to their dower, and have exclusive right to it under the terms of the marriage contract, in practice 'the amount thereof due to her varies according to circumstances. She may be entitled to the whole dower, half of it, or may have no dower at all' (*ibid.*). Men are also required to maintain a wife in the style to which she has been accustomed, to pay for the suckling of children and to abide by the terms of the marriage contract. But of course in practice the degree to which these rights are observed varies considerably from country to country and from branch to branch of Islamic schools. What women are entitled to and what they get are very different. Married women are not expected to assert their proprietorial rights. They are not to bring conflict, but peace. They are to be help-mates and obedient partners. They are required to become part and parcel of their new families; not only to embrace the new ascribed role of wifehood, but also to excel at it. Within a year or two they are expected to give birth, preferably to a son, and to transmit the positive family 'values' intact to the next generation.

Thus for women the loss of early identity, loss of name and independence is merely the beginning of what some may call 'real' life and 'real' responsibilities. Although, strictly speaking, married life should be about complementarity and mutual obligations, it is, on the whole, women who are expected both to change and to cope. This means the adoption of a new role, new ways and new mores. Generally this is not expected to be a negotiated settlement, but rather an integration of the female into the family of the husband. Yet women, who are expected to discard themselves so readily, are also expected to transmit eternal values and identities to their children. This, particularly in contexts where the group is a minority, and a beleaguered one at that, is hard, if not impossible to achieve successfully.

Modesty and Morality

When it comes to transmittable values, more than anything it is morality that is at issue for Muslim women. All those that I have been talking to in the past ten years are unanimous in their defence of *izzat*, or *aberu*, the honour of the family, which can be turned into shame with the slightest transgression. Shame amongst Muslim minorities is an almost unforgivable crime; the group is merciless and unforgiving to those who transgress. Salman Rushdie is a clear and much publicized example. But there are many cases of daughters, wives or sisters being beaten to death, burned or grievously harmed by their kin for transgressing. Although some of these cases are reported in the Western media, the majority are not.

There are even more women who are disowned, allowed to disappear in the 'mire of Western immorality' and cut off never to be seen again by their family. In most of these cases the transgression has been an 'inappropriate' marriage or a suspected extra-marital relationship. Since women are defined as dependent, as 'guarded' by their men, then any transgression denotes a failure not only of the women, but also and particularly of their menfolk and hence the entire family.

Given the centrality of marriage and the need to have a good name and a good reputation to capture a husband at all, the major effort of mothers is directed towards ensuring that their daughters are moral and modest. In practice morality for women is all too often articulated in terms of sexual purity and apparent modesty. In this domain garments acquire an extraordinary importance; the good woman is the one who covers her hair and her legs. Modesty is defined by the head-scarf, the *shalwar kamiz* and the length of a girl's hair and its style.[7]

Young Muslim men dress and generally behave in ways which are not easily distinguishable from their Western counterparts. Many assert their birthright to do so. Although their parents frown at drinking and smoking, the best amongst them may refrain from taking these habits home, but many feel quite free to mix and play with with their contemporaries of all races, beliefs and colours. Yet the same young men all too often expect their sisters, future wives and daughters to behave in a distinctly different way; to dress in the way that their mothers and grandmothers had done, to remain separate from the host society and to retain the identity that is so dear to the heart of the immigrant society.

There is an entire gamut of definition of immodest clothing for women, where I know of none for men living in the West. At one extreme we have the current view of the Iranian *Hezbollah*, the party of God, who call any woman who is showing a single strand of hair 'immodest' and subject to seventy lashes and assume that 'nakedness' is showing anything other than the face and the hands. Hence morality and propriety is about shrouding women in black garments. Even colours are viewed as sexually provocative and therefore women are not permitted to wear bright 'suggestive' *chadors* (veils).

Although there are Muslim women who wear the veil in the West, none go quite as far as the Iranians. The more prevalent definition of 'nakedness' here is in terms of showing one's legs. For centuries Muslim Pakistani women have had no compunction about showing their midriff and wearing relatively low-cut tops under their saris, but they have consistently hidden their legs. The obsession with hidden legs remains prevalent amongst the immigrant community in West Yorkshire. Girls who are allowed to go to swimming classes when they are young are abruptly taken away at puberty. Athletic young women are no longer permitted to compete wearing gym clothes and sport becomes a taboo domain, often merely because its participants have bare legs.

There are of course advantages to the veil[8] and many Muslim women are consciously choosing to adopt it as a symbol of political independence, nationalism, revivalism and as a conscious rejection of Western values. They have evolved and developed a new sense of self and a new perspective on their place in society and history.

This same identity, which has gone through changes and has evolved and developed through time in all the home towns of the migrants, has been held static in its embodiment in the West. The immigrants in Bradford, like immigrants everywhere, have ossified some of the values of their past, and have demanded rigid adherence to these unchanging roles. In the context of a changing world, a changing Europe and evolving Islamic concepts of self and identity, the immigrants have retained an idolized idea of the past and have imposed the duty on their women to guard and maintain this identity and to nurture it and transmit it to the next generation.

Perhaps the only way that this ascribed identity could be guarded and passed on is by separating the women both from the host society and from the emerging and evolving literature and discussions about Islam that emanate from the Middle East and elsewhere. Perhaps it is necessary for women to be blinkered, if they are to transmit the unwritten laws of morality that they must obey.

Many years ago when I was working with a group of second-generation Muslim women reading through the Quran, our group met with severe opposition for seeking to find our own answers in the holy text. We were told in no uncertain terms that we must go to male interpreters and listen to their interpretation of the text. As ignorant, unlearned women we had no right to go to our own holy book and seek to understand the laws of Islam. But those women who did go to the mosque and to Islamic classes were not taught the meaning of the texts; they learned the words and knew how to recite them perfectly. The quest for the meanings remained very much in the hands of the men. The Shias have for some years now been discussing and disputing the question of interpretation and whether or not a particular group of learned men should interpose their knowledge between people and God.[9] Muslim women too are beginning to question the demands of imposed ignorance.

But the values that they are expected to transfer within minority groups are not necessarily those of Islam; they are a combination of cultural, customary and idealized views, learned through second-hand transmission by young women born here, from older women born in a different epoch, in a different place and raised for a different life. As one of my respondents, Mrs B., reported:[10]

We have to teach our children two separate sorts of things; one is about cooking and cleaning and things like that. The other is about *sharme* and manners. We also have to teach them about religion and their own history and background, about the family.

I do my best to pass on things that I was taught by my elders so they can pass them on to their children. Maybe not everything, but most of what we were taught was right and we should pass it on.

Mrs B., who was born and raised in Uganda and moved to Britain in 1968, recalled that life was much easier then; for one thing she did not have to work long hours as a machinist to make a living. The combination of forced migration and full-time work made her self-assigned tasks much harder to accomplish:

> Things are difficult here. It was different for us. We were taught to look after the whole family: aunties, uncles, cousins. But things are different here, because girls have to go to school. When they get back from school they have homework and household work as well. We can't expect them to do as much for the family as we did. . . .
>
> In our days our parents didn't want to send their daughter to school; they preferred that we stayed at home and learn to cook and sew and look after the family. They wanted us to respect our elders and never answer back. We were taught not to complain about a husband, no matter what. . . . We were told the same things by everybody. If you went to the neighbours they said the same thing. But here if you go to your neighbour they are different from you. They have a different religion, different ways of life, different views about children. We cannot learn the same things from them.

Grandmothers like Mrs B. feel for their daughters who have to cope with ever more difficult circumstances:

> Times were better when my daughter was growing up. But things are not the same, you have to be careful, children get bad influences from outside their homes from friends or neighbours who set bad examples.

It is in this context of being 'the other', 'the alien', that Muslim women have to reflect a sense of self, a firm identity and a variety of moral values to their children. Often this is done by contrasting 'us' and 'our values' with those of the host society. For example, Mrs A., a young mother who came over from East Africa when she was a child, and is now living with her husband's extended family, explained:

> I teach them about other religions and tell them that ours is the best.

Mrs J., a young widowed daughter-in-law who came from Pakistan with her parents when she was in her teens, also talked of the problems of both working and raising her young children and giving them the 'correct' upbringing:

> I tell them about religion and the bad things in these – Sikhs, Hindus, Jewish, Christianity – and explain what sacrifices our ancestors have done for us and this is the best religion in the world.

But her daughter Y. is also learning about religions at school and has a somewhat different view:

We are taught about other religions in our schools. I like it. It broadens the mind. It changes your attitude. You think that other people have their own ways which is OK; when you thought that only one religion was good and the others were not.

The Media

Immigrant mothers are continuously battling against a barrage of contradictory information and values that pour out of the educative system and the media. In all the houses that I went to, as well as my own, the television is almost always on, and more often than not there is a young person glued to it. It is a curious companion. Mrs T., an affluent matriarch who had come over from Pakistan in the 1960s and who now presides over the extended household, remarked:

After school my children watch TV and read the Holy Quran.

What they acquire from the television is diametrically opposed to what they read in the holy book. What the television imparts is a language that is not spoken at home, even an English language that is different from the one their parents wish them to speak; manners and attitudes that are alien and norms and values that are opposed to those advocated by the family.

None of the women that I talked to identified with the Western media. Most saw it as a window into the lives of their neighbours and an opportunity to see how the others lived. Mrs B. said:

The TV is on all the time. It's always about different people. It's not about us. I think people live more or less like you see on TV. But I wouldn't like my children to live like them.

This view was endorsed by Mrs K. who moved from Pakistan in the late 1970s because of the better professional opportunities offered to her husband here:

English customs and culture is good for them, but not for us. I don't like their freedom. If you go out you see girls and boys on the street together. . . .

They tell everything on TV. No this is not good. This never happens in our country.

You know these children who grow up here, they watch a lot of TV. You know how they talk about sex and it's also taught at school. Then children come and ask parents. In Pakistan this would not happen.

The second and third generations are less worried about the morality advocated by the television soaps. S., a vivacious young granddaughter of a millworker, as well as most of the other young respondents, felt that *Coronation Street, Brookside* and *East Enders*, as well as *Neighbours*, were like 'real' lives: that across the road, or down the next street, there were white people living such lives. But on the whole the young women I talked to did not want to share these lives. They were weary of the rampant 'immorality' and, as S. told me,

They don't seem too happy, do they? So why should I want to be like them?

Nevertheless they liked watching the soaps, even though they found no common grounds with their characters. As S. told me,

I like watching *Dallas* and *Dynasty*, I like the clothes and the glamour and all that. It's like fairyland.

But mothers were weary of the television. Although it was usually on, they rarely watched it. Most said they did not have the time; many did not find it really interesting. But all worried about its impact on their daughters. Some, like Mrs T., sent daughters, but not sons, out of the room 'when TV shows rude films'. Others blamed it it for the fashions it introduced to the household. Mrs B. complained that it made her daughter adopt 'a very funny hairstyle'. Mrs T. said:

My oldest daughter is very fashion conscious. I try and explain to her that this is not right.

Yet her 12-year-old granddaughter is planning to become a fashion designer – perhaps proof that Mrs T. is right to distrust the television.

In the end, as Mrs H. explained, it's a matter of luck and the best that mothers can do is be philosophical about it all:

Children learn a lot of things from television and school. But it all depends on how lucky you are. If you are lucky they are alright. But if you are not lucky they go their own way.

She should know; a grandmother who came from Pakistan in 1958, Mrs H. has been a garment-making homeworker for most of her life, and has successfully combined work and childcare. Her view is echoed by Mrs A.:

God gives you good children, same as brains. The way God gives them some are brainy and some are not.

It is worth noting that it is not only the British media which are at variance with the values of Muslim society. Many of the Pakistani videos and films which are regularly rented and enjoyed by the Muslim families also reflect a never-never world where women are prey to the whims of strong assertive men who extract vengeance on those women who are too proud, tame those who are too unruly. Often impoverished peasant boys end up marrying the rich, arrogant young girls, daughters of their landlords or whatever, who, strictly speaking, are not of a compatible class and whom they would be hard put to keep in the style to which they are accustomed. In all these films the young actress has at least one and often numerous singing and dancing scenes dissolving romantically in the arms of her admirer. Arranged marriages are not advocated and the heroes and heroines are often star-crossed lovers moving mountains to reach each other – hardly a message suited to the demands of Muslim families in West Yorkshire (Zia, 1992).

Given these contradictory images of reality, romance and happiness, it is hard not to understand the dilemma faced by mothers like Mrs B.:

These days it is very difficult to guide children. . . . You have to do your best, to tell the girls to preserve their *izzat* till they get married and after marriage when they go to in-laws' home then they should respect their in-laws and be careful from their brothers-in-law.

Sadly these are not values that are reflected in the media.

Education

There would be no problem and no conflict if the society where the younger women are raised did, as it had done for their mothers, endorse and perpetuate the accepted standards of morality and the mothers' norms and values, developing some, discarding others and replacing a few with new and revised versions. But where the immigrant community lives, the hosts are perceived as fundamentally 'immoral'. Yet the children are sent to 'their' schools, are trained by 'their' teachers and in most cases immersed in 'their' television. Continuously the youngest generation is subject to a barrage of ideas, information and values that mothers have to define as wrong, unacceptable and positively wicked. But they strive and do their best to counter the worst and back the best that the system has to offer. As Mrs B. explained:

Children go to school and see different things and they see different things at home and get very confused. They are having a double life.

They think that what they see outside their homes is the real thing. But we have to tell them about life. We have to do the teaching and the caring and the loving.

Parents strive to give their children, boys and girls, the very best education that they can. Education is seen as a passport to success and children are encouraged to do their best and achieve both good grades and the approval of their teachers.[11] From an early age immigrant children have to learn to cope with double standards about education. At home the school is seen as central, important and beneficial; the youngsters are told to respect the teachers, obey the rules and behave properly. At school they meet racism, discrimination and bullying; yet they are too fond of their parents to report back. They learn to tell them less than the truth at home and to cope the best they can at school. As Saifullah Khan has pointed out,

> It is through the school's lack of contact with community aspirations and systems of support and education, and the lack of recognition of the child's existing social and linguistic skills that children of ethnic minorities assess the relative value placed upon their identity and affiliations. (1982, p. 211)

If they wish to succeed, to gain any degree of approval from their teachers, then they must learn both the texts and the subtexts of the material that they are taught: the history that denies their existence, the geography that places their 'homes' at the periphery,[12] the literature that has no place for their language and their poetry. The host society is claiming its right to integration, the hegemony of an affluent class of white citizens has permeated the education system and those who learn it well manage to move up the grades. As Verity Saifullah Khan explains:

> In England the dominant (sub)culture of the society is reproduced in the schooling of children based on middle-class values and expectations. It is not just individual teachers but, more fundamentally, the organizational and conceptional strategies of the institution, and its relationship with the local working-class cultures, which produces structural disadvantage and personal rejection. (1982, p. 199)

Nevertheless parents expect their children to 'do well at school'. It is not always easy for them to cope. It is remarkable that these children do not end up rejecting both their parents' and the schools' values. Miraculously they survive and forge their own personalities and realities through this confusing moral maze.

I found that younger girls, at primary school, have a somewhat easier time; in part because they are less aware of the discrimination within the curriculum and in part because they are less restricted and mix more freely with the other children. They are allowed to play games and go swimming; some of the middle-class parents also send their primary school daughters to Brownies and similar British youth groups. They are also more likely to allow their daughters to go to friends' houses to play and have them back, although often this is done warily; Mrs B. explained:

> My granddaughter likes to go to her play at her friend's house. But I always tell her not to go inside their houses, because you don't know what kind of people come to their houses.

So even the young carry the awareness of being different, of a threat lurking in the houses they don't know. Of course all children grow up with a sense of themselves, and of the otherness of neighbours, but in the case of Muslim children this is tinged with the experiences of racism, and the distrust that it brings about. Many of these youngsters were aware of racism, but able to cope. They were born in this country, knew the language, were learning the mores and were well aware of their rights; this was particularly true of the middle-class children. Ten-year-old M., born and raised by a middle-class family of Pakistani descent, told me:

> This lass called me a 'nigger' at the swimming baths. So I told her 'I don't know what this means, but I know that it's against the law to call me names and if you are not careful I'll ask my mum to take you to the police station!'

It is less easy for older girls who have to tread on a tightrope of double identities, double values and double standards. Secondary school is a problem both for parents and children. The choices for single-sex girls' schools are limited and costly. Most of those parents who could afford to do so, and some who could hardly afford it, bought private tuition for their children, boys and girls, and did their best to help them through the entrance exams of the few single-sex girls' schools that were available. Now there is also an all-girl Muslim school in Bradford, but of necessity this school too has to charge a fee.

There is of course a tension between the conflicting demands that parents make of their daughters. Sons are expected to excel at school, to gain a degree or professional qualifications whenever possible and to get a job. Daughters, however, are faced with a more complex prospect. Mrs J., talking about her 9-year-old daughter, said:

> I'd like my daughter to become a doctor, because we need a lady doctor.
> I'd allow her to go to a co-ed school, but we need separate medical schools.

At the same time, Mrs J. felt that

> The place of a woman is at home. She should stay at home and look
> after her children and husband, because this is our way and the way
> our religion tells us to be. For educated women this is difficult. But
> this is the proper behaviour.

The girls who go to mixed schools soon learn how to create a distance
between themselves and the 'others' – boys and girls. Even those going to
single-sex school soon realize the difference between them. It is through the
difficult years of adolescence that education, both formal and informal, moral
and intellectual, becomes a major problem. Too young to appreciate the
advantages of 'difference', too old to be blind to rampant racism, too good
to smoke behind the bike sheds or experience drinking a drop of alcohol at
lunch breaks, the young women find it difficult to bridge the identity gap, to
form close friendships with their white classmates. Those who do meet the
united opposition of their friends and family and are sometimes driven to
precipitous decisions.

Two sisters from a strict Pakistani millworking family, who had been
chaperoned to and from school by their father, who wore their head-scarf to
and from school and who were closely watched, 'broke out'. To the amaze-
ment of all, at 16 they cut their hair, left home and moved to a different city
in pursuit of jobs. Their family was shamed and ostracized and they in turn
refused to have any more to do with their daughters. For the past five years
none of their relatives have spoken to them. Still they consider themselves
lucky to have escaped the wrath of the family. Eventually both girls married
white men; they remained outsiders, uncertain of what the norms and values
of their married family were and unsure of what they themselves retained to
offer their children.

I talked to one of them, P., who was pleased to have a job and to be
independent and who said that she liked the insularity of her nuclear household. Her husband's parents disapproved of her and her parents disapproved
of him, there was no one either of them could go to and she felt that this
might well be a blessing. She was not resentful about her childhood and the
family, but she preferred her new lifestyle, even though she felt insecure and
uncertain about it. She told me:

> It wasn't that I didn't love my mum and dad, but I wanted to have
> a job, a life of my own, I wanted to make my own decisions and I
> wanted to be free. Besides I did not want to go back 'home' and was
> worried about having to marry a cousin and having to leave.

It is difficult to grow up in one society, learn its values and still retain a
vision and a will to return to a different world. But most of the Muslim girls
do manage to do just that. They retain a sense of self, of who they are and

where they belong, in opposition to the barrage of racism that they face. For many the revivalism of the the 1980s has been almost literally a 'God send'.

Revivalism and the New Identity

The return to the faith was a gradual development after the 1979 Iranian revolution and as the media in the West slowly and grudgingly came to terms with a new image of Islam. Although what was reflected in the media was not flattering,[13] it denoted power, independence and a sense of importance; the West was even afraid of what the Muslims might do. For many youngsters, caught in the web of conflicting values, demands, ideas and moralities, none of which they found totally convincing, this new vision provided an ideal worth supporting. There was at last a clear indication that Islam and the Muslims were not inferior. On the contrary, they were both righteous and powerful.

In the jungle that is the school play ground it was possible to assert a sense of superiority, and, while I know of no Muslim girl who can come up with the traditional cliché 'my dad is a policeman' to intimidate her classmates, many could say 'I am a Muslim' and bask in the reflected glory of the violent media images of sword-bearing warriors of Islam attacking the Western liberals!

More than that, the ideas of the veil, of separation of space and of womanhood according to Islam began gaining ground. In part this was the result of the better understanding that some young women gained of Islam itself and what it offered to women, in part it was the result of the debates about revivalism that have been echoing through the community.

In the 1980s many a young Muslim woman found that she could *choose* to forge a new Islamic identity, one that conferred dignity on the adoption of some form of veil, and made them part of the great anti-imperialist Islamic movement. The mood was echoed across Europe and gradually the isolation felt in the schools for being the outsiders, both in the classroom and the playground, was replaced by the awareness of belonging to a revitalized, forceful religion that was gaining power and momentum across the world.

The French episode over the refusal to allow two young Muslim women wearing head-scarves access to school, in October 1989, helped to fuel the anger and add to the conviction of young Muslim women in England and elsewhere that the veil was a means of asserting a revolutionary right to their cultural heritage and religious obligations. They could feel themselves to be part of a rebellion that had a political context, and a solidarity with the great mass of Muslims.

The feeling of strength and separation gained momentum during the war against Iraq. The Western powers united to demonstrate beyond doubt what the Muslims had known, that the world order was about the supremacy of the

West at all costs.[14] At the same time they realized that despite it all the Muslim community could be strong, righteous and defiant.

Women in West Yorkshire and the Salman Rushdie Crisis

Much has been written about Khomeini's *fatwa* on Salman Rushdie in March 1989 and its reverberations in West Yorkshire.[15] But there has been little or no attention paid to the implications of the some of the issues that emerged on the lives of women in the region.

Since the *fatwa* and the subsequent unrests and episodes, particularly in Bradford, there has been a tendency amongst the embattled Muslims in the city and the region to claim a unitary identity and postulate a cohesion of views and values that they do not necessarily adhere to in practice. It should be noted in passing that the earlier *fatwa* by Khomeini demanding the death of Saddam Hussein did not meet with a similar acclaim amongst the Muslims. The proclaimed unity is reflected in the public political face of Islam, presented most forcefully by Kalim Sadighi and the Islamic Parliament. But this politicization does little to help the private dilemmas of young women growing up as immigrants in the West. All too often the intended solidarity of Islam, though entered into as political action by the men in the family, is represented, at times none too willingly, by their womenfolk in general and the way they are expected to dress and behave and the kinds of jobs and professions that they are encouraged to choose.

The situation is exacerbated by the severe cutbacks on health and welfare provisions in the region as a whole and in Bradford in particular. Women as major recipients and providers of social services have proved most vulnerable to cuts. Those identified as less than submissive have also suffered not only at the hand of racist managers but also through male Muslim employers who vigilantly monitor the activities of Muslim women working in their organizations. A climate of fear and oppression has been created that extends to the areas of research and scholarly pursuits. Female Muslim social workers have had to behave and write with much circumlocution or say nothing at all to keep their jobs. For women without formal paid employment the situation is worse.

Faced with a contracting labour market, a hostile host community and a forbidding patriarchal kin community, Muslim women resist the ascribed identities of obedience, submission and propriety at their peril. Losing face, or failing to conform to the much stricter demands of modesty imposed by the most conservative elements of the community and endorsed as a sign of solidarity by the rest, involves hardship not only for the individual women, but also for their kin. Those involved with women's centres and women's issues are considered suspect and overtly and covertly controlled. The community has defined itself in peril, many of its members have chosen to break their traditional political links with the left and have reverted to an idealized vision of Islam and its politics in the Middle East. The vision includes munificent Saudi and Iranian governments, who are assumed to be considerably more generous in theory than they are in practice. Faced with constant harassment and real threats from militant white youths it is easy to argue the case for an absolute need for cohesion and united action. But this unity and cohesion often pose severe limitations on women.

Women Grow Up and Ideals Grow Weak

For Muslim women, the experience of subordination and discrimination was, for the 1980s and the early 1990s, altered quite markedly. Despite the recession, the intensification of racism and ever fewer job opportunities; despite the bleak economic outlook for many of the women concerned individually and despite the continuing harassment and open attacks on minorities as a whole and Muslims in particular, the community had a vision, an ideological consciousness of its own righteousness. Even though this was tinged with the reality of defeat of Iraq, defeat of Iran, defeat of Muslims, still the combination of faith and a touch of martyrdom provided an unprecedented form of strength. Muslims everywhere were united as one, and Muslim women belonged to this united group. For many young women that I talked to, abandoning Western hairstyles and donning a scarf was a small price to pay – one that many were more than willing to pay.

Returning to talk to the second and third generation of women in 1992, I find a more sombre mood. There are of course those who have faith, and whose vision of a united Islam is both empowering and positive. They are usually the youngest group, still at school, still with the future to live. But amongst the second generation, women who are now working, many with the social services, the education services, the local councils and what some critics call the 'race relations industry', the mood is less than euphoric. In practice, when it comes to workplace support, to economic and professional alliances, many have found the gender divide between Muslim men and women to be unbridgeable. To succeed they are expected to represent the immaculate face of Islam, which women in public places are not permitted to transgress. But, since the mores of morality, modesty and transgression are so fluid, it is hard for most of them to comply at all times. In particular they are expected to maintain a respectful silence and not to protest on 'women's issues'. Feminism is viewed balefully as a main culprit for the derailment of minority honour; it is hailed as the ultimate weapon of the British middle-class hegemony and its most pernicious one where Muslim women are concerned.

For many women, the conflicts that such views cause are proving destructive, in both the personal and professional domains. It is time that the Muslim community as a whole and its men as a group begin to reconsider the demands made of their women and to move towards a position that allows these women to *choose* the combination of identities that suits them, rather than to be forced to adopt ascribed identities that do not add up to a coherent whole.

Notes

1 I am most grateful for the very helpful comments by the authors in this volume on the earlier draft of this chapter. All mistakes and misrepresentations, however, are entirely my responsibility.
2 Paperneck (1971).
3 I am most grateful to Sheila Allen for pointing out to me long ago that this sociological method was an acceptable choice in certain circumstances; coming from the background of economic studies, I was only too grateful to be freed of the necessity to launch on some form of stratified sampling. Nevertheless the groups interviewed do include a cross-section of classes.
4 This does not mean that politically all Muslim minorities are united; nevertheless efforts for setting up organizations such as the Islamic Parliament in London are rooted in the assertion of this assumed unity.
5 See for example Nasir (1990), amongst many more.
6 For further details see Afshar (1982).
7 For a detailed discussion see Ram (1990).
8 See for example Afshar (1990a).
9 See for example Ali Shariati (n.d.).
10 I am grateful to Mrs Usha Verma for conducting, recording and transcribing most of the interviews used in this article.
11 For further discussion see Afshar (1989); Kallie (1987); Pryce (1979), amongst many more.
12 I think that Hafiz Mirza's paper 'Some Reflections on the European Perimeter', presented at the conference on Islam in a changing world in Bradford in September 1992, where he argues convincingly that at best we should refer to Europe as 'West Asia', should become compulsory reading for all Asian schoolchildren.
13 For a revealing discussion see Yasmin Alibhai-Brown's plenary address at the conference on Islam in a changing Europe in September 1992.
14 For detailed discussions see, for example, Brittain (1991) and Gittings (1991).
15 See, for example, Bowen (1992), amongst many more.

References

AFSHAR, HALEH (1982) 'Khomeini's Teachings and their Implications for Women', in TABARI, AZAR and YEGANEH, NAHID (Eds) *In the Shadow of Islam*, Zed, pp. 79–90.

AFSHAR, HALEH (1989) 'Education: Hopes, Expectations and Achievements of Muslim Women in West Yorkshire', *Gender and Education*, vol. 1, no. 3, pp. 261–72.

AFSHAR, HALEH (1990a) 'The Veil Gives Us Power', *The Independent*, 20 November.

AFSHAR, HALEH (1990b) 'Sex, Marriage and the Muslim', *The Sunday Correspondent*, 18 November.

ALIBHAI-BROWN, YASMIN (1992) Plenary address at the Conference on Islam in a Changing Europe, Bradford University, September.

BRITTAIN, VICTORIA (Ed.) (1991) *The Gulf Between Us, The Gulf War and Beyond*, London, Virago.

BOWEN, D.G. (Ed.) (1992) *The Satanic Verses: Bradford Responds*, Bradford and Ilkley College.

GITTINGS, J. (Ed.) (1991) *Beyond the Gulf War: The Middle East and the New World Order*, London, Catholic Institute for International Relations.

HAERI, SHAHLA (1989) *The Law of Desire: Temporary Marriage in Iran*, London, I.B. Tauris.

HILLI, MUHAQQIQ NAJIM AL-DIN ABU AL-QASIM JA'FAR (1968) *Sharayal-Islam*, Islamic law, translated from Arabic to Persian by YAZDI, A. AHMAD and DANISH PAZHUH, M.T., University of Tehran Press 1347.

KALLIE, JOHN (1987) 'Asian School Leavers and Their Aspirations', unpublished PhD thesis, Oxford Polytechnic.

KANDIYOTI, D. (1991) 'Islam and Patriarchy: A Comparative Perspective', in KEDDIE, N. and BARON, B. (Eds) *Women in Middle Eastern History*, Yale University Press, pp. 23–44.

LUTZ, HELMA (1991) 'Migrant Women of "Islamic background", Images and Self-Images', Occasional paper no. 11, Middle East Research Associates, Amsterdam, December.

MIRZA, HAFIZ (1992) 'Some Reflections on the European Perimeter', paper presented at the Conference on Islam in a Changing World, Bradford, September.

NASIR, JAMAL J. (1990) *The Status of Women under Islamic Law, and under Modern Islamic Legislation*, London, Graham and Trotman.

PAPERNECK, H. (1971) 'Purdah in Pakistan', *Journal of Marriage and Family*, August.

PRYCE, K. (1979) *Endless Pressure*, Harmondsworth, Penguin.

RAM, KALPANA (1990) 'Women's Hair, Coiled and Uncoiled', paper delivered as part of Women Studies Seminars, University of York.

SAIFULLAH KHAN, V. (1982) 'The Role of the Culture of Dominance in Structuring the Experience of Ethnic Minorities', in HUSBAND, C. (Ed.) *'Race' in Britain: Continuity and Change*, Hutchinson, pp. 197–216.

SHARIATI, ALI (n.d.) *Tashiyeh Alavi va Tahsiyeh Safavi*, Alavid and Safavid Shiism, Hoseiynieh Ershad.

ZIA, AFIYA (1992) MA dissertation, University of York.

Section III

Racism and Sexism at Work

Chapter 8

'Race' and 'Culture' in the Gendering of Labour Markets: South Asian Young Muslim Women and the Labour Market[1]

Avtar Brah

Introduction

Feminist critiques of gender-blind approaches to the study of labour markets have demonstrated that gender relations do not simply articulate with labour markets, but, rather, are part of the very fabric of labour markets as they have developed. That is, gender is a constitutive element in the formation of labour markets. Studies show that gender underpins such aspects as the definition of skill, the construction of the division between full-time and part-time work, the differential between men's and women's wages, segregation of the labour market into 'men's jobs' and 'women's jobs', the nature and type of hierarchies sustained by cultures of the workplace, and the experience of paid work in the formation of identities (see Beechey, 1988, for an overview). Much less attention has been paid to issues associated with 'race', culture and ethnicity in the gendering of labour markets (but see, for instance, Westwood, 1984; Westwood and Bhachu, 1988; Phizacklea, 1990; Walby, 1990; Bhavnani, 1991). It is crucial, in my view, to conceptualize the labour market as mediated by 'race', class, gender, ethnicity, age, disability and sexuality.

But how are such links to be theorized? The task is made even more complex when we note a general tendency in the literature to theorize the macro and micro levels of analysis as separate, almost 'independent levels'. My own interest resides in trying to understand how the macro and micro inhere. My aim in this paper is to outline a framework which foregrounds the interconnectedness of the macro and the micro in explicating *racialized gendering* of labour markets. I offer this framework as part of an attempt to theorize more adequately young Muslim women's relationship to the labour market in Britain, but the framework will have a wider applicability. In seeking to understand how the issue of paid work features in women's lives it is important to address what the women themselves say about such matters. But my argument is that analysis of women's narratives must be framed against wider economic, political and cultural processes in non-reductive ways. In the framework that I propose structure, culture, and agency are conceptualized as inextricably linked, mutually inscribing formations.

Discussions on the subject of South Asian young Muslim women's employment tend to be dominated by a concern with statistics which point to lower economic activity rates for this category of women compared with other groups of Asian and non-Asian women in Britain. Much less attention has been paid to the realities behind the statistics. Why are young Muslim women under-represented in the labour market? What is the nature and range of factors that limit young Muslim women's fuller participation in the labour market? What are the continuities and discontinuities in the life histories of those young women not engaged in paid work as compared with those who are in employment? What are the similarities and differences in the labour market experiences of different categories of Muslim women, as, for example, married women compared with unmarried women, or women recently arrived from Pakistan as compared with those who have been brought up in Britain? How are educational institutions and government training schemes perceived and experienced by Muslim women? Such questions have rarely been addressed by previous research but form the core of a recently completed study (Brah and Shaw, 1992). Here I analyze how questions of paid employment are featured in the narratives of the women we interviewed; how these narratives provide instances of the ways in which women's individual biographies intersect with changing socio-economic and political conditions of present-day Britain. That is how the 'discursive' and the 'material' are encountered in the everyday of lived experience.

A Framework for Analysis

But how are such encounters to be theorized? Discussions of Muslim women's participation in the labour market are suffused with 'culturalist' explanations. It is argued that Muslim women are prevented from taking up paid employment by Muslim men. The racialized themes in such discourses are now well documented (cf. Parmar, 1982; Brah and Minhas, 1985; Brah, 1987, 1992; Lutz, 1991). Such explanations fail to take into account a variety of factors that are central to an understanding of the *racialized gendering* of labour markets in contemporary Europe. A second aim of this article is to suggest a framework which, it is hoped, could better explain labour market issues as they relate to Muslim women. Although developed with specific reference to

Muslim women the framework should have a wider applicability. I do not believe that analyses of women's employment necessarily demand a general theory of gender that can subsequently be deployed in analyzing the specific instance of paid work. Rather, I favour analysis of historically specific gendered processes that avoid demarcating 'public' and 'private' as analytically separate domains, but which are able to interrogate the social construction of these spheres as distinct social spaces. Social labour is thus understood as gendered in historically variable forms. Such variation is embedded within histories of slavery, colonialism, imperialism, and the currently evolving global order that is underpinned by 'G Sevenism'.

I would emphasize the importance of studying the articulation between different forms of social differentiations empirically and historically, as contingent relationships with multiple determinations. Within such a framework a study of young Muslim women and the labour market would need to address how the labour of this category of women is

(a)   socially constructed;
(b)   represented in discourse;
(c)   constituted by and is constitutive of labour markets; and
(d)   framed within personal narratives and collective histories.

It will be evident from the above that there is no suggestion of a binary divide within this formulation between culture and structure. A concept of culture that is evoked here does not reference a fixed array of customs, values and traditions. Rather, culture is conceptualized as a process; a nexus of intersecting significations; a terrain on which social meanings are produced, appropriated, disrupted and contested. Cultural specifities remain important but they are construed as fluid modalities, as shifting boundaries that mediate stuctures and relations of power. Hence, structure and culture are enmeshing formations. The one is not privileged over the other. What is of greater significance is how structures – economic, political, ideological – emerge and change over time in and through systems of signification, and how they in turn shape cultural meanings.

In using such a framework in order to understand the relationship of young Muslim women to the labour market it would be necessary to deconstruct the concept of 'Muslim woman' as it has been constituted in British discourse. We would need to consider to what extent and in what ways these social representations construct 'Muslim woman' as a racialized category, and how these stereotypes might serve to structure their position in the labour market. In so doing we would be highlighting processes whereby labour markets become racially gendered. Simultaneously, we would need to examine how women position themselves with respect to such discourses. In other words, what light do women's personal narratives throw on the way in which such discursive significations are implicated in their personal and social identities? Do women occupy oppositional or non-oppositional subject positions within such discourses? Do their own perceptions of themselves reinforce or contest social meaning embodied in such discourses?

The point I wish to stress is that it is crucial to make a distinction between 'Muslim woman' as a category of discourse and Muslim women as concrete historical subjects with varying and diverse social and personal biographies and social orientations.

There are at least seven other dimensions that are central to the framework I am proposing. These are equally critical in explaining the nature, extent and patterns of Muslim women's participation in the labour market. These are:

(1) the history of colonialism and imperialism that framed the patterns of post World War Two migrations into Western Europe;
(2) the timing of migration;
(3) the restructuring of the national and global economies;
(4) the changing structure of the regional and local labour markets;
(5) state policies, especially on immigration control;
(6) racial discrimination in the labour market; and
(7) segmentation of the labour market by gender, class, age and ethnic background.

I now elaborate this framework drawing out its implications for understanding issues of 'race' and ethnicity with respect to gendered labour markets. In the first section I consider how the seven dimensions listed above inscribe the terrain on which young Muslim women's relationship to the labour market is negotiated. I then go on to outline the nature of social imagery through which Muslim women are socially constructed in Britain and the impact of these on how Muslim young women are positioned in relation to the labour market. This is followed by an examination of the narratives of women we interviewed with the aim of understanding how women themselves view issues concerning paid work and how they experience the labour market.

Grounding the Narratives in the Historical Perspective

So how would such a framework inform a study of young Muslim women and the labour market, such as the one we made?

Firstly, its emphasis on a historical perspective draws attention to the colonial background that frames the formation of South Asian communities in Britain. The colonial relationship, as is now well known, was a complex and contested relationship which not only involved economic and political domination but was also underpinned by gendered forms of racism. For instance, as Mies (1986) points out, colonial regimes of accumulation were centrally implicated in class-mediated changes in the organization and structure of families and households in metropolitan societies as much as they were in the colonies. The emergence of the notion of a 'family wage' in Western societies, she argues, owes not a little to the extraction of surplus from the colonies. Certain weaknesses in parts of her argument notwithstanding (cf. Walby, 1990) Mies demonstrates the centrality of gender and racialization processes as constitutive elements in the development of a global economy. Patriarchal systems of the colonizers and the colonized have been interconnected since long before the post World War Two migrations from the subcontinent.

A historical perspective also focuses attention on the conditions under which immigrant labour was deployed in post-war Britain. The economic boom from 1945 until the late 1960s that helped to draw a growing number of white British women into the labour force also led to the recruitment of workers from Britain's former colonies. Both sets of workers were employed predominantly in low-waged sectors of the economy. Segregation of the labour market by gender meant, however, that male and female workers were concentrated in different sectors of the economy.

Asian women experienced the labour market not simply through their gender but also as racialized subjects. Even within a gender-segregated labour market they occupy a distinctive position compared with white women. Overall, a higher proportion of women than men in Britain are engaged in part-time work. This pattern of employment is often taken as a major contributory factor towards women's low pay. However, a higher proportion of Asian women than white women are in full-time employment. Yet their earnings are lower compared with white women. Whereas the overall pattern for women in Britain is that they are concentrated in the service industries, Asian women are more commonly found in the low-paid, semi-skilled and unskilled work in the manufacturing sector, particularly in the clothing and textile industries which have recently been in decline. Evidence also shows that even in those industries where women predominate, Asian women are concentrated in the lowest-level jobs. Unemployment rates among Asian women are much higher compared with white women (Brown, 1984; Beechey, 1986; Bruegel, 1989).

In the early phase of post-war migrations, Pakistani men had arrived predominantly without their female kin. The class position of these men as low-waged workers resident in declining inner areas of British cities was to have a crucial effect on the nature and type of employment on offer to Pakistani women as they began to arrive. Within the framework that I am proposing, the argument that fewer Pakistani women enter the labour market primarily due to 'cultural reasons' would need to be interrogated rather than thrown out of court without consideration. Leaving aside for the moment the question of what these 'cultural reasons' might or might not be, I briefly consider below the impact of timing of migration, economic change, immigration control and racism in structuring job opportunities for Pakistani women.

Timing of Migration and Post-War
Socio-Economic Change

Pakistani women migrated to Britain later than women from India (mostly Sikh and Hindu women). The former arrived mainly in the late 1960s and early 1970s. As a consequence, Asian women who entered the labour market in the early phase of the post-war migrations were mainly Sikh and Hindu women. These Asian women took up paid employment at a time of economic growth and relative stability. Mass production concentrated in factories, centralized forms of work organization and managed national markets were a key feature of this phase. Most Asian women, including the small number of Muslim women in employment at the time, found paid work doing semi-skilled and unskilled jobs generated by this form of production.

There was a fundamental restructuring of the economies of the advanced industrial societies from the 1970s. The global economy became increasingly dominated by the multinationals, with their new international division of labour, and their greater autonomy from the control of nation-states. The decline in the old manufacturing sector, where Asian workers have been concentrated, led to a large-scale job loss. Simultaneously there was growth of jobs in the service sector. This transition entailed a rise of 'flexible specialization' leading to more decentralized forms of labour process and a greater emphasis on contracting-out of functions and services. New types of small businesses proliferated within national economies. There was an increase in low-status, part-time work and a variety of forms of 'homeworking' (Mitter, 1986; Allen and Massey, 1988; Jensen *et al.*, 1988; Hall and Jacques, 1989; Phizacklea, 1990; Nazir, 1991).

It will be evident from the above that Muslim women arriving in Britain in the late 1960s and early 1970s would have encountered the labour market in a period of major economic restructuring and recession. Whilst this resulted in contraction of certain types of jobs, there was an expansion, as we noted, of small businesses, especially those reliant upon the 'putting out' system. The ready availability of paid work that could be carried out from home would have appeared a realistic option to Muslim women with young families to care for. Over a period of time, as homeworking became an established pattern, more and more women were likely to be drawn into it through kinship and friendship networks. In other words, the growing involvement of Muslim women in homeworking during this period could not be explained simply in terms of 'cultural constraints'.

The relationship of Pakistani women to the labour market cannot be fully understood without an appreciation of the significance of region and locality. The South Asian groups are concentrated in specific regions. The highest concentrations of Pakistanis are found in the London and South-East region, with substantial settlements also in Yorkshire, Humberside and the North-West region. Patterns of change in the economy at the regional and local level have been critical in shaping the structures of job opportunities in specific areas of

Birmingham where our study was conducted. During the 1980s major job losses occurred in the West Midlands, especially in manufacturing where there has been a concentration of Asian workers. Between 1981 and 1984 Birmingham city declined twice as fast as the region as a whole (Birmingham City Council Report). The devastating impact of this change on Asian households may be gauged when we note that according to the 1971 Census just over 60 per cent of male workers of Pakistani and Indian origin in the West Midlands worked in the manufacturing industries. Asian women too have been concentrated in manufacturing, principally in textiles and clothing. Whilst there has been a relative increase in employment in the service sector, this is primarily in those enclaves where the Asian workforce is as yet not strongly represented. Moreover, Asian workers have been employed in large numbers in the secondary labour market. Birmingham City Council's 1986 Review of Economic Strategy points to an expansion in secondary sector jobs. The report highlights a steady growth of low-paid employment, and of self-employment at lower levels of the income scale. Such local trends circumscribe the nature and type of employment available to young women.

The impact of immigration legislation on Asian families is now well-documented. Social constructions of Asian marriage and family systems as a 'problem for British Society' have been pivotal in the legitimation of British immigration policy. Images of 'tidal waves' of Asian men scheming to circumvent immigration restrictions through the arranged marriage system were commonly invoked in the justification of immigration control. Whilst the Asian male was defined as a prospective worker posing a threat to the employment prospects of white men, Asian women were defined in immigration law as 'dependants'. The social imagery of Asian women as hapless dependants who would most likely be married off at the earliest possible opportunity has played an important role in shaping the views that teachers or careers officers might hold of young Muslim women's education and employment prospects. Such professionals have an important role to play in encouraging or discouraging young Muslim women from pursuing certain types of education or employment (Cross *et al.*, 1990; Brah, 1987, 1992).

There is now an extensive literature that documents direct and indirect discrimination in the labour market in terms of access to employment, promotion and training (see Daniel, 1968; Brooks and Singh, 1978; Brown, 1984; Drew *et al.*, 1991). Such discriminatory practices are constituted in and through a variety of racialized discourses that construct the racialized Other in stereotypic terms as inherently 'different'. Just as patriarchal discourses may represent women's labour as 'different' and/or inferior, racialized discourses call into question the abilities, aptitudes, cultural attributes, and the general suitability of a group for certain types of jobs and positions within the employment hierarchy. Evidence shows that teachers, careers officers, and employers can all be implicated in practices that have life-long adverse consequences for individuals (Lee and Wrench, 1983; Brah, 1986; Cross *et al.*, 1990; Drew *et al.*, 1991).

Images, Representations and Lived Culture

Where Asian women are concerned racialized discourses articulate with those of gender and class in the social representations of this category of women in Britain. There is a long history of Orientalisms embedded in literature, paintings, drawings, photography, 'scientific' discourse, political debate, state policies and practices and in common sense. The 'oriental female', especially the Muslim woman, came to occupy a position of the quintessential other in this discursive space (see Said, 1978; Kabbani, 1986). Whether she is exoticized, represented as ruthlessly oppressed and in need of liberation, or read as a victim/enigmatic emblem of religious fundamentalism, she is often perceived as the bearer of 'races' and cultures that are constructed as inherently threatening to the presumed superiority of Western civilizations. But we should not necessarily assume a one-to-one direct correspondence either between colonial representations of groups who were 'orientalized' (Arabs, Turks and Indians, for example, have been orientalized in different ways), or between colonial representations and contemporary discourses. There are continuities as well as discontinuities across this discursive field. Hence, social images of Pakistani women in present-day Britain may in part derive from colonial representations of Muslims in colonial India but, essentially, they are an integral component of the field of representation associated with the Pakistani presence in post-war Britain. Such social imagery connects also with discourses of 'the Muslim' in Western Europe. There would seem to be substantial overlap in the available imagery of young Muslim women in different parts of Western Europe (Parmar, 1982; Brah and Minhas, 1985; Lutz, 1991; Brah, 1987, 1992).

But how do such images of Muslim or other Asian women affect their employment trajectories? They do so when, as noted above, these stereotypes are translated in such fields as education, training and employment into practices that have adverse effects on women's position with respect to the labour market. For example, the notion of 'cultural constraints on Muslim women' can come into play and underpin a myriad of practices involving teachers, education and training guidance providers, recruitment and personnel officers, and so on. The general currency of such notions on a wide scale through media consumption means that they have become sedimented into a collective common sense. Their influence, therefore, can be multivariate, conscious and unconscious, and insidious. Their effectiveness, however, depends upon the degree, extent, and manner in which they are activated under given economic, cultural and political circumstances.

To highlight the discourse of 'cultural constraints' as ideology is not to deny the importance of culture. But what do we mean when we speak of cultural constraints? In discussions of Muslim women the 'cultural constraint' that is most frequently invoked is the institution of 'purdah' – a series of norms and practices which limit women's participation in public life. It is important to point out that this social concept and its manifestation varies from one historical period to another, from one country to another, and from one social group to another. Even within the same social group its patterns of observance can differ considerably along class, caste and other dimensions (cf. El Saadawi, 1980; Sharma, 1983). Nor is this institution specific to Muslims in the Asian subcontinent. Versions of 'purdah' are also observable amongst Hindus and Sikhs. Indeed Sharma (1983) suggests that in its broader meaning referring to a complex of ideologies and practices that shape the nature and form of women's participation in public life the concept may have some applicability in all societies. In this sense, the segregation of the labour market by gender in Britain, for instance, could be understood as a set of patriarchal ideologies and practices that are not entirely different from 'purdah'. Nevertheless, it is important to acknowledge the specificity of Islamic forms of 'purdah' but without viewing the institution as fixed and unchanging. What is particularly relevant is the specific ways in which 'purdah' manifests itself differently among different Muslim and other South Asian communities in Britain and the extent and manner in which it articulates with other British patriarchal ideologies and practices. The point I wish to stress is that Asian patriarchal discourses and practices in Britain do not exist outside discursive and material practices that are endogenous to British society; rather they are articulating configurations that are interwoven into the fabric of British social formations.

The lived cultures that young Muslim women inhabit are highly differentiated, varying according to such factors as country of origin, rural/urban background of households prior to migration, regional and linguistic background in the subcontinent, class position in the subcontinent as well as in Britain, and regional location in Britain. British Asian cultures are not simply a carry-over from the subcontinent, but, rather, they are organically rooted in regional and local specificities within Britain. Hence, Asian cultures of London may be distinguished from their counterparts in Birmingham. Similarly, East London Asian cultures have distinctive features as compared with those from West London. Of course, there are commonalities, but what they are would vary depending upon whether one is attempting to establish particularities of religion, or language (e.g. Punjabi cultures have their own specificities compared with Gujarati or Bengali cultures) or class. In the everyday lives of women these are not separate but intersecting and enmeshing realities. They cannot be disaggregated into 'Asian' and 'British' components. They are fusions such that 'Asian British' is a new ensemble created, reproduced or transformed in and through everyday social practices. The structural and cultural dimensions we have referred to in the preceding sections delineate the social terrain in which the everyday is experienced.

In view of the foregoing it is critical, as I pointed out earlier, that we distinguish between 'young Pakistani women', as an object of social discourse, and young Pakistani women as concrete historical subjects. The latter are diverse and heterogeneous people who occupy a multiplicity of subject positions. As is the case with other social agents, their everyday lives are constituted in and through intersecting discourses, material practices and matrices of power embedded in these.

In the next section we examine how our respondents viewed issues of paid employment in relation to themselves as well as to women in general. We examine the ways in which women's responses represent a range of strategies of accommodation, complicity, resistance, struggle, transgression – as they negotiate varying structures of power in their everyday lives. The aim is to explore how wider social structures are encountered in the lived cultures that the women inhabit.

To Work Or Not To Work?

There is growing acknowledgment that paid employment is only one form of work. Although wage labour has existed for many centuries, the almost total dependence of households on a wage is a relatively recent phenomenon. In Europe, where it is now the dominant pattern, it only dates from the nineteenth century.

It is a commonplace to say that women have always worked. In most societies, however, some of the most demanding work that women perform, viz., housework, childcare, and caring work for other members of the family, is rarely regarded as 'work', such that the notion of 'work' is now a synonym for paid work. Whilst many women engaged in paid forms of work, whether inside the house in some form of homeworking or on employers' premises, the ideology of the male breadwinner is still pervasive in advanced industrialized societies (see Leonard and Speakman, 1986; McRae, 1989).

In less industrialized countries the subsistence sector is comparatively large and the demarcation between productive work and work for creation of use values is less clear. Women may be involved in a variety of tasks which simultaneously form part of the market economy and of the production of goods and services directly for consumption within the household (Beneria and Sen, 1981; Young and Walkowitz, 1981; Redclift, 1985). In South Asia women perform a wide range of economic activities both inside and outside the home. In urban Pakistan women may work in a variety of professions such as teaching, medicine and social work. Women may also be found in some of the lowest-status forms of paid work including road and building construction, municipal street sweeping, and domestic service. In the rural areas women are likely to be responsible for the care of domestic animals and processing of food for preservation and storage; they may undertake specialized forms of agricultural work such as transplanting of rice, and take part in general sowing and harvesting of crops; and they may weave, sew and produce handicrafts alongside other domestic and childcare responsibilities (Papaneck, 1971; Nazir, 1991). In other words, Pakistani women who migrated to Britain are likely to have been involved in a variety of economic activities prior to migration. What would be new when they migrated would not be the prospect of 'working' but rather the experience of paid work in an advanced indus- trialized economy.

There is a dearth of research case lore from which to develop a systematic picture of the labour market realities of young Muslim women. Much of the research carried out relates to the migrant generation (Dahya, 1974; Saifullah Khan, 1974; Jeffery, 1976; Anwar, 1979). One exception is a pilot study involv- ing a dozen households where the author interviewed daughters, mothers and grandmothers (Afshar, 1989). In this account we encounter women employed largely as homeworkers, although some women had worked in mills before the birth of their children; or as unpaid workers in a family business; and, in some cases, as 'career women'. Clearly, these women were economically active although few would be included in formal statistics.

In formulating a strategy for our study we decided to interview five categories of women: those who were not seeking paid employment; women engaged in paid work (both those working on employers' premises and home- workers); unemployed women; trainees on government training schemes; and students in courses in further or higher education. This range of women were interviewed because of our belief that in order to fully understand why some Muslim women do not enter the labour market we need to know why groups of others already have done so. Furthermore, it is important to know what perceptions and aspirations are represented amongst those enrolled on courses in education and training.

The most striking aspect of the responses we received was that an over- whelming majority of the women we interviewed considered it was important for women to do paid work. Irrespective of whether or not they were them- selves keen to find employment, this was a consistent echo in the interviews. What is its significance, especially in cases where individual women said that they were not looking for paid work? I would suggest that this response represents a critical commentary on those views that assert the exclusion of women from the labour market as desirable. It interrogates the hegemonic claims of such perspectives. Women's earnings were considered by our re- spondents as an indispensable contribution to the income of households. Equally, paid work was valued for offering women a measure of independence, and providing them with a sense of confidence. When performed outside the home paid work was seen as providing much needed networks of contacts beyond those of family and kinship. Employment outside the home was seen as an antidote to the boredom and isolation of staying at home. Workplace friendships were experienced as a source of fun. From our interviews it was evident that sharing a joke, teasing, engaging in casual banter, sharing out items of lunch brought from home, gossiping, offering a sympathetic ear to workmates experiencing problems, sharing 'a moan' against employers, etc., were some of the elements that went into the making of workplace cultures. Contradictions of gender, ethnicity, racism, class, generation, seemed to be played out in all their complexity. Importance attached by women to workplace cultures is also attested by ethnographic studies of women in the workplace (Pollert, 1981; Westwood, 1984).

If the great majority of women emphasized that it was important for women to undertake paid work why were some of them not seeking employment? All the women in this category – both married and single – cited housework and other caring responsibilities as taking up most of their time. The single women often had to share responsibility for looking after their younger brothers and sisters, or, in some cases, their nephews and nieces. In instances where a mother suffered ill health, the single women had to assume the overall responsibility for the household. There was no doubt that these women perceived housework and other forms of caring work such as childcare, care of elderly parents-in-law or that of other members of the extended family, as 'work'.

How can I look for other work, I can't even finish my housework. I have plenty of work to do: wash, iron, make dinner and all that. My mum can't do it because of poor health, so I have to do the housework. (18-year-old single woman)

Housework takes up all my time. There are eight of us at home. Cooking, cleaning the house, washing clothes, ironing – it never finishes. (20-year-old single woman)

I have four children, a girl and three boys. . . . I have my hands full. Besides, if I did work I would have to place the children in a nursery. That costs more than the wage I would earn. (married young woman)

Whilst these women are not alone in finding domestic responsibilities onerous, there are two factors that have a particular bearing on this group. Firstly, these women often had responsibility for larger-than-average households, which sometimes included members of the extended family. Secondly, domestic appliances such as washing machines or dishwashers that might relieve the pressures of housework were not a common feature of many households, especially those facing difficult material circumstances in a period of high unemployment. A similar finding is reported by Shaw (1988). It is worth bearing in mind that Pakistani households in Birmingham have been among the hardest hit by job losses in the area. We came across families where several members of the household were unemployed. Of course, low income amongst Pakistani families derives also from the concentration of Pakistanis in low-paid jobs.

The family background prior to migration of women who were not seeking paid work did not differ in any significant way from that of women in employment or those who were unemployed. The families of the majority of women in all three categories originate from rural parts of Pakistan. Hence, rural origin by itself cannot be taken as a sufficient indicator of whether or not young Pakistani women were in the labour market. Nor did marital status emerge as a particularly important determinant of women's propensity to seek paid work. Although single women were more likely to be economically active, they were also strongly represented amongst those not seeking work.

One factor, that did seem to be significant with respect to our respondents' participation in the labour market was their length of stay in Britain. We found that the great majority of women who were active in the labour market were born here or arrived here as children. In contrast, most of the women who were not seeking employment came to Britain as teenagers and, as a consequence, their experience of schooling in Britain was limited. In Pakistan they had attended mainly village schools. In Britain the majority had left school without achieving any formal qualifications, and some experienced difficulty in using English for purposes of communication. Such women often perceived their lack of formal qualifications and their limited facility in the English language as a barrier to 'good jobs'.

> Sitting at home you get bored. But finding jobs is not easy. I have to learn English first.

> At the moment I don't know. When I have learnt English and other things I'll see whether I want to work or not. English is a big problem for me.

These women were not unaware of jobs in the secondary sector, especially in the clothing industry in Birmingham where employers asked no questions about knowledge of English or other types of formal qualifications. But the young women categorized them as 'bad jobs' with low rates of pay and poor working conditions. Such jobs held little attraction for the women since these would merely impose an extra burden on existing demands on their time from other domestic responsibilities, without any of the advantages of a well-paid job with good working conditions.

We noted earlier that women's position in the labour market is defined not simply by the structure of the labour market or the needs of the economy but also by patriarchal ideologies which define women's position in society. Social norms about 'women's work' and 'men's work' underpin the unequal division of labour in the household and the occupational segregation of the labour market by gender, and underlie processes whereby a substantial number of women may never enter the labour market. Patriarchal ideologies have a bearing on all women in Britain but they may take specific forms in relation to young Muslim women. Notions of 'purdah', as has already been pointed out, vary enormously among Muslim groups. But where families do wish to observe such norms the prospect of women going out to perform paid work causes deep concern because it is thought to signal the inability of men to provide for the economic maintenance of the household. The generalized ideology of male as breadwinner, common in Britain and other Western countries, emerges in this particular system of signification as 'family honour'. The prospect of young women working away from home unchaperoned would be seen to provide fertile ground for malicious gossip that would threaten a single woman's position of respectability.

Contrary to the stereotype, however, only about a quarter of our respondents gave their families' opposition to women holding jobs away from the home on the grounds of '*izzat*' and 'purdah' as the major reason why they were not doing paid work. But when opposition occurred constraints could be quite stringent:

> My parents want me to stay at home. . . . The relatives are the same as well. They say 'she shouldn't go out'. . . . I don't even sign on. I think they wouldn't mind me doing homeworking. . . . If I was at home they could keep an eye on me. If I went to a factory they might think I will go somewhere else with a friend, or I might find a boyfriend.

> My parents didn't let me out of the house. Straight home from school, do the housework and stay in. Didn't see my friends. My Mum is stricter than my Dad. Dad used to say 'let them go out', but she wouldn't. She said people would talk.

Patriarchal norms and practices cannot, however, be regarded totally as 'external' constraints. Different women may position themselves differently within patriarchal discourses. How did those young women who were not looking for employment locate themselves in relation to cultural practices that serve to exclude women from the labour market? In some cases the young women echoed the gender-specific injunctions that underpin the concept of '*izzat*'.

> When women work outside the home it brings '*Be Izzti*' [dishonour] on the family. I do not think women should work. I would not want a daughter of mine to work! (Translated)

Other women opposed the view which holds that women should not work outside the home. But their responses to the personal circumstances that had led to their own exclusion from the labour market differed considerably. Currently unable to take up paid work due to the opposition of her parents, one young woman lived in hope that her future husband would be more liberal on the subject. A second young woman whose parents had not considered it appropriate for unmarried women to work outside the home, and who was married soon after leaving school, found that her husband too was not in favour of her finding a job. Feeling isolated and bored at home she feels quite disenchanted with this aspect of her life. But she is determined to ensure that her daughter gets similar opportunities to her son. Her own life might have been constrained by cultural norm of male as breadwinner but she is keen to negotiate a different future for her daughter. A third woman who was a 24-year-old young mother with three children could not take up employment because of childcare responsibilities but she was planning to train as a nursery nurse when her children were older. Her husband and in-laws were supportive of her job aspirations. It is evident that young Pakistani women who are outside the labour market constitute a diverse and differentiated category of individuals.

Dilemmas of Paid Work

Muslim women may be under-represented in those forms of paid work which are accessible to statistical collation. But they are far from absent in the labour market. Evidence suggests, as we noted earlier, that a substantial proportion of these women may be engaged in homeworking. Furthermore, Muslim women are also employed in a range of manual, office and clerical, as well as professional jobs in Britain. This range was reflected amongst our employed respondents with three working in a clothing factory; one was self-employed as a graphic designer; one was a primary school teacher; another worked for the local authority in a middle-range advisory post; three worked in the voluntary sector, as community workers or advice workers; and two worked from home as homeworkers. Another twelve women were unemployed.

A common characteristic of women who were in employment or those who were unemployed was their determination to find jobs. They placed great emphasis on the need for women to be economically active:

I think men and women should have equal rights. If men work why can't women. Women are not just there to do the housework.

I strongly disagree with those who think that women should not work outside the home. Well, why should they stay at home? Why can't men stay at home?

I think that both men and women should work. You can't live on one person's wages. . . . It is important to me not to be dependent on anyone – my Mum or husband. I am ambitious for myself.

A substantial proportion of our respondents belonged to families who were fairly flexible about women holding jobs. In some cases parents had been positively supportive of the education and career ambitions of their daughters:

When I decided to look for jobs my parents were not overjoyed. But they didn't stop me either.

My parents left the choice to me: you can stay at home or go to work just as long as you don't give me a bad name and people can't point the finger.

My parents were very encouraging. They said, 'do what you want to do'.

Where families were initially reluctant the women used a variety of strategies of persuasion to obtain consent, often recruiting the support of sympathetic relatives or family friends to help negotiate a desired outcome. Academic and professional jobs are especially highly regarded amongst Asian groups. Even those families who might at first disapprove of a daughter pursuing higher education/professional qualifications for fear that the young woman may become 'wayward' as one respondent put it, feel quite proud once she has achieved such qualifications.

Economic necessity emerged as one of the single most important reasons why women found employment outside the home:

At first I didn't work because my parents didn't want me to. Dad is unemployed now. It is hard. I am looking for work now.

Well it is hard because my Mom doesn't really want me to have a job. But we have been forced to because we've got no money. . . . My parents want me to sew at home [homeworking]. Loads of girls my age [17] do it around here. But I don't want to.

When my father retired of ill health we actually had to support ourselves. . . . There's no way my sisters could have got married right – the dowry, the jewellery and hiring the hall, feeding the guests – all that – without previous employment.

The effects of immigration legislation were also cited as influencing women's decision to participate in the labour market. Our respondents argued that the law discriminates against Asians, and the young women are particularly caught up in this through the 'primary purpose' clause which places the onus on an applicant from the Asian subcontinent married to a British-born Asian woman to provide the burden of proof that the marriage was not contracted primarily for the purpose of immigration to Britain. The immigration rules also stipulate that a woman (or a man) wishing to bring their spouse over to live in Britain must be able to support them without recourse to public funds. Families are often divided across continents due to these laws, and the women who wish to sponsor a spouse must find employment in order to provide proof of being able to support a spouse without recourse to public funds (see Sondhi, 1987).

Whatever the reasons given for being in the labour market, and irrespective of the level of social importance attached to women's employment by individual women, paid work was not always experienced as an unequivocal advantage. Managing the 'double shift' of domestic and paid work was likely to be exhausting. For many women involved in combining these two types of work, the day could start as early as 5.00 or 6.00 a.m. In the evening their domestic chores or other activities such as tasks related to homeworking may not be completed until 10.00 or 11.00 p.m. (see case studies cited in the Report).[2]

Our interviews with homeworkers support the evidence from other studies that points to low wages, insecurity of employment, boredom and isolation, unbearable pressures resulting from sudden deadlines imposed at short notice by suppliers, and overall lack of employment protection, as characteristic features of homeworking (see Bisset and Huws, 1984; Allen and Wolkowitz, 1987). This should not be taken to imply, however, that women working from employers' premises considered themselves as being better off. Indeed several women working outside the home in low-waged, non-unionized sectors of the economy complained bitterly about conditions of work. Any attempts at unionization of the workforce, they said, could result in dismissal. Fear of 'the sack' was likely to act as a deterrant against collective action. As one woman put it, 'They treat you like animals' but everyone feared 'the sack because you can't get a job that fast'. Whether associated with homeworking or with work carried out from employers' premises, poor working conditions were deplored across the board. Women condemned such conditions even though they might have no option themselves but to accept such employment through lack of choice.

Overall, homeworking was regarded by the women as the least favoured form of paid work. They described it as sheer drudgery and exploitation. They saw it as reinforcing social isolation and leading to loneliness, and in some cases to acute forms of depression. Correspondingly, low-skilled forms of 'factory work' or non-manual work were also met with little enthusiasm, although they were generally preferred over homeworking. Women wanted 'good jobs' 'with decent pay' and a positive working environment. Yet they possessed a fairly realistic assessment of the limited range of jobs available to the majority of Asian women. Living in working-class areas of decaying urban centres women were sensitive to the structures of the local labour market. They spoke of how homeworking, certain types of factory work, or, at best, low-skilled low-paid non-manual work in the service sector had become the norm for Asian girls in the minds of local employers, teachers, education and guidance advisors, as well as amongst sections of the Asian communities. There is not the space here to discuss our respondents' experiences of education, the government training schemes, and the education and training guidance services. Suffice it to say that it was clear that low expectations and stereotyped perceptions of Asian girls, their aspirations, abilities and cultures on the part of educational professionals were seen by the women as a major obstacle to Asian girls' success in the labour market. Also cited as a major obstacle to success was racism and discrimination in the labour market.

Racism is a problem. It is easier for white people to get jobs. If a white person advertised a job he would probably want a white person to do it.

It is difficult for us. They give the white people jobs first and then us last.

There are some white people who do not like Asian people. When they see them on the streets they shout abuse and swear words. It makes me really angry. Some employers don't like to give jobs to Asians.

Q: Do you think people can get jobs if they try hard enough?
A: Yes, of course – of course there's loads of jobs out there, providing you are white, you've got loads of jobs to go to . . .
Q: Why do you say that?
A: Because the employers are prejudiced – definitely.

Conclusion

It can be seen that women's personal narratives show them to be positioned differentially within and across a variety of discourses. Whilst a majority of the women endorse the view that women should have the right to undertake paid forms of work outside the home, and in so doing challenge patriarchal notions of males as breadwinners, other women reinforce patriarchal values. There is no one-to-one correspondence between what they believe and the reality of whether or not they are actually engaged in paid work, the latter being mediated by a host of other factors such as the nature and extent of their caring responsibilities, the financial circumstances of the household, the structure of opportunities available in the local market, encouraging/discouraging attitudes on the part of their 'significant others' such as parents, in-laws and spouses, and processes of racial discrimination as they operate in relation to labour markets. Yet their beliefs, ideals and social orientations are not irrelevant. They provide the psychic and social grid from which the minutiae of everyday life are negotiated. For instance, those women who placed a strong emphasis on the importance of women doing paid work were likely to be persistent in their pursuit of strategies that improved their own or other women's position in the labour market even if such a goal was to be deferred for a generation and achieved through daughters, or partially gained by supporting friends or female relatives. In the case of women who already held jobs, encounters with paid forms of work embodied all the contradictions of gender, class and racism as the women sought to balance the 'double shift' of combining domestic responsibilities with paid work, as they came face to face with simultaneously racialized and gendered forms of class exploitation either as homeworkers or in low-waged occupations on employers' premises, or when they came across racism in professional jobs. In other words, the micro world of individual narratives constantly references and foregrounds the macro canvass of economic, political and cultural change. This would seem to highlight the analytical purchase of the framework I have proposed.

Overall, we found that the young women's relationship to the labour market was structured by a multiplicity of ideological, cultural and structural factors, such as the impact of the global and the national economy on the local labour markets; ideologies about women's position in relation to caring responsibilities and paid work; women's own social and political perspectives on such issues, that is, how they might 'feel' as well as 'think' about them; the role of education in the social construction of gendered job aspirations; and racism. In other words, structure, culture, and agency; the social and the psychic are all implicated. They are all integral to the framework of analysis I have outlined.

Notes

1   This paper was originally published in *New Community*, vol. 19, no. 3, April 1993, pp. 441–58.
2   This study focuses upon young women of predominantly Pakistani background living in Birmingham. It is a qualitative study, carried out during 1988/9, which involved fifty-five in-depth interviews with individuals and group discussions with fifty women in the age range 16–24. The women had family origins in the Mirpur district of Azad Kashmir and Punjab. Most of the families came to Britain from rural parts of the subcontinent, but about a sixth of them had urban backgrounds prior to migration. The young women's parents worked mainly in manual occupations (Brah and Shaw, 1992).
The research was funded and published by the Department of Employment. The Research Paper is available from: Research Management Branch, Employment Department, Room W441, Moorfoot, Sheffield S1 4PQ.

References

AFSHAR, H. (1989) 'Gender Roles and the "Moral Economy of Kin" among Pakistani Women in West Yorkshire', *New Community*, vol. 15, no. 2.

Avtar Brah

ALLEN, J. and MASSEY, D. (1988) *The Economy in Question*, London, Sage.
ALLEN, S. and WOLKOWITZ, C. (1987) *Homeworking: Myths and Realities*, Basingstoke, Macmillan Education.
ANWAR, M. (1979) *The Myth of Return*, London, Heinemann Educational.
BEECHEY, V. (1986) 'Women's Employment in Contemporary Britain', in BEECHEY, V. and WHITELEGG, E. *Women in Britain Today*, Milton Keynes, Open University Press.
BEECHEY, V. (1988) 'Rethinking the Definition of Work: Gender and Work', in JENSON, J., HAGEN, E. and REDDY, C. (Eds) *Feminization of the Labour Force*, Cambridge, Polity.
BENERIA, L. and SEN, G. (1981) 'Accumulation, Reproduction and Women's Role in Economic Development: Boserup Revisited', *Signs*, 7, 2.
BHAVNANI, K-K. (1991) *Talking Politics*, Cambridge, Cambridge University Press.
BISSET, L. and HUWS, U. (1984) 'Sweated Labour: Homeworking in Britain Today', Pamphlet No. 33, London Low Pay Unit.
BRAH, A. (1986) 'Unemployment and Racism: Asian Youth on the Dole', in ALLEN, S., WATON, A., PURCELL, K. and WOOD, S. (Eds) *The Experience of Unemployment*, British Sociological Association with Macmillan Press.
BRAH, A. (1987) 'Women of South Asian Origin in Britain: Issues and Concerns' *South Asia Research*, vol. 7, no. 1, pp. 39–54 (reprinted in BRAHAM, P., RATTANSI A. and SKELLINGTON, R. (Eds) (1992) *Racism and Antiracism*, London, Sage).
BRAH, A. (1992) 'Difference, Diversity and Differentiation', in DONALD, J. and RATTANSI, A. (Eds) *Race, Culture and Difference*, London, Sage.
BRAH, A. and MINHAS, R. (1985) 'Structural Racism or Cultural Conflict: Asian Girls in British Schools', in WEINER, G. (Ed.) *Just A Bunch of Girls*, Milton Keynes, Open University Press.
BRAH, A. and SHAW, S. (1992) *Working Choices: South Asian Young Muslim Women and the Labour Market*, London: Department of Employment, Research Paper no. 91.
BROOKS, D. and SINGH, K. (1978) *Aspirations versus Opportunities: Asian and White School Leavers in the Midlands*, London, Commission for Racial Equality.
BROWN, C. (1984) *Black and White Britain*, London, Policy Studies Institute.
BRUEGEL, I. (1989) 'Sex and Race in the Labour Market', *Feminist Review*, no. 32, Summer.
CROSS, M., WRENCH, J. and BARNETT, S. (1990) *Ethnic Minorities and the Careers Service: Investigation into Processess of Assessment and Placement*, London, Department of Employment, Research Paper no. 73.
DAHYA, B. (1974) 'The Nature of Pakistani Ethnicity in Industrial Cities in Britain', in COHEN, A. (Ed.) *Urban Ethnicity* (A.S.A. Monograph 12), London, Tavistock Publications.
DANIEL, W.W. (1968) *Racial Discrimination in England*, Harmondsworth, Penguin.
DREW, D., GRAY, J. and SIME, N. (1991) *Against the Odds: The Educational and Labour Market Experiences of Black Young People*, Sheffield, TEED Youth Cohort Series.
EL SAADAWI, N. (1980) *The Hidden Face of Eve*, London, Zed Press.
HALL, S. and JACQUES, M. (1989) *New Times*, London, Lawrence and Wishart.

JEFFERY, P. (1976) *Migrants and Refugees*, Cambridge, Cambridge University Press.

JENSEN, J., HAGEN, E. and REDDY, C. (Eds) (1988) *Feminization of the Labour Force*, Cambridge, Polity.

KABBANI, R. (1986) *Europe's Myths of Orient*, Basingstoke, Macmillan.

LEE, G. and WRENCH, J. (1983) *Skill Seekers*, Leicester, National Youth Bureau.

LEONARD, D. and SPEAKMAN, A. (1986) 'Women in the Family: Companions or Caretakers?', in BEECHEY, V. and WHITELEGG, E. *Women in Britain Today*, Milton Keynes, Open University Press.

LUTZ, H. (1991) '*Migrant Women of "Islamic Background": Images and Self-Images*', Amsterdam, Middle East Research Associates, Occasional Paper no. 11.

McRAE, S. (1989) *Flexible Working Time and Family Life*, London, Policy Studies Institute.

MIES, M. (1986) *Patriarchy and Accumulation on a World Scale*, London, Zed.

MITTER, S. (1986) *Common Fate, Common Bond: Women in the Global Economy*, London, Pluto.

NAZIR, P. (1991) *Local Development in the Global Economy: The Case of Pakistan*, Aldershot, Avebury.

PAPANECK, H. (1971) 'Purdah in Pakistan', *Journal of Marriage and Family*, August.

PARMAR, P. (1982) 'Gender, Race and Class: Asian Women in Resistance', in CENTRE FOR CONTEMPORARY CULTURAL STUDIES *The Empire Strikes Back*, London, Hutchinson.

PHIZACKLEA, A. (1990) *Unpacking the Fashion Industry*, London, Routledge.

POLLERT, A. (1981) *Girls, Wives, Factory Lives*, London, Macmillan.

REDCLIFT, N. (1985) 'The Contested Domain: Gender, Accumulation and the Labour Process' in REDCLIFT, N. and MINGION, E. (Eds) *Beyond Unemployment*, Basil Blackwell.

SAID, E. (1978) *Orientalism*, New York, Pantheon Books/London, Routledge and Kegan Paul.

SAIFULLAH KHAN, V. (1974) *Pakistani Villagers in a British City*, Unpublished PhD thesis, University of Bradford.

SHARMA, U. (1983) *Women, Work and Property in North-West India*, London, Tavistock Publications.

SHAW, A. (1988) *A Pakistani Community in Britain*, Basil Blackwell.

SONDHI, R. (1987) *Divided Families*, London, Runnymede Trust.

WALBY, S. (1990) *Theorizing Patriarchy*, Oxford, Blackwell.

WESTWOOD, S. (1984) *All Day, Every Day*, London, Pluto.

WESTWOOD, S. and BHACHU, P. (Eds) (1988) *Enterprising Women: Ethnicity, Economy and Gender Relations*, London, Routledge.

YOUNG, K. and WALKOWITZ, C. (Ed.) (1981) *Of Marriage and the Market: Women's Subordination in International Perspective*, London, CSE Books.

Chapter 9

A Single or Segregated Market?
Gendered and Racialized Divisions

Annie Phizacklea

Introduction

Originally theories of occupational segregation were developed to explain why both women and black people generally were crowded into certain sectors of the labour market and not others. Not surprisingly these blanket theories were not very satisfactory because the processes of gendering and racialization may have similar outcomes but they have their own histories and their own dynamics. So the debates diverged leaving the question of black and ethnic minority women outside the theoretical boundaries.

Certainly in Britain and the US there is a lively academic and political debate about the continued gendering of jobs and the real cost of that to women in their wage packets. My long-term concern has been to make those debates sensitive to the impact of racialization and suggest how such a sensitivity can help us bring together both the demand and supply side factors in understanding occupational segregation. Towards that end I began, in the early 1980s, to look at national employment statistics, stratified by ethnic/ nationality grouping, in Britain, France and what was then West Germany and also to carry out micro-level research which aimed to paint a fuller picture than aggregate data can provide (see, for example, Phizacklea, 1983, 1987, 1988, 1990). Those early researches led me to the conclusion that the subordinate position of minority women within some Western European labour markets introduced another layer of occupational segregation within the narrow band of jobs into which women were already crowded (Phizacklea, 1983). In 1992 I re-examined the same national data sets and, as we shall see later in this chapter, in Britain and France, at least, there appeared to have been some bridging of the gap between majority and ethnic minority women's employment levels. Nevertheless, I go on to suggest a number of factors which may make this seeming improvement illusory. In the final section I use the case of home-based work in Coventry to illustrate how these factors operate to produce and reproduce racialized disadvantage and occupational segregation.

The political face of Europe has changed dramatically over the last decade, not only with the demise of the so-called 'communist bloc' but also with efforts to forge greater European Community integration. I want to start by contextualizing the more specific questions around occupational segregation, within a critical evaluation of the supposed benefits of the Single European Market for those 15 million or so long-term ethnic minority residents of Europe who over the last decade have been the front-line victims of rising unemployment and the rising tide of racial violence and murder.

Equal Opportunities in the Single Market?

The freedom of movement provision of the Single European market does, in theory, allow any citizen of an EC country to travel to and settle in any other member country for the purpose of taking employment, establishing oneself in self-employment, running a business or providing or receiving a service. In addition, the husband or wife and children if under 21 of that worker, even if they are not EC citizens, will have the right to settle in the new country. Nevertheless, many of Europe's 15 million long-term ethnic minority group members regard these so called 'benefits' with some scepticism. Why? There are at least four reasons: Firstly, despite clear evidence of an increase in overt racism, often expressed through violence and murder throughout the Community, there is no collective political will to address the issue of real legal protection for not only black and ethnic minority citizens but also the millions of long-term settlers without such citizenship.

The horrifying racist murders in Rostock, Mölln and Solingen in Germany have rightly been given headline status (see for example *Observer*, 6 June 1993) yet equally horrifying racist attacks and murders have often gone unreported in Britain and France. Just as right-wing politicians and the National Front in Britain successfully shifted the terms of debate to the right in the 1970s (Miles and Phizacklea, 1984) so Jean-Marie Le Pen's Front National has done the same in France in the 1980s (Lloyd and Waters, 1991). The Pasqua law passed in 1986 tightened immigration controls and claimed to be a measure against 'clandestine immigration and imported delinquency'. Even the rhetoric of Le Pen has come to pervade political discourse around immigration and settlement in France, particularly since the victory of the right in the French national elections in March 1993. Within weeks of its election, the new government 'reassured' the nation that it would 'crack down' on illegal immigrants in France. In Germany the right-wing Republican Party got only 1 per cent of the vote in Baden-Württemberg (Germany's richest state) in 1988. In 1993 it captured 11 per cent (*Observer*, 6 June 1993).

Throughout the European community, member states have been quick to agree on cooperation between national police authorities and interior ministries on asylum seekers and immigration generally. The stereotype of the economic migrant posing as a political refugee was articulated at a European summit meeting in Luxembourg by John Major, who warned against the 'rising tide' of immigrants and asylum seekers washing into Europe:'We must not be wide open to all-comers just because Rome, Paris and London are more attractive than Bombay or Algiers' (*Independent*, 29 June 1991). What is completely missing from this negative stance and corresponding agenda is a commitment on how best to tackle racial discrimination and racial violence on a community-wide basis.

The second factor as to why there is scepticism about the Single European Market relates to who gets the jobs within Europe. Citizens of what are referred to as 'third countries' might as well be called third-class workers in the European hierarchy. Between 1986 and 1989 a quarter of a million 'British subjects' (people whose 'British' passports had become devalued) had to pay to become British citizens. But many other British residents, for instance many born in India, have understandably not chosen to do so because their home country does not allow dual citizenship. Even though these same people may have lived in Britain all their lives, they not only will have great difficulty in working elsewhere in Europe, they will have to continue to apply for a visa even to cross the Channel. Germany may have one of the largest 'immigrant' populations in Europe but this needs to be seen within the context of its highly restrictive nationality law (Germans-by-blood) whereby the German-born children of 'immigrants' are denied citizenship, a system which institutionalizes third-class European status in nationality law.

The third reason for scepticism is linked to the above. Many black and ethnic minority people in Europe fear that those who are regarded as 'racially' similar Eastern Europeans will be given preferential treatment in the competition for jobs and housing. East-West migrations are substantial. For instance, in just one year, 1989, a quarter of a million Poles and 98,000 Soviets migrated to Germany, and of the 121,000 people seeking asylum in Germany that year, 40 per cent were Eastern European (SOPEMI, 1990). This is even before we consider the impact that reunification and subsequent recession and unemployment has had on the position of the five million long-term ethnic minority residents, Turks constituting the largest group.

Finally, evidence is presented below which shows that labour markets have remained segregated by gender and racialization and it could be argued that the Single Market is likely to further polarize this. For instance, in the case of Britain, according to longitudinal data collected by the Department of Employment, there has been a significant increase in the occupational category defined as corporate managers and administrators over the last decade. The growth in this category has been most marked amongst women and paralleled by increased earnings (Elias and Gregory, 1992). Nevertheless when we break these figures down by ethnicity we find that minority women are over-represented in areas of occupational decline and under-represented in the growth areas. While there are plenty of well qualified ethnic minority women moving into the growth areas their numbers are still small compared to those seemingly locked into the declining, low-pay, low-skill sectors of manufacturing and the manual sectors of women's work, for instance contract cleaning. Mobility is, of course, another option for the better qualified but black and ethnic minority EC national job applicants will have even less redress elsewhere in Europe against racial discrimination than they currently do under the inadequate British race relations legislation.

For those less well qualified evidence collected on a Europe-wide basis suggests that those with limited or no skills are becoming less mobile, concentrating on the local labour market and the informal economy (Eurostat, 1989).

There is a real danger here that the increased racial polarization that we have witnessed occurring in the United States during the 1980s could be happening in Britain and perhaps more widely in Europe too. While the 1980s saw a big increase in women's representation amongst the managerial and professional ranks in the US, it was also a decade of savage cuts in welfare programmes. It has been argued that this has led to a further racialized polarization amongst women, with white women at the top and black women disproportionately clustered at the bottom of the economic scale (Power, 1988, p. 145).

Ten years ago I argued that the subordinate position of minority women within Western European labour markets introduced another layer of occupational segregation within the narrow band of jobs into which women generally have been crowded. The next section examines the same data sets ten years on and considers whether there has been any bridging of the employment gap over the last decade.

Minority Women in Britain, Germany and France Ten Years On

Before considering any figures on occupational segregation and the representation of majority and minority women within the labour force, it is necessary to emphasize some of the many problems which beset such a comparative exercise. Unlike Britain, other European countries do not use the category 'ethnic minority' statistically. Rather, aggregate data refers to 'foreigners'. Thus the category 'foreigner' does not include persons who belong to ethnic minorities but who hold the citizenship of the member country. This is further complicated by the fact that data for Britain is now presented in two ways. The categories 'white' and 'ethnic minority group' are retained for domestic consumption (for instance Labour Force Surveys), but for the purposes of European-wide statistics anyone who does not possess British citizenship becomes classified as a 'foreigner', in line with the other member states (see SOPEMI, 1990, p. 91). Despite these and many more problems of comparability, one can discern certain trends in the three countries over the last decade.

For Britain, Labour Force Surveys indicate that in 1987–8 ethnic minorities constituted 4.7 per cent of the population of working age. A glance at aggregate data suggests that the gap in job levels between black and white women is much less than between black and white men and in the last ten years that gap has been further bridged. But this interpretation of the trends needs to be qualified in the following ways: during recessionary periods black women are far more likely to become unemployed than white women and even in a period, such as 1987–8, which was not regarded as an employment 'trough', 16 per cent of black women were unemployed compared to 9 per cent of white women (for men the figures were 17 per cent and 10 per cent respectively). The marked differences in unemployment levels led analysts at the Policy Studies Institute to argue, as early as 1982, that the bridging of the gap is largely illusory, much of the change being due to the fact that black women in the poorest jobs have become unemployed and those in the better jobs have become a larger proportion of all those in employment (Brown, 1984, p. 179).

Another factor, which is important in comparing black and white women's job levels, is that black women are much more likely to work full-time (40 per cent compared to 27 per cent of white women). As we shall see in the home-based work case study this can be explained with reference to household finances and the greater dependency that the black households have on the mother's earnings. The 1982 PSI report provides evidence to show that in all types of household the earned income per person is lower among Caribbeans than among whites and is particularly low in Asian households (Brown, 1984, p. 231). In addition it has been argued that, while full-time work lifts many white women out of low-pay ghettos, this is far less true for black women (GLC, 1986, p. 114).

The final point that needs to be made is that large categories, such as 'professional and managerial', hide more than they reveal. For instance, if we unpack this category we find that close to half the Caribbean women within it are working in the Health Service in nursing grades, while white women are more likely to be represented in administrative grades. Thus, while Caribbean women remain over-represented in the Health Service, Asian women are over-represented in the clothing industry (and national figures underestimate their involvement in clothing manufacture), in both cases ethnic 'niches' within traditional sectors of 'women's work'.

In France 'foreign' women are still more likely to be found in manufacturing than French women, twice as likely to be unemployed and less likely to be found in the more 'desirable' sectors of 'women's' work. Nevertheless, the gap between French and 'foreign' women's job levels has, at an aggregate level, shrunk over the last decade (INSEE, 1989).

There is less evidence to suggest that the gap is shrinking in Germany, though the trends over the decade are interesting. In the early 1980s there was clear evidence that 'foreign' women were taking the brunt of manufacturing job losses, thus acting as a 'buffer' to German women. Data for 1990 indicates a rise in employment for German and 'foreign' women across all sectors of the economy, though 'foreign' women are still more likely to be located in manufacturing industry (42 per cent) than German women (24 per cent) and more likely to be located in the manual sectors of 'women's work' (Sonderdruck. Sozialversicherungspflichtig Beschäftigte, June 1990).

To reiterate, if we interpret the trends at face value there is some evidence to suggest that the large gap in job levels apparent ten years ago between majority and minority women has to some extent been bridged in Britain and France. But this is aggregate data relating to employment in the formal economy and needs to be treated with a good deal of caution. Moving our level of analysis down in scale we uncover a rather different picture and this is what my colleague Carol Wolkowitz and I found in Coventry in the first phase of a research project that we carried out on home-based work.

Racialized Divisions at Home

The first in-depth phase of our 1990 research on home-based work was designed to uncover what, if any, ethnic differences exist amongst Coventry home-based workers. A full account of the research methodology and findings as a whole can be found in our book *Working at Home* (1994). Our findings suggest that, within the shared constraints that all women with children experience, there are ethnic differences in levels of employment that force families into a situation where inadequate benefits have to be supplemented by low-waged home-based work. Unlike white women, Asian women in Coventry were not represented at all in the better-paid, less onerous clerical home-based work available in the city.

For the manual workers in the sample, the issues which arise out of ethnic segregation are not only differences in hourly earnings but also differences in hours, regularity and the intensity of work. This is particularly acute in the Coventry clothing industry, a major employer of Asian women, because of the extent to which employers are themselves in a 'master-servant' relationship in the subcontracting chain of production.

All nineteen Asian women that we interviewed in Coventry were manual workers, fifteen of whom were involved in clothing assembly, most earning well below the Wages Council minimum. The work of the other Asian home-workers was even more poorly paid. Two assembled Christmas crackers and were earning, in 1990, between 8 and 16 pence an hour. Another was packing nappies for 53p an hour and one was a childminder charging only 33p per hour per child. This was far less than white childminders were charging. The Asian childminder was not registered and she explained she could not register because at the rates her clients could afford she had to care for more children than registered childminders are permitted in order to make it financially viable for herself.

Amongst the thirty white homeworkers interviewed nine were clerical workers. The latter earned more for less hours and had a fair amount of control over their work flow. While homeworking wages generally are low by any standard, there was a difference between Asian and white women in Coventry, with two-thirds of the Asian women earning between 75p and £1.50 an hour, compared to white homeworkers' earnings of £2.00 an hour or more.

The Coventry homeworking labour force reproduced the occupational segregation that is evident in the external labour market. The impact of racialization and ethnicity on the working lives of Asian women is demonstrated by their concentration in a narrower band of jobs and their exclusion from the better-paid and less onerous clerical work available in the city. If they have sewing skills their hourly earnings are low. If not they are usually thrown into even more poorly paid assembly work.

Equally important are differences in the place of homework in the women's lives and its role in the household economy. The very long hours worked by the Asian women reflect economic need. Sixty per cent worked 45 hours or more and a third over 60 hours a week. Twelve of the Asian households but only three of the white ones depended on Income Support and the Asian households had more children to support. In fact, the only advantage that some Asian women could see in homeworking was that they could bring some money into the household in order to supplement their inadequate benefits. As one Asian woman explained,

My husband is unemployed. We cannot manage on the Income Support we receive. The children constantly need some form of clothing or shoes. My husband has gone for an interview today.

One of the questions we asked was whether the respondent was happier working at home or whether she would prefer to go out to work 'if that were possible'. The answers showed a clear difference between Asian and white women. Slightly over half the white women said that they preferred to work at home as against only two of the Asian women. The other Asian women responded that they were neither happier nor unhappier working at home, which suggests that they felt that they had no choice.

We also asked the respondents if working at home 'made for an easy-going day'. While three-quarters of the white clerical workers responded that it did, none of the Asian women agreed. As one explained:

work is always there to be done, housework, homework – I shout at the children most of the time, I lose my temper quickly. I don't have as much time for the children as I would like. The homework is messy and this creates more work for me.

While there is a good deal in common between the working conditions of the Asian and white homeworkers, the Asian women were much more likely to be dependent on benefit or trying to manage on a very low income. As a consequence they were being thrown into homework that was so badly paid that they had to work very long hours. So why are Asian women not getting access to the better paid forms of homework in Coventry? Part of the explanation is the informal recruitment processes so typical of homeworking. Contrary to popular belief, none of the Asian women in our sample acquired their jobs through relatives. Rather, where it exists, the recruitment of kin can discriminate against minority women. For instance, the better-paid electronics homework carried out by white women in Coventry was brought home by husbands who worked in the factory. The better-paid clerical homework was acquired through word of mouth as was the bow-making. Some years ago the Council for Racial Equality investigated recruitment practices at the Massey Ferguson plant in Coventry and uncovered a similar process of indirect racial discrimination reproduced through informal recruitment practices. In addition, some of the ethnic differences in earnings and the intensity of work reflect the position of the suppliers of homework in the economy. For instance, the clothing industry in Coventry is dominated by Asian entrepreneurs who occupy a subordinate position in the subcontracting production chain for a low-value-added product where labour costs constitute a high proportion of total costs (Phizacklea, 1990).

Employment Segregation and the Impact of Immigration Policy

Supply-side explanations for occupational segregation by sex have emphasized women's 'domestic reponsibilities' as the key to their disadvantaged and occupationally crowded position in the labour market. For minority women their supposed 'language deficiencies' and 'lack of skills' are routinely added and trotted out as explanations for their doubly disadvantaged position. There is little doubt that employers take advantage of these gendered and racialized ideologies (see Phizacklea, 1983). While language can constitute a problem for some women, the last Policy Studies Institute study of racial disadvantage at work indicated that this is far less of a problem than is commonly thought (Brown, 1984).

What is often overlooked is the role of the state in shaping job status through immigration policy. Obviously this is formally the case with specific recruitment policies and work permit allocations but state intervention is apparent in less direct forms in the case of family reunion. Since the early 1970s and the banning of new worker entries throughout the European Community the major migration flows have been related to family reunion, asylum seekers and refugees.

In the case of family reunion the entry of spouses and dependants is only allowed if a sponsor can provide evidence that he or she can support and accommodate them without recourse to 'public funds' (particularly benefits). Not only is the family then forced to settle without state support, there are also residence conditions for non-contributory benefit claims and in some countries a waiting period before access to the labour market is granted. All of these factors push families who are struggling to reconstruct their lives in the migration setting into poverty and often women into work in the informal economy.

Conclusions

Aggregate data on the occupational distribution of majority and minority women in Britain, France and Germany might at face value provide grounds for cautious optimism in so far as the large gap in job levels that existed ten years ago appears to have been bridged slightly in Britain and France at least. My own view is that one would need to be very wary of coming to such a conclusion.

The aggregate data on employment tells us nothing about the much higher rates of unemployment amongst minority men and women, about the hours that they work, about their pay, about the formation of 'ethnic niches' within national labour markets nor about the overall level of household income, all factors which we need to consider if we are going to gain a more complete picture of what is really going on.

What really is a priority on the policy front is a radical change in EC member states' attitudes to tackling racial discrimination combined with an aggressive commitment to the pursuit of equal opportunities. Without this there is little that can be regarded as beneficial in the Single Market for Europe's ethnic minorities.

References

BROWN, C. (1984) *Black and White Britain: The Third PSI Survey*, London, Heinemann.
ELIAS, P. and GREGORY, M. (1992) *The Changing Structure of Occupations and Earnings in Great Britain, 1975–1990*, Institute for Employment Research, University of Warwick.

GREATER LONDON COUNCIL (1986) *The London Labour Plan*, London, GLC.

INSEE (1989) *Enquête Emploi*.

LLOYD, C. and WATERS, H. (1991) 'France: One Culture and One People?', *Race and Class*, 32(3), pp. 49–66.

MILES, R. and PHIZACKLEA, A. (1984) *White Man's Country: Racism in British Politics*, London, Pluto.

PHIZACKLEA, A. (Ed.) (1983) *One Way Ticket: Migration and Female Labour*, London, Routledge and Kegan Paul.

PHIZACKLEA, A. (1987) 'Minority Women and Economic Restructuring: The Case of Britain and the Federal Republic of Germany', *Work, Employment and Society*, vol. 1, no. 3, pp. 309–25.

PHIZACKLEA, A. (1988) 'Entrepreneurship, Ethnicity and Gender', in WESTWOOD, S. and BHACHU, P. (Eds) *Enterprising Women*, London, Routledge.

PHIZACKLEA, A. (1990) *Unpacking the Fashion Industry: Gender, Racism and Class in Production*, London, Routledge.

PHIZACKLEA, A. and WOLKOWITZ, C. (1994) *Working at Home*, London, Sage.

POWER, M. (1988) 'Women, the State and the Family in the US: Reagonomics and the Experience of Women', in RUBERY, J. (Ed.) *Women and Recession*, London, Routledge.

SONDERDRUCK. SOZIALVERSICHERUNGSPFLICHTIG BESCHÄFTIGTE (June 1990) Bundesanstalt für Arbeit, Nurnberg.

SOPEMI (1990) *Continuous Reporting System on Migration*, OECD, Paris, 1991.

Chapter 10

The Tension between Ethnicity and Work: Immigrant Women in the Netherlands

Helma Lutz

This article tries to unravel the 'enlightened' policies of assimilation through the labour market adopted by the Dutch government. The analysis focuses on the meaning of ethnicity for immigrant women in the Netherlands and its implications for their chances on the labour market. It is argued that the measures taken effectively assimilate immigrant women, marginalizing the majority of them in third-class workers' status in the informal sector. When some of the inappropriate policies created to facilitate the employment of immigrant women are explored it can be seen that it is because they lack a clear understanding of the demands and positions of women that such policies have proved completely ineffective. Furthermore in the Netherlands, as in much of Europe, minority policies on the labour market must be interpreted in the context of the dismantling of the welfare state. The article concludes that the new Europe of 'open borders' creates more 'closed doors' for immigrant women rather than an elevation of opportunities.

Talking and writing about the labour market position of immigrant women in almost any West European country is terribly frustrating. One has to sum up depressing tables showing a continuous decline of formal labour market participation and a tremendous augmentation of insecure, unregistered work. The most common explanation for this is the economic crisis and the reorganizational process, technological innovations in industrial society tending to shift away from unskilled to educated labour, leaving the 'unskilled' and drop-outs to the care of the welfare state. On the other hand it is stressed that the welfare state – at least in the Netherlands – has become prohibitive (impossibly expensive) and its institutions have come under tremendous pressure. Among different aspects left out of sight in this common explanation is the role of the state, the government's policy in the process of deterioration and erosion of immigrant women's employment situation. As Amina Mama (1986) has analyzed the situation in Britain, I will focus on the effects of

Table 10.1 Registered unemployment, by sex, total numbers and percentage of the working population of the group

	total (×100)			percentage of the working population in the group		
	men	women	total	men	women	total
Indigenous Dutch	375.5	219.4	594.9	12	16	13
Surinamese	13.0	6.7	19.7	27	25	27
Antillians	3.2	1.9	5.1	21	27	23
Turks	18.6	7.6	26.2	40	58	44
Moroccans	13.5	3.3	16.8	41	49	42

Source: Min. of Social Affairs, 1 Jan 1988

official Dutch policy-making for immigrant women. Mama argued that access to the labour market had already been severely limited for black women by historical and contemporary racial and sexual divisions and that above that the government exploits the economic crisis 'as a means to erode away the welfare state' (Mama, 1986, p. 202). I will keep her argument as a guideline in this article, though the British and the Dutch situations seem to be significantly different. In the Netherlands ethnicity rather than 'race' has become the main concept in the state policy which will be subject of this article. Next to this the technological innovation and reorganization of the main industries began in the Netherlands at least five years later than in Britain and it is only since the end of the 1980s that the devastating effects of this process for 'ethnic' minorities have become publicly known and discussed. Relating the analysis of the effects of labour market change and state policy to theoretical notions of the intersection between ethnicity, class and gender relations informs us about the underlying power structures and their relevance for immigrant women. In this sense the situation in the Netherlands is not so special but the elements of this case can be found in other European countries as well.

Defining the Problem

A look at the (un)employment rates shown in table 10.1 confirms the assumption that female immigrants have been affected by the recession of the 1980s even more than their male counterparts: the *registered* unemployment rates for women of virtually all minority groups (which in the Dutch context comprise colonial migrants: Surinamese, Antillians and Moluccan, as well as labour migrants: Turkish and Moroccan) outnumber those for men. Though there is a slight indication that, since 1988, the situation has improved (see table 10.2) this does not prove that the situation in general has changed. According to recent information the recession in the Netherlands has been overcome and the GNP has, in fact, been growing since 1984, but immigrants, male and female, did not benefit much from this amelioration (see Klooster-man and Knaack, 1992). Registered unemployment of immigrant women is now significantly higher than that for indigenous Dutch women, whereas in the 1970s it was the other way round. Immigrant women then outnumbered indigenous women in official labour market participation figures. What happened?

In the early 1980s women's emancipation policies in the Netherlands had initiated a wide range of programmes to improve the situation of women in general. The percentage of labour participation by Dutch indigenous women was extremely low in comparison with other Western and West European countries. According to an OECD report of 1986 it was estimated at 28 per cent and was the second lowest in the EEC, next to Ireland, whereas it was 34 per cent in the FRG and 43 per cent in the United States. Between 1987 and 1991 the percentage rose to the EEC average of 53 per cent (see Kloosterman, 1993, p. 6).

This served policy-makers as an indication of the tremendous improve-ment in the position of women. According to the National Association for the Economic Independence of Women, however, these figures are misleading. There is no other country within the EEC in which the majority of women work in part-time jobs. On the whole, the number of hours women work has not gone up at all. Hence more women work the same hours as before, apparently for lower wages. Despite the official Dutch government policy of encouraging women's labour participation, the result is disappointing because it has obviously not led to a significant redistribution of work, housework and care work (see Volkskrant, 11.7.1991). According to a recent study, even in households with a double income, the husband's share in caretaking for children and household obligations is not more than a third of the wife's investment (v. d. Lippe, 1993, p. 149).

Nevertheless, there is an overwhelming tendency for increased female labour market participation which is supported by government campaigns and via a new law which makes employment compulsory for young women after school age. The images of 'women and work' are, therefore, changing in the Netherlands. While it had been regarded as quite undesirable for women to work and to 'mother' at the same time, and the economy had been focusing on the working father with a sufficient salary, nowadays it is much easier to request public childcare facilities. With regard to this changing image I have to underline that this is concerned with the image of Dutch indigenous woman-hood. With regard to women's position one has to realize that it has been in-digenous women who have gained from this development. While indigenous women were supposed to be able to meet the needs of the formal sector of the economy (educated labour) immigrant women became the losers of this decade.

The Dutch economy nowadays, as elsewhere in Europe, has increasingly tended to divide into a small primary sector on the one side and a large secondary and tertiary sector on the other side. The primary sector, which is characterized by the stable employment of educated employees, is dominated by the indigenous population (male and female), whereas we find the majority of immigrants, again male and female, in the poor working conditions and instability of employment in the secondary sector and in the rapidly increasing sector of the hidden economy. The vast majority of the garment industry, the flower industry, the food service industry and the whole area of domestic help is dependent on immigrant female and illegal (mostly male) work. In summary, this development is an obvious confirmation of Floya Anthias' statement that 'the gender division of the dominant ethnic group as well as the prevailing dominant images of the "other" affect ethnic minority women's position in society in general and access to the labour market in particular' (Anthias, 1991, p. 38).

Before I go into some more detail on the question of how and to what degree the different groups of immigrant women have been affected by developments in the labour market, I want to focus on state policy and images of immigrant women in policy-making.

State Policy for Immigrant Women

In the European context Dutch politics have gained a considerable reputation on behalf of liberal policy-making for minorities, including ethnic minorities. In 1979 it was officially acknowledged that Dutch society was no longer mono-cultural but multi-cultural and that the society and its institutions would have to take this change into account. The first overall policy report on ethnic minorities acknowledged that the non-Dutch population was no longer resident in the Netherlands on a temporary basis but that it had settled there permanently. This acknowledgment concerned colonial migrants such as the Surinamese, Antillian and Moluccan as well as 'labour' migrants, Turkish and Moroccan being the largest of them. The 1979 report leading to the first policy document on ethnic minorities, which passed through the Dutch parliament in 1983, set out guidelines for improving the marginal social and economic status of these 'ethnic minorities' (see also Lutz, 1993a). This document contains a small but typical note on immigrant women. I quote from this document:

The majority of these women lead isolated lives. Their skills and knowledge are too limited for them to be able to function independently in a complex industrialized society. They have little or no knowledge of the Dutch language, and they lack opportunities to orientate themselves in the society surrounding them . . . minority women have hardly taken advantage of the opportunities they are offered through the emancipation policy for support of self-organization. (Min. v. Bi. Za., 1983, p. 124)

Although on the same page there is a subordinate clause in which it is acknowledged that 'working' immigrant women outnumber the indigenous working female population, this fact is not in the slightest way drawn upon in the rest of the document. Here, as well as in the majority of other reports, we find two recurring arguments. First of all, the majority of immigrant women, no matter what background and education they have, are lumped together into one category and presented in terms of one prevailing image: the isolated dependent woman. Secondly, there is a strong emphasis on the backwardness of immigrant women, their incapacity to adjust to 'modern' society and its way of life and their lack of appropriate schooling and qualifications.

Although, throughout Dutch policy on ethnic minorities in general and this document in particular, a distinction is made between the ethnic or cultural background of immigrant women (we usually find Turkish and Moroccan women lumped together into the category 'Muslim women' which is a cultural definition, while Creole and Hindu women from the former Dutch colony Surinam are defined as Surinamese women, thus defined in terms of their former national country of origin), the commonalities in the image-creating process are striking: the dominant perception assumes that immigrant women are *different* and have to be seen and approached as different. This difference is overwhelmingly seen as an antagonism in relation to the Western female standard which serves as the standard for defining 'womanhood' in society. What an immigrant woman does, what she thinks and how she defines herself is seen as a digression from the Western female standard. The immigrant woman becomes the 'other' by definition. Though this standard is hardly ever mentioned as such explicitly, one generally encounters an image of Western woman as triumphant in the realization of equal rights and social equality. According to this image Western women have become straightforward and autonomously successful beings whose gendered life has been freed of major contradictions and ambivalence. I have argued elsewhere (see Lutz, 1991b, p. 23) that this dominant approach reflects the 'host' societies' contact with the immigrant rather than providing us with information about immigrants themselves. In other words, it is not the immigrant woman or her assumed lack of social competence, but rather a socio-genetical assignment with a political function, in which the indigenous Westerner (male and female) becomes a citizen through the othering of the immigrant. This proces of 'othering' can be traced throughout Dutch policy on minorities, in particular state policies for immigrant women.

In the emancipation policy of the 1980s migrant women were one of the target groups of a special programme (VEM, 'Vrouwen Emancipatie

Minderheden'), a minority women's emancipation project. This project was started in 1983, scheduled until 1988 and finally concluded in 1990. By the end of 1990 the Minstry of the Interior (Home Office) had invested Fl. 6.5 million in the VEM project. From the final report (Mi. v. So. Za., 1992a) one gets the impression that the whole project was an overall success; from a close reading of the evaluation, however, I come to the opposite conclusion.

'Care' as a Core Notion in the State Policies for Immigrant Women

The document of 1983, from which I quoted above, had set out guidelines for the project development. In the document four main areas of importance were stressed: (a) education (development of Dutch language courses, training for the development of a cadre and management for self-organization); (b) development of vocational training programmes in the field of health, care and social work; (c) development of material, providing information for immigrant women about Dutch society; (d) job creation. In the outline of the programme, target (b) was linked to the programme target (d); in other words, most of the small-scale educational and vocational training projects developed within the VEM program were limited to the areas of health, care and social work. Some of the projects such as the 'family helper training', set up for Turkish and Moroccan women, were disastrous failures due to a lack of interest in participation in the training programmes. With regard to the output of the projects, one can only note the failure of the programme. By the end of 1988 only 100 immigrant women had been helped to attain a secure job, while statistics totalled 36,456 registered unemployed immigrant women at that time (see *Onderweg*, 1990, p. 6). From the final report we understand that a lot of empathy and money was put into the recruitment of immigrant women for the training projects and into the development of educational (vocational) training material. The material can be used elsewhere and is spread among immigrant women's (self-)organizations nationally. While it is noticeable that in the final report the unequal relation between expenditure (Fl. 6.5 million out of which 2 million were spent on the work creation projects) and output (jobs for 100 women) is not mentioned at all, it is even more striking that we search in vain for a paragraph of critical evaluation of the implicit and explicit core notions of the whole programme.

First of all there are indications that the projects were set up without consulting migrant women at the level of implementation (see Kempadoo, 1990, p. 9). As in many cases of the Dutch policy on minorities, these projects were planned at the tables of administration.

Secondly, the projects were meant to give immigrant women an orientation towards jobs and professions which require skills for traditional women's work such as medical care, social work and related areas, such as interpreters for the health sector. The document of 1983 which sets out the agenda for the projects underlines the desirability of training immigrant women for the health care sector, as interpreters, nurses and family-helpers (Mi. v. Bi. Za., 1983, p. 130). It is not mentioned that this area of work had and still has considerable problems with a shortage of professional staff, because of its low salaries and shift-work. One can conclude that immigrant women are/were to be channelled into those professions, seen as undesirable for indigenous women. At the same time another project – established outside the VEM policy – the Vrouweninformaticaschool (school for women on information studies) which offers a vocational training program in new (computer) technologies was set up for immigrant women and is tremendously successful, with long waiting lists. It nevertheless had to struggle for survival and government support; one can assume that this direction of orientation counteracts the traditional orientation of the VEM projects. One of the emerging problems in the case of training was immigrant women's lack of Dutch diplomas. Diplomas from elsewhere, especially those from outside the EEC, were not and still are not seen as equal credentials. This has forced numerous immigrant women to repeat to a large extent training concerning diplomas which they already held, and this is very likely to have had a demotivating effect on immigrant women's ambitions. For those who wanted to participate in a programme but held a diploma in a more technical or service area (banking), training was not available and these women were channelled into the health sector as well. In conclusion one can say that the definition of gender at the level of policy-making is dominated by Dutch (or Western) paradigms which deny the historical contexts of non-Western femininity and the specific experiences and needs of immigrant women.

'Care' as an area which is traditionally assigned to women underpins the job creation policies for immigrant women while at the same time immigrant women are lumped into the associated female image: woman as natural 'caretaker'. Because immigrant women are regarded in traditional terms one could say that the policies themselves play a part in the creation of this image. Though this may be an unintentional effect of policy-making it seems to me noticeable that the traditional image of immigrant women becomes a self-fulfilling prophecy as a result of state policies.

The image of immigrant women as much more attached to traditional female values than indigenous women is contradicted by studies elsewhere. Morokvasic (1991), Phizacklea (1990) and Anthias (1991) point out that immigrant women are more likely to work full-time because their salary contribution to the household budget is crucial. The lack of childcare facilities, which still is a tremendous problem for women in general in the Netherlands, reinforces the inclination of immigrant women to accept homeworking for subcontracters (especially in the textile industry), making it possible to combine care for children and earning a salary. Because it is assumed that – for the majority of women in general and immigrant women in particular – the money earned from paid labour is an *additional* contribution to the household budget, very little research has been done on immigrant women as breadwinners. From Dutch data we know that there are groups of immigrant women for whom the familialist orientation is not applicable. There is, for instance, one group which consists primarily of single-parent households, the Surinamese Creole women (see van Horn-Gooswit *et al.*, 1992). These women are in fact breadwinners for their children – whether they are able to earn the money through paid labour or not. One can conclude that research in this area is still dominated by gender stereotypes as well as ethnic stereotypes. In the next section I will elaborate the intersection between gender, ethnicity and work in the Dutch context on the basis of case studies. I want to connect this to more general theoretical notions on the issue.

'Ethnicity': Boundaries of the Dutch Labour Market?

First I want to turn briefly to the fact that different groups of immigrant women have been affected by the labour market situation differently. Out of approximately 15 million people in the Netherlands (in 1990) 7.5 million are women, of whom 6.9 million are registered as indigenous 'Dutch' women. Out of 600,000 non-Dutch women 327,000 are not registered as members of 'ethnic minorities', which is to say that these women hold EEC membership or they are US citizens or Japanese citizens. The following are considered as the largest 'ethnic' groups: Surinamese (81,000 females), Turkish (63,000 females), Moroccan (49,000 females), Antillian and Aruban (29,000 females), Chinese (10,000 females). Those are followed by Spanish, Yugoslavian, Italian, Cape Verdean, Portuguese, Vietnamese, Greek and Tunisian (source: Min. v. So. Za., 1992b). While the largest group of immigrant women, Surinamese women, holds Dutch citizenship (90 per cent), the majority of the second and third largest groups, Turkish and Moroccan, do not hold this status. Data in the Netherlands are collected according to ethnic criteria given by the administration (place of birth and place of birth of the parents) and not according to self-registration or national membership (citizenship). This kind of ethnic registration is nevertheless a hot issue in the Netherlands: the advocates point to the necessity of it in order to make positive action programmes applicable, while the opponents emphasize the dangers of misuse, referring to the fate of the Dutch Jews under the occupation by fascist Germany (90 per cent were deported to concentration camps). The discussion of ethnic registration reflects in fact another discussion, namely the question of whether the state should engage in labour market policies or not. Although in a report published in 1989, the WRR (Scientific Council of Government Policy) has pleaded for the implementation of 'contract compliance', according to the Canadian model, the Dutch employers' federations are strongly opposed to this proposal.

Table 10.2   Non-working persons (age 15–64), persons registered for employment and registered unemployment, by sex and ethnicity, 1990 (as percentage of the population aged 15–64)

	non-working		registered for employment		registered unemployment	
	men	women	men	women	men	women
Indigenous Dutch	6	11	4	10	4	4
Immigrants	21	25	17	20	16	13
Turks, Moroccans	37	44	31	33	27	26
Surinamese, Antillians	27	32	21	26	24	19
Other immigrants	13	19	10	16	9	8
Total	7	12	5	11	5	5

Source: Enquête beroepsbevolking, Statistiek geregistreerde werkloosheid, CBS 1992

Since the voice of this lobby is powerful the government has not yet come up (and probably will not come up) with such a law. I have argued elsewhere (see Lutz, 1993a) that the Dutch state *de facto* intervenes considerably on behalf of immigrants in the labour market – as the labour market nowadays is seen as a crucial mediator on the road to the emancipation and integration of ethnic minorities. Government investment in the improvement of the social position of ethnic minorities has reached the level of Fl. 800 million per year (see Lutz, 1993a). Nevertheless there is an absence of any serious evaluation on the spending of the money and no evaluation at all of the implicit notions underlying this policy. Another omission is the absence of the acknowledgment that racism is a structural characteristic of society in general and the labour market in particular. The presence of racism or racist effects can be easily seen from case studies (for further information see Lutz, 1993a).

As table 10.2 shows, Turkish and Moroccan women, of all immigrant women, are most affected by unemployment. A general assumption is that the reason for this has to be seen in their lack of schooling and the absence of language capacities. But if we turn to Surinamese women, whose labour market participation is considerably lower than that of indigenous Dutch women, this explanation does not hold ground.

Surinamese women happen to hold the same level of education as indigenous Dutch women (see Jaarsma, 1991, p. 19) but nevertheless the majority of them are found in the three least-paid and lowest-status categories of the labour market. And though there is quite a considerable number of Surinamese women who have been able to reach the middle and higher rungs of the status ladder (see Essed, 1990), this number does not correspond in any respect to that of those with good levels of education. A recent study (Sansone, 1992) has shown that among the lowest educated young Creole women there is a tremendous tendency towards teenage motherhood and dropping out of school (Sansone, 1992, pp. 203ff.). The young women then usually live on welfare which gives them some economic independence from their parents or their lovers. As the amount of welfare almost equals the amount one could earn through official employment and as there is, as already mentioned, a lack of childcare facilities, in this situation the young mothers try to earn additional money from work in the hidden economy, such as babysitting or cooking for others. Many of these young women have tried to find formal employment for some time and many of them have experienced explicit or implicit racism when they are refused jobs.

For better-educated Surinamese women in middle-range business, such as banking and services, research shows that employers prefer white employees above immigrants, although they would hardly confess that overtly as a selection criterion (see Oosterhuis and Glebbeek, 1988). As I have emphasized earlier, the care sector (hospitals) is one of the open sectors to those with middle-range diplomas because it is poorly paid.

Uneducated Turkish and Moroccan women in the Netherlands are almost driven out of the official labour market into the hidden economy or they become helping members in a family business. Turkish and Moroccan women are more or less seen as the group which is less equipped for the labour market in general. Lack of language capacity and the lack of minimal diplomas is considered responsible for this situation. A second reason is seen in the 'cultural unfitness' of these two groups, linked to the notion of their Muslim background. Looking at the schooling situation of second-generation Turkish and Moroccan girls confirms the expectation that the daughters will not climb up the status ladder much higher than their mothers: 90 per cent of the girls have completed secondary modern schooling, obtaining a diploma which is of hardly any value. Though Turkish and Moroccan children have followed Dutch education for almost twenty years, there is still a strikingly small number of students from these groups in higher education and universities.

Studies on Turkish immigrant women with a college or university education indicate that the majority of them are engaged in 'ethnic work' such as social work or native language teaching of immigrant children (Bovenkerk *et al.*, 1991; Gowricharn, 1989). My case study (see Lutz, 1991a, 1993a, 1993b) focused on the experiences of better-educated women from Turkey living in the Netherlands and West Germany. These women were involved in work with and for compatriots in different institutions of social work: social welfare, community work and teaching. Summarizing some conclusions of this study, it turned out that these women's ethnic membership both facilitated and constrained their participation in the labour market. Taking various aspects of their career development into account, it became obvious that this area of work was one of the few employment sectors open to them, which finally had channelled those who held a diploma in other professional areas into this sector. Due to the organization of the sector of social work for immigrants (short-term projects of a non-structural, temporary nature) the career prospects are very limited. Above that, discrimination played a serious role in blocking or preventing upward mobility. Though the inclusion of 'ethnic' social workers is a requirement for the emancipation process of the community, it became obvious that it was not these women's 'professional competence' which was acknowledged by their employers and indigenous colleagues, but rather their 'ethnic' capacities which were appreciated. I have argued elsewhere (see Lutz, 1993a) that if one considers ethnicity in the case of the Turkish female social workers as a commodity for negotiating access to the labour market, one has to emphasize the feasibility of this commodity. Their case is an example of ethnic segmentation of the labour market which exists due to boundary signification: because of the assumption that Turks have characteristics in common which stand in a meaningful contrast to the characteristics of the Dutch classifier. In other words: the whole area of ethnic social work is dependent on state policies. It can easily disappear as soon as government policies cease to define an ethnic group as a problem category. This case study has also shown that next to the structural limitations Turkish immigrant women as *actors* call upon their cultural, social and gender resources. The active involvement in the bargaining process of these women became obvious in numerous situations where they *call upon* ethnicity in order to act as an advocate or spokeswoman for the community. I will return to this in my concluding remarks.

What are the alternatives for those who cannot meet the requirements of the official labour market? Most of the Turkish women can be found in the ethnic niches: family businesses like grocery stores and working for the clothing industry. Both sectors are significantly under-researched, so that there is a lack of sound data. What Floya Anthias has shown for the Cypriot community in London (see Anthias, 1992), namely the fact that women have a central role in the ethnic economy, while they are also exploited, often doing unpaid work, and that patriarchal control of them is intensified by and through the organization of work, seems to be true for the Turkish communities in the Netherlands as well.

From recent studies on the clothing industry in the Netherlands we can derive tentative views on the experiences of some thousands of immigrant women working for subcontractors in the clothing industry (Smit and Jongejans, 1989; v. Putten, 1988). Much of the clothing industry has been restructured and been brought back from the free-trade areas of developing countries to Western Europe or the United States by way of subcontracting small entrepreneurs (Benetton was the first and is the most 'successful' example of this). Since in the Dutch context the majority of these subcontractors are Turks a whole new job area has been created as part of the ethnic economy. The work is either done by homeworking women or by illegal workers recruited from Turkey. On first sight homeworking for women has its advantages as it is supposed to enable women to work and take care of their children. But studies on homeworking women (see Allen and Wolkowitz, 1986) have shown that working in one's own home as a means of working autonomously and being able to combine work more easily with other obligations is misleading. The time pressures of delivery and the payment by piece leaves the responsibility for the whole production process to the individual women, whether there are family troubles or not. The disadvantages of this kind of work outweigh the advantages: 'Homeworking is very far from being a boon to women, for instead of liberating them from or reducing the burden of the "double day" it intensifies the pressure of both waged work and unpaid domestic labour' (Allen and Wolkowitz, 1986, p. 263). In the case of the 'ethnic' economy women may be even more exploited as community loyalty and community control work in favour of the compatriot (male) employer.

In conclusion, I claim that there are clear indications for ethnic segmentations in the Dutch labour market. Above that I want to emphasize that the intersection of gender and ethnicity lies at the bottom of this process. Immigrant women are expected to be inclined to work in traditional, often feminized, areas of the labour market because as I mentioned earlier their contribution to the household income is seen as additional rather than crucial. The opportunities offered to them are bound to traditional notions of 'natural' female capacities which serve as legitimations for their incorporation into the feminized segments of the labour market, such as (health) care, social work, the service sector etc. State emancipation policies, instead of challenging this situation, tend rather to (re)produce it by introducing work creation projects in these very areas. Though there are significant commonalities between the situations of women of different immigrant groups in the Netherlands, there are also considerable differences. At the dawn of a unified Europe questions of ethnic background are gaining more and more significance, nowadays emerging in discussions on citizenship and the welfare state. The discussion on the limitations of the welfare state, presently a hot public issue in the Netherlands, concentrates on the question as to whether the state is responsible for immigrants or not. For those immigrants who hold a Dutch passport (which is not true for the majority of Turks and Moroccans), the government can hardly legitimate exclusion politics on the basis of national membership. Former colonial immigrants like the Surinamese, Moluccans or Antillians can be more assured of access to welfare state facilities than former labour migrants (though the arrival of numbers of 'problematic' youngsters from the Antilles has caused a debate on how the government can prevent them from coming). Turks and Moroccans who have worked for the benefit of the Dutch economy for nearly thirty years, on the other hand, cannot easily be thrown out of the country either. What the government, nevertheless, tries to do, is to limit the number of (official) newcomers. As the family unification or in many cases rather the family foundation process (second-generation young males and females get married to partners from Turkey or Morocco) is in full swing, bringing in up to 20,000 persons per year, the Ministry of Justice tries to restrict this immigration by imposing certain conditions (proper housing, minimum income) on the applicants. This again will effect the career planning of young men and women, as those who want to marry have to work for the required family income and are likely to give up their study plans.

Helma Lutz

The necessary debate on citizenship and the individual and collective requirements for becoming an accepted member of a national state within the European community has not been conducted at all, neither in the Netherlands nor elsewhere in Europe. Within such a debate it will be important to look carefully at the underlying aspects of ethnicity, gender and class, not just understanding them as a whole but analyzing their intersections and the special effects they create.

References

ALLEN, SHEILA and WOLKOWITZ, CAROL (1986) 'Homeworking and the Control of Women's Work', in FEMINIST REVIEW (Ed.) *Waged Work: A Reader*, London, Virago.

ANTHIAS, FLOYA (1991) *'Gendered Ethnicities and Labour Market Processes in Britain'*, paper presented at the conference 'Transitions' at the Science Center for Social Research/Labour Market and Employment Unit, 13/14 May, Berlin.

ANTHIAS, FLOYA (1992) *Ethnicity, Class, Gender and Migration: Greek Cypriots in Britain*, Aldershot, Avebury.

BOVENKERK, FRANK, BROK, B.D. and RULAND, L. (1991) 'Meer, Minder of Gelijk', *Sociologische gids*, jarg XXXVIII, 3, pp. 174–86.

CBS (CENTRAAL BUREAU VOOR DE STATISTIC) (1989) *Minderheden in Nederland*, Stichting Vademecum.

ESSED, PHILOMENA (1990) *Understanding Everyday Racism*, PhD, University of Amsterdam.

GOWRICHARN, R. (1989) *Verschillen in werkloosheid en etnische afkomst*, Rotterdam, Onderzoeksrapport Gemeentelijke Sociale Dienst.

V. HORN-GOOSWIT, SYLVIA, ZUIDVEEN, JENNIFER and CAMPBELL, WILFRED (1992) *Samen Werken, Samen Zorgen: Herverdeling Betaalde en Onbetaalde Arbeid onder Surinaamse Mannen en Vrouwen*, LOSV report, Utrecht.

JAARSMA, RIA (1991) *Hoe Kom Je van B naar A?: Handreiking voor Trajectontwikkeling ten Behoeve van Allochtone Vrouwen*, s'Gravenhage.

KEMPADOO, K. (1990) 'Construction of Black and Migrant Womanhood and the Women's and Minorities Policy in the Netherlands', paper presented at the conference 'The Social Construction of Minorities and their Cultural Rights in Western Europe', Leiden, 12–14 Sept.

KLOOSTERMAN, ROBERT (1993) 'Het Onafwendbare einde van de Nederlandse Verzorgingsstaat?', *FACTA, Sociaal-Wetenschappelijk Magazine*, 1, 1, February, Amsterdam.

KLOOSTERMAN, ROBERT and KNAACK, RUUD (1992) *Het Nederlandse Model: Kansen en Bedreigingen van de Verzorgingsstaat*, Amsterdam University Press.

V.D. LIPPE, TANJA (1993) *Arbeidsverdeling Tussen Mannen en Vrouwen*, Amsterdam, Thesis Publishers.

LUTZ, HELMA (1991a) *Welten Verbinden: Türkische Sozialarbeiterinnen in den Niederlanden und der Bundesrepublik Deutschland*, Frankfurt a.m., IKO Verlag.

LUTZ, HELMA (1991b) *Migrant Women of 'Islamic Background': Images and Self-Images*, Middle East Research Associates paper no. 11, Amsterdam.

LUTZ, HELMA (1993a) 'Migrant Women, Racism and the Dutch Labour Market', in SOLOMOS, JOHN and WRENCH, JOHN (Eds) *Racism and Migration in Western Europe*, London and New York, Berg.

LUTZ, HELMA (1993b) 'In Between or Bridging Cultural Gaps? Migrant Women from Turkey as Mediators', *New Community*, no. 1, University of Warwick.

MAMA, AMINA (1986, first published in 1984) 'Black Women and the Economic Crisis', in FEMINIST REVIEW (Ed.) *Waged Work: A Reader*, London, Virago.

MIN. V. BINNENLANDSE ZAKEN (1983) *Minderhedennota*, s'Gravenhage.

MIN. V. SOCIALE ZAKEN EN WERKGELEGENHEID (1992a) *Eindrapportage van het Project Vrouwen en Minderhedenbeleid*, s'Gravenhage, Staatsuitgeverij.

MIN. V. SOCIALE ZAKEN EN WERKGELEGENHEID (1992b) *Emancipatie in Cijfers*, nov. staatsuitgeverij, s'Gravenhage.

MOROKVASIC, M. (1991) 'Fortress Europe and Migrant Women', *Feminist Review*, no. 39.

Onderweg, 7ejrg., no. 1, feb. 1990, Ministerie voor Sociale Zaken en Werkgelegenheid, s'Gravenhage.

OOSTERHUIS, G. and GLEBBEEK, A. (1988) 'Ras en Geslacht bij de Personeelsselectie', *Mens en Maatschappij*, 63 jrg., nr. 3.

PHIZACKLEA, A. (1990) *Unpacking the Fashion Industry*. London, Macmillan.

V. PUTTEN, MAARTJE (1988) *Made in Heaven*, Amsterdam.

SANSONE, LIVIO (1992) *Schitteren in de Schaduw: Overlevingsstrategien, Subcultuur en Etniciteit van Creoolse Jongeren uit de Lagere Klasse in Amsterdam 1981–1990*, Het Spinhuis.

SMIT, MARIJKE, and JONGEJANS, LORETTE (1989) *C & A De Stille Gigant*, Amsterdam, SOMO.

Volkskrant, 11.7.1991 'Vrouwen Moeten aan de Slag, Maar Herverdeling Werk – Hou Maar'.

WETENSCHAPPELIJKE RAAD VOOR HET REGERINGSBELEID (1989) *Allochtonenbeleid*, s'Gravenhage.

Chapter 11

Violence Against Women:
Experiences of South African
Domestic Workers

Bunie M. Matlanyane Sexwale

We are called girls. We are called maids.
It is like we are small.
It is like we are children.

We are told what to do
We are told what to say
We are told what to think
We are told what to wear.

We are women. We are mothers.
Our bodies are strong from hard work.
Our hearts are big from suffering.

We struggle against hunger.
We struggle against poverty.
We struggle against sickness.
We struggle against suffering.

We are women. We are mothers.
Too much work can break our bodies.
Too much suffering can break our hearts.

Our problem is that we live alone.
Our problem is that we work alone.
Our problem is that we suffer alone.

But we find friendship if we meet together.
And we find answers if we talk together.

And we find strength if we work together.
And we find hope if we stand together.
(Thula Baba, Raven 1987:11)

Introduction

Part of the reality that remains to be unravelled if a future South Africa is to be truly non-racial, non-sexist and democratic is the plight of domestic workers. Together with farm workers they constitute the majority of the most downtrodden of black people in general, of the working class and of black women in particular.

Domestic workers are defined by a number of interrelated characteristics. They are part of the colonized and oppressed who, to date, continue to struggle for their right to 'self-determination'. They are black in the context of a country where the world's escalating problem of racism has been taken a step further – beyond common forms of institutionalization to explicit and blatant legalization. They are workers, but the law in South Africa does not recognize them as such; legally they are just 'servants' subject to the whims of their employers, the so-called 'masters and madams', a relationship reminiscent of aspects of slavery and feudalism. Although some men work in this sector, over 90 per cent of domestic workers are women (SADWU, undated); the non-recognition of their work can also, therefore, be understood in the context of the kind of separation between 'productive' and 'non-productive' work where domestic services – usually taken as women's duty – are relegated to the so-called 'private sphere of reproduction' and labour thus expended is poorly, if at all, remunerated.

This paper focuses on violence against black women domestic workers (employed in white households) whose lives spell the centre of convergence for gender, race, class, and national oppression – underscored by their legal non-recognition. It is organized as follows: the second section gives a brief historical background to the violence that surrounds black women and labour relations in domestic service. In the third section, domestic workers' experiences of different forms of violence are described, while their resistance, organization and action against the violence against domestic workers are dealt with in the fourth section. As much as possible these two sections give space to domestic workers' narrations of their experiences from interviews or secondary sources such as (auto)biographies and newspapers.[1] The fifth part gives some concluding remarks.

The paper does not set out to advance any new theory of violence generally, violence against women, black people nor workers specifically; neither does it go into the glaringly unreliable statistics on violence against women and against domestic workers. The complex but growing domestic service sector in the Black communities requires special and urgent attention but cannot justifiably form part of this undertaking. To lay the ground this introduction ends with a brief look at the problematic concept of violence against women.

Violence against women

Following the February 1990 events that marked a watershed in social and political life in South Africa, many exiles have been returning home, permanently or for visits. Upon her return from one such visit, a friend recounted her experiences, joys and pains. One of the things which she had not realized she had terribly missed in the decade spent in exile was men shouting '*Dodlhu, hei, hei!*' and whistling whenever she went by – to her, an acknowledgment of her femininity which she very much appreciated. The same year, I returned home to my shaken and angered teenage daughter; a compatriot who had been visiting the house had attempted to kiss her in a way that made her feel sexually harassed.

These two examples fall in that area of abuse which is most slippery and perhaps controversial. The reactions of the women differ tremendously, one feeling clearly violated while the other is flattered. Neither is unique in her interpretation which informs her reaction. Many women within the same or different age, class, space and cultural contexts, could have reacted in either way, some appreciative while others find both objectionable violation and sexual harassment. Like most dominant ideologies, the ideology of patriarchy is so powerfully ingrained in our minds and behaviour, so much so that mechanisms of gender oppression tend to be understood and defended (even by some of its victims) as the norm, the culture and/or tradition, private/family affairs, which must never be questioned. Even glaringly horrendous violations such as rape and assault, sometimes with grievous bodily harm or murder, also remain clouded with either silence or controversy, and in many societies condoned, especially, though not exclusively, when such aggressions are by husbands and partners, or by whites against black people. In between the extremes of sexual objectification and ambiguous kisses on the one hand, and rape and murder on the other, lie a range of abuses, violence, which we women experience consistently.

> It is as if an invisible electrified fence surrounds us. We can easily bump into it in straying beyond the confines of behaviour they [men] have mapped out as appropriate for us, and when we do, the electric shock is of their aggression. (Wilson, 1983, pp. 11–12)

It is difficult to define violence against women. The range covered by forms of abuse is wide. Women, activists, academics, feminists, professionals, different disciplines, laws, cultures, are in no easy agreement. Since the last decade or so, attempts to conceptualize violence against women with a view of working out strategies to combat it are on the increase. The common view has traditionally been that which emphasizes a combination of use of force and physical evidence thereof. This is evident not only in legal debates and practice, but also in some feminist writing and politics. For instance, Mama asserts, 'For the broader international women's movement, north, south, east, and west, violence against women has generally been articulated as the *crude use of physical force* to coerce women into the subordinate position afforded them by patriarchal societies' (Mama, 1989, p. 4; emphasis mine). I take the position that such articulation as claimed in this quotation concentrates only on limited areas of violence and ignores some equally important ones. Focusing only on 'crude use of physical force' in fact excludes some experiences of violence eloquently articulated by South African domestic workers, themselves a part of 'the broader international women's movement' located in the South. It seems crucial to emphasize that violence against women often entails a sophisticated and systematic wearing down of a woman's autonomy and self-esteem on spiritual, emotional and mental levels, well before the first blow is struck – which partly explains many women's attitude of self-abnegation – physical violence being about the last stage of execution. Also, violence against women is in a high number of instances devoid of physical contact, which makes it elusive and difficult to define. Often women experience gender violence but have no recourse because not only do they have no external bruising but they have not even been touched physically; to my belief and experience, this does not make it any the less violent.

It is useful to pause at this point and ask why the violence against women? Some attribute it fundamentally to misogyny, hating women, as in the following example:

Misogynist expressions range from gender biases against female children and women which have debilitating, negative effects on their lives, to battering and sexual/psychological abuse of females of all ages (rape, incest etc). Murder is the most extreme form it assumes. (McFadden, 1991, p. 41)

This view has been criticized as falling short of explaining some forms of violence against women, particularly those perpetrated by other women or by white men against black women. To misogyny Meena suggests adding racism, intention to humiliate, and 'the psychological feeling of helplessness which women have been socialised into' (Meena, 1991, esp. p. 42). Examining most of the analyses (for instance Wilson, 1983; Mama, 1989; McFadden, 1991; Meena, 1991; Schuler, 1992; Mies, 1986; Kedijang, 1990) one sees a common thread, patriarchy – women's subordination, exploitation and oppression (usually closely related to the construction and control of female sexuality and generally to the control of different aspects of women's lives, women being seen as minors, dependants, and outright property of men). As Schuler observes, it is this understanding of violence against women being an expression and mechanism of power over women, embedded in gender relations, ascribed by patriarchal domination, which has led many activists to define gender violence as 'any act involving use of force or coercion with an intent of perpetuating/promoting hierarchical gender relations' (APWLD quoted in Schuler, 1992). Schuler, however, goes on to criticize this definition for its breadth. I propose an understanding of gender violence which recognizes in addition to its patriarchal roots, that contrary to its portrayal as mainly occurring as short and sharp injections, violence is a process, relying on a range of mechanisms, subtle or obvious; geared at many varying but closely inter-related levels, the spiritual, emotional, the psychological, and, last but not least, the sexual and physical. These levels may occasionally be separate but often they occur in sequence or in combination, and are mutually reinforcing – in fact, I believe that the physical and sexual gender violence would not be so widely tolerated were it not predominantly a sequel to and backed by the emotional and psychological degradation which the sexual/physical, in turn, reproduce. Because of the inherent tensions underlying power and gender relations, gender violence often lies latent until it is sparked off or 'bursts'.

Highlighting the concept of power, and the diversity of levels, forms, and contexts in relation to gender violence allows us to understand even those (relatively fewer) acts that are perpetrated by women. Power is dynamic, not static; it also defines relationships. Thus, although black men are the beneficiaries of the power defining gender relations, say in the home, they are relatively powerless in the streets vibrant with racist assaults where white people enjoy the power. Similarly a white woman who is an employer will be more powerful at the workplace, or at home in relation to her (male and female) employee(s), although she in turn may be subservient to her spouse. The same woman's 'class and white power' may be totally irrelevant in a situation where the deciding factor is the supremacy of 'gender power'.

Violence against women covers all racial, ethnic, cultural and religious groups, all social classes, all ages, whatever sexual preference or orientation; it occurs worldwide, in diverse economic and ideological contexts, in rural and urban settings. So widespread is violence against women that to Mies it 'seems the main common denominator that epitomizes women's exploitation and oppression' (Mies, 1986, p. 169). That said, however, we ought to acknowledge that although many forms of violence against women are common across the board, some forms and/or their incidence are strictly related to one's positioning in terms of the diversity of our realities, in time and space. Since gender is socially and historically constructed, violence against women, a manifestation of gender relations, of power relations, is therefore necessarily responsive to these diverse realities. For instance, while female genital mutilation was practised in Europe until about the 1930s, today it occurs in isolated cases, yet it is currently widespread in some parts of Africa, among certain groups. Similarly, dowry deaths and bride burning are currently specific to

India, and the escalating reported cases of sexual abuse of the mentally disabled and the aged in care are currently a phenomenon of the Western world. Also, during periods of economic, political and social upheaval and uncertainties, violence against subordinated groups, against women, often escalates.

Such appears to be the case in South Africa. Black women who are domestic workers are subjected to all the economic, social and political violence of apartheid. They are not immune to the escalating horrors presently sweeping through the country. They commute on the same trains, live in the same townships, urban and rural areas, attend the same funerals and walk in the same streets and alleys where killing, maiming and general harassment has become the order of the day. Some live and work in areas presently dominated by the neo-nazi and other white right-wing constituencies who have openly sworn to unleash terrorism if the results of the imminent election spell black majority rule. They are part of the same trade union movement and other organizations struggling through contemporary challenges. This systemic violence affects women, children and men; it also affects them differently. Black women also experience personal and institutional gender violence at the level of the home/household, work, organizations, the wider community, and the state. The dialectical combination of the varying aspects of their oppression renders domestic workers extremely vulnerable to forms of violence which permeate life and labour relations. It is important to keep that in mind while concentrating in this paper on violence which occurs at or around the workplace. These gender relations of labour cannot be understood outside their historical context.

Historical Background

The boers took our land and broke our families up. They forced us to work for them. Now, after 100's of years, we still have no legal rights. We still earn starvation wages. We get no rest, no peace. We grow their food and we look after their children. But we are hungry and our children, who we never see, are dying. We cannot go on like this. We demand at least the same rights as other workers. (SADWU pamphlet)

For the indigenous African peoples of Southern Africa colonization and capitalist penetration have been a bitterly violent affair. Brutal wars were waged upon them by the two settler colonial regimes, the British and the Dutch Boers which, although sometimes in conflict with each other, acted in concert to create in 1910 a white settler state which further disenfranchised the indigenous population and consolidated power in the hands of the settler. The equally crippling ideological drive for the colonization of the mind spearheaded by European missionaries, and the brutalization of African culture, deserve mention. Through the medium of the state, economic and extra-economic coercion was resorted to in the creation of the African proletariat – initially envisioned to be oscillatory, migratory and male – and its correlative, the settler bourgeoisie.

Although these processes are here listed separately for clarity, they all constitute an interrelated and dynamic process of the violent transformation from pre-capitalist to capitalist relations of production which underlined the economic, social, psychological and political dispossession and subjugation of the indigenous peoples. Together they served the interest of international and settler capital and of the settler state, to the benefit and privilege of the white settler community at large. They laid the roots for the apartheid system, a system whose entire history is fraught with violence.

Unlike Europe where capitalism is believed to have ushered in civil liberties for all citizens, for colonial subjects civil liberties were curtailed; they became a monopoly of the white minority. The Africans, of course, never took their subjugation sitting down. However, as the indigens perfected their methods and strategies to combat their oppression and exploitation, the settler state and nation and their international allies perfected their repressive strategies until their ultra-violent apartheid in its military, economic and political manifestations devastated lives of black South and Southern African children, women and men, while also psychologically maiming their own white women, men and children, irrespective of whether they ultimately did or did not actively or passively support apartheid.

An important but often overlooked part of this violent process is its effect on gender relations. Black women came to bear the brunt of these racially constituted and structured state policies and their implementation. The creation of a predominantly black female domestic work force, today operating under conditions of super exploitation and oppression, employed by members of all races, all ethnic groups, and both genders, can be traced back to the process mentioned above.

The nation of South Africa comprises different communities the conjunction of whose economic, political, social and cognitive structures and processes birth present-day reality of complex and dynamic relations between and among women and men. It is certainly informative to look historically at social and gender relations as far as they can separately and collectively be traced in each of the nationalities and their sub-groups. This however is not the place for such a task except for brief observation.

Among the few scholars who have worked on this area, controversy surrounds the nature of gender relations within communities of Southern Africa prior to conquest. The major part of the problem is that the history of these societies was passed orally from generation to generation. The geographic and cultural dislocation resulting from colonialism and 'modernization' has made the preservation of that history difficult. Another problem is that written history was solely in the hands of the members of the colonizing nation, the majority of whom were direct or indirect agents of imperialism, interested in the justification and perpetuation of the status quo. Their racist and sexist accounts cannot do justice to the history of the oppressed. Thus the bulk of this history remains still to be (re)written.

Nevertheless, two views dominate contemporary debates. The first is aptly captured in the words of Guy who 'delineates certain social features which were common to all pre-capitalist societies in Southern Africa ... and argues that these features suggest that these societies were based upon the appropriation of women's labour by men' (Guy, 1990, p. 33). 'There was a clear sexual division of labour under the control of the husband/father' (*ibid.*, p. 34; see also Kimble, 1983). Molokomme's (1991) work, while following this same trend, points out that men's control of the means of production was not absolute, thus suggesting flexibility.

The second view belongs to those who believe that patriarchy and matri-archy defined African gender relations in different parts of the continent and that the universalization of patriarchy was a later, European-influenced development.

> Contrary to the more popularly held view, African women on a con-tinent wide scale enjoyed great freedom and had both a legal and social equality which, among other things enabled them to become effective heads of state and military strategists and to portray the dynamism of both gender relations and their history over time and space in all these communities. (Qunta, 1987, p. 23)

What should be remembered is that these societies were numerous and varied. Some had developed into sizeable and relatively powerful political and economic entities, while others remained smaller. Gender relations could not have been identical. Cock (1984) writes about differential treatment and attitudes of settlers towards domestic workers of different ethnicity in the nineteenth century. One might ask to what degree this had to do, in part, with the workers' cultural and historical backgrounds, including socialization, attitudes and mechanisms of coping with the experience of imperialism and changing production relations. Another part, of course, would be attributable to the attitudes towards domestic service and workers in Europe from where the employers emigrated.[2]

It is beyond the scope of this paper to go deeper into these debates. Suffice it to note that, whatever the case may have been, British imperialism has not been known to promote equitable (race, class and) gender relations. Instead, where their interests coincided, they collaborated with local male power elites to facilitate and deepen control over women, as in the Lesotho case where they sought to discourage female labour migration to South African farms and industrial cities (Kimble, 1983; Matlanyane Sexwale, 1989).

> Where women held positions of power and indigenous concepts linked to flexible gender constructions in terms of access to power

and authority mediated dual-sex divisions, the new Western concepts introduced through colonial conquest carried strong sex and class inequalities supported by rigid gender ideology and construction. (Amadiume, 1987, p. 119)

Two groups formed the largest and most powerful of the white settler tribes; in addition to the British were the Dutch. Their laws, policies and practice would naturally be influenced by, among other things, their patriarchal traditions, which would in turn impact on and be influenced by their inter-action with the indigens and other groups. British capital dominated the mining (and subsequently other) industry while the Dutch Afrikaners ulti-mately became significant in the agricultural sector. The story of social, gender and labour relations in Victorian England and its degradation and dehumani-sation of especially the peasant and working class women and children forms an important backdrop. The Dutch Calvinist religious background which permeates the Afrikaner existence informs their specific brand of patriarchy, their love/hate relationship with other white tribes, and their fear and hatred of black people – to them the 'children of Ham' (Gardner, 1991, pp. 8–12). The combination militates aggressively against Afrikaner women who are expected to maintain apartheid by preserving the cultural and racial 'purity' of the Afrikaner race. Add institutionalized, eventually legislated white su-premacy which has been emotionally, psychologically, physically and system-atically instilled in the minds, hearts and lives of the whites, to understand patriarchy blended together with racism and classism in the relationship between these whites and their workers, black and women.

The demographic distribution of the Africans resulting from, *inter alia*, earlier wars was reinforced by a consortium of laws and regulations, forcible removals and relocations, in an attempt to confine Africans to a mere 13 per cent of South Africa, the richest 87 per cent being reserved for exclusive access and control by the whites (4.5 million, i.e., 15.6 per cent of the entire population according to the 1985 census). Though there has been evidence of black women directly coerced into domestic service by the colonists (Cock, 1984, pp. 198–9), forced labour was targeted initially mainly at men. The plan was for the women to remain in these 'reserves'[3] engaged in production and reproduction geared at subsidizing and sustaining the dominant system. Before long, however, conditions in the reserves degenerated and demands of monetization, poverty, landlessness and deteriorating relationships between men and women, forced women out of the 'reserves' in search of opportun-ities in the industrial centres and white farms. Thus the gender composition of migration and of the labour force, especially the domestic service labour market, was transformed.

Although black men and white women have taken up domestic work in white homes, for them it has been a place of first entry into the labour market from which most have ultimately moved, and to which some return during periods of unemployment.[4] For most black women it has been a job for life, passed on through generations, competing only with farm work, beer brewing and other activities on the parallel market. Throughout the years of white rule this historically violent relationship between capital and labour, between on the one hand the ruling classes and nation, and on the other the subordinated, has been reproduced at different levels and in various forms. The domestic service sector has been plagued with violent labour relations with roots traceable to this background, and it cannot be assumed that they will automatically vanish with the demise of political apartheid.

The Violence as Described by Domestic Workers

Where does the social, psychological and emotional violence begin and fester?

I start work at six and knock off at the earliest at eight in the night. I clean the house, make up the beds, feed and clean the baby. In between I take care of the family washing. If the baby is awake when I take the washing outside to hang, then I put the baby on my back. I have to rush to prepare lunch for the family and feed the baby. There is no time for my lunch. I have to play with the child, if it doesn't want to sleep then I cannot iron.

On Saturdays and Sundays I work until ten in the morning except once a month when I have both days off.

No one is allowed to visit me. They have a big dog. They never explained to me why they don't want visitors but maybe it is because they don't trust black people or black men. (interview, Baleka)

I worked at the kitchen . . . as soon as I finished scrubbing the house, cleaning it, then I would go to the butchery . . . I started work at six.

That was the work we did. It would strike eleven, twelve [midnight], we used not to sleep. Before we notice it would be morning. (interview, Jelase)

Let me say, I worked there in Zastron at the home of one old Boer woman. At this time when other people had knocked off, me, I would be in the bedroom grinding nose tobacco . . . of this very woman . . . and sifting it with a stocking. EVERY DAY!

Isn't it, me, I was dumb, not knowing what was what. I did not know what discrimination was when you live in a Boer's place. You see I regarded her as if she was a person like other people I was used to . . . One time I took a brush and combed my hair . . . she found hair on this brush. *Joo 'na 'na ooe! Ha!* She fought me. Every day whenever she was cross she would take the brush, put it in water with Dettol, and I would wash it.

But one thing painful about the Boers, *k'ore*, even in the kitchen when there are chairs, you cannot sit on those chairs. You will be on your feet like that every day of your life. You must not be found eating in the same dish they eat in. You may not have tea in the cups they drink in. The point is, everything they use you may not use. You use only things they have set aside for you . . . even keeping it you may not keep it where they keep theirs. (interview, 'Metlakhola)

For the first time/I am a mother to my child./I carried my other children/for nine months./I fed them with my milk/To make them strong./But even as they made me happy,/they made me sad./I knew I must send them away. (Raven, 1987, p. 12)

My firstborn, Sipho,/was just eleven months/when the Inspectors came./They gave me 24 hours to take him/to my sister./I can still hear him crying./He didn't understand. (*ibid.*, p. 13)

I have walked to the station/five times to send a child away./It doesn't matter if it is my own child/or a sister's child./I feel the same sickness/and sadness in my heart. It is such a terrible thing for a mother/ to send her child away./It is such a terrible thing for a child/to lose her mother. (*ibid.*, p. 70)

Always when we go to the station/we see mothers/taking their children home./Sometimes the madam says/the baby must go./Sometimes the police find them./Sometimes the mother loses her job./Then she must go back to the/homelands with her baby.

For me the saddest thing in my life/was to take my children on the train/and come back without them. For Matshepo it was even worse./She took Teboho home./A month later her baby was dead. (*ibid.*, p. 72)

Still I have no time to feed my child/when she is hungry./I have looked after many white babies./I never let them go hungry./It makes me like a mad person./My child is hungry./I have food to give her./But I cannot feed her/when she is hungry. Every white child/I looked after was happy./I looked after them so nicely./But with my own children it is different./I sent Thoko, Sipho and Jabu away./I felt I am a bad mother/to leave my children. (*ibid.*, p. 39)

Thus, an ordinary week wasn't that bad. I worked from seven in the morning to eight-thirty at night, Monday to Friday; and seven to two-thirty in the afternoon on Saturday; and Sunday, eight to ten-thirty. No, it wasn't a bad job for a domestic servant. Moreover, I had my baby with me, a luxury and a privilege. Most domestic workers are sleep-ins: they live on the premises. The law forbids members of their families, including spouses, to live with them. Some employers turn a blind eye to the glaring signs indicating the frequent visits of a spouse: booming, obviously male voice, heavy footsteps in the middle of the night and the same steps, now departing, at crack of dawn; the heaped plate or indeed, two plates carried by the maid to her room at night; the maid's laundry hanging on her wash line, shirts several sizes too large for her, man's underpants, etc. The law says it is forbidden, the wise employer may choose not to see the black man walking in her very yard! That the Garlands let me keep my baby with me made me see them as kinder than most and for that favour I would tolerate many an infringement! (Magona, 1990, p. 124)

So Pule sleeps with his wife/in her room./Last night they were sleeping/when the police came./Pule showed them his pass./He told them that he had a job. They didn't listen./They threw him in the back/of the landrover with the dogs./They said he was in the area illegally. (Raven, 1987, p. 77)

It is a heavy punishment/for sleeping with your wife./To get arrested,/ to be sent back to the homelands/and to lose your job. (*ibid.*, p. 78)

I was to work the longest and hardest hours . . .
  Mrs Paporokoulus was not only a harsh medem, she was, by far, the most unreasonable and, I thought, least blessed with any intelligence. (Magona, 1990, p. 133)

[The verbal contract had been stated by Mr P, 'a man of short English words, No smoking, no drinking, no boyfriend. Polish floor, machine; washing, machine. No cooking. You, . . . eat food from the Astoria. Thirty rand a month' (*ibid.*, p. 131).
  Food, albeit the same food everyday – for which Magona would have to wait up till 1 a.m.! – and the 30 rand was the only part of the verbal contract ever performed by her employers. The executing party, the overseer, was the wife who, regarding the working conditions, would 'contradict her husband on virtually every clause' (*ibid.*, p. 133)].

One of the extras I used to do for this family [the Garlands] was reading the children to sleep. This task, clearly outside the scope of our verbal contract, did not bring me any extra money. It necessitated my spending an hour or two of my own time 'in the kitchen', a metonymy for being on duty inside the house. However the recognition that I could read, that I was capable of higher duty, that I was not limited to sweeping, scrubbing, scouring and steam-ironing; in short, that I, although a servant, had a brain, did a lot for my battered ego. It more than compensated the absence of pecuniary gain. (Magona, 1990, p. 127)

Sexual harassment and rape

However, bad as that sounds, nothing beat the guest who became too familiar, overstepping not only the boundaries of servant and employer classes, unbecoming as that may be, but overstepping racial and colour lines – and that was illegal! Somehow, and this happened only once to me while I was working for this family, a servant is left with the bad after-taste of having, even unknowingly, invited the unwanted attention. The feeling of shame at having made a spectacle of oneself – for how could a black woman, a servant, begin to think of herself as an object of desire when she was hard put to it going on believing that she was more than a beast of burden? (Magona, 1990, p. 125)

The door was not closed. I have no clothes on because I'm just changing. My employer just pushed the door open and kept it right there. 'Okay, I understand but please close the door because I've got no clothes on'. He's very cross. (interview, Baleka)

An adult female, a live-in domestic was employed by a male in Bellevue. Some time in 1989, her employer arrived at his house and found her in the kitchen. He touched the domestic worker in the region of her private parts saying that her 'thing' is big. The worker then took exception to this act, got angry and walked out of the kitchen. When the employer noticed that she was cross, he chased her out of his premises with a firearm. He locked the domestic worker's room and the gates.

The domestic worker then reported the matter to the police. Two days later she was accompanied by the police to get her belongings. On arrival, the employer refused to release the worker's possessions alleging that she had stolen certain of his belongings.

This matter was reported to a lawyer who instructed the police to accompany the worker to collect her belongings and should the employer fail to release same, a charge would be laid against him. The employer subsequently released the worker's belongings. (SADWU records cited in Kedijang, 1990, p. 16)

I had just started to work for a family in Jeppestown. My master was not working far and he used to come during the day. When I was working, he used to follow me around and touched my breasts and private parts.

. . . I was afraid of him. When he was home, I spent time working outside.

. . . I was even afraid to tell madam because she would be angry with me and she may even shoot me. I have heard of people who are shot because of these things. (Kedijang, 1990)

The president of the domestic workers' union tells of some of the escalating rape and attempted rape incidents. In one, the domestic worker was forced into group sex by two brothers, her employers. In another case in February 1992, a domestic worker was raped by her white employer. Attracted out of the servant's quarters by the crying of their baby who had been left on the floor and her own screaming, her husband came to her rescue.

But he couldn't do anything more. He says he was afraid to beat up the white man lest he got shot. So they came to the office of SADWU. And the husband was crying when he related this. He was so angry that he plans to remove all their belongings from the backyard and then do something about the employer. He was prepared to die the way he was so angry. Of course, the law cannot do anything and the union can't do anything. (interview, Senna Motlhasedi)

And you know that some of our black women hate to tell people that they've been raped. They hide it, they don't want to be seen or to tell the story of what happened. Some of them don't even come to the office we just get it from hearsay... Because they don't want to expose themselves in front of the court I think. Or they are frightened that if they say this then the employer, the white man is going to kill them. So this case is very difficult even for the union to deal with. Ja, because of the humiliation that the women usually go through to prove that they have been raped. It's very, very difficult life and it's an on-going thing. It's really an on-going thing now. It is on the increase. (interview, Senna Motlhasedi)

Physical violence

Overall the situation is getting worse for domestic workers, especially after the unbanning of the ANC. One woman was pushed out – this is violence, why the employer cannot just tell me to 'get out of my house!' instead of pushing me? – The story of that old woman is that she was watching TV when Mandela was to come out. All over the country people waited next to their TVs because Mandela only came out late, people watched from 9 and he was released late afternoon. The woman with her friends were dancing and quite happy. As they were clapping the employer came out, 'this is my house not ANC house!' She was pushed out of the house. She had worked there for twenty-five years and earned R350, no overalls, no food rations.

Many workers have been tortured by the employers. They ask them 'are you a member of ANC or Inkatha? Who do you like between Mandela and Buthelezi? Do you like De Klerk?' And it is very, very dangerous with the workers because they stay there, they work, alone, isolated. We don't know how many they have killed. (interview, Senna Motlhasedi)

Evelyn Mthethwa, a domestic worker, was insulted, beaten and thrown out of the gate of her employers' house for requesting her wages. The wife of the household also beat her using kitchen utensils and said Mthethwa was lucky not to have been killed by their dogs. Mthethwa returned to the house from hospital after receiving twelve stitches to her forehead, only to be met by two policemen who, without speaking, kicked her, punched her and hit her with the butt of a gun and a sjambok. They tortured her psychologically, making her run towards their van then tripping her before she could reach it, so they could again kick her all over her body. She was then taken into the house bleeding badly, and forced to clean it from top to bottom. When finished she was bundled into the back of a van with a sheep the policemen had been given by Mr and Mrs Chris Badenhorst, her employers, as a reward for their efforts (*Star*, 27 Jan. 1992; *Sowetan*, 22 Jan. 1992).

Master came to my room and said to me, 'somebody is coming into my yard when I'm not here'. So I said, 'no, no one comes because you told me so'. Then he told me to start work at 4.00 hours when madam goes to work. I explained that I took a sleep-in job because I don't want to start too early and 6 is already quite early, it's too much. But he insisted. When I said no, he just smacked me right on the face. I ran into the house to report to madam. She also joined the beating. I don't know why. He said, 'Out here bloody fucking *Kaffir bitch*' and continued beating me. I was bleeding. The swimming pool was full. He pushed me right in, every time I tried to come out he pushed me back in. I'm just screaming. No one is coming to this house, until the phone rang. The wife went to answer the phone and call the husband. I ran trying to find a police station until I found one. By this time I'm *wet* and it is *cold* because it is May. I report to them what happened. Policeman phoned Mr Smit. When he's finished he put the phone down and sprayed my eyes with tear gas and told me, 'John Smit said you stole something from them'. I asked him, 'you believe Mr Smit because he's white?'

Mr Smit did not give me my money, notice, wages. [Another] policeman said I'd better find a lawyer, 'John Smit said he'll shoot you if you come near his house again'. They're all Afrikaans. Went to lawyer and through lawyer I got the notice and wages. When I'd gone with the policeman he'd refused to pay me because he said I'd taken something from the house.

I'll never forget that. I can't swim. If the phone hadn't rang I'd have died! (interview, Baleka)

The testimonies reveal various mechanisms through which the autonomy and self-esteem of the domestic workers are systematically eroded, developing or enhancing vulnerability: the low wages, the long working hours, the multiple tasks, the isolation, the less than human treatment, the humiliation, the pangs of mothers forced by the wishes of their employers and by state regulation to abandon their children at a tender age, plunging them into dire living conditions, while the mothers instead nurture the children of their employers! Needless to stress, the psychological impact on the worker is a recurring theme irrespective of the category under which the atrocities are sorted. In excerpt after excerpt the interlinkages of the different forms of gender violence – emotional, psychological, sexual and physical – remain vivid. Although these get to be acted out between individuals at a family or household level, their facilitation is institutional and systematic.

One other aspect that stands out is the collaboration between the white employers, the state and its apparatus. Having been assaulted by the employers, Baleka and Mthethwa were further abused by the police, who, in a less bizarre situation, would have been expected to protect the survivor of the violence – none of the aggressors have been brought to book! Both women's employers are white, one suburban and the other rural, and so, in these cases, were the police officers. But beyond white solidarity and white patriarchal power, there is yet another reinforcing factor. It is in order to assume that outside their state function back in their households, the police officers are also employers of black (women) domestics; research has suggested that almost all white South African families employ domestic workers (Cock, 1984). On the other hand, the brutality of the employers is facilitated by the position of the workers whose vulnerability is a consequence of the system, further weakened, as we shall see in the next section, by the absence of legal protection, and by lack of resources to file complaints in those cases where this might have been a possibility.

Often, discussions of domestic service emphasize the relationship between the *women* employers and the *women* workers (Rollins, 1985; Cock, 1984). One of the striking things revealed by these accounts is that the ultimate power rests with the man, the 'head' of the household. It is Mr Paporokoulus who dictates the contract; the wife is an executing agent, although in relation to the domestic worker she is powerful. It is the male employers who sexually and physically assault the female employees, with the wife's collaboration. The white women are involved in verbal abuse, emotional and psychological torture, but I have not thus far come across cases where they independently dare to physically attack the black woman; instead, when they wish the worker to be thus punished, they appeal to the men. Kedijang (1990) notes cases where this was used as a threat. While this goes to show the gender of power, of brute force, the white woman's role demonstrates not only the dynamism of power but also divisions between and among women.

Bunie M. Matlanyane Sexwale

What Is Being Done: Resisting and Organizing

'Comrade, your supper is ready.'

Domestic workers face the largest obstacles to organizing and unionizing. In fact the very conditions discussed above as those making them vulnerable in relation to violence act as obstacles for unionization. But history has shown that oppression does not necessarily lead to weakness; often, women (and men) facing great adversity are quite militant in their struggles. In 1986 SADWU, the South African Domestic Workers' Union, was launched, an act of bravery and defiance in the face of state-imposed illegality. The existence of SADWU has to be understood as part of the history of unionization of black workers in South Africa which has been a long and difficult part and parcel of the resistance against colonialism, apartheid and capitalist exploitation. After a long period of their being outlawed, and following consistent labour action, the state and employers were forced to succumb to black workers' determined demands for recognition of independent trade unions. By 1986 COSATU, the Congress of South African Trade Unions, a powerful union federation, was launched; SADWU was to be one of its affiliates. Since the February 1990 unbanning of political organizations, COSATU entered into a tripartite alliance concerned with democratic change, led by the ANC (African National Congress).

SADWU's affiliation to COSATU is of unquestionable advantage to the small union, which remains technically unrecognized (legally and otherwise) because domestic workers are not recognized as workers. However, problems surface when it comes to gender concerns. Although they have reached some level of serious self-criticism, planning and strategizing, being, as organizations usually are, microcosms of society, ANC and its ally, COSATU, are still by and large male-dominated. It is not surprising, then, that, coming from a union with an overwhelmingly female membership, SADWU's President has mixed feelings about the nature of solidarity among the allies and affiliates. Three sentiments are apparent in her utterances. As an individual member of ANC herself she constructively criticizes the organization but also looks up to it as a site of necessary struggles – working-class, race and gender – but also as a competent structure to lead towards a non-racial, non-sexist democracy. She says with striking confidence of the Mthethwa case: 'We have appealed to the ANC for help because there is nothing we can do. Something is already being done'. Then she criticizes ANC and COSATU for not having full understanding of the oppression and exploitation of domestic workers: 'And if one can just sit down and think about it, it totally differs from the other workforce. So we're getting support from COSATU, but it is a mass support.' She shows appreciation of overburdened structures due to the present conditions and demands, but also a frustration understandable in one involved on a daily basis with grassroots demands. And lastly she finds self-criticism by SADWU appropriate:

We have to sort out our internal problems and inefficiency. We have to articulate our requests to COSATU and ANC much clearer and in a more structural way, through the already established channels.

Right from its inception, SADWU has given itself tasks to confront the many tiers of exploitation and oppression faced by its constituency, and demands basic human rights, workers' rights and women's rights. The following demands aptly reflect the misery of working conditions in domestic service: a minimum living wage set at R450 since 1986, three weeks' paid leave, fourteen days' paid sick leave, two months' maternity leave with pay and one month's notice upon dismissal, including allowing the worker to find alternative accommodation. In the rare cases where any of these benefits have been enjoyed by some workers, it has been purely as favours extended according to the wishes of employers or resulting from pressure from the union.

Demands levelled at the government plead legal recognition and reform. The first is for farm and domestic workers to be covered by the Labour Relations and Basic Conditions of Employment Acts. The second is that the Wage Act should be extended to cover the domestic service sector. Lastly, in collaboration with COSATU, SADWU demands twelve days' public holidays per annum, which will include May Day and Soweto Day (SADWU newsletter, undated). The first two have been addressed to the state in a tripartite National Manpower Commission, a structure involving representatives of SADWU, COSATU and the government Department of Manpower, which has met since 1990. The irony of this structure, remarks SADWU's president, is that apart from the SADWU representatives, most of the other negotiators are also actually employers of domestic workers, thus there is a danger that they may represent their own interests as employers, without openly admitting them. This could be a stumbling block.

The employers and the state are tackled through an intricate multi-pronged strategy of negotiation, protest and worker mobilization in collaboration with other unions, political organizations and professionals.

However, even were legal reform achieved, SADWU would still face a number of obstacles including, among others, enforcement, individual employers' attitudes and insecurity, as the following accounts indicate.

Employers' attitudes and reactions to SADWU

The reactions of the employers to SADWU, described below, should be understood in the general context of a power relationship and the threat to the powerful of a possibility of losing some of their power. Again this rotates around the race, class and gender hierarchy enacted through labour relations.

Bunie M. Matlanyane Sexwale

I worked for three years eight months in Gleenwood, paid R120 start. Work every day till Saturday 1 o'clock. Off Sunday. No long weekend. I buy my own food and utensils – cups, plates, etc. After one year I complained. They say they have no money. They'd give me R10. The man works for the university! That's when I joined SADWU. SADWU tried to negotiate with employer to improve wage and give me food, uniform and he start to shout me and fight me. He told me to leave the union because they are liars. One day he told me to leave SADWU or leave their house. (interview, Baletse)

In the case of the worker dismissed for celebrating the release of Mandela, we [SADWU] phoned the employer to negotiate leave, notice pay and wages. The employer's response was she must go to Mandela who must pay her, give her pension – 'I don't see why, after working for me for so long, the woman should rejoice when Mandela is released'. Ultimately we got her wages and notice pay. No pension. No leave pay. (interview, Senna Motlhasedi)

My madam doesn't know I've joined SADWU. She has told me that Nelson Mandela is bad, that ANC is a killer. So I don't want her to know that I'm a member. When she asks me about my political affiliation I say I'm neutral. But she thinks that Gatsha Buthelezi is the best man. If you're SADWU they know SADWU is affiliated with COSATU and therefore with the ANC. (interview, Maleshoane)

My employers resisted and don't like me joining SADWU but they had nothing to fear because I attend to SADWU business in my own free time, my working hours and wages and conditions are okay. I start at 7, break for one hour at 9, 10 to 1 o'clock, then 2 to 5. I earn R400 which is bad but far better than domestic workers who earn R100. Salaries in Natal are very poor. (interview, Nondaba)

'Is SADWU not involved with ANC?' I said SADWU is involved with COSATU. She doesn't like COSATU because of link with ANC. One day [March 1992] I's going to a Communist Party rally. So I wore my SACP T-shirt. After rally I went back to work, on Sunday night. Then employer came straight to my room and told me 'I don't want this T-shirt. It is for communists. If you don't want to leave this shirt, leave my job'. (interview, Baleka)

Ja, definitely, sure, we involve other organizations, since now ANCWL has got its own structure we would like them to help us organize this kind of marches . . . and some other things more especially on women. . . .
And of course our members are becoming aware. They are joining marches on anything that is taking place, affecting women no matter COSATU or ANC.

They are even wearing now the colours of ANC. Even at the workplaces some of them have been dismissed because they wear the T-shirt of SACP, the party. They are nice and tired. You know they cannot tell the employers that they are members of ANC. But they can tell, it's a T-shirt. When they start asking they say ja, of course I am. I can't be a member of De Klerk, of NP, AWB or CP [the white political parties]. There are some other workers who are very, very strong. . . .

But some workers don't want to tell the employers that they are members. Even if they know that the employers are members [of ANC]. Because they feel threatened that if they know they might dismiss them. But I say to them if they are members of ANC it means they are comrades. So if you can just sit down with your employer at the end of the day I don't think that you are going to call your madam, madam any more. You're going to call out, '*comrade, your supper is ready!*' . . .

It can be a very lovely country. That is how we're going to kill this madam, master and maid. Then you just going to call them comrade, comrade. . . . But at least that step of saying 'No, today we are going to an ANC meeting together'. Like when you go to church, the employers respect you so much. Because whenever you say to them I have to work, chop-chop, and go to church, then they always say, 'You don't have to wash the dishes, I'll do that for you, you can go to church because you're going to be late'. But why not ANC? And why not SADWU? And it's up to us. (interview, Senna Motlhasedi)

Social behaviour is always complex and people react differently to different situations due to several influencing factors. Some employers (a regrettably small number) have reacted positively to SADWU's existence and given support to the union. Some use it as a centre of referral or advice whenever in doubt about aspects of their relationship with their employees. A group of women in Kilarney, a rich Johannesburg suburb, organized themselves and invited SADWU for a discussion around SADWU and its relationship with the ANC. They were taken aback by an assertive and astute president who challenged them.

Let us now forget about ANC and SADWU, let us discuss us as women. Why can't we come together? Because you are woman, you are affected sometimes the same as me, sometimes you're not enjoying your riches because there are some difficulties/contradictions between you and men, as a woman. So they agreed to another meeting somewhere between April and June. . . . So I think now they can see change. And they can see that SADWU is really pushing and since now the discussion on domestic workers at the National Manpower, I think they feel fear because the Wage Act is in question. . . . Most employers we met in that area are paying their domestic workers R500-R600 [per month]. Then they feel they can also do something to educate other employers on how its very important for now to come together so that our union does not become a threat. (interview, Senna Motlhasedi)

How is SADWU dealing with the violence?

Still bleeding, ten days after being seriously assaulted by her employers, Evelyn Mthethwa took her case to SADWU, where she received immediate support and commitment, although she was not a member of the union. Senna Motlhasedi commented: 'The farm is very far from town. Our office in that area is very far in Van der Bijl Park. We still haven't reached some of the areas to organize. We need to have a field worker to go to some of those areas still'.

Having been interviewed by SADWU and some journalists, she was advised to come back to the SADWU office the following day for legal and medical assistance. To everyone's worry, she has vanished. SADWU has appealed for ANC intervention.

Mthethwa's case is not an isolated one but part of an alarming rate of violence by whites against black women and men especially in the rural areas. A few days before her assault, on the same farm, a black man, Letsoalo, was killed during a row over the mating of his dog and a white-owned one. Such is the depth of racial hatred festering among the white farming communities. Coincidental to her disappearance, the journalist who exposed her case has received threatening telephone calls accusing her of being a white sell-out. It is not difficult to imagine that both the employers and the police would want to cover up their excesses.

Having been raped by her employers, a woman was discovered by a SARHU (South African Railways and Harbours Union) activist dumped at Park Station in Johannesburg. He accompanied her to the SADWU offices.

Then we took this woman to the doctor. And after that we took her to the lawyers. But nothing was done to the employers. That is what is frustrating me so much. The employers are just going to be exposed in the newspapers or wherever. But it is nothing very strong because of what I will say. Even if you take the matter to the police they do not arrest the employers. (interview, Senna Motlhasedi)

At this moment we have got no lawyers because the lawyers are demanding a lot of money. We have no progressive lawyers who can help us even though we haven't got money. Not especially with cases like this. Lawyers for Human Rights also need some money. (interview, Senna Motlhasedi)

Concluding Remarks

Instead of drawing conclusions, I choose at this stage to end only with some remarks.

What I have done in this paper is to underline the fact that violence against women as a manifestation of gender relations is historically, culturally and socially determined. The testimonies of the domestic workers interviewed, and those gleaned from secondary sources, convey a wide range of experiences of violence. Many women, particularly black women, will recognize themselves in some of the cases cited; yet the peculiarity of violence against domestic workers stands out.

Some factors that ring through these women's eloquent voices repeatedly emphasize the commonality of their experience. The long, long hours to which they are subjected reinforce their isolation; their very low wages, brutal working conditions and lack of social and material benefits keep them within the spiral of perpetual dependence on their ultra-exploitative and oppressive occupation. In short, the horrible working conditions related above emphasize the psychological and emotional violence of domestic service in apartheid South Africa and highlight the specificities of sexual and physical violence the women experience. It is also clear that these forms of violence coincide.

One of the harshest realities those ruled forcibly by the minority regime have had to face is the collusion between many elements of white society and the coercive state machinery, especially the military and the police. Of the many frustrations articulated in the narratives, the non-validation of the humanness of domestic workers is extremely impressive. It is the absence of any legal rights whatsoever; but it is more – the ugly face of racism, classism and sexism manifested at different levels.

The events of February 1990 which ushered in a new era in the life and politics of South Africa appear to have also enhanced the violence which has featured through the years, escalating at particular moments in history. There seems to be a clear prevalence of insecurity among white employers which can be explained as a fear of losing their power. Such is the fear that some white patriarchs decide to kill their wives and children and then themselves, and ironically, this is made easy by their white privilege which entitles them to own any number of guns. This fear is also reflected in the escalation of violence against domestic workers.

Equally impressive, though in a totally different way, is the determination of the oppressed to overcome their oppression. The very existence of SADWU, its affiliation to COSATU and through that its alliance with the ANC, reflect an understanding of domestic workers' exploitation and oppression. SADWU's strategies to combat violence against domestic workers is currently through, first, making the violence visible through media exposure which relies on sympathetic journalists and editors; and second, facilitating workers' access to professional assistance such as lawyers, doctors, etc. This is hampered by the union's growing lack of financial resources and by the shortage of people who through sympathy and/or commitment could give these services voluntarily. Thirdly, SADWU provides support such as accompanying the women to the points where service might be accessible. This is limited by the smallness of the number of SADWU workers (related in part to lack of finance) and to the multiplicity of jobs they have to perform. The financial problem is actually becoming quite serious as those who have hitherto been the main external funders show growing reluctance to continue their support.

Legal reform and creation of a climate conductive to unionization, however, will not automatically change the racist and patriarchal ideology underlining the relations discussed in this chapter. Neither can waging a war on one front lead to winning a battle. Reflecting on the testimonies, the current focus seems to be on the important task of dealing with the after-effects. There is a need for a rigorous gender analysis and networking geared towards the development of additional strategies which focus on gender relations in their complexity. What has been addressed here is a small, albeit worrying, part of a much bigger challenge. If the overall problem of violence against women (wherever they exist and work) is to be combated, there is need for a much more concerted effort, for a stronger women and gender focused organization than exists in contemporary South Africa and indeed in the world. There is also a need for coordinated strategies to tackle gender oppression and gender violence at all levels: household, workplace, community, national and international levels.[5]

You are not Alone

Woman, crouched down low in the corner
Woman, feeling blood pour from your mouth
Woman, watching the man you love, the man
you hate, the man you love and hate
Watching, the man you hate, the man you
love, the man you hate to love
beat you and abuse you
Woman, the pain you feel is the pain of many generations.
The pain you share with so many other souls.
The pain which you alone feel doomed to know.
Lying to your family, lying to your friends, lying to yourself.
Woman your tears can nurture growth of spirit.
Your blood can feed the strength so deep inside.

Break the chain that holds you locked within 'that woman'.
Swing the chain and gather back your pride.
You are not alone.
You are not to blame.
Your shame is all of our shame
Your blame is all of our pain.
Child see your mother father beat you.
Child you are also not to blame.
Your pain is their shame, is our pain and shame and blame.
Child, just hold to the promise not to repeat the cycle
and remember
You Are Not Alone.

(Lennie St Luce, 1989)

Notes

I owe the greatest debt to the Southern African domestic workers who have shared aspects of their experiences, and mention Violet Senna Motlhasedi, the President of the South African Domestic Workers' Union, SADWU, herself a domestic worker, who engaged me in long perceptive and sometimes emotionally disturbing discussions, periodically interrupted and made lighter by our toyi-toyi dances to the music of 'Amaqabane – the comrades'; I dedicate this paper to them all. My heart felt appreciation to Madelein Maurick who conducted some of the interviews and shot slides; to my extended family and friends Jose Tegels, Michelle Williams, Lennie St Luce, Matsobane Sexwale and Yahaya Hashim for all their encouragement and support; to KAIROS for sharing their resources on south Africa; and to the contributors to this volume for their useful comments on an earlier draft. Responsibility for any errors of omission, interpretation and otherwise, remains mine.

1   The testimonies owe origin in part from the Basotho Women Migrants Oral History research project which I undertook from 1983. Not less than 90 per cent of these migrant women from Lesotho working in South Africa had been domestic workers. Three trends have influenced the writing of this chapter, the brutal battery of my sister in 1991, my involvement with SADWU support, and efforts by a group of us Southern African women to analyze women's experiences as a crucial starting point for the process to influence strategy and gender policy formulation during this transitional period. The more recent testimonies are part of this on-going project. Elsewhere (1989) I debate ethical, political and methodological concerns and issues arising from the use of oral history as a research method. Other contributors to this book discuss methodological questions more fully.

2   For comprehensive historical discussion of this see Cock, 1984, and Rollins, 1985; the latter traces domestic service historically right back from slavery.

219

3   Later to be dubbed Bantustans or Homelands according to the whims of the apartheid policy-makers.
4   There is now a small number of white women re-entering the domestic service job market, according to Violet Senna Motlhasedi of SADWU, as a result of the current economic recession.
5   A sequel to this chapter is a working paper proposing concrete measures.

Abbreviations

ANC   African National Congress
ANCWL   African National Congress Women's League
AWB   Afrikaanerweerstandsbeweging
COSATU   Congress of South African Trade Unions
CP   Conservative Party
INKATHA   Inkatha Freedom Party
NP   National Party (ruling party)
SACP   South African Communist Party
SADWU   South African Domestic Workers' Union

References

AMADIUME, I. (1987) *Male Daughters, Female Husbands: Gender and Sex in an African Society*, London, Zed.

BBC TV (1991) *An Act of Love: Family Killings in South Africa*, Everyman.

COCK, J. (1984) *Maids and Madams: A study in the politics of exploitation*, Johannesburg, Raven.

GARDNER, J.H. (1991) *Impaired Vision, Portraits of Black Women in The Afrikaans Novel 1948–1988*, Amsterdam, VU University Press.

GUY, J. (1990) 'Gender Oppression in Southern Africa's Precapitalist Societies,' in WALKER (Ed.) *Women and Gender in Southern Africa*, Cape Town, James Currey; London, David Philip.

HUMAN RIGHTS COMMISSION (1991) Human Rights Update, Dec. (1991) Area Repression Report, Dec. (1990–1992) Weekly Repression Reports.

KEDIJANG, M. (1990) *The best kept secret: Domestic workers as victims of violence*, Project for the study of violence Wits, Johannesburg.

KIMBLE, J. (1983) '*Runaway wives*': Basotho Women, Chiefs and the colonial State, c. 1890–1920, Paper presented to the women in Africa seminar, School of Oriental and African Studies, University of London.

MCFADDEN, P. (1991) 'The Reality of Hating Women', SAPEM, vol. 4, no. 12.

McKENDRICK, B. and HOFFMAN, W. (Eds) (1990) *People and Violence in South Africa*, Cape Town, Oxford University Press.

MAGONA, S. (1990) *To My Children's Children*, Africa South New Writing, South Africa, Claremont.

MAMA, A. (1989) *The Hidden Struggle, Statutory and Voluntary Sector Responses To Violence Against Black Women In The Home*, London Race and Housing Research Unit, UK.

MATLANYANE SEXWALE, B.M. (1987) 'The "New Lesotho's" Prospects For Democracy', A Background to the January 1986 Coup d'Etat, ISS, The Hague.

MATLANYANE SEXWALE, B.M. (1989) 'If Only God Can Help Me Go To Khauteng', Experiences of Migrant Women Workers of Lesotho (mimeo) Presented at the launching conference of the AAWORD Kenya Chapter, Nairobi.

MATLANYANE SEXWALE, B.M. and ROSTE, J. (1989) A Life of Endless Struggle: Migrant Women Workers of Lesotho (mimeo) Research report to NORAD, Oslo.

MEENA, R. (1991) 'Can Women Combat Violence Against Them?' in SAPEM, Harare, vol. 5, no. 2.

MIES, M. (1986) *Patriarchy and Accumulation on a World Scale: Women and The International Division of Labour*, London, Zed.

MOLOKOMME, A. (1991) *Children of The Fence, The Maintenance of Extra-marital Children Under Law and Practice in Botswana*, Phd Thesis, Rijksuniversiteit, Leiden.

PIZZEY, E. (1974) *Scream Quietly Or The Neighbours Will Hear*, UK, Penguin.

QUNTA, C. (1987) *Women in Southern Africa*, London, Allison and Busby.

RAVEN PRESS (1987) *Thula Baba*, Johannesburg.

ROLLINS, J. (1985) *Between Women: Domestics and their employers*, Philadelphia, Temple University Press.

SCHULER, M. (1992) 'Violence Against Women: an international Perspective', in EVENHUIS, W. *et al.* (Eds) *BASTA Women against violence: strategies and action to stop violations of women's human rights*, work conference reader, Amsterdam.

VOGELMAN, I. (1990) 'Debunking Some Myths Of The "Sex monster" Syndrome', Weekly Mail, Johannesburg, Jan. 26 to Feb. 1.

VOGELMAN, I. (1990) *The Sexual Face of Violence, Rapists on Rape*, Johannesburg, Raven Press.

VOGELMAN, I. (1990) 'Violent crime: rape', in McKENDRICK and HOFFMANN (Eds), pp. 96–131.

WILSON, E. (1983) *What Is To Be Done About Violence Against Women?*, UK, Penguin.

Newspapers and Newsletters,
SADWU, Newsletter (undated)
Star, Jan. 27, 1992
Sowetan, Jan. 22, 1992
Weekly Mail, several issues 1990–1992

Chapter 12

Racism and Sexism in Academic Practice: A Case Study

Haideh Moghissi

Racism is commonly understood as prejudicial opinions about and behaviours towards members of racial, ethnic, cultural, religious, or linguistic groups who are considered to be inherently inferior to one's own. Anthony Appiah categorizes 'racial prejudice' as

> [t]he tendency to assent to false propositions, both moral and theoretical, about races – propositions that support policies or beliefs that are to the disadvantage of some race (or races) as opposed to others, and to do so even in the face of evidence and argument that should appropriately lead to giving those propositions up. (Appiah, 1990, pp. 15–16)

According to this definition, racially prejudiced statements and practices are those that use people's racially attributed characteristics to justify discrimination and exclusion. A major problem in combating racism, however, is that it is not always easy to identify racialist attitudes and practices. Not only are racist attitudes and practices often disguised under more benign notions, but racism changes its character, forms and actors according to the setting within which it operates. For example, the racism of educated intellectuals, which is the subject of my paper, is not necessarily conscious and does not directly originate from holding 'other' as inherently inferior. Sometimes, this 'otherness' might seem exotic and as such interesting. It can even generate attraction and fascination. But this fascination is often irrelational, that is they cannot associate with the 'other' individual on equal terms, and their relationship embodies some power relations that preclude equality. The inequality in relation to power, whatever that power might mean, complicates and obstructs interracial communication and relations. In other words, our 'otherness' prevents them from seeing us as individuals, as ourselves. It prevents them from understanding us and relating to us. Often they might not even try to understand us.

It is usually harder to reveal the subtle, unconscious racism of intellectuals and the incredible tolerance of racism in academic institutions than to expose a man in the street who commits overt racism. Most academics disguise their racist attitudes and practices more competently, and hide and suppress challenges to such beliefs more effectively, by resorting to more benign notions and seemingly neutral criteria, such as academic freedom and academic excellence. This is also true for sexist and misogynist attitudes and practices. It is also the case that most intellectuals suffer from a 'cognitive incapacity', to borrow Anthony Appiah's term, to recognize racism, particularly their own racism. Underlying the notion of 'excellence' in such cases is the belief that being qualified and being coloured and/or female are mutually exclusive.

Almost no one likes to be considered racist. In fact often people who inflict racism are not even aware of the harm done and are surprised, even offended, when individuals who are the object of the harm understand their actions as racist. This is particularly the case in those institutions and communities which present and preserve an idealized imagery of liberalism, openness and diversity, such as universities, for most liberal and left educators tend to understand racism only in terms of overt words and actions deriving from malicious intentions and fail to recognize that highly educated and otherwise gentle and civil individuals can also be guilty of prejudicial perceptions and practices.

The racist and sexist behaviours and practices in academia typically do not include hard and convincing-beyond-doubt evidence, such as bodily harm or explicit derogatory statement. This, however, does not make racism and sexism in academia more benign – far from it. Academic institutions produce knowledge and reproduce the ideological make-up of every society. Through educating and training the future elite of every society their intellectual produce has far-reaching impacts on the whole society. Moreover, one always finds the racism of intellectuals more harmful. This is not only because it takes one off-guard. It is also because intellectual racism requires that we put our energies into a battle that need not and should not exist, blocking the way for communication and cooperation in other social and political battlegrounds.

The subtle, unconscious and seemingly innocent racist actions and behaviours of intellectuals take many forms. The experience of a recent grievance process I went through at a Canadian university helped me to observe the many faces of racism or ethnocentrism of intellectuals. This account of the events in this case is inevitably personal and experiential. But personal accounts of racism and sexism always relate to experiences with which many can empathize. Personal stories can provide new insights into what individuals can expect and prepare for if they decide to break the silence and confront racism and sexism, particularly through legal and institutional procedures established for that purpose.

The grievance itself is not our concern here. It arose from a hiring process designed to recruit 'bright new scholars' and increase the proportions of women and people of colour at the University. I was one of two short-listed internal candidates, asked to prepare a presentation which, in the end, I was not given the opportunity to deliver. The other internal candidate (incidentally a white male) was invited to give a presentation and subsequently nominated by the Politics Department for hire. I felt my deliberate exclusion from the competition was manifestly discriminatory and the result of the negative viewing of factors other than my academic qualifications, namely my 'race' and gender, and also of anti-feminism. Thus, I demanded an explanation for my unexpected, eleventh-hour exclusion or the rejection of my application. Indeed I was not even informed that I had been rejected. However, not only was I not provided with an explanation, but I was treated completely as a non-person at the time of the decision. I filed a formal grievance hoping that an open confrontation with the racist practices of the university would help those who do not recognize the existence of racism in academic practice to come face to face with this reality and do something about it. This was a somewhat naive expectation, as the subsequent events demonstrated. For it was based on the assumption that it was lack of information about the existence of racism that explained why there is no aggressive anti-racist campaign, comparable to anti-sexist militancy, in academic institutions. The grievance hearings, which continued for six months, helped me to see that, while lack of concrete information or knowledge about racist structures and relations is a problem, the main reason for the persistent survival of racism is that the pain and anger racism cause are not seen as a collective injury by most white intellectuals, male or female. I could observe for myself what Edward Said has identified as the problem of helplessness, impotence and fragmentation due to specialization; that is being drawn only by virtue of expertise and 'being above all causes' (Said, 1991, pp. 15–16).

When it comes to taking sides in an anti-racist campaign, however, the problem is more profound. The immobility on race issues, I think, is directly related to the fact that white people experience race as a privilege and that, without being aware of it, they benefit from racist structures and relations. For white intellectuals to understand racism requires a fundamental change in the way they see things, understand and interpret them and particularly in the way they relate to others. To recognize the dehumanizing impact of racism and sexism, and particularly to do something about it, requires a willingness to examine and re-examine and challenge one's understanding of racism and sexism, in favour of those who live with and survive racism and sexism. It requires challenging the meanings, standards, values and practices that preclude equality and genuine autonomy for some sorts of people.

A Lesson in Systemic Racism and Sexism

In challenging the adverse decision of the Appointment Committee through a quasi-legal procedure within the University, I sought several goals. First, I was hoping that by making those whose actions and decisions victimize others hear about the effects of their actions they would positively alter their conscience and behaviour in future. This would prevent the repetition of similar injustice and inhumanity. Second, I sought to draw attention to the fact that, if we are serious about combating racism, sexism and other dehumanizing prejudices, we must make individuals accountable for the decisions they make behind closed doors. Finally, I believed that the open hearing of a case involving racism and sexism would serve an educational purpose. I hoped that the hearings would alert not only conservatives, but particularly liberal and left academics, to the many faces and forms of racism and sexism, something that they might be guilty of. The University Grievance Board, after several months of hearings, which were open to the University community, decided that I had been 'the victim of unfair treatment at the hands of the University', and that I had 'a reasonable apprehension of systemic bias'. The Board recommended that the University Principal (President) apologize on behalf of the University for the treatment I had received. It also recommended that the Principal write letters to three men on the Appointment Committee to acknowledge 'the stressful and embarrassing position' they had experienced, and to 'encourage' their future participation in similar processes.

The Board also recommended that the University undertake other efforts in order to ensure the appearance of fairness in its employment procedures and criteria. This included the active involvement of women and people of colour in appointment decisions and the fair assessment of feminist scholarship. The Board's recommendations were viewed by the University's feminist and anti-racist communities as having a far-reaching and long-term significance for other universities and institutions across Canada. Many thought that they would give heart to others who aspire to a more diverse, inclusive and open environment for academic institutions.

Where the existence of discrimination and bias has been so long denied, the mere acknowledgment of the problem was a victory. But I felt the grievance was won when I refused to surrender to the authority of the Head of Department and his colleagues in their judgment of me and my work a year earlier. In any setting where uniformity, vanity and conformity are celebrated to intimidate and silence dissenting voices, to speak out loudly is a victory in itself. However, the Board's decision was a disappointment, as it refused to acknowledge the professional and moral responsibility of individual members of the Appointment Committee. It carefully avoided saying what it should have said, that is, identifying the exact nature of the discrimination I grieved against and the individuals responsible for it. Instead, it whitewashed those responsible, made excuses for their actions and decisions, showed much consideration and sympathy for their discomfort, and tried to appease them by criticizing my conduct and praising their behaviours. Consequently, the Board made it easy for the Principal of the University to refuse once more to acknowledge his institutional responsibility for discriminatory and hurtful practices within the University, and to make specific individuals accountable for the wrong done to others. In fact, in his letter to the three members of the Appointment Committee, he wrote that he was 'very happy' to recognize that their behaviour had been 'exemplary'.

This denied the most sought-for goal of my grievance, which was making individuals accountable for their actions and decisions that marginalize and injure others. I so wanted to bring home to them that systemic racism and sexism in all instances is practised and perpetuated through the actions and behaviours of individuals. Throughout the hearings, I argued that we must seek to understand how individuals carrying out institutional processes can become agents of systemic biases.

The Board's Report demonstrated vividly the paradox of a procedure that has been devised to give the appearance of fairness. When the idea of justice is to 'appear fair' only, it is possible to confuse who is the victim and end up treating the discomfort of the victimizer with the pain and anguish of the victims. This only serves the status quo.

In many cases, people who inflict racism and sexism are not even aware of the harm they are doing. When confronted, they show surprise and find objectionable the victim's understanding of their actions. In such cases, not only do their prejudiced perceptions and practices cause harm to individuals, but they also help to institutionalize inequality and to systemically exclude those perceived as different by their refusal to acknowledge the problem and to do something about it. In other words, they 'consciously' participate in institutionalizing discriminatory practices.

The virulent refusal of the Appointment Committee members to accept any form of responsibility, throughout the hearings, exposed the 'arrogant eyes', to use Marilyn Frye's term (Frye, 1983, p. 67) through which they viewed others. The fact that the whole process did not create even a crack in their wall of resistance, showed that I did not achieve the first goal. They did not listen to what I said with the same care that they gave to their own defence. The many words that passed between us could not fill the gap between our different ways of thinking. All the efforts made to make them see that racism is not necessarily about careful and detailed plans, drawn up by people with malicious intentions, to inflict harm to members of non-dominant ethnic groups and cultures, came to nothing. A Committee member, incidentally a white woman, thought my allegation of racism was 'ludicrous', because she herself had not heard any racist remarks from the members of the Committee in the hiring process. She claimed authority on racism because she is married to an Asian Canadian. She could not see that loving or living with a person of colour would not insulate one against racist assumptions. Neither could she and others appreciate the brutalizing impact of her self-righteous attitudes and her appropriation of the real pain of racism.

If I take the Board's Report and its recommendation as the only outcome of the grievance, then I also did not achieve my second goal. As mentioned earlier, the Board persistently refused to blame or even to acknowledge the individual responsibility of these men in the perpetration of systemic racist, sexist and anti-feminist biases. Although it recognized that I had reasonable grounds for apprehending such biases, it only blamed the Head for 'administrative error', for 'lack of communication' and for his 'unprofessional and unfair' behaviour. However, I think the grievance and, more specifically, the hearings had enormous educational value for me and for many people who attended the hearings. The messages communicated were often insidious and covert but at times open and performative. It was this aspect of the ordeal that I take as an important achievement.

Even though the individuals who inflicted racism and sexism were only concerned with denying that fact and protecting themselves, I believe the hearings created an awareness about the many faces of racism and sexism. It provided an opportunity for many to learn that racism and sexism do not necessarily consist of careful and detailed malicious plans. More often than not, they are about using one's own particular sex, culture and experience as the reference point or yardstick for the 'evaluative judgment' of different cultures, standards and practices. Racism is about how we perceive difference, how we value other sources of knowledge, and how, regardless of intention, the outcomes of prejudiced perceptions and practices institutionalize inequality and exclude those perceived as different.

When I filed my formal complaint, I had no illusions about equity and impartiality in legal or quasi-legal procedures, for, as Audre Lorde put it, 'the master's tools will never dismantle the master's house'. We cannot 'use the tools of a racist patriarchy to examine the fruits of that same patriarchy', because then 'only the most narrow perimeters of change are possible and allowable' (Lorde, 1984, pp. 110–11). The University administration did not even try 'to appear impartial', or to respect their own rhetoric and offer the appearance of fairness. This was obvious in the University's differential treatment of its own officials, namely the Department Head who was represented by the University's lawyer and the Employment Equity Advisor, who was ostracized and isolated, since her testimonies had confirmed my apprehensions of racism and sexism. Hence she showed 'disloyalty' to the institution. The behaviour of members of the Board and their differential treatment of the parties and their evidence were also a reconfirmation that, in a society built on power and privilege differentials, the credibility of one's words and evidence very much depends on one's position in the hierarchy of power. The Board generally accepted as evidence all that was said by the other party and their witnesses at face value. If they said that they did not have racist and sexist bias, if their colleagues testified that they had never heard them making any racist or derogatory remarks, and if they said that they had often 'talked' and even 'socialized with people of colour', the Board seemed to accept this as evidence that they could not have racist perceptions. In other words, it was the viewpoints, standards and value system of the white men on the other side of the table that the Board used to interpret events, actions and reactions in the course of the grievance.

Throughout the hearings, I felt a tremendous sense of powerlessness. The only way I could deal with this and the intimidating formalities of the hearings, and 'the white wall of resistance' on the other side of the table – as a friend identified the sitting arrangement in the hearings – was to express and show my anger. It was a way to hang on to my own identity and reject the identity they wanted to mould for me. As the Afro-American feminist, June Jordan, notes, this is all a question of power. 'At the minimum we have the power to stop cooperating with our enemies. We have the power to stop the courtesies and to let the feelings be real' (Jordan, 1989, p. 114). I was trying to deconstruct the power structure that was very much present in the room. If I did not respect the orderliness as much as the chair of the Grievance Board liked, it was because he did not always keep the order with the same care, courtesy and leniency. While our witnesses were repeatedly cut off, this was not done even once to the other side. Not even half of the concern for the reputation of the men was shown to me. I was not granted even half as much sympathy or respect as was shown to the other side and its witnesses. The evidence presented to the Board and the kind of people who testified in support of each side, and the Board's differential treatment of the parties, demonstrated the clear-cut racial, gender and ideological alignments within the University. The hostile remarks in the Board's report about my conduct and statements showed that, during the course of the hearings, the Board was troubled by only one thing and that was my behaviour. It saved its harshest words for me, because I had embarrassed the polite, cooperative white men by my anger and by my refusal to meet them on their terms and in their fashion. By juxtaposing my 'bad' behaviour with the 'good' behaviour of these white men, the Board portrayed me as a trouble-maker. I was 'unfair', and 'unduly personal', I 'interrupted speakers' and 'talked out of turn'. They were 'helpful', 'eloquent', 'conscientious' and 'compelling'. In this way, it appeared as if my character and conduct were on trial.

The reasons for my anger were numerous. I felt a continued attempt to make me invisible, to intimidate and silence me. For example, the Board told me I 'looked Caucasian' and asked why I considered myself a woman of colour. In other words, I was invisible. I was an invisible visible minority. Gradually, I realized why they persistently talked of other people's 'personal agenda', and sarcastically referred to people who were committed to a 'cause'. They were puzzled. I irritated them because I did not conform to the cultural image they had of a woman from the Orient. After all, wasn't I supposed to be quiet, submissive and obedient? Wasn't I to let others think and act for me? So, they thought someone must have induced me into grieving.

It was quite astounding to see the degree of ignorance apparently held by these senior academics about basic concepts and facts relating to racism and ethnocentrism. So we had to spend much time defining racism and explaining what constitutes racist perceptions and practices. The judgment of the members of the Appointment Committee and their reaction to my works was also firmly and unambiguously situated within the rigid malestream scholarship which finds feminist research 'overdetermined', 'non-objective' and 'emotional'. They argued that my research was 'concentrated heavily on giving the women's side of the story'. They also asserted that I 'did not pose a very important question'. Since the work was about a feminist movement in a Middle Eastern Islamic society, the defeat of feminists was 'predetermined'. It did not require an explanation.

These comments recalled what Edward Said has so brilliantly argued about 'orientalism', that it is the Eurocentric view of the Mediterranean Orient constructed by Occidental scholars. It is a collective imagination of the Orient constructed on the basis of Occidental images as a paradigm to study 'their' mentality, culture and politics. For example, when the assertions of one member of the Appointment Committee were challenged for his lack of knowledge of Middle Eastern politics and culture, he claimed he was familiar with the region, as a result of 'chatting with people from the Middle East and ordering books for the University library'. Obviously he did not think Middle Eastern politics to be so complex as to require serious scholarship and specialized training. The ignorance about women's political movements in Middle Eastern societies, some dating back to the turn of the century, had led them to think that the fate of what they called 'Western' feminism in a Middle Eastern country was 'counterintuitive'. Thus, it did not deserve scholarly investigation and research.

I wondered how this could be so obvious. From an Orientalist perspective, all Middle Eastern countries are irrational and parochial societies, which lack intellectual sophistication. The stereotypes, popularized by the American media in recent decades, after Khomeini's confrontation with the Carter Administration and Saddam Hussein's conflict with Bush, perpetrate an image of Middle Eastern people as terrorists and hostage-takers, who love dictators and despots, and of Middle Eastern women as subservient, domesticated and silent.

The members of the Appointment Committee, I believe, failed to appreciate either the enormous intellectual, cultural and philosophical traditions of Middle Eastern societies or the numerous major uprisings against despots and colonial powers. They had failed to recognize this heritage because, being educated in an orientalist tradition that originates in Greek, Roman and Renaissance philosophy, they did not notice or appreciate this. As is the case with paradigms, those who are situated in a particular paradigm have difficulty appreciating what is not defined as valuable within that paradigm. Indeed, they would even have difficulty identifying phenomena defined by another paradigm. If asked what happened during the twelve centuries between the collapse of the Roman empire and the Renaissance, when Europe was in the so-called Dark Ages and the Middle East was a flourishing centre for science, philosophy and poetry, what would they say? It is the same for feminisms. As orientalists take white, Eurocentric values and standards to define and interpret the important problems and questions, so many who are comfortable with male-dominated, conservative standards and practices have difficulty appreciating the significance of feminist questions. Despite all the seemingly value-free, neutral assumptions of Orientalists, orientalism is of course primarily ideological in nature. This means that terms like 'excellence', 'academic merit' and so on cannot be taken for granted; they are also paradigmatic. Anyone who fits the criteria defined by the paradigm is let in by the gatekeepers, and gets to exist. If she exists in the right way, according to the dogma, she might even qualify for 'excellence'.

Many well-established feminist scholars have documented the hostility of various academic disciplines to feminist thought and methodology. Ann Innis Dagg, for example, has noted several factors that make it especially difficult for feminists to get hired and to achieve tenure and promotion:

> [F]eminist research will usually be judged by predominantly male tenure committees, few of whom are familiar with feminist research. 'Yet lack of knowledge doesn't seem to deter these people from judging feminist literature.' As well, feminist research often has a political basis, which offends men who prefer more academic and less immediately useful work. (Dagg, 1992)

Anecdotal evidence suggests that some feminists, including law scholar Catharine MacKinnon, were denied university positions early in their careers and have had to fight their way through the academy. Feminist sociologist, Marylee Stephenson, who helped launch Women's Studies in Canada, was denied tenure at McMaster University, because her research which involved women reflecting on their changing role was considered 'inadequate', despite her 'clearly outstanding' teaching record and service to the community (Dagg, 1992).

Political Science, in particular, has long been the monopoly of conservative men. It is still very resistant to feminist ideas and methodology and quite dismissive of feminist research. Feminist political scientists have documented the hostility they face and the disrespect they receive if they do feminist work and try to include women's concerns and voices in the field. This is because feminist challenges inevitably lead to a redefinition of public life and politics themselves.

Naomi Black, a well-known feminist political scientist at York University, Canada, has written about her own experience in moving from International Relations to the study of women and politics, and the hostility she has faced and now faces from her arrogant and chauvinistic colleagues. She has been accused of doing propaganda, instead of political science, and has often been asked how it is possible to do research when she knows what answer she is looking for. Of course, no such question is asked of colleagues who study, say, decolonization, or work on South Africa, or write about the life and work of their favourite politicians or political thinker (Black, 1987).

Feminists who try to get a hearing for women in politics are reclaiming a sphere monopolized by men. Consequently, in their research they cannot rely on readily available documents and records of political events which have been mostly recorded by men. If they have been recorded by women, it has often been by women who don't see women as political actors, or give women's voices authority to interpret social realities. Feminist researchers, therefore, are creating a 'methodological rebellion' that is not acceptable to traditionalist scholarship.

Feminist scholars must often rely on interviews, women's stories and observation, so-called 'soft material' to complement traditional sources or 'hard material'. These sources are seen as causing 'methodological violations', a 'rebellion against decontextualising research', as Jill McCalla Vickers has put it. This is 'the basis of charges by disciplinary traditionalists that feminist research is not "real" research, especially in the sense of certifying the research for such things as tenure and promotion or in the sense of taking [feminist] ideas seriously' (McCalla Vickers, 1989, p. 41). Moreover, feminist scholars are not detached and unengaged in their research as the traditional approach to research supposedly requires. This is unacceptable to the anti-feminist academic establishment, not because their work is not unbiased (since no work is unbiased), but because it is biased in the wrong way. Given the hostility towards feminist scholars, it is easy to understand why only 18 per cent of professors in Canadian universities are women and many of these are not feminists or are actively anti-feminist (Dagg, 1992).

It is extremely difficult for me to separate the racist, sexist and ideological biases of those who dealt with me or to define the exact nature of the prejudice that accounted most for the treatment I received. Neither is there a need to do so. As Adorno and his colleagues, in their studies of prejudice, showed, there is always a correlation between a man's hostility towards one minority group and his hostility against a wide variety of others. 'In some cases it might be that the individual merely repeats opinions which are taken for granted in his social milieu and which he has no reason to question; in other cases it might be that the individual has chosen to join a particular group [and adopt its opinion] because it stood for ideals with which he was already in sympathy' (Adorno *et al.*, 1950, p. 9).

On closer examination of the events and the evidence presented to the Board, I now believe that racialist views and perceptions were more influential than sexist bias in the judgment of the Appointment Committee of me and my work. Had I been a white woman, these men would have acted more tactfully. They would undoubtedly have extended to me the minimal courtesy which would have given their decision a more polite appearance. My feminist research and politics, while a strong negative factor in the assessment of my work, provided these men with the pretext to give their racist perceptions and judgments an academic character.

Expressing and Dealing with Anger

The grievance was a disillusionizing learning process. In retrospect, I think, I was most disheartened in seeing the racism of the people who consider themselves liberals, since I did not expect much from conservative scholars entangled in the cobwebs of the ideas of the seventeenth and eighteenth centuries. It was, of course, sad to see that in democratic societies also rights and wrongs, values and counter-values, are defined from the perspective of those (often white) men, who have the authority for making definitions and imposing them on others, and that difference and non-conformism are not tolerated when they threaten the status quo. But I was more astounded by the racism of the so-called progressives, including some self-proclaimed Marxist academics, and by how limited and narrow was their understanding of racial-ist attitudes and behaviours, and how blind they could be to their own racism. Often white progressive academics think their friendly and courteous rela-tionship with non-white faculty and students, their occasional participation in anti-racist meetings, and their contribution to Amnesty International, can disinfect them against racist infections.

One member of the Appointment Committee, a self-proclaimed Marxist, who throughout the process was careful not to distance himself from the rest of the men, constantly referred to the tyranny of the 'politically correct'. He persistently alluded to the conspiracy of people with a personal agenda, people who in his view had seduced me to grieve. In my view, he did not appreciate that this was in itself a racist remark, and that it exposed his cultural myth about a woman from the Orient. Ironically the term 'politically correct' was used by the men who were not only 'correct' in their politics but have the 'correct' gender, 'correct' colour, 'correct' ideology, and 'correct' connections for silencing others. I was equally disappointed by the paralysing impact of identity politics on some feminists and lesbian activists. It is always sad to see how hollow rhetoric about common oppression and common cause is, when it comes to combating oppression in areas that do not affect some of us personally, and to see the divisive impact of the rise of a hierarchy of oppres-sion and the creation of what Juliet Mitchell years ago called 'a more-oppressed than thou' campaign (Mitchell, 1973, p. 178). In saying this, I am not denying the fact that often many people of colour also tend not to be as dedicated to combating sexism and homophobia as they are to anti-racist activities. But it is also true that it is anti-racism that draws the least attention from the progressive and feminist faculty and students. And, arguably, it is mostly the people of colour in universities whose voices are not heard and whose presence is unnoticed. It is when outrageous practices are directed against people of colour that they invoke the mildest reactions from the liberal and left intel-lectuals, feminists quite often included. Very often, the anger and bitterness irritates them. It causes them discomfort, and they are unable to appreciate, respect and share the anger which is often the only dignity one has against the violating effects of racism. They tend not to acknowledge the fact that bitterness, as Lynne McFall has noted, is a 'moral achievement', if 'the real choice is between bitterness and cynicism' (McFall, 1991). The only effective way to survive the injuries inflicted upon racism's victims is to be angry, to show that anger and to act upon it.

The fact is that in the absence of a habit of or commitment to self-evaluation, many intellectuals conveniently limit their commitment to anti-racism to the level of abstraction. They have little time, energy and mental capacity to spare, when anti-racism leaves the realm of theory. Some can comfortably and arrogantly place themselves above politics of race or gender in academia by resorting to grand theories that are supposed to bring the world revolution. Others see the need for change, but do not see that change cannot happen without collision with power and with the gatekeepers. In the words of Audre Lorde, 'those of us who stand outside the circle of this society's definition of acceptable women; those of us who have been forged in the crucibles of difference . . . [know all too well that] survival is not an academic skill. It is learning how to stand alone, unpopular and sometimes reviled' (Lorde, 1984, p. 112).

These facts are often hidden from many white intellectuals. Sometimes it takes amazingly little time for them to be sucked into the conservative and conformist structures and relations of academic institutions. Their radical ideas and politics are conveniently stored, to be dusted and used only in the community of friends, when there is absolutely no risk to their tenure or promotion. Their politics is a politics of whisper, not one of outrage and noise. Many mean well. But they simply cannot see that the politics of conformity and the politics of protest have little to do with how secure our positions are. They are more about whether or not we see living as an inescapable site for taking sides, as Gramsci noted. If you do not take sides with justice and truth out loud, you are taking sides with injustice and lies through your silence. There is no middle way for intellectuals.

References

ADORNO, T., FRENKEL-BRUNSWIK, ELSE, LEVINSON, DANIEL, J. and SANFORD, R. NEVITT (1950) *The Authoritarian Personality*, New York, Harper and Brothers.

APPIAH, KWAME ANTHONY (1990) 'Racism', in GOLDBERG, DAVID T. (Ed.) *Anatomy of Racism*, Minneapolis, University of Minnesota Press.

BLACK, NAOMI (1987) ' "The Child is Father to the Man": The Impact of Feminism on Canadian Political Science', in TOMM, WINNIE (Ed.) *The Effects of Feminist Approaches on Research Methodologies*, Waterloo: Wilfred Laurier University Press, pp. 225–43.

DAGG, ANN INNIS (1992) 'Feminism Reviled: Academic Non-Freedom at Canadian Universities', *Canadian Woman Studies*, 12, 3 (Spring), pp. 89–92.

FRYE, MARILYN (1983) *The Politics of Reality: Essays in Feminist Theory*, California, The Crossing Press.

JORDAN, JUNE (1989) *Moving Towards Home*, London, Virago.

LORDE, AUDRE (1984) *Sister Outsider*, Trumansberg, N.Y., The Crossing Press.

Haideh Moghissi

McCALLA VICKERS, JILL (1989) 'Memoirs of an Ontological Exile: The Methodological Rebellions of Feminist Research', in MILES, ANGELA and FINN, GERALDINE, *Feminism from Pressure to Politics*, New York/Montreal, Black Rose Press.

McFALL, LYNNE (1991) 'What is Wrong with Bitterness?', in CARD, CLAUDIA *Feminist Ethics*, Lawrence, Kan., University Press of Kansas, pp. 146–60.

MITCHELL, JULIET (1973) *Women's Estate*, Harmondsworth, Penguin.

SAID, EDWARD (1978) *Orientalism*, New York, Pantheon Books/London, Routledge and Kegan Paul.

SAID, EDWARD (1991) 'The Intellectuals and the War', *Middle East Report*, July–August.

Selected Bibliography

Abbott, Pamela and Wallace, Claire (1990) An Introduction to Sociology: Feminist Perspectives, London, Routledge.

Abrahams, R.D. (1976) Talking Black, Bowley, Mass., Newbury House Publishers.

Acker, Joan, Barry, Kate and Esseveld, Joke (1983) 'Objectivity and Truth: Problems in Doing Feminist Research', Women's Studies International Forum, vol. 6, no. 4, pp. 423–35.

Adams, M.L. (1989) 'There's No Place Like Home: On the Place of Identity in Feminist Politics', Feminist Review, no. 31.

Adie, K. (1993) contribution to Keating, R. 'When Reporters Go Over the Top', The Guardian, 18 January.

Adorno, T., Frenkel-Brunswik, Else, Levinson, Daniel, J. and Sanford, R. Nevitt (1950) The Authoritarian Personality, New York, Harper and Brothers.

Afshar, H. (1989) 'Gender Roles and the "Moral Economy of Kin" among Pakistani Women in West Yorkshire', New Community, vol. 15, no. 2.

Afshar, Haleh (1982) 'Khomeini's Teachings and their Implications for Women', in Tabari, Azar and Yeganeh, Nahid (Eds) In the Shadow of Islam, Zed, pp. 79–90.

Afshar, Haleh (1989) 'Education: Hopes, Expectations and Achievements of Muslim Women in West Yorkshire', Gender and Education, vol. 1, no. 3, pp. 261–72.

Afshar, Haleh (1990a) 'The Veil Gives Us Power', The Independent, 20 November.

Afshar, Haleh (1990b) 'Sex, Marriage and the Muslim', The Sunday Correspondent, 18 November.

Ahmad, W.I.U. (Ed.) (1992) The Politics of Race and Health, Race Relations Research Unit, University of Bradford.

Alibhai-Brown, Y. and Montague, A. (1992) The Colour of Love, London, Virago.

Allen, J. and Massey, D. (1988) The Economy in Question, London, Sage.

Allen, S. (1972) 'Plural Society and Conflict', New Community, vol. 1, no. 5.

Allen, S. (1989a) 'Social Aspects of Citizenship', Public Lecture, Queen's University, Belfast, May.

Allen, S. (1989b) 'Women and Citizenship: The British Experience', paper presented to the International Seminar on The Participation of Women in Politics and Decision Making Processes, Istanbul.

Allen, S. (1991) 'Diversity and Commonality: Building a Dialogue', paper presented at the International Conference 'Building a Europe without Frontiers: The Role of Women', Athens, November.

Allen, S. and Macey, M. (1992) 'Some Issues of Race, Ethnicity and Nationalism in the "New" Europe: Re-Thinking Sociological Paradigms', paper presented at the BSA Annual Conference, University of Kent.

Allen, S. and Wolkowitz, C. (1987) Homeworking: Myths and Realities, Basingstoke, Macmillan Education.

Allen, S., Anthias, F. and Yuval-Davis, N. (1991) 'Diversity and Commonality: Theory and Politics', Review Internationale Sociologies, 2.

Allen, Sheila and Wolkowitz, Carol (1986) 'Homeworking and the Control of Women's Work', in Feminist Review (Ed.) Waged Work: A Reader, London, Virago.

Alonso, Ana Maria (1988) 'The Effects of Truth: Representations of the Past and the Imagining of Community', Journal of Historical Sociology, vol. 1, no. 1, pp. 33–58.

Alonso, W. and Starr, P. (Eds) (1987) The Politics of Numbers, New York, Russell Sage Foundation.

Amadiume, I. (1987) Male Daughters, Female Husbands: Gender and Sex in an African Society, London, Zed.

American Public Health Association (1992) 'Policy Statements Adopted by the Governing Council of the American Public Health Association November 13, 1991', American Journal of Public Health, vol. 82, no. 3, pp. 476–94.

Amos, V. and Parmar, P. (1984) 'Challenging Imperial Feminism', Feminist Review, no. 17.

Amos, V. and Parmar, P. (1984) 'Challenging Imperialist Feminism', Feminist Review, no. 17, pp. 3–19.

Anderson, M. (1992) 'The History of Women and the History of Statistics', Journal of Women's History, vol. 4, no. 1, pp. 14–36.

Anthias, F. (1990) 'Race and Class Revisited – Conceptualising Race and Racisms', Sociological Review.

Anthias, F. (1992) Ethnicity, Class, Gender and Migration, Aldershot, Avebury.

Anthias, F. and Yuval-Davis, N. (1983) 'Contextualising Feminism: Gender, Ethnic and Class Divisions', Feminist Review, no. 15.

Anthias, Floya (1992) Ethnicity, Class, Gender and Migration: Greek Cypriots in Britain, Aldershot, Avebury.

Anwar, M. (1979) The Myth of Return, London, Heinemann Educational.

Appiah, Kwame Anthony (1990) 'Racism', in Goldberg, David T. (Ed.) Anatomy of Racism, Minneapolis, University of Minnesota Press.

Bacchi, C.L. (1990) Same Difference: Feminism and Sexual Difference, Sydney, Allen and Unwin.

Bailey, D.A. and Hall, S. (1992) 'The Vertigo of Displacement', Ten 8, vol. 2, no. 3, pp. 15–23.

Ballard, R. (1979) 'Ethnic Minorities and the Social Services', in Saifullah Khan, V. (Ed.) Minority Families in Britain, London, Macmillan.

Banks, M., Bates, I., Breakwell, G., Bynnes, J., Emler, N., Jamieson, L. and Roberts, K. (1992) Careers and Identities, Milton Keynes, Open University Press.

Barnes, M. and Maple, N. (1992) Women and Mental Health: Challenging the Stereotypes, Birmingham, Venture Press.

Barrett, M. (1987) 'The Concept of Difference', Feminist Review, no. 26.

Barrett, M. (1992) 'Words and Things: Materialism and Method in Contemporary Feminist Analysis', in Barrett, M. and Phillips, A. (Eds) Destabilizing Theory: Contemporary Feminist Debates, Cambridge, Polity.

Barrett, M. and Roberts, H. (1978) 'Doctors and their patients: the social control of women in General Practice' in Smart, C. and Smart, B. (Eds) Women, Sexuality and Social Control, London, Routledge and Kegan Paul.

Barth, F. (1969) Ethnic Groups and Boundaries, London, George Allen and Unwin.

Bates, Inge, Clarke, John, Cohen, Phil, Finn, Dan, Moore, Robert and Willis, Paul (Eds) (1984) Schooling for the Dole? The New Vocationalism, London, Macmillan.

Baudrillard, J. (1989) Selected Writings, ed. M. Poster, Cambridge, Polity.

Baudrillard, J. (1990) Revenge of the Crystal: A Baudrillard Reader, London, Pluto.

Bauman, J. (1986) Winter in the Morning, London, Virago.

Bauman, Z. (1978) Hermeneutics and Social Science, London, Hutchinson.

Bauman, Z. (1991) Modernity and the Holocaust, Cambridge, Polity.

Bauman, Z. (1992) Intimations of Postmodernity, London, Routledge.

Beauvoir, S. de (1974) The Second Sex, Harmondsworth, Penguin.

Bebbington, P., Hurry, J. and Tennant, C. (1981) 'Psychiatric Disorders in Selected Immigrant Groups in Camberwell', Social Psychiatry, 16, pp. 43–51.

Beechey, V. (1986) 'Women's Employment in Contemporary Britain', in Beechey, V. and Whitelegg, E. Women in Britain Today, Milton Keynes, Open University Press.

Beechey, V. (1988) 'Rethinking the Definition of Work: Gender and Work', in Jenson, J., Hagen, E. and Reddy, C. (Eds) Feminization of the Labour Force, Cambridge, Polity.

Beheria, L. and Sen, G. (1981) 'Accumulation, Reproduction and Women's Role in Economic Development: Boserup Revisited', Signs, 7, 2.

Bell, C. (1928) Civilisation, Harmondsworth, Penguin.

Benton, T. (1977) Philosophical Foundations of the Three Sociologies, London, Routledge and Kegan Paul.

Berktay, F. (1993) 'Looking from the "Other" Side: Is Cultural Relativism a Way Out?', in de Groot, J. and Maynard, M. (Eds) Women's Studies in the 1990s: Doing Things Differently?, London, Macmillan.

Bernard, R-P. (1991) 'AIDS/HIV by Age/Gender: Global Review in 22 Panels', AIDS-Forschung, vol. 6, no. 11, pp. 577–93.

Bhabha, H. (1983) 'The Other Question . . .', Screen, vol. 24, no. 6, pp. 18–36.

Bhaskar, Roy (1989) Reclaiming Reality, London, Verso.

Bhat, A., Carr-Hill, R. and Ohri, S. (1988) Britain's Black Population: A New Perspective, Aldershot, Gower.

Bhavnani, K-K. (1991) Talking Politics, Cambridge, Cambridge University Press.

Bhavnani, Kum-Kum (1988) 'Empowerment and Social Research', TEXT, vol. 8, no. 1, pp. 41–51.

Bhavnani, Kum-Kum (1991) Talking Politics: A Psychological Framing for Views from Youth in Britain, Cambridge, Cambridge University Press.

Bhavnani, Kum-Kum (1993) 'Talking Racism and the Editing of Women's Studies', in Richardson, Diane and Robinson, Vicki (Eds) Introducing Women's Studies, London, Macmillan.

Bisset, L. and Huws, U. (1984) 'Sweated Labour: Homeworking in Britain Today', Pamphlet No. 33, London Low Pay Unit.

Black, Naomi (1987) '"The Child is Father to the Man": The Impact of Feminism on Canadian Political Science', in Tomm, Winnie (Ed.) The Effects of Feminist Approaches on Research Methodologies, Waterloo: Wilfred Laurier University Press, pp. 225–43.

Bloor, M., Goldberg, D. and Emslie, J. (1991) 'Ethnostatics and the AIDS Epidemic', British Journal of Sociology, vol. 42, no. 1, pp. 131–8.

Blumer, H. (1969) Symbolic Interactionism: Perspective and Method, Englewood Cliffs, N.J., Prentice-Hall.

Bobo, J. and Seiter, E. (1991) 'Black Feminism and Media Criticism: The Women of Brewster Place', Screen, vol. 32, no. 3, pp. 286–302.

Boserup, E. (1970) Women's Role in Economic Development, London, Allen and Unwin.

Bourdieu, P. (1986) Distinctions: A Social Critique of the Judgement of Taste, London, Routledge and Kegan Paul.

Bovenkerk, Frank, Brok, B.D. and Ruland, L. (1991) 'Meer, Minder of Gelijk', Sociologische gids, jarg XXXVIII, 3, pp. 174–86.

Bowen, D.G. (Ed.) (1992) The Satanic Verses: Bradford Responds, Bradford and Ilkley College.

Boyne, R. and Rattansi, A. (Eds) (1990) Postmodernism and Society, London, Macmillan.

Brah, A. (1986) 'Unemployment and Racism: Asian Youth on the Dole', in Allen, S., Waton, A., Purcell, K. and Wood, S. (Eds) The Experience of Unemployment, British Sociological Association with Macmillan Press.

Brah, A. (1987) 'Women of South Asian Origin in Britain: Issues and Concerns', South Asia Research, vol. 7, no. 1, pp. 39–54 (reprinted in Braham, P., Rattansi, A. and Skellington, R. (Eds) (1992) Racism and Antiracism, London, Sage).

Brah, A. (1991) 'Questions of Difference and International Feminism', in Aaron, J. and Walby, S. (Eds) Out of the Margins, London, Falmer Press.

Brah, A. (1992) 'Difference, Diversity and Differentiation', in Donald, J. and Rattansi, A. (Eds) Race, Culture and Difference, London, Sage.

Brah, A. and Minhas, R. (1985) 'Structural Racism or Cultural Conflict: Asian Girls in British Schools', in Weiner, G. (Ed.) Just A Bunch of Girls, Milton Keynes, Open University Press.

Brah, A. and Shaw, S. (1992) Working Choices: South Asian Young Muslim Women and the Labour Market, London: Department of Employment, Research Paper no. 91.

Brah, Avtar (1987) 'Women of South Asian Origin in Britain: Issues and Concerns'

South Asia Research, vol. 7, no. 1, pp. 39–54 (reprinted in Braham, P., Rattansi, A. and Skellington, R. (Eds) (1992) Racism and Antiracism, London, Sage).

Brah, Avtar and Shaw, Sobia (1992) Working Choices: South Asian Young Muslim Women and the Labour Market, London, Department of Employment (Research Paper No. 91).

Bridenthal, Renate, Grossman, Atina and Kaplan, Marion (Eds) (1984) When Biology Became Destiny: Women in Weimar and Nazi Germany, New York, Monthly Review Press.

Brittain, Victoria (Ed.) (1991) The Gulf Between Us, The Gulf War and Beyond, London, Virago.

Brooks, D. and Singh, K. (1978) Aspirations versus Opportunities: Asian and White School Leavers in the Midlands, London, Commission for Racial Equality.

Broverman, D., Clarkson, F., Rosenkrantz, P., Vogel, S. and Broverman, I. (1970) 'Sex-Role Stereotype and Clinical Judgements of Mental Health', Journal of Consulting and Clinical Psychology, 34, pp. 1–7.

Brown, C. (1984) Black and White Britain: The Third PSI Survey, London, Heinemann.

Bruegel, I. (1989) 'Sex and Race in the Labour Market', Feminist Review, no. 32, Summer.

Bryan, Beverley, Dadzie, Stella and Scafe, Suzanne (1985) The Heart of the Race, London, Virago.

Buehler, J.W. (1992) 'The Surveillance Definition for AIDS', American Journal of Public Health, vol. 82, no. 11, pp. 1462–4.

Buehler, J.W., Berkelman, R.L. and Stehr-green, J.K, (1992b) 'The Completeness of AIDS Surveillance', Journal of Acquired Immune Deficiency Syndromes, vol. 5, no. 3, pp. 257–64.

Buehler, J.W., Hanson, D.L. and Chu, S.Y. (1992a) 'The Reporting of HIV/AIDS Deaths in Women', American Journal of Public Health, vol. 82, no. 11, pp. 1500–5.

Buehler, J.W., Stroup, D.F., Klaucke, D.N. and Berkelman, R.L. (1989) 'The Reporting of Race and Ethnicity in the National Notifiable Diseases Surveillance System', Public Health Reports, vol. 104, no. 5, pp. 457–65.

Burkitt, I. (1991) Social Selves: Theories of the Social Formation of Personality, London, Sage.

Butt, J., Gorbach, P. and Ahmad, B. (1991) 'Equally Fair?', London, Race Equality Unit.

Callinicos, A. (1989) Against Postmodernism: A Marxist Critique, Cambridge, Polity.

Campbell, C.A. (1990) 'Women and AIDS', Social Science and Medicine, vol. 30, no. 4, pp. 407–15.

Carby, H. (1982) 'White Woman Listen! Black Feminism and the Boundaries of Sisterhood', in Centre for Contemporary Cultural Studies The Empire Strikes Back, London, Hutchinson, pp. 212–36.

Carby, H. (1986) 'Sometimes It Jus Bes Dat Way', Radical America, vol. 20, pt. 4, pp. 9–22.

Carpenter, L. and Brockington, I.F. (1980) 'A Study of mental Illness in Asians, West

Indians and Africans Living in Manchester', British Journal of Psychiatry, 137, pp. 201–5.

Carrithers, M. (1992) Why Humans Have Cultures, Oxford, Oxford University Press.

Castro, K.G., Valdiserri, R.O. and Curran, J.W. (1992) 'Perspectives on HIV/AIDS Epidemiology and Prevention from the Eighth International Conference on AIDS', American Journal of Public Health, vol. 82, no. 11, pp. 1465–70.

CBS (Centraal Bureau voor de Statistic) (1989) Minderheden in Nederland, Stichting Vademecum.

Centers for Disease Control (1982) 'Update on Acquired Immune Deficiency Syndrome (AIDS) – United States', MMWR – Morbidity and Mortality Weekly Report, vol. 31, no. 37, pp. 507–8, 513–14.

Centers for Disease Control (1983) 'Immunodeficiency among Female Sexual Partners of Males with Acquired Immune Deficiency Syndrome (AIDS) – New York', MMWR, vol. 31, no. 52, pp. 697–8.

Centers for Disease Control (1989) 'Update: Acquired Immune Deficiency Syndrome – United States, 1981–1988', MMWR, vol. 38, no. 14, pp. 229–36.

Centers for Disease Control (1990) 'AIDS in Women – United States', MMWR, vol. 39, pp. 845–6.

(Charles), H. (1992) 'Whiteness – The Relevance of Politically Colouring the "Non"', in Hinds, H., Phoenix, A. and Stacey, J. (Eds) Working Out: New Directions in Women's Studies, London, Falmer Press.

Chin, J. (1990) 'Current and Future Dimensions of the HIV/AIDS Pandemic in Women and Children', The Lancet, vol. 336, no. 8709, pp. 221–4.

Christian, B. (1987) 'The Race for Theory', Cultural Critique, Spring, pp. 51–63.

Christian, B. (1990) 'What Celie Knows That You Should Know', in Goldberg, D.T. (Ed.) Anatomy of Racism, Minneapolis, University of Minnesota Press, pp. 135–45.

Chu, S.Y., Hammett, T.A. and Buehler, J.W. (1992) 'Update: Epidemiology of Reported Cases of AIDS in Women Who Report Sex Only With Other Women, United States, 1980–1991', AIDS, vol. 6, no. 5, pp. 518–19.

Cochrane R. (1977) 'Mental Illness in Immigrants to England and Wales: an analysis of Mental Hospital Admissions 1971' Social Psychiatry, 12, pp. 2–35.

Cochrane R. and Stopes-Roe, M. (1981) 'Psychological Symptom Levels in Indian Immigrants to England – A Comparison with the Native English', Psychological Medicine, 11, pp. 319–27.

Cock, J. (1984) Maids and Madams: A study in the politics of exploitation, Johannesburg, Raven.

Cohen, A. (1969) Custom and Politics in Urban Africa, Berkeley, University of California Press.

Cohen, A. (1974) Two Dimensional Man, Berkeley, University of California Press.

Cohen, A. (1981) The Politics of Elite Culture, Berkeley, University of California Press.

Collins, P.H. (1990) Black Feminist Thought, London, Unwin Hyman.

Collins, Patricia Hill (1990) Black Feminist Thought: Knowledge, Consciousness and the Politics of Empowerment, Boston and London, Unwin Hyman.

Conger, John (1973) Adolescence and Youth: Psychological Development in a Changing World, New York, Harper International Edition.

Connelly, N. (1988) Care in the Multiracial Community, London, Policy Studies Institute.

Cooperstock, R. and Lennard, H. (1979) 'Some Social Meanings of Tranquillizer Use', Sociology of Health and Illness, 1, 3, p. 33.

Cope, R. (1989) 'The Compulsory Detention of Afro-Caribbeans under the Mental Health Act', New Community, 15(3), April, pp. 343–56.

Cross, M., Wrench, J. and Barnett, S. (1990) Ethnic Minorities and the Careers Service: Investigation into Processess of Assessment and Placement, London, Department of Employment, Research Paper no. 73.

Curran, V. and Golombok, S. (1985) Bottling it up, London, Faber and Faber.

Dagg, Ann Innis (1992) 'Feminism Reviled: Academic Non-Freedom at Canadian Universities', Canadian Women's Studies, 12, 3 (Spring), pp. 89–92.

Dahya, B. (1974) 'The Nature of Pakistani Ethnicity in Industrial Cities in Britain', in Cohen, A. (Ed.) Urban Ethnicity (A.S.A. Monograph 12), London, Tavistock Publications.

Daniel, W.W. (1968) Racial Discrimination in England, Harmondsworth, Penguin.

Davis, A. (1981) Women, Race and Class, London, The Women's Press.

Davis, A. (1990) 'Black Women and Music: A Historical Legacy of Struggle', in Braxton, J.M. and McLaughlin, A.N. (Eds) Wild Women in the Whirlwind: Afro-American Culture and the Contemporary Literary Renaissance, New Jersey, Rutgers University Press, pp. 3

Davis, Angela (1971) 'Reflections on the Role of the Black Woman in the Community of Slaves', Black Scholar, December, pp. 3–15.

Davis, Angela (1981) Women, Race and Class, London, The Women's Press.

Dean, G., Walsh, D., Downing, H. and Shelley, E. (1981) 'First admissions of native-born and immigrants to psychiatric hospitals in south-east England in 1976' British Journal of Psychiatry, 139, pp. 506–512.

Derrida, J. (1978) Writing and Difference, London, Routledge and Kegan Paul.

Diop, C.A. (1974) The African Origin of Civilisation: Myth or Reality, USA, Lawrence Hill & Co.

Donald, J. and Rattansi, A. (Eds) (1992) 'Race', Culture and Difference, London, Sage.

Drew, D., Gray, J. and Sime, N. (1991) Against the Odds: The Educational and Labour Market Experiences of Black Young People, Sheffield, TEED Youth Cohort Series.

Easterbrook, P.J., Margolick, J., Saah, A.J. et al. (1992) 'Racial Differences in Rate of CD4 Decline in HIV-1 Infected Homosexual Men', Abstract MoC 0064 in Index File: V1: Final Programme and Oral Abstracts, Eighth International Conference on AIDS, Amst

Eichler, Margritte (1988) Non-Sexist Research Methods, London, Allen and Unwin.

El Saadawi, N. (1980) The Hidden Face of Eve, London, Zed Press.

El-sadr, W. and Capps, L. (1992) 'The Challenge of Minority Recruitment in Clinical Trials for AIDS', Journal of the American Medical Association (JAMA), vol. 267, no. 7, pp. 954–7.

Elias, N. (1982) Power and Civility (The Civilising Process, vol. 2), New York, Pantheon Books.

Elias, N. (1982) State Formation and Civilisation: The Civilising Process, vol. 2, Oxford, Blackwell.

Elias, P. and Gregory, M. (1992) The Changing Structure of Occupations and Earnings in Great Britain, 1975–1990, Institute for Employment Research, University of Warwick.

Ellerbrock, T.V., Bush, T.J., Chamberland, M.E. and Oxtoby, M.J. (1991) 'Epidemiology of Women with AIDS in the United States, 1981 through 1990', Journal of the American Medical Association (JAMA), vol. 265, no. 22, pp. 2971–5.

Epstein, A.L. (1978) Ethos and Identity, London, Tavistock.

Essed, Philomena (1990) Everyday Racism, Claremont, CA, Hunter House.

Evans, B.G., Gill, O.N. and Emslie, J.A.N. (1991) 'Completeness of Reporting of AIDS Cases', British Medical Journal, vol. 302, no. 6789, pp. 1351–2.

Febvre, L. (1973) A New Kind of History and Other Essays (ed. by P. Burke, trans. by K. Folia), London, Routledge and Kegan Paul.

Fee, E. and Fox, D.M. (Eds) (1988) AIDS: The Burdens of History, Berkeley, CA, University of California Press.

Fee, E. and Fox, D.M. (Eds) (1992) AIDS: The Making of a Chronic Disease, Berkeley, CA, University of California Press.

Felski, R. (1989) 'Feminist Theory and Social Change', Theory, Culture and Society, vol. 6.

Fine, M. (1988) 'Sexuality, Schooling and Adolescent Females: The Missing Discourse of Desire', Harvard Educational Review, vol. 58, no. 1 (Feb.), pp. 29–53.

Fisher, B.M. and Strauss, A.L. (1978) 'Interactionism', in Bottomore, T. and Nisbet, R. (Eds) A History of Sociological Analysis, London, Heinemann.

Flax, J. (1987) 'Postmodernism and Gender Relations in Feminist Theory', Signs, vol. 12, no. 4.

Foucault, M. (1989) The Archaeology of Knowledge, London, Routledge.

Fox, R.G. (Ed.) (1990) Nationalist Ideologies and the Production of National Culture, Washington, American Antrhopological Association.

Francis, E. (1989) 'Black People, "Dangerousness" and Psychiatric Compulsion', in Brackx, A. and Grimshaw, C. (Eds) Mental Health Care in Crisis, London, Pluto.

Fraser, Nancy (1989) Unruly Practices: Power, Discourse and Gender in Contemporary Social Theory, Minneapolis, University of Minnesota Press.

Frazer, E. (1988) 'Teenage Girls Talking about Class', Sociology, vol. 22, no. 3, pp. 343–58.

Friedan, B. (1963) The Feminine Mystique, London, Gollancz.

Frye, Marilyn (1983) The Politics of Reality: Essays in Feminist Theory, California, The Crossing Press.

Fuller, M. (1980) 'Black Girls in a London Comprehensive School', in Deem, R. (Ed.) Schooling for Women's Work, London, Routledge and Kegan Paul, pp. 52–66.

Furnham, Adrian (1985) 'Youth Unemployment: A Review of the Literature', Journal of Adolescence, vol. 8, pp. 109–24.

Gardner, J.H. (1991) Impaired Vision, Portraits of Black Women in The Afrikaans Novel 1948–1988, Amsterdam, VU University Press.

Gayle, J.A., Selik, R.M. and Chu, S.Y. (1990) 'Surveillance for AIDS and HIV Infection among Black and Hispanic Children and Women of Childbearing Age, 1981–1989', MMWR – Morbidity and Mortality Weekly Report, vol. 39, no. SS-3, pp. 23–30.

Gertig, D.M., Marion, S.A. and Schecter, M.T. (1991) 'Estimating the Extent of Underreporting in AIDS Surveillance', AIDS, vol. 5, pp. 1157–64.

Giddens, A. (1979) Central Problems in Social Theory, London, Macmillan.

Giddens, A. (1991) Modernity and Self Identity, Cambridge, Polity.

Gilman, S.L. (1992) 'Black Bodies, White Bodies: Towards an Iconography of Female Sexuality in Late Nineteenth Century Art, Medicine and Literature', in Donald, J. and Rattansi, A. (Eds) 'Race', Culture and Difference, London, Sage, pp. 171–98.

Gilroy, P. (1987) 'There Ain't no Black in the Union Jack', London, Hutchinson.

Gilroy, P. (1990) 'One Nation Under a Groove: The Cultural Politics of "Race" and Racism in Britain', in Goldberg, D.T. (Ed.) Anatomy of Racism, Minneapolis, University of Minnesota Press, pp. 263–83.

Gilroy, P. (1992) 'The End of Antiracism', in Donald, J. and Rattansi, A. (Eds) 'Race', Culture and Difference, London, Sage.

Gittings, J. (Ed.) (1991) Beyond the Gulf War: The Middle East and the New World Order, London, Catholic Institute for International Relations.

Goldberg, D. and Huxley, P. (1980) Mental Illness in the Community: The Pathway to Psychiatric Care, London, Tavistock.

Gordon, L. (1991) 'On "Difference"', Genders, no. 10.

Goulbourne, H. (1991) Ethnicity and Nationalism in Post-Imperial Britain, Cambridge, Cambridge University Press.

Gouldner, A.W. (1971) The Coming Crisis of Western Sociology, London, Heinemann.

Gowricharn, R. Verschillen in werkloosheid en etnische afkomst, Rotterdam, Onderzoeksrapport Gemeentelijke Sociale Dienst.

Greater London Council (1986) The London Labour Plan, London, GLC.

Greenwood, A. (1993) 'Ethnic Minorities' Mental Health: The Case for a Specialist Unit', Ethnic Minorities Current Awareness Bulletin, vol. 4, part 2 (March 1993), pp. i–ii.

Grewal, Shabnam, Kay, Jackie, Landor, Liliane, Lewis, Gail, and Parmar, Pratibha (Eds) (1988) Charting the Journey: Writings by Black and Third World Women, London, Sheba Feminist Publishers.

Griffin, Chris (1985) Typical Girls? Young Women from School to the Job Market, London, Routledge and Kegan Paul.

Griffiths, Dorothy and Saraga, Esther (1979) 'Sex Differences and Cognitive Abilities: A Sterile Field of Enquiry?', in Hartnett, O., Boden, G. and Fuller, M. (Eds) Sex Role Stereotyping, London, Tavistock, pp. 17–45.

Grosz, Elizabeth (1987) 'Feminist Theory and the Challenge to Knowledges', Women's Studies International Forum, vol. 10, no. 5, pp. 475–80.

Gutman, H. (1976) The Black Family in Slavery and Freedom, 1750–1925, New York, Vintage.

Guttentag, M., Salasin, S. and Belle, D. (Eds) (1980) The Mental Health of Women, New York, Academic Press Inc.

Guy, D.J. (1992) '"White Slavery", Citizenship and Nationality in Argentina', in Parker, A., Rosso, M., Sommer, D. and Yaeger, P. (Eds) Nationalisms and Sexualities, New York, Routledge.

Guy, J. (1990) 'Gender Oppression in Southern Africa's Precapitalist Societies,' in Walker (Ed.) Women and Gender in Southern Africa, Cape Town/James Currey, London, David Philip.

Habermas, J. (1987) The Philosophical Discourse of Modernity, Cambridge, Polity.

Haeri, Shahla (1989) The Law of Desire: Temporary Marriage in Iran, London, I.B. Tauris.

Hahn, R.A. (1992) 'The State of Federal Health Statistics on Racial and Ethnic Groups', Journal of the American Medical Association (JAMA), vol. 267, no. 2, pp. 268–71.

Hall, C. (1983) 'Many People with HIV "Do Not Know They Are Infected"', The Independent (London), 1 February, p. 3.

Hall, S. (1992) 'New Ethnicities', in Donald, J. and Rattansi, A. (Eds) 'Race', Culture and Difference, London, Sage, pp. 252–60.

Hall, S. and Jacques, M. (1989) New Times, London, Lawrence and Wishart.

Hall, Stuart and Jefferson, Tony (Eds) (1975) Resistance through Rituals: Youth Subcultures in Post-War Britain, London, Hutchinson.

Haraway, Donna (1988) 'Situated Knowledges: The Science Question in Feminism and the Privilege of Partial Perspective', Feminist Studies, vol. 14, no. 3 (Fall), pp. 575–600.

Haraway, Donna (1989) Primate Visions, London, Routledge.

Harding, S. (1986) The Science Question in Feminism, Milton Keynes, Open University Press.

Harding, S. (Ed.) (1987) Feminism and Methodology, Milton Keynes, Open University Press.

Harding, Sandra (1991) Whose Science? Whose Knowledge?, Ithaca, Cornell University Press.

Harré, R. (1979) Social Being: A Theory for Social Psychology, Oxford, Blackwell.

Harré, R. (1983) Personal Being: A Theory for Individual Psychology, Oxford, Blackwell.

Harrison, G., Owens, D., Holton, A., Neilson, D. and Boot, D. (1988) 'A Prospective Study of Severe Mental Disorder in Afro-Caribbean Patients', Psychological Medicine, 18, pp. 643–57.

Harriss, K. (1989) 'New Alliances: Socialist Feminism in the Eighties', Feminist Review, no. 31.

Hartsock, N. (1987) 'Rethinking Modernism', Cultural Critique, Fall.

Hartsock, Nancy (1983) 'The Feminist Standpoint: Developing the Ground for a Specifically Feminist Historical Materialism', in Harding, S. and Hintikka, M.

(Eds) Discovering Reality: Feminist Perspectives on Epistemology, Metaphysics, Methodology, and Phi

Hebdige, D. (1988) Hiding in the Light, London, Comedia.

Hebdige, D. (undated) 'Reggae, Rastas & Rudies: Style and the Subversion of Form', Stencilled Occasional Paper, no. 24, Race Series, Birmingham, Centre for Contemporary Cultural Studies.

Hemsi, L.K. (1967) 'Psychiatric Morbidity of West Indian Immigrants', Social Psychiatry, 2, pp. 95–100.

Henry, F. (1983) Victims and Neighbours: A Small Town in Nazi Germany Remembered, Vergin and Garvey.

Herek, G.M. and Glunt, E.K. (1988) 'An Epidemic of Stigma: Public Reactions to AIDS', American Psychologist, vol. 43, no. 11, pp. 886–91.

Hewitt, Nancy (1985) 'Beyond the Search for Sisterhood: American Women's History in the 1980s', Social History, vol. 10, October.

Hilli, Muhaqqiq Najim al-Din Abu al-Qasim Ja'far (1968) Sharayal-Islam, Islamic law, translated from Arabic to Persian by Yazdi, A. Ahmad and Danish Pazhuh, M.T., University of Tehran Press 1347.

Hitch, P.J. and Clegg, P. (1980) 'Modes of Referral of Overseas Immigrant and Native-born First Admissions to Psychiatric Hospital', Social Scientific Medicine, vol. 14A, pp. 369–74.

Hobsbawm, E. (1984) 'Mass-Producing Traditions: Europe, 1870–1914', in Hobsbawm, E. and Ranger, T. (Eds) The Invention of Tradition, Cambridge, Cambridge University Press.

hooks, B. (1981) Ain't I a woman?, London, Pluto.

hooks, b. (1984) Feminist Theory: From Margin to Centre, Boston, South End Press.

hooks, b. (1989) Talking Back: Thinking Feminist, Thinking Black, London, Sheba Feminist Publishers.

hooks, b. (1991) Yearning, London, Turnaround.

hooks, b. (1992) discussion of C. West 'The Postmodern Crisis of Black intellectuals', in Grossberg, L., Nelson, C. and Treichler, P. (Eds) Cultural Studies, London, Routledge, p. 700.

Howell, E. and Bayes, M. (1981) Women and Mental Health, New York, Basic Books Inc.

Human Rights Commission (1991) Human Rights Update, Dec. (1991) Area Repression Report, Dec. (1990–1992) Weekly Repression Reports.

Hurtado, A. (1989) 'Relating to Privilege: Seduction and Rejection in the Subordination of White Women and Women of Color', Sings, vol. 14, no. 4, pp. 833–55.

Husband, C. (1986) 'Racism, Prejudice and Social Policy', in Coombe, V. and Little, A. (Eds) Race and Social Work: A Guide to Training, London, Tavistock.

Hutnik, N. (1992) Ethnic Minority Identity: A Social Psychological Perspective, Oxford, Clarendon Press.

Ickovics, J.R. and Rodin, J. (1992) 'Women and AIDS in the United States: Epidemiology, Natural History, and Mediating Mechanisms', Health Psychology, vol. 11, no. 1, pp. 1–16.

INSEE (1989) Enquete Emploi.

Jaarsma, Ria (1991) Hoe Kom Je van B naar A?: Handreiking voor Trajectontwikkeling ten Behoeve van Allochtone Vrouwen, s'Gravenhage.

Jarvie, I.C. (1964) The Revolution in Anthropology, London, Routledge and Kegan Paul.

Jayaratne, Toby Epstein and Stewart, Abigail (1991) 'Quantitative and Qualitative Methods in the Social Sciences: Current Feminist Issues and Practical Strategies', in Fonow, Mary Margaret and Cook, Judith A. (Eds) Beyond Methodology: Feminist Scholarship

Jeffery, P. (1976) Migrants and Refugees, Cambridge, Cambridge University Press.

Jensen, J., Hagen, E. and Reddy, C. (Eds) (1988) Feminization of the Labour Force, Cambridge, Polity.

Jordan, June (1989) Moving Towards Home, London, Virago.

Joseph, G. and Lewis, J. (1981) Common Differences: Conflicts in Black and White Feminist Perspectives, New York, Anchor Press/Doubleday.

Kabbani, R. (1986) Europe's Myths of Orient, Basingstoke, Macmillan.

Kallie, John (1987) 'Asian School Leavers and Their Aspirations', unpublished PhD thesis, Oxford Polytechnic.

Kandiyoti, D. (1991) 'Islam and Patriarchy: A Comparative Perspective', in Keddie, N. and Baron, B. (Eds) Women in Middle Eastern History, Yale University Press, pp. 23–44.

Kay, J. (1991) The Adoption Papers, Newcastle, Bloodaxe.

Keating, R. (1993) 'When Reporters Go Over the Top', The Guardian, 18 January.

Kedijang, M. (1990) The best kept secret: Domestic workers as victims of violence, Project for the study of violence Wits, Johannesburg.

Kelly, G.A. (1955) The Psychology of Personal Constructs, New York, Norton.

Kempadoo, K. (1990) 'Construction of Black and Migrant Womanhood and the Women's and Minorities Policy in the Netherlands', paper presented at the conference 'The Social Construction of Minorities and their Cultural Rights in Western Europe', Leiden, 12–1

Keyfitz, N. (1987) 'The Social and Political Context of Population Forecasting', in Alonso, W. and Starr, P. (Eds), The Politics of Numbers, New York, Russell Sage Foundation.

Kimble, J. (1983) 'Runaway wives': Basotho Women, Chiefs and the colonial State, c. 1890–1920, Paper presented to the women in Africa seminar, School of Oriental and African Studies, University of London.

Kloosterman, Robert (1993) 'Het Onafwendbare einde van de Nederlandse Verzorgingsstaat?', FACTA, Sociaal-Wetenschappelijk Magazine, 1, 1, February, Amsterdam.

Kloosterman, Robert and Knaack, Ruud (1992) Het Nederlandse Model: Kansen en Bedreigingen van de Verzorgingsstaat, Amsterdam University Press.

Knowles, C. and Mercer, S. (1992) 'Feminism and Antiracism: An Exploration of the Political Possibilities', in Donald, J. and Rattansi, A. (Eds) 'Race', Culture and Difference, London, Sage.

Krieger, N. (1993) 'Analyzing Socioeconomic and Racial/Ethnic Patterns in Health and Health Care', American Journal of Public Health, vol. 83, no. 8, pp. 1086–7.

Ladner, J.A. (1971) Tomorrow's Tomorrow, Garden City, N.Y., Doubleday.

Laing, R.D. (1965) The Divided Self, Harmondsworth, Penguin.

Lal, B.B. (1986) 'The "Chicago School" of American Sociology, Symbolic Interactionism, and Race Relations Theory', in Rex, J. and Mason, D. (Eds) Theories of Race and Ethnic Relations, Cambridge, Cambridge University

Lancet, The (1993) 'Heterosexual AIDS: Pessimism, Pandemics, and Plain Hard Facts', Editorial, 3 April, vol. 341, pp. 863–4.

Lazreg, Marnia (1990) 'Feminism and Difference: The Perils of Writing as a Woman on Women in Algeria', in Hirsch, Marilyn and Keller, Evelyn Fox (Eds) Conflicts in Feminism, New York, Routledge, pp. 326–48.

Le Doeuff, Michele (1987) 'Women and Philosophy', in Moi, Toril (Ed.) French Feminist Thought: A Reader, Oxford, Basil Blackwell, pp. 181–209.

Lee, G. and Wrench, J. (1983) Skill Seekers, Leicester, National Youth Bureau.

Lee, S.M. (1993) 'Racial Classifications in the US Census: 1890–1990', Ethnic and Racial Studies, vol. 16, no. 1, pp. 75–94.

Lees, S. (1986) Losing Out, Harmondsworth, Penguin.

Leonard, D. and Speakman, A. (1986) 'Women in the Family: Companions or Caretakers?', in Beechey, V. and Whitelegg, E. Women in Britain Today, Milton Keynes, Open University Press.

Littlewood, R. and Lipsedge, M. (1982) Aliens and Alienists, Harmondsworth, Penguin.

Lloyd, C. and Waters, H. (1991) 'France: One Culture and One People?', Race and Class, 32(3), pp. 49–66.

Lorde, A. (1984) Sister Outsider, New York, The Crossing Press.

Lutz, H. (1991) 'Migrant Women of "Islamic Background": Images and Self-Images', Amsterdam, Middle East Research Associates, Occasional Paper no. 11.

Lutz, Helma (1991) 'Migrant Women of "Islamic background", Images and Self-Images', Occasional paper no. 11, Middle East Research Associates, Amsterdam, December.

Lutz, Helma (1991a) Welten Verbinden: Türkische Sozialarbeiterinnen in den Niederlanden und der Bundesrepublik Deutschland, Frankfurt a.M., IKO Verlag.

Lutz, Helma (1991b) Migrant Women of 'Islamic Background': Images and Self-Images, Middle East Research Associates paper no. 11, Amsterdam.

Lutz, Helma (1993a) 'Migrant Women, Racism and the Dutch Labour Market', in Solomos, John and Wrench, John (Eds) Racism and Migration in Europe in the 1990s, London and New York, Berg.

Lutz, Helma (1993b) 'In Between or Bridging Cultural Gaps? Migrant Women from Turkey as Mediators', New Community, no. 1, University of Warwick.

Lyotard, J-F, (1984) The Postmodern Condition, Manchester, Manchester University Press.

Mac an Ghaill, M. (1988) Young, Gifted and Black: Student-Teacher Relations in the Schooling of Black Youth, Milton Keynes, Open University Press.

MacKinnon, C. (1987) Feminism Unmodified, Harvard, Harvard University Press.

Magona, S. (1990) To My Children's Children, Africa South New Writing, South Africa, Claremont.

Magura, S., O'Day, J. and Rosenblum, A. (1992) 'Women Usually Take Care of Their Girlfriends: Bisexuality and HIV Risk among Female Intravenous Drug Users', The Journal of Drug Issues, vol. 22, no. 1, pp. 179–90.

Mama, A. (1989) The Hidden Struggle, Statutory and Voluntary Sector Responses To Violence Against Black Women In The H, Lond Race and Housing Research Unit, UK.

Mama, Amina (1986, first published in 1984) 'Black Women and the Economic Crisis', in Feminist Review (Ed.) Waged Work: A Reader, London, Virago.

Mann, J., Tarantola, D.J.M. and Netter, T.W. (Eds) (1992) AIDS in the World: A Global Report, Cambridge, MA and London, Harvard University Press.

Marx, K. (1973) Grundrisse, Harmondsworth, Penguin.

Mason, D. (1986) 'Introduction Controversies and Continuities in Race and Ethnic Relations Theory', in Rex, J. and Mason, D. (Eds)Theories of Race and Ethnic Relations, Cambridge, Cambridge University Press.

Matlanyane Sexwale, B.M. (1987) 'The "New Lesotho's" Prospects For Democracy', A Background to the January 1986 Coup d'Etat, ISS, The Hague.

Matlanyane Sexwale, B.M. (1989) 'If Only God Can Help Me Go To Khauteng', Experiences of Migrant Women Workers of Lesotho (mimeo) Presented at the launching conference of the AAWORD Kenya Chapter, Nairobi.

Matlanyane Sexwale, B.M. and Roste, J. (1989) A Life of Endless Struggle: Migrant Women Workers of Lesotho (mimeo) Research report to NORAD, Oslo.

McCalla Vickers, Jill (1989) 'Memoirs of an Ontological Exile: The Methodological Rebellions of Feminist Research', in Miles Angela and Finn Geraldine, Feminism from Pressure to Politics, New York/Montreal, Black Rose Press.

McCombs, S.B., McCray, E., Wendell, D.A., Sweeney, P.A. and Oronato, I.M. (1992) 'Epidemiology of HIV-1 Infection in Bisexual Women [Letter]', Journal of Acquired Immune Deficiency Syndrome, vol. 5, no. 8, pp. 850–2.

McCrone, D. (1992) Understanding Scotland: The Sociology of a Stateless Nation, London, Routledge.

McFadden, P. (1991) 'The Reality of Hating Women', SAPEM, vol. 4, no. 12.

McFall, Lynne (1991) 'What is Wrong with Bitterness?', in Card, Claudia Feminist Ethics, Lawrence, Kan., University Press of Kansas, pp. 146–60.

McFarland, J. (1988) 'The Construction of Women and Development Theory', Canadian Review of Sociology and Anthropology, vol. 25, no. 2.

McGovern, D. and Cope, R.V. (1987) 'First Psychiatric Admission Rates of First and Second Generation Afro-Caribbeans', Social Psychiatry, 22, pp. 139–49.

McKendrick, B. and Hoffman, W. (Eds) (1990) People and Violence in South Africa, Cape Town, Oxford University Press.

McRae, S. (1989) Flexible Working Time and Family Life, London, Policy Studies Institute.

McRobbie, A. (1991) Feminism and Youth Culture: From 'Jackie' to 'Just Seventeen', London, Macmillan.

McRobbie, Angela (1982) 'The Politics of Feminist Research: Between Talk, Text and Action', Feminist Review, no. 12, pp. 46–62.

Mead, G.H. (1934) Mind, Self and Society, from the Standpoint of a Social Behaviourist, Chicago, Chicago University Press.

Meena, R. (1991) Can Women Combat Violence Against Them? in SAPEM, Harare, vol. 5, no. 2.

Mercer, K. (1984) Black communities experience of psychiatric services, International Journal of Social Psychiatry, 3, 1 and 2.

Mercer, K. and Julien, I. (1988) 'Race, Sexual Politics and Black Masculinity: A Dossier', in Chapman, R. and Rutherford, J. (Eds) Male Order: Unwrapping Masculinity, London, Lawrence and Wishart, pp. 97–165.

Mies, M. (1986) Patriarchy and Accumulation on a World Scale: Women and The International Division of Labour, London, Zed.

Mies, Maria (1983) 'Towards a Methodology for Feminist Research', in Bowles, Gloria and Duelli Klein, Renate (Eds) Theories of Women's Studies, pp. 117–39.

Miles, A. (1981) The Mentally Ill in Contemporary Society, Oxford, Blackwell.

Miles, A. (1988) Women and Mental Illness, Brighton, Wheatsheaf.

Miles, R. (1982) Racism and Migrant Labour, London, Routledge and Kegan Paul.

Miles, R. (1987a) 'Recent Marxist Theories of Nationalism and the Issue of Racism', British Journal of Sociology, vol. XXXVIII, no. 1.

Miles, R. (1987b) 'Racism and Nationalism in Britain', in Husband, C.H. (Ed.) 'Race' in Britain: Continuity and Change, London, Hutchinson.

Miles, R. (1989) Racism, London, Routledge.

Miles, R. and Phizacklea, A. (1984) White Man's Country: Racism in British Politics, London, Pluto.

Milner, D. (1975) Children and Race, Harmondsworth, Penguin.

Min. v. Binnenlandse Zaken (1983) Minderhedennota, s'Gravenhage.

Min. v. Sociale Zaken en Werkgelegenheid (1992a) Eindrapportage van het Project Vrouwen en Minderhedenbeleid, s'Gravenhage, Staatsuitgeverij.

Min. v. Sociale Zaken en Werkgelegenheid (1992b) Emancipatie in Cijfers, nov. staatsuitgeverij, s'Gravenhage.

Minkoff, H.L. and DeHovitz, J.A. (1991) 'Care of Women Infected with the Human Immunodeficiency Virus', Journal of the American Medical Association (JAMA), vol. 266, no. 16, pp. 2253–8.

Miraz, H.S. (1992) Young, Female and Black, London, Routledge.

Mirza, Hafiz (1992) 'Some Reflections on the European Perimeter', paper presented at the Conference on Islam in a Changing World, Bradford, September.

Mitchell, Juliet (1973) Women's Estate, Harmondsworth, Penguin.

Mitter, S. (1986) Common Fate, Common Bond: Women in the Global Economy, London, Pluto.

Modleski, T. (Ed.) (1986) Studies in Entertainment: Critical Approaches to Mass Culture, Bloomington and Indianapolis, Indiana University Press.

Molokomme, A. (1991) Children of The Fence, The Maintenance of Extra-marital Children Under Law and Practice in Botswana, Phd Thesis, Rijksuniversiteit, Leiden.

Morokvasic, M. (1991) 'Fortress Europe and Migrant Women', Feminist Review, no. 39.

Morokvasic, M. (1992) 'Chez nous, la Guerre', in Morokvasic, M. (Ed.) Yugoslavie: Logiques De L'Exclusion, Peuples Mediterraneens, Paris, Revue Trimestrielle, no. 61.

Morrissey, M. (1989) Slave Women in the New World, Lawrence, Kansas, University Press of Kansas.

Murrain, M. (1993) 'New stats on women and AIDS with new definition', Discussion on Women's Studies List, WMST-L@UMDD.BITNET, 14 June.

Nasir, Jamal J. (1990) The Status of Women under Islamic Law, and under Modern Islamic Legislation, London, Graham and Trotman.

Nazir, P. (1991) Local Development in the Global Economy: The Case of Pakistan, Aldershot, Avebury.

Ngcobo, L. (Ed.) (1988) Let It Be Told: Essays by Black Women in Britain, London, Virago.

Nicholson, L. (Ed.) (1990) Feminism/Postmodernism, London, Routledge.

Nicoll, A. (1991) 'Global HIV/AIDS: Women and Children First', Current AIDS Literature, vol. 7, no. 6, pp. 213–14.

Norris, C. (1992) Uncritical Theory, London: Lawrence and Wishart.

Obbo, C. (1989) 'Sexuality and Economic Domination in Uganda', in Anthias, F. and Yuval-Davis, N. (Eds) Women, Nation, State, London, Macmillan.

Ohri, S. (1988) 'The Politics of Racism, Statistics and Equal Opportunity: Towards a Black Perspective', in Bhat, A., Carr-Hill, R. and Ohri, S. (Eds) Britain's Black Population, Aldershot, Gower.

Omi, M. and Winant, H. (1986) Racial Formation in the United States, London and New York, Routledge and Kegan Paul.

Onderweg, 7ejrg., no. 1, feb. 1990, Ministerie voor Sociale Zaken en Werkgelegenheid, s'Gravenhage.

Oosterhuis, G. and Glebbeek, A. (1988) 'Ras en Geslacht bij de Personeelsselectie', Mens en Maatschappij, 63 jrg., nr. 3.

Oppenheimer, G.M. (1988) 'In the eye of the storm: The Epidemiological Construction of AIDS', in Fee, E. and Fox, D.M. (Eds) AIDS: The Burdens of History, Berkeley, CA, University of California Press.

Oppenheimer, G.M. (1992) 'Causes, Cases, and Cohorts: The Role of Epidemiology in the Historical Construction of AIDS', in Fee, E. and Fox, D.M. (Eds) AIDS: The Making of a Chronic Disease, Berkeley, CA, University of California Press.

Osborne, N.G. and Feit, M.D. (1992) 'The Use of Race in Medical Research', Journal of the American Medical Association (JAMA), vol. 267, no. 2, pp. 275–9.

Osmond, M.W., Wambach, K.G., Harrison, D.F. Byers, J., Levine, P., Imershein, A. and Quadagno, D.M. (1993) 'The Multiple Jeopardy of Race, Class, and Gender for AIDS Risk among Women', Gender & Society, vol. 7, no. 1, pp. 99–120.

Papaneck, H. (1971) 'Purdah in Pakistan', Journal of Marriage and Family, August.

Parmar, P. (1982) 'Gender, Race and Class: Asian Women in Resistance', in Centre for Contemporary Cultural Studies The Empire Strikes Back, London, Hutchinson.

Parmar, P. (1989) 'Other Kinds of Dreams', Feminist Review, no. 31.

Passerini, Luisa (1987) Fascism in Popular Memory, Cambridge, Cambridge University Press.

Patton, C. (1986) Sex and Germs: The Politics of AIDS, Montreal and Buffalo, Black Rose Books.

Penfold, S. and Walker, G. (1984) Women and the Psychiatric Paradox, Milton Keynes, Open University Press.

Petersen, L.R., Doll, L., White, C., Chu, S. and the HIV Blood Donor Study Group (1992) 'No Evidence for Female-to-Female HIV Transmission among 960,000 Female Blood Donors', Journal of Acquired Immune Deficiency Syndromes, vol. 5, no. 9, pp. 853–5.

Petersen, W. (1987) 'Politics and the Measurement of Ethnicity', in Alonso, W. and Starr, P. (Eds), The Politics of Numbers, New York, Russell Sage Foundation.

Phillips, D.L. (1971) Knowledge from What? Theories and Methods in Social Research, Chicago, Rand McNally and Co.

Phizacklea, A. (1987) 'Minority Women and Economic Restructuring: The Case of Britain and the Federal Republic of Germany', Work, Employment and Society, vol. 1, no. 3, pp. 309–25.

Phizacklea, A. (1988) 'Entrepreneurship, Ethnicity and Gender', in Westwood, S. and Bhachu, P. (Eds) Enterprising Women, London, Routledge.

Phizacklea, A. (1990) Unpacking the Fashion Industry: Gender, Racism and Class in Production, London, Routledge.

Phizacklea, A. (Ed.) (1983) One Way Ticket: Migration and Female Labour, London, Routledge and Kegan Paul.

Phizacklea, A. and Wolkowitz, C. (1994) Working at Home, London, Sage.

Pinto, R.T. (1970) A Study of Psychiatric Illness among Asians in the Camberwell Area, unpublished MPhil thesis, University of London.

Pizzey, E. (1974) Scream Quietly Or The Neighbours Will Hear, UK, Penguin.

Pollert, A. (1981) Girls, Wives, Factory Lives, London, Macmillan.

Poovey, M. (1988) 'Feminism and Deconstruction', Feminist Studies, vol. 14, no. 1.

Power, M. (1988) 'Women, the State and the Family in the US: Reagonomics and the Experience of Women', in Rubery, J. (Ed.) Women and Recession, London, Routledge.

Probyn, E. (1992) 'Technologising the Self: A Future Anterior for Cultural Studies', in Grossberg, L., Nelson, C. and Treichler, P. (Eds) Cultural Studies, London, Routledge, pp. 501–12.

Pryce, K. (1979) Endless Pressure, Harmondsworth, Penguin.

Qunta, C. (1987) Women in Southern Africa, London, Allison and Busby.

Ramazanoglu, C. (1989) Feminism and the Contradictions of Oppression, London, Routledge.

Ravan Press (1987) Thula Baba, Johannesburg.

Redclift, N. (1985) 'The Contested Domain: Gender, Accummulation and the Labour Process', in Redclift, N. and Mingion, E. (Eds) Beyond Unemployment, Basil Blackwell.

Reid, E. (1992) 'Gender, Knowledge and Responsibility', in Mann, J., Tarantola,

D.J.M. and Netter, T.W. (Eds) AIDS in the World, Cambridge, MA and London, Harvard University Press, pp. 657–67.

Rex, J. (1986) Race and Ethnicity, Milton Keynes, Open University Press.

Rich, A. (1984) On Lies, Secrets and Silence: Selected Prose 1966–1978, London, Virago.

Richardson, Ken, Spears, David and Richards, Martin (Eds) (1972) Race, Culture and Intelligence, Harmondsworth, Penguin.

Riley, D. (1988) 'Am I That Name?' Feminism and the Category of 'Women' in History, Basingstoke, Macmillan.

Riley, K. (1981) 'Black Girls Speak for Themselves', Multiracial Education, vol. 10, no. 3, pp. 3–12.

Roberts, Helen (Ed.) (1981) Doing Feminist Research, London, Routledge and Kegan Paul.

Rollins, J. (1985) Between Women: Domestics and their employers, Philadelphia, Temple University Press.

Rose, Hilary (1983) 'Hand, Brain and Heart A Feminist Epistemology for the Natural Sciences', Signs, vol. 9, no. 1.

Rose, Hilary and Rose, Stephen (Eds) (1976) The Radicalisation of Science: Ideology of/In the Natural Sciences, New York, Macmillan.

Rose, T. (1990) 'Never Trust a Big Butt and a Smile', Camera Obscura, vol. 123, May, pp. 110–31.

Rosenkrantz, P., Vogel, S., Bee, H., Broverman, I. and Broverman, D. (1968) 'Sex-Role Stereotypes and Self-Concepts in College Students', Journal of Consulting and Clinical Psychology, 32, pp. 287–95.

Rosenthal, Robert (1966) Experimental Effects in Behavioural Research, New York, Appleton.

Rothenberg, P. (1990) 'The Construction, Deconstruction, and Reconstruction of Difference', Hypatia, vol. 5, no. 1.

Rowbotham, S. (1972) Women, Resistance and Revolution, London, Allen Lane.

Russell, M. (1982) 'Slave Codes and Liner Notes', in Hull, G.T., Scott, P.B. and Smith, B. (Eds) All the Women Are White, All the Blacks Are Men, But Some Of Us Are Brave, New York, Feminist Press, pp. 129–41.

Rust, P.C. (1993) '"Coming Out" in the Age of Social Constructionism: Sexual Identity Formation among Lesbian and Bisexual Women', Gender & Society, vol. 7, no. 1, pp. 50–77.

Said, E. (1978) Orientalism, New York, Pantheon Books London, Routledge and Kegan Paul.

Said, Edward (1991) 'The Intellectuals and the War', Middle East Report, July–August.

Saifullah Khan, V. 'The Role of the Culture of Dominance in Structuring the Experience of Ethnic Minorities', in Husband, C. (Ed.) 'Race' in Britain: Continuity and Change, Hutchinson, 1982, pp. 197–216.

Saifullah Khan, V.J. (1974) Pakistani Villagers in a British City: The World of the Mirpuri Villager in Bradford in his Village of Origin, unpublished PhD thesis, University of Bradford.

Saifullah Khan, V.J. (1976) 'Perceptions of a Population: Pakistanis in Britain', New Community, 5.

Saifullah Khan, V.J. (1977) 'The Pakistanis: Mirpuri Villagers at Home and in Bradford', in Watson, J.L. (Ed.) Between Two Cultures, Oxford, Blackwell.

Saifullah Khan, V.J. (1979) 'Work and Network: South Asian Women in South London', in Wallman, S. (Ed.) Ethnicity at Work, London, Macmillan.

Sandoval, Chela (1991) 'US Third World Feminism', Genders, no. 10, Spring, pp. 1–24.

Sansone, Livio (1992) Schitteren in de Schaduw: Overlevingsstrategien, Subcultuur en Etniciteit van Creoolse Jongeren uit de Lagere Klasse in Amsterdam 1981–1990, Het Spinhuis.

Sashidharan, S. (1989a) 'Epidemiology, Ethnicity and Schizophrenia', Paper given to Special Committee on Psychiatric Practice and Training in British Multi-Ethnic Society, Royal College of Psychiatrists.

Sashidharan, S. (1989b) 'Schizophrenic or Just Black?', Community Care, 5 October.

Scharf, E. and Toole, S. (1992) 'HIV and the Invisibility of Women: Is there a Need to Redefine AIDS?', Feminist Review, no. 41, pp. 64–7.

Schermerhorn, R.A. (1970) Comparative Ethnic Relations, New York, Random House.

Schneider, B.E. (1992) 'AIDS and Class, Gender, and Race Relations', in Huber, J. and Schneider, B.E. (Eds), The Social Context of AIDS, Newbury Park, CA, SAGE Publications.

Schoenbaum, E.E. and Webber, M.P. (1993) 'The Underrecognition of HIV Infection in Women in an Inner-City Emergency Room', American Journal of Public Health, vol. 83, no. 3, pp. 363–8.

Schuler, M. (1992) 'Violence Against Women: an international Perspective', in Evenhuis, W. et al. (Eds) BASTA Women against violence: strategies and action to stop violations of women's human rights, work conference reader, Amsterdam.

Scott, J.H. (1992) 'From Foreground to Margin: Female Configuration and Masculine Self-Representation in Black Nationalist Fiction', in Parker, A., Russo, M., Sommer, D. and Yaeger, A. (Eds) Nationalisms and Sexualities, New York and London, Routledge, pp

Secretaries of State for Health, Social Security, Wales and Scotland (1989) Community Care in the Next Decade and Beyond: Policy Guidance, London, HMSO.

Seidman, S. (1992) 'Postmodern Social Theory as Narrative with a Moral Intent', in Seidman, S. and Wagner, D.G. (Eds) Postmodernism and Social Theory, Oxford, Blackwell.

Sharma, U. (1983) Women, Work and Property in North-West India, London, Tavistock Publications.

Shaw, A. (1988) A Pakistani Community in Britain, Basil Blackwell.

Shayne, V.T. and Kaplan, B.J. (1991) 'Double Victims: Poor Women and AIDS', Women & Health, vol. 17, no. 1, pp. 21–37.

Sheldon, T. and Parker, H. (1992) 'The Use of "Ethnicity" and "Race" in Health Research: A Cautionary Note', in Ahmad, W.I.U. (Ed.) The Politics of Race and Health, Bradford, Race Relations Research Unit, University of Bradford.

Sherif, Carolyn Wood (1987) 'Bias in Psychology', in Harding, S. (Ed.) Feminism and Methodology, Milton Keynes, Open University Press, pp. 37–56.

Sherr, L. (1991) 'Women and Children', Aids Care, vol. 3, no. 4, pp. 423–32.

Skeggs, B. (1991) 'Challenging Masculinity and Using Sexuality', British Journal of Sociology of Education, vol. 22, no. 3, pp. 343–58.

Skeggs, B. (1991a) 'A Spanking Good Time', Magazine of Cultural Studies, no. 3.

Skeggs, B. (1991b) 'Postmodernism: What is all the Fuss About?', British Journal of the Sociology of Education, vol. 12, no. 2.

Skellington, R. and Morris, P. (1992) 'Race' in Britain Today, London, Sage, in association with the Open University.

Smit, Marijke, and Jongejans, Lorette (1989) C & A De Stille Gigant, Amsterdam, SOMO.

Smith, A.D. (1986) The Ethnic Origins of Nations, Oxford, Blackwell.

Smith, D. (1988) The Everyday World as Problematic, Milton Keynes, Open University Press.

Smith, Dorothy (1988) The Everyday World as Problematic: A Feminist Sociology, Milton Keynes, Open University Press.

Smith, L. (1962) 'Autobiography as a Dialogue between King and Corpse', quoted in Rich, A. (1984) On Lies, Secrets and Silence: Selected Prose 1966–1978, London, Virago.

Solomos, J. (1989) Race and Racism in Contemporary Britain, London, Macmillan.

Sonderdruck. Sozialversicherungspflichtig Beschäftigte (June 1990) Bundesanstalt für Arbeit, Nurnberg.

Sondhi, R. (1987) Divided Families, London, Runnymede Trust.

SOPEMI (1990) Continuous Reporting System on Migration, OECD, Paris, 1991.

Spelman, E. (1988) Inessential Woman, London, The Women's Press.

Spickard, P.R. (1989) Mixed Blood: Intermarriage and Ethnic Identity in Twentieth Century America, Madison, University of Wisconsin Press.

Spillers, H.J. (1984) 'Interstices: A Small Drama of Words', in Vance, C. (Ed.) Pleasure and Danger: Exploring Female Sexuality, London, Pandora, pp. 73–101.

Spivak, G.C. (1988) In Other Worlds, London, Routledge.

Spivak, G.C. (1990) The Post-Colonial Critic, London, Routledge.

Spivak, G.C. (1992) 'Woman in Difference: Mahasweta Devi's "Douloti the Bountiful"', in Parker, A., Rosso, M., Sommer, D. and Yaeger, P. (Eds) Nationalisms and Sexualities, New York, Routledge.

Squire, Corinne (1989) Significant Differences: Feminism and Psychology, London, Routledge.

Stacey, Judith (1988) 'Can there be a Feminist Ethnography?', Women's Studies International Forum, vol. 11, no. 1, pp. 21–7.

Stahl, A. (1992) 'The Offspring of Interethnic Marriage: Relations of Children with Paternal and Maternal Grandparents', Ethnic and Racial Studies, vol. 15, no. 2.

Stanfield, J.H. II (1993) 'Epistemological Considerations', in Stanfield, J.H. II and Dennis, R.M. (Eds) Race and Ethnicity in Research Methods, Newbury Park, CA, SAGE Publications.

Stanley, L. (1990) 'Recovering Women in History from Feminist Deconstructionism', Women's Studies International Forum, vol. 13, nos 1/2.

Stanley, Liz (Ed.) (1990) Feminist Praxis, London, Routledge.

Stanley, Liz and Wise, Sue (1979) 'Feminist Research, Feminist Consciousness and Experience of Sexism', Women's Studies International Forum, vol. 1, no. 3.

Stanton, D., Chaisson, R.E., Rucker, S. et al. (1992) 'Impact of the 1992 AIDS Case Definition on the Prevalence of AIDS in a Clinical Setting', Abstract PoC 4460 in Index File: V2: Poster Abstracts, Eighth International Conference on AIDS, Amsterdam, 19– .

Steward, S. and Garratt, S. (1984) Signed, Sealed and Delivered: Of Women in Pop, London, Pluto.

Stiehm, J.H. (1982) 'The Protected, the Protector, the Defender', Women's Studies International Forum, vol. 5, nos 3/4.

Stone, K.M. and Peterson, H.B. (1992) 'HIV, Heterosexual Transmission, and Women', Journal of the American Medical Association (JAMA), vol. 268, no. 4, pp. 520–3.

Thomas, W.I. and Znaniecki, F. (1918–20) The Peasant in Europe and America, 5 vols., Chicago, Chicago University Press.

Thompson, S. (1990a) ' "Drastic Entertainments": Teenage Mothers' Signifying Narratives', in Ginsburg, F. and Lowenhaupt-Tsing, A. (Eds) Uncertain Terms: Negotiating Gender in American Culture, Boston, Beacon Press, pp. 269–81.

Thompson, S. (1990b) 'Putting a Big Thing Into a Little Hole: Teenage Girls' Accounts of Sexual Initiation', Journal of Sex Research, vol. 27, no. 3.

Thorogood, N. (1989) 'Afro-Caribbean Women's Experience of the Health Service', New Community, 15(3), April, pp. 319–34.

Treichler, P.A. (1988) 'AIDS, Gender, and Biomedical Discourse: Current Contest for Meaning', in Fee, E. and Fox, D.M. (Eds) AIDS: The Burdens of History, Berkeley, CA, University of California Press.

Treichler, P.A. (1992) 'AIDS and HIV Infection in the Third World: A First World Chronicle', in Fee, E. and Fox, D.M. (Eds) AIDS: The Making of a Chronic Disease, Berkeley, CA, University of California Press.

v. Horn-Gooswit, Sylvia, Zuidveen, Jennifer and Campbell, Wilfred (1992) Samen Werken, Samen Zorgen: Herverdeling Betaalde en Onbetaalde Arbeid onder Surinaamse Mannen en Vrouwen, LOSV report, Utrecht.

v. Putten, Maartje (1988) Made in Heaven, Amsterdam.

v.d. Lippe, Tanja (1993) Arbeidsverdeling Tussen Mannen en Vrouwen, Amsterdam, Thesis Publishers.

Venn, C. (1992) 'Subjectivity, Ideology and Difference: Recovering Otherness', New Formations, no. 16, pp. 40–62.

Vogelman, I. (1990) 'Debunking Some Myths Of The "Sex monster" Syndrome', Weekly Mail, Johannesburg, Jan. 26 to Feb. 1.

Vogelman, I. (1990) The Sexual Face of Violence, Rapists on Rape, Johannesburg, Ravan Press.

Vogelman, I. (1990) Violent crime: rape, in McKendrick and Hoffmann (Eds), pp. 96–131.

Volkskrant, 11.7.1991 'Vrouwen Moeten aan de Slag, Maar Herverdeling Werk – Hou Maar'.

Walby, S. (1990) Theorizing Patriarchy, Oxford, Blackwell.

Walby, S. (1992) 'Post-Post-Modernism? Theorizing Social Complexity', in Barrett, M. and Phillips, A. (Eds) Destabilizing Theory, Cambridge, Polity.

Walkerdine, V. (1987) Surveillance, Subjectivity and Struggle: Lessons from Pedagogic and Domestic Practices, University of Minnesota, Center for Humanistic Studies.

Walkerdine, V. (1989) 'Femininity as Performance', Oxford Review of Education, vol. 15, no. 3, pp. 267–79.

Wallace, M. (1979) Black Macho and the Myth of the Superwoman, London, John Calder.

Wallace, M. (1992) 'Negative Images: Towards a Black Feminist Cultural Criticism', in Grossberg, L., Nelson, C. and Treichler, P. (Eds) Cultural Studies, London, Routledge, pp. 654–72.

Ware, Vron (1992) Beyond the Pale: White Women, Racism and History, London, Verso.

Webb, J. (1993) '"Gender Offenders" Skew Results in Many Studies', New Scientist, 20 February, vol. 137, no. 1861, p. 20.

Weinreich, P. (1986) 'The Operationalisation of Identity Theory in Racial and Ethnic Relations', in Rex, J. and Mason, D. (Eds) Theories of Race and Ethnic Relations, Cambridge, Cambridge University Press.

Weinreich, P. (1989) 'Variations in Ethnic Identity: Identity Structure Analysis', in Liebkind, K. (Ed.) New Identities in Europe, Aldershot, Gower.

West, C. (1992) 'The Postmodern Crisis of Black Intellectuals', in Grossberg, L., Nelson, C. and Treichler, P. (Eds) Cultural Studies, London, Routledge, pp. 689–706.

Westwood, S. (1984) All Day, Every Day, London, Pluto.

Westwood, S. and Bhachu, P. (Eds) (1988) Enterprising Women: Ethnicity, Economy and Gender Relations, London, Routledge.

Wetenschappelijke Raad voor het Regeringsbeleid (1989) Allochtonenbeleid, s'Gravenhage.

Willis, Paul (1978) Learning to Labour, London, Saxon House.

Wilson, A. (1987) Mixed Race Children, London: Unwin Hyman.

Wilson, E. (1983) What Is To Be Done About Violence Against Women?, UK, Penguin.

Winn, S. and Skelton, R. (1992) 'HIV in the U.K.: Problems of Prevalence, Sociological Response and Health Education', Social Science and Medicine, vol. 34, no. 6, pp. 697–707.

Winship, J. (1985) '"A Girl Needs to get Streetwise": Magazines for the 1980s', Feminist Review, no. 21, Winter, pp. 25–47.

Young, I.M. (1990) Justice and the Politics of Difference, Princeton, Princeton University Press.

Young, K. and Walkowitz, C. (Ed.) (1981) Of Marriage and the Market: Women's Subordination in International Perspective, London, CSE Books.

Young, L. (1990) 'A Nasty Piece of Work: A Psychoanalytic Study of Sexual and Racial Difference in "Mona Lisa"', in Rutherford, J. (Ed.) Identity: Community, Culture, Difference, London, Routledge, pp. 188–207.

Yu, E.S.H. and Liu, W.T. (1992) 'US National Health Data on Asian Americans and Pacific Islanders: A Research Agenda for the 1990s', American Journal of Public Health, vol. 82, no. 12, pp. 1645–52.

Zenie-Ziegler, Wiedad (1988) In Search of Shadows: Conversations with Egyptian Women, London, Zed Books.

Zia, Afiya (1992) MA dissertation, University of York.

Notes on Contributors

Haleh Afshar teaches Politics and Women's Studies at the University of York. She worked as a journalist and as a civil servant in Iran before the revolution and remains active in Iranian politics. Her research interests are centred on women, Islam and Iran. For the past decade she has been working with Muslim women in West Yorkshire and conducting a three-generational study. She is a founder member of the Development Studies Association's Women and Development Study Group and is its joint convenor. With Mary Maynard, she is the joint editor of the Women's Studies at York/Macmillan series. She has edited *Iran: A Revolution in Turmoil* (1985), *Women, Work and Ideology* (1985), *Women, State and Ideology* (1987), *Women, Poverty and Ideology in Asia* (with Bina Agarwal) (1990), *Women and Adjustment Policies in the Third World* (with Carolyne Dennis) (1992), and *Women in the Middle East* (1993).

Anne Akeroyd is a lecturer in the Centre for Women's Studies, the Centre for Southern African Studies and the Department of Sociology at the University of York. She took a PhD in Social Anthropology at University College, London. Her current main teaching and research interests are in HIV/AIDS; feminist and gender research methods, qualitative research and Information Technology issues; social research ethics; ethnic minorities; and southern Africa (position of women, development, health, gender and human rights). She is currently working on an analysis of media reporting of HIV/AIDS. Recent papers include: 'Gender, Food Production and Poverty Rights: Constraints on Women Farmers in Southern Africa' in H. Afshar (Ed.), *Women, Development and Survival in the Third World* (1991); 'Personal Information and Qualitative Research Data: Some Practical and Ethical Problems Arising from Data Protection Legislation' in N.G. Fielding and R.M. Lee (Eds), *Using Computers for Qualitative Research* (1991); and 'The Socio-Cultural Contexts of AIDS in Africa: An Ethnographic Review' in G.G. Bobd, J. Kreniske, I.S. Susswe and J. Vincent (Eds), *AIDS in Africa and the Caribbean: The Documentation of an Epidemic* (forthcoming). Anne Akeroyd has been a member of the Executive Council of the Association of Social Anthropologists of the Commonwealth, of the Councils of the Royal Anthropological Institute and of the African Studies Association of the UK, and of the Standing Committee on Library Materials on Africa.

Sheila Allen is Professor of Sociology at the University of Bradford and a former president of the British Sociological Association. She has researched and published extensively in the areas of race and ethnic relations, gender, and work and employment. She recently completed a study of women and business enterprise.

Kum-Kum Bhavnani is presently in the Department of Sociology at the University of California, Santa Barbara. She teaches Feminist Studies and Critical Social Psychology. Her intellectual interests include an exploration of the intersections of 'race', gender and class in feminist epistemology, as well as conducting research using the framework of social representations theory in social psychology. She has published a number of articles and her book, *Talking Politics*, was published in 1991.

Avtar Brah teaches in Birkbeck College at the University of London. Her research addresses the intersections between 'race', ethnicity, gender and class through a variety of studies concerned with: intergenerational continuity and change; cultural identities; unemployment; and a gendered youth labour market. Recently, she has been involved in researching, with Alison Kaye, the relationship of Asian and Somali women to the educational guidance system. Presently, her research is concerned with diaspora identities.

Helma Lutz is a sociologist and lecturer at the University of Utrecht, Department of General Social Science. Her main areas of research and teaching interests are ethnic relations, women's studies, racism, and multi-cultural society. She has published in German, Dutch, French and English. Her main publications include *Welten Verbinden. Türkische Sozialarbeiterinnen in der Niederlanden und der Bundesrepublik Deutschland* (1991); 'Migrant Women of "Islamic Background" – Images and Self Images', Occasional Paper, MERA, Amsterdam (1991); 'Cultural/Ethnic Identity in the Safety Net of Cultural Hegemony', *European Journal of Intercultural Studies* (1990); and 'Migrant Women, Racism and the Dutch Labour Market' in J. Solomos and J. Wrench (Eds), *Racism and Migration in Europe* (forthcoming).

Bunie M. Matlanyane Sexwale is currently a trainer at the Women and Development Training Programme of the Training and Communication Department, the Royal Tropical Institute (KIT), Amsterdam. She has been a research associate at the Institute of Social Studies, The Hague, where she also participated in teaching activities, mainly on the Women and Development MA programme. An ANC activist, she is also a member of several networks and the women's and other movements for social justice in Africa and internationally.

Mary Maynard is a senior lecturer in Sociology and coordinator of the Centre for Women's Studies at the University of York. Her books include: *Sexism, Racism and Oppression* (with A. Brittan, 1984); *Women, Violence and Social Control* (edited, with J. Hanmer, 1987); *Sociological Theory* (1989); *Women's Studies in the 1990s: Doing Things Differently?* (edited, with J. de Groot, 1993). She is author of a number of articles on feminism and Women's Studies, most recently 'The Re-Shaping of Sociology? Trends in the Study of Gender', *Sociology* (1990), and 'Violence towards Women' in D. Richardson and D. Robinson (Eds), *Introducing Women's Studies* (1993).

Haideh Moghissi teaches Women's Studies at Queen's University, Kingston, Canada. She is currently writing a book, *Populism and Feminism in Iran*, which looks at why women's struggle did not develop into a strong and autonomous movement against the fundamentalist assault on women's legal rights and personal and social freedoms.

Annie Phizacklea lectures in Sociology at the University of Warwick. She is the author of many articles and books on the interrelationship of race and gender and its effects on women's position in the workplace, including *Unpacking the Fashion Industry: Gender, Racism and Class in Production* (1990) and *Working at Home* (with C. Wolkowitz) (1994); and she is the editor of *One Way Ticket: Migration and Female Labour* (1983).

Beverley Skeggs now teaches Women's Studies at Lancaster University, having previously been in the Department of Education and the Centre for Women's Studies at the University of York. From her earliest ethnographic research, her work has concentrated on how power relations are lived. This focus comes from a desire to locate the sites of and possibilities for social change. Her work analyzes how young women, using cultural resources to which they have access, construct their identities in relation to institutionalized and structural constraints. The results of this work have been published in a variety of journals and will soon culminate in a book. She has also published a book on *The Media*.

Erica Wheeler is a PhD student doing research in the area of black people and mental health. She is primarily concerned with doing research with and for black users of mental health services and the politics of their carers. Erica is the Chair of the Black Mental Health Resource Centre, which offers counselling support and therapy, *inter alia*, to African-Caribbeans and Asians in Leeds. The Centre is the only black voluntary organization of this kind in Yorkshire. From September 1990 to November 1992, Erica Wheeler was a research fellow at the University of Leeds, in the Department of Sociology and Social Policy, where her research involved the evaluation of housing, support and aftercare for black/minority mentally ill people.

Index